Edited by Magda Fahrni and Robert Rutherdale

Creating Postwar Canada
Community, Diversity, and Dissent
1945-75

D1319301

UBCPress · Vancouver · Toronto

16 15 14 13 12 11 10 09 08   5 4 3 2 1

Printed in Canada on ancient-forest-free paper (100% post-consumer recycled)
that is processed chlorine- and acid-free, with vegetable-based inks.

Library and Archives Canada Cataloguing in Publication

Creating postwar Canada : community, diversity, and dissent, 1945-75 /
edited by Magda Fahrni and Robert Rutherdale.

Includes bibliographical references and index.
ISBN 978-0-7748-1384-6 (bound); 978-0-7748-1385-3 (pbk.)

1. Canada – History – 1945- 2. Canada – Social conditions – 1945- 3. Canada –
Economic conditions – 1945- 4. Social change – Canada – History – 20th century.
I. Fahrni, Magdalena, 1970- II. Rutherdale, Robert Allen, 1956-

FC164.C74 2007   971.063   C2007-904427-1

Canadä

UBC Press gratefully acknowledges the financial support for our publishing
program of the Government of Canada through the Book Publishing Industry
Development Program (BPIDP), and of the Canada Council for the Arts, and
the British Columbia Arts Council.

This book has been published with the help of a grant from the Canadian
Federation for the Humanities and Social Sciences, through the Aid to Scholarly
Publications Programme, using funds provided by the Social Sciences and
Humanities Research Council of Canada.

Printed and bound in Canada by Friesens
Set in Stone by Artegraphica Design Co. Ltd.
Copy editor: Robert Lewis
Proofreader: Megan Brand
Indexer: Patricia Buchanan

UBC Press
The University of British Columbia
2029 West Mall
Vancouver, BC V6T 1Z2
604-822-5959 / Fax: 604-822-6083
www.ubcpress.ca

Contents

Illustrations

Acknowledgments

It has been a great pleasure to work with UBC Press on the production of this book. The efficiency, professionalism, and encouragement of our editor, Jean Wilson, were much appreciated, as was the work of Ann Macklem, Megan Brand, and George Maddison. We would like to thank the two anonymous reviewers, whose comments helped to strengthen this collection. We would also like to acknowledge the generous financial support of the Aid to Scholarly Publications Programme. Finally, our thanks go to Amélie Bourbeau and Yasmine Mazani, graduate students in the Department of History at the Université du Québec à Montréal, for their help in preparing the manuscript for publication.

Abbreviations

ACHA	American College Health Association
AGEUM	Association générale des étudiants de l'Université de Montréal
AMS	Alma Mater Society
ARENA	Adoption Resource Exchange Program of North America
Auto Pact	Automotive Trade Products Agreement
AWS	Association of Women Students
CAPs	*comités d'action politique*
CIC	Committee for an Independent Canada
CLA	Canadian Linguistics Association
CMA	Canadian Medical Association
CPR	Canadian Pacific Railway
CRAN	Conseil régional d'aménagement du Nord
CSC	Children's Service Centre
CUS	Canadian Union of Students
FAL	Feminist Action League
FANE	Fédération des Acadiens de la Nouvelle-Écosse
FLN	Front de libération nationale
FLQ	Front de libération du Québec
FTA	Free Trade Agreement
GATT	General Agreement on Tariffs and Trade
HBC	Hudson's Bay Company
ICBM	intercontinental ballistic missile
ICC	International Control Commission
ITO	International Trade Organization
IUD	intra-uterine device
LSD	lysergic acid diethylamide
MFN	most-favoured-nation
MSP	Mouvement syndical politique
NAFTA	North American Free Trade Agreement
NATO	North American Treaty Organization

NORAD	North American Aerospace Defense Command
ODS	Open Door Society
OISE	Ontario Institute for Studies in Education
OJC	Ordre-de-Jacques-Cartier
PA	Parti Acadien
PEO	Programme of Equal Opportunity
PQ	Parti Québécois
RCMP	Royal Canadian Mounted Police
RCSW	Royal Commission on the Status of Women
RIN	Rassemblement pour l'indépendance nationale
RMA	Retail Merchants Association
RMC	Royal Military College
SANB	Société des Acadiens du Nouveau-Brunswick
SEC	Security and Exchange Commission
SHS	Student Health Services
SNA	Société nationale acadienne
STR	special representative for trade negotiations
TAC	Therapeutic Abortion Committee
TWL	Toronto Women's Liberation
UBC	University of British Columbia
UCC	Upper Canada College
UGEQ	Union générale des étudiants du Québec
UN	United Nations
UQAM	Université du Québec à Montréal
USJ	Université Saint Joseph
VWC	Vancouver Women's Caucus

Introduction

Magda Fahrni and Robert Rutherdale

In 1967 the first McDonald's restaurant in Canada opened its doors in the Vancouver commuter suburb of Richmond, British Columbia. Not far away, at approximately the same time, unmarried students at the University of British Columbia were demanding access to the birth control pill. A few months later, at the other end of the country, Acadian students at the Université de Moncton held noisy demonstrations demanding that their French-language institution receive funding commensurate with the Acadian proportion of New Brunswick's population. These three historical moments, drawn from three of the essays in this book, suggest the diversity of the symbols and the battlegrounds of postwar Canada.

Over the past decade, much exciting work has been undertaken on the postwar years in Canada. This book represents the convictions of its editors and authors that there is a place for a collective project that showcases some of this new research, that draws together individual microstudies and case studies in an effort to assess the meanings of this period for Canada as a whole, its regions, and its citizens. A call for papers was sent out by the editors to a number of historians working in the field of postwar Canada, and the result is thirteen essays probing various aspects of this era. Some of these essays are the work of senior scholars; others are studies drawn from recent doctoral research. While several essays adopt a pan-Canadian perspective, most employ a narrower lens, examining particular cities, provinces, or geographical constructs such as "the North" or "English Canada."

Unlike a number of other studies of postwar Canada, this book does not take as its central focus Canada's response to, involvement in, or version of the Cold War.[1] Instead, the new research selected for inclusion in *Creating Postwar Canada: Community, Diversity, and Dissent* takes the form of political and social histories of nations, nationalisms, social movements, families, consumer cultures, and countercultures. In contrast to much of the North American historiography, moreover, many of these essays insist on the importance of local or regional contexts, debates, and identities. While the

Canada that emerges from these studies is firmly situated within North America, we also see in many of these essays citizens responding to continentalism, to the process of "Americanization," and in some cases to the process of "Canadianization." The "imagined communities" considered in the first section of this book – the Canadian North, Quebec, Acadian New Brunswick, and English Canada – all had specificities that set them apart to some degree from our image of a North American "norm" and thus from much of the North American historiography of the postwar era. Like the contributors to another recent edited collection, the authors and editors of *Creating Postwar Canada* do not necessarily share "a fully agreed-upon project"; rather, we propose here "a diversity of perspectives and approaches."[2] This diversity is evident in the topics addressed in this collection but can also be found in the scale and perspective adopted by the authors: histories of day-to-day life rub shoulders here with broad examinations of ideological, political, and economic change.

Assessing the Postwar Period

Sustained attention to the social, political, and cultural history of postwar Canada is relatively recent. In part, this is because the intervening years have provided the distance necessary to pinpointing the characteristics of the postwar years that made them a coherent historical period. Moreover, a new generation of scholars, not yet born in the immediate postwar years, has come along to critically interrogate the era. In contrast to the recent collection edited by Nancy Christie and Michael Gauvreau, *Cultures of Citizenship, 1940-1955*, this book examines the thirty years between 1945 and 1975, a period referred to by historians of France, Belgium, and Switzerland as "les trente glorieuses" and by British historian Eric Hobsbawm as the "Golden Age."[3] Taken together, these "thirty glorious years" are generally hailed in Canada and elsewhere as an extended moment of unprecedented prosperity, developed welfare states, high modernity, and advanced capitalism. The editors of this collection concur with Christie, Gauvreau, and other scholars who argue that the immediate postwar years must in many ways be considered separately from what followed: the legacy of the Great Depression and the imperatives of postwar reconstruction shaped the 1940s to an important degree and made of those years something rather different from the 1950s and certainly from the 1960s and 1970s.[4] Moreover, those who lived through the "Sixties," in English Canada, Quebec, and French Canada, appear to have felt that they were part of an era unlike the 1950s.[5] While we recognize that the postwar era was not monolithic, we nonetheless see a historical coherence in the period known as the "trente glorieuses" – a label that applies, in our opinion, as well to Canada as it does to western Europe.

We see six aspects of the era as particularly important. The first is that this was a prolonged period of prosperity, albeit a prosperity that was unevenly shared and that came later to certain regions of the country than to others.[6] The postwar economic boom can be attributed, first, to high consumer demand, fuelled in part by high rates of family formation. This boom was also due to the sustained demand, on the part of the United States, for Canadian resources – "new staple" industries such as mining, oil, and gas. After 1948 Canada benefited from European purchases made with American money under the terms of the Marshall Plan. New social-welfare benefits, in addition to the gains made during and immediately after the war by an organized labour movement on a more secure footing, ensured that some sectors of the working class benefited from this prosperity. A Fordist regime premised on high wages and state regulation of industrial relations allowed for consumption that was in some ways truly "mass." The very idea of "discretionary" or "disposable" income – income that could be "thrown away" on "extras" rather than carefully allocated to essentials – revealed in some of the essays published here must have seemed radically new to most postwar Canadians.[7] Yet postwar prosperity had its limits. For one thing, it began slowly, as the Canadian economy experienced transitional shocks during the reconstruction period. Moreover, the minor recession of 1957-61 dampened the economic optimism of the 1950s and gave hints of the stagflation that would characterize the Canadian economy after 1973. Finally, the regional disparities that had long characterized the country's economy persisted. In the long term, a postwar prosperity dependent on exports to the United States and on American investment tied Canada's economic fate more tightly than ever to that of its neighbour to the south.[8]

A second key characteristic of the period is population growth. The number of Canadians nearly doubled in these years, from 12.1 million in 1945 to 22.7 million in 1975.[9] This growth was partly spurred by the baby boom, which demographers locate in the years extending roughly from 1946 to 1962. More than simply a demographic concept, "generation" acquired social and political meaning, and the children born of the baby boom ensured that the postwar years would leave an indelible mark on the collective memory of Canadians and Quebecers. Postwar population growth was also attributable to the massive waves of immigration that began in the late 1940s. This immigration changed the ethnic make-up of Canada considerably. While Canada's population had long been more diverse than was suggested by the rhetoric of two "founding" peoples, this diversity became much more pronounced in the decades after the war as those who were soon termed "New Canadians" arrived not only from Britain but also from Italy, Germany, the Netherlands, Poland, Greece, Hungary, the West Indies, and increasingly, from the 1970s onward, from China, Vietnam, Hong Kong,

Haiti, Latin America, South Asia, and the Middle East.[10] The baby boom, postwar immigration, and the growing numbers of youth and married women entering the formal labour market ensured that the Canadian paid labour force expanded considerably in the postwar decades.[11]

A third marker of the period is the extensive urbanization and suburbanization that took place across the country. Neither of these phenomena were new in the postwar years, but they took place at accelerated rates and in parts of the country that had remained relatively rural until the war. As sociologist Gilles Paquet notes, for instance, the number of Quebecers who urbanized in the 1940s matched the total for the entire preceding century.[12] Urbanization and suburbanization meant the growth of networks of freeways, boulevards, new town centres, and new configurations of home and work. They spurred on building booms in both residential and commercial construction, which created an abundance of new jobs for both long-established Canadians and the newly arrived. What geographer Richard Harris calls the "creeping conformity" of Canada's postwar suburban peripheries was due, in large part, to the displacement of owner-built housing by the North American phenomenon of the "corporate suburb."[13]

A fourth characteristic of the period is the establishment and growth of the welfare state. Initially, this development took place principally at the federal level, as Ottawa used the new constitutional powers and financial resources acquired during the war years to implement such important measures as unemployment insurance, family allowances, veterans' benefits, and more generous old-age pensions. While these measures had their limits, they nonetheless represented an undeniable shift in ways of thinking about poverty, citizenship, and the proper role of the state. Those measures that were universal, such as family allowances, represented a drastic rupture with private charity and with earlier state measures premised on parsimony, classic liberal individualism, and "less eligibility."

A fifth phenomenon not dissociable from the period is Canada's complicated and sometimes difficult relationship with the United States. Neighbour, cultural "cousin," long-time trading partner, and beginning in the 1940s, wartime ally and then Cold War ally, the United States truly was the elephant in the North American bed, as Pierre Elliott Trudeau's useful aphorism suggested. Historians commonly cite the Gouzenko affair of 1945 as marking the beginning of Canada's Cold War and the resulting, sometimes intense, pressures for political and social conformity. However, the American empire went beyond the diplomatic and the political: cultural products such as magazines, movies, and beginning in the 1950s, television also advertised the American way of life in the postwar decades.[14] As several of the essays in this collection demonstrate, resistance to American influence on Canadian culture, politics, and economic life was important in the postwar decades and perhaps increasingly so by the end of the 1960s. Yet by the

1970s it was also clear that Canada was integrated into the continental economy as never before and that its economic wellbeing was increasingly dependent on decisions made in the United States.

The social movements commonly grouped together under the rubric of the "Sixties" are a final phenomenon that we see as essential to any history of the postwar era. These movements ranged from those widely seen as political, such as the American civil rights movement, opposition to US involvement in Vietnam, new nationalisms in Quebec, Acadia, and English Canada, and the emergence of the New Left, to those that explicitly sought to expand definitions of the political, such as women's liberation, gay rights, student protests, and countercultural movements that insisted on the significance of music, fashion, illegal drugs, and "free love." These movements, like other key aspects of the period, remind us of the extent to which postwar Canada was integrated into and attuned to what was happening elsewhere in the Western world. Ho Chi Minh City, Haight-Ashbury, Mai '68, the Prague Spring, and Selma, Alabama: the names of these places and moments, among others, were familiar to most postwar Canadians.

Historiography

Writing in 1989, the authors of *Canada since 1945: Power, Politics, and Provincialism* insisted that "No part of Canada's history is as neglected or as misunderstood as that of the past forty years."[15] In the nearly two decades since the revised edition of *Canada since 1945* was published, things have changed. Postwar Canada can now hardly be said to be barren historiographical terrain. This collection of new research contributes to the growing literature on the political, social, and cultural history of postwar Canada as well as to a number of more specific historiographies, notably those of nationalism, gender and the family, and consumer cultures.

There now exist edited collections and syntheses dealing with the postwar period in Canada.[16] The syntheses focus largely on political developments, emphasizing in particular the expanded role of government in the lives of Canadians after the Second World War. They insist on the significant degree of centralization that took place during and after the war, with the federal government assuming a greater role in the economy and in the provision of social welfare. Such a perspective was seen as early as 1976, at the very end of the "trente glorieuses," in Donald Creighton's classic and somewhat cranky polemic *The Forked Road: Canada, 1939-1957.*[17] The accent on the state is likewise evident in *Canada since 1945,* which in some ways is the standard academic overview of the period. Organized around prime ministers – with sections on Mackenzie King, St. Laurent, Diefenbaker, and Pearson – party politics are front and centre in this synthesis. It is a generally optimistic portrait of the period. The authors argue that "Canadian history is a success story – an account of coping with troubles and triumphing over adversities." Between 1945 and 1975, they claim, Canada enjoyed "thirty years of unprecedented economic advance" and much improved living standards. Acknowledging that this "is a book about our own times" and that these are "events through which the authors have lived," they are even somewhat nostalgic about the immediate postwar decades, what they term "the relatively centralized but outward-looking Canada of the forties and fifties."[18]

A rather different perspective can be found in Alvin Finkel's *Our Lives: Canada after 1945*, an overview of the years since the end of the Second World War that is in some ways a reaction to the upbeat version of Canadian history seen in *Canada since 1945*.[19] Finkel acknowledges the unprecedented prosperity of the postwar era but argues that this prosperity was unevenly shared. Like *Canada since 1945*, Finkel's text combines a strong emphasis on political events with an interest in economic, social, and cultural developments. An interpretive synthesis of existing works, *Our Lives* does not showcase new research but does provide a less rosy counternarrative to that provided by *Canada since 1945*.

A number of other studies explore Canada's place in the military, diplomatic, and political alliances of the Cold War. Denis Smith's *Diplomacy of Fear*, for instance, argues that Canadians in the early Cold War years "found not security but new anxiety." Smith also claims that Canada was not simply a pawn of the United States but that it had its own reasons for participating in the Cold War.[20] Other works go beyond the high politics of the Cold War to examine its impact on political culture and civil society. We think here of Reg Whitaker's and Gary Marcuse's *Cold War Canada*, of Gary Kinsman, Dieter Buse, and Mercedes Steedman's edited collection *Whose National Security?* and of Richard Cavell's edited collection *Love, Hate, and Fear in Canada's Cold War*.[21] This last collection is a cultural history, a book that examines the "discursive practices" of the Cold War in Canada. In it we see the ways that the regulation of postwar sexuality, in particular, was imbricated with Cold War thinking. Although the insights of these books are important to our understanding of postwar Canada, the editors and authors of the present collection depart from an exclusive focus on the Cold War. As American historian Lizabeth Cohen has recently argued, the Cold War was not necessarily "the fundamental shaper" of postwar society. An overriding preoccupation with the Cold War, Cohen argues in her book *A Consumer's Republic*, "can obscure other crucial developments."[22]

One of these "other crucial developments" in the postwar years, and one that has attracted a great deal of attention from historians, was the implementation of a postwar welfare state. James Struthers' *The Limits of Affluence*, for instance, reminds us of the importance of public welfare measures in these years of supposed widespread prosperity.[23] Some researchers have focused on "the Ottawa men" – the planners and politicians who established the formal structures of these new state measures.[24] Others have examined the development of specific programs such as unemployment insurance, family allowances, and veterans' benefits.[25] Studies of federal and provincial measures by scholars such as Ruth Roach Pierson, Nancy Christie, and Ann Porter deconstruct the gendered thinking that structured such programs.[26] Yves Vaillancourt's overview of state welfare in Quebec between 1940 and 1960 and Dominique Marshall's analysis of family allowances and compulsory schooling in Quebec remind us that the implementation of such programs was a key component of relations – and frequently, of conflict – between Ottawa and the provinces in the postwar years.[27] Shirley Tillotson's *The Public at Play: Gender and the Politics of Recreation in Post-War Ontario* examines the place of organized leisure in the postwar welfare state but also the relationship between welfare and liberal democracy.[28] This literature showcases the interventionist liberalism of the period, an ideology and a tendency shared by other Western societies at the same moment. In Canada the social-welfare measures of the wartime and immediate postwar years were part and parcel of Ottawa's "New National Policy" and meant a considerable centralization of powers. Studies of the 1960s onward, in contrast, tend to emphasize a certain decentralization, with the provinces "repatriating" many of the powers and responsibilities acquired by Ottawa during and immediately after the Second World War. Quebec's Quiet Revolution, which involved rapid and thoroughgoing state building at the provincial level, was to some degree echoed in other provinces, notably those of western Canada.[29]

In Quebec, in particular, there exists an abundant literature on the 1940s and 1950s and on what has come to be known as *Duplessisme* or the *grande noirceur* (Great Darkness). Traditionally, the *grande noirceur* of the postwar years was seen as a conservative period during which Premier Maurice Duplessis and the Catholic Church exercised considerable, even authoritarian, control over political and social life in the province. Since the 1970s, however, an entire generation of historians (labelled "revisionist" by Ronald Rudin or "modernist" by Gérard Bouchard)[30] has called into question the "darkness" of this *grande noirceur*.[31] An even more extensive historiography examines the rapid political and social changes generally grouped under the rubric of the Quiet Revolution. Over the past quarter-century, many – perhaps most – historians of Quebec have argued that the Quiet Revolution did not suddenly begin with the election of Jean Lesage's Liberals in June 1960. They insist, rather, that the Quiet Revolution had long roots that stretch back to the Second World War, to the Great Depression of the 1930s, even, in some cases, to the late nineteenth century.[32] What is certain is that by the end of the Second World War, Quebec was an industrialized, largely urbanized society. Far from being the ideologically monolithic, conservative, clerical society implied by the term *grande noirceur,* the postwar period in Quebec increasingly appears to have been one during which traditional forms of authority were contested and new voices were heard in political life and especially in civil society, such as those of the labour movement, student movements, movements affiliated with the Action catholique, and intellectuals and artists.[33] Moreover, it is abundantly clear that divisions existed within the Catholic Church and that progressive elements within the church were often the source of social change in the postwar years.[34]

Analysis of the social history of postwar Canada was launched, to some degree, by the publication in 1996 of Doug Owram's *Born at the Right Time: A History of the Baby-Boom Generation.* A study constructed around the idea of generation, *Born at the Right Time* addresses questions of family, domesticity, consumption, student movements, and countercultures in these years. François Ricard's *La génération lyrique* might be seen as its Quebec equivalent, with a similar focus on the demographic, social, and political ramifications of this storied generation.[35] Within the broad category of social history, an abundance of works explore family and gender roles in postwar Canada. These works are attuned to historiographical developments in the United States, where initial historical interpretations of the postwar period tended to depict the era as almost uniformly prosperous, conservative, and conformist. Women, in particular, were assumed to be safely ensconced in suburbia amid the comforts of consumer goods. This perspective is best represented by Elaine Tyler May's *Homeward Bound: American Families in the Cold War Era.*[36] This 1988 publication has become a classic in the field of postwar North America, often used as a point of departure and sometimes as somewhat of a "straw-book," a book from which many historians of postwar North America now distance themselves. It remains useful, however, in that it reminds us that the "postwar demographic explosion" was a temporary disruption of long-term trends. It was also a pioneering study in that it drew explicit connections between political and familial values in the postwar United States.

May's perspective has been called into question by more recent American studies, such as Joanne Meyerowitz's edited collection *Not June Cleaver: Women and Gender in Postwar America, 1945-1960* and Sylvie Murray's *The Progressive Housewife: Community Activism in Suburban Queens, 1945-1965.*[37] In Canada, however, most historians of gender and the family in the postwar period have been "revisionist" almost from the start, calling into question the supposed complacency, conformity, and universal prosperity of the postwar era and emphasizing women's political activism even during the "doldrum years" of the 1940s and 1950s.[38] Mary Louise Adams' study of postwar campaigns to encourage conformity through sex education suggests that such conformity was not easily achieved. Mona Gleason's *Normalizing*

the Ideal likewise underlines the concerted efforts of psychologists and
tional professionals to construct the "normal" in postwar English Canada.[39]
Veronica Strong-Boag's research on women in postwar suburbs and Valerie
Korinek's study of *Chatelaine* and its readers uncover a range of experiences
among postwar women, while Joan Sangster's *Earning Respect* reveals the growing importance of married women's paid work in the postwar years despite
social pressures for them to confine their work to the home. Franca Iacovetta's
Such Hardworking People: Italian Immigrants in Postwar Toronto studies men
and women who departed in numerous ways from postwar prescriptions
that assumed an economically comfortable, Anglo-Celtic model.[40] Joy Parr's
edited collection *A Diversity of Women: Ontario, 1945-1980* includes studies
of urban, suburban, and rural women, consumption, labour activism, wage-
earning women, immigrant women, First Nations women, and francophone
women in Ontario in the years between the end of the Second World War
and 1980. Yet alongside this diversity and what Parr in her "Introduction"
calls the "permissive moment" between 1968 and 1972, there existed, she
argues, conformity, consensus, denial, and anxiety.[41] Finally, Marlene Epp,
Franca Iacovetta, and Frances Swyripa's edited collection *Sisters or Strangers?*
reminds us once again of the variety of experiences lived by postwar women,
experiences that varied not only according to their urban or rural settings,
their social class, and whether they were married or unmarried, but also
according to their racial and ethnic ascriptions and identities.[42] All of these
works contribute to our understanding of postwar women and of postwar
families. Our knowledge of fatherhood and of postwar masculinity has been
similarly enriched through studies by historians Robert Rutherdale,
Christopher Dummitt, and Vincent Duhaime.[43]

A final literature that inspires this collective work and to which it contributes is the growing historiography of consumption and consumerism.
One of the key recent studies of consumption in the international literature
is Lizabeth Cohen's *A Consumers' Republic.* There are many ways, Cohen
acknowledges, to write the history of the postwar United States; she has
chosen to do so through the history of mass consumption. She insists on
the importance in the United States of the "pursuit of prosperity" in the
decades following the Second World War. The vision of what she calls the
"consumers' republic" placed mass consumption at the centre of plans for a
prosperous postwar America. Cohen refuses, however, to settle for an uncomplicated portrait of a "Golden Era" that extended from 1945 to 1975,
arguing that a "period of unprecedented affluence did much more than
make Americans a people of plenty."[44] Joy Parr's *Domestic Goods,* a key Canadian contribution to the international literature on consumption, likewise
forces us to rethink conventional wisdom. Parr paints a picture of postwar
Canada that is one of scarcity rather than abundance, of caution rather
than abandon. It is a study of consumption "precisely located in time and

in geographical and social space," a study that insists on local experiences of consumption and of the postwar period.[45] Like Parr's book, many of the essays in the present collection focus on the local, the regional, the distinctive, the departure from American patterns. *Domestic Goods* exemplifies the recent historiographical interest, perhaps especially for the postwar years, in the consumer/citizen pairing, another theme taken up in the present collection. Wartime economic controls, Keynesian policies, and Cold War politics encouraged a certain degree of convergence between citizenship and consumption in the 1940s and 1950s.[46] They also remind us that consumption and consumerism must be examined through the lens of political economy, not simply through that of self-expression.[47]

The essays in this book thus draw on the existing postwar historiography, both Canadian and international, and on criticisms of this historiography. They nuance common understandings of postwar continentalization and "North Americanness" by insisting on the importance of community, or communities, in the postwar years – communities that were sometimes national, often local, and occasionally defined by sex, gender, class, occupation, age, ethnicity, "race," or ideology. In response to what was once the received wisdom, namely that postwar Canada was characterized by ideological homogeneity and Cold War consensus, these essays join other recent studies of the postwar period in emphasizing diversity and dissent while nonetheless recognizing the important pressures that existed for conformity.

The Essays

Imagining Postwar Communities
The thirteen essays in this collection are divided into two broad categories: those dealing with "imagined" postwar communities and those examining forms of diversity and dissent. The essays in the first section examine the various nations that made up postwar Canada and the various expressions of national sentiment articulated during these years. To allude to Benedict Anderson's idea of "imagined communities," as we do in the title of our first section, is not to imply that these communities were not real or that the bonds of nation and belonging were not meaningful for individuals. It is to argue, rather, that such communities existed within, and were structured by, systems of meaning, representations, and symbols.[48]

Linked to the redefinition of Canadian identities in the wake of the Second World War was the "discovery" and colonization of a "new" region of Canada: the North. If some postwar Quebecers and Canadians were attempting to dismantle imperial and colonial legacies, Joan Sangster's study of southern constructions of Inuit peoples reminds us that the Canadian state stepped up its colonization projects in the far North throughout this period, in part as a response to what were seen to be Cold War imperatives.

Sangster's essay reveals how a vast region unknown to most postwar Canadians was made familiar to a southern readership through white women's travel narratives and the pages of *The Beaver*. It thus demonstrates that nations were "imagined" from without as well as from within. Sangster's article also underlines the way that gender and race were central to constructions of nation. In this study, the travel narratives of white women sojourning in Arctic communities as nurses, teachers, or the spouses of physicians, missionaries, or Hudson's Bay Company traders offer a revealing set of colonial "gazes." According to Sangster, the conviction of these white, formally educated, southern Canadian women that they were "modern, rational, progressive, and scientifically superior" shaped their sense of the otherness of Inuit people. Such certitudes also structured their imagining of the Canadian "South." As Sangster writes, "portrayals of the Inuit as stubborn adherents to a premodern culture could only reinforce existing power relations, perpetuating Canada's distinctive brand of internal colonialism which involved not only 'geographical incursion' but also the *ideological* construction of a hierarchy of white progress, culture, and history."

Although the Second World War threw some extreme forms of nationalism into disrepute, the second half of the twentieth century saw the resurgence of nationalist aspirations around the globe. Decolonization movements, national awakenings, and ethnic revivals took place in such parts of the world as Vietnam, Cuba, Algeria, Brittany, the Basque country, and Catalonia. The most striking example of this in the Canadian setting was the transformation of national identities in Quebec. While nationalism was by no means a new phenomenon in Quebec or in French Canada, it took new forms in the postwar years, particularly the 1960s. If in the immediate postwar years the most public defender of provincial autonomy was Premier Maurice Duplessis and his political party, the Union nationale, other, more progressive nationalist voices emerged in the 1950s, such as the historians belonging to the École de Montréal and the "neo-nationalists" who worked with their federalist counterparts on the journal *Cité libre*. The reforms of the Quiet Revolution, in the 1960s, were undertaken under the auspices of a liberal, interventionist, progressive nationalism centred more closely on Quebec than on older political entities such as "French Canada."

As Éric Bédard's essay shows, on the heels of the Quiet Revolution, many in Quebec demanded recognition of their society's distinctiveness in the form of new political structures, notably sovereignty-association or independence. Bédard's work also reveals that the technocratic reforms implemented in Quebec in the 1960s shared the political stage with other nationalist currents, inspired by decolonization movements around the world (the civil rights movement in the United States, for instance, along with uprisings in Algeria and Vietnam) and by contemporary countercultural influences. Some of the most radical demands for independence came from the Front de libération du Québec (FLQ), a movement inspired in part by Algeria's Front de libération nationale (FLN). Bédard's intellectual history of *felquiste* thought argues for the existence of both millenarian and "spontaneous" currents within the FLQ. His innovative article contends that faith and spirituality were not lost amid the mid-twentieth-century secularization of Quebec society and institutions. Rather, his reading of the FLQ publication *La Cognée* suggests that while religious institutions appeared to have lost their following during these years, the spiritual was invested in other objectives, such as the movement for the independence of Quebec.[49]

The nationalism and interventionist liberalism of Quebec's Quiet Revolution were echoed elsewhere in the country. Joel Belliveau's essay recounts the little-known story of the social and political transformations – indeed, the ideological paradigm shifts – experienced by New Brunswick's Acadian community in the postwar years. During the *trente glorieuses*, in a parallel Quiet Revolution of sorts, Acadian New Brunswick embraced the ideology of "participation" – that is, integration into New Brunswick's and Canada's formal political and economic structures. By the late 1960s, however, the participationist ideology was being called into question by a neo-nationalist ideology that advocated autonomy and differentiation – that is, separate institutions for the French speakers of the region – rather than integration.

While perhaps less dramatic, English Canada underwent its own nationalist awakening in the 1960s and 1970s. Although the 1951 Report of the Massey Commission suggested a distinct lack of national consciousness in the immediate postwar years, this would rapidly change. With political, economic, and cultural ties to Great Britain receding into the past, English Canadian national identity became defined in relation to, and often in opposition to, the United States.[50] Such a redefinition frequently took shape on the cultural front, as efforts were made to develop a distinctly Canadian literature and to establish better-funded Canadian universities staffed by Canadian scholars. Concern about Canada's economic autonomy was also pressing, as was the desire to claim some political autonomy, particularly in the context of Cold War politics and American involvement in Vietnam. Federal nation-building policies such as welfare-state measures were accompanied by national anxieties, such as those evident in the Massey Report, in George Grant's *Lament for a Nation*,[51] in the economic nationalism of Walter Gordon, in the "Waffle" movement within the New Democratic Party, and in the founding of the Canadian Automobile Workers in the early 1980s.

Such national anxieties were the backdrop to the invention of "Canadian English" in the 1950s and its promotion in the 1960s, developments analyzed in Steven High's essay in this collection. Through an examination of a series of new Canadian dictionaries of English, containing distinct vocabulary, spellings, and pronunciations, High points to the ways that language served as a marker of national difference. The "small differences" identified and occasionally celebrated by linguists, educators, and the media were used to distinguish Canada from Great Britain and especially from the United States in the postwar years.

Similarly concerned with postwar English Canadian nationalism, Robert Wright's essay studies the incomplete and uneven trajectory of Canadian author and editor Peter C. Newman from free-market liberalism to nationalism. Wright constructs his analysis of Newman's political thought "not only in the light of his five-decade writing career but also in the context of the resurgence of continentalism as the predominant economic paradigm in post–Free Trade Agreement (FTA) North America and the concomitant rise of neo-liberalism as its ideological handmaiden." One of the country's most prolific political commentators, Newman had also become by the early 1970s one of the staunchest defenders of Canadian nationalism. Yet Wright argues that Newman never entirely abandoned his fundamental belief in liberalism. In hindsight, as Wright argues, it is clear that Newman's conflicted views reflected Canada's own economic policy quandaries in the 1960s and early 1970s. How could the country best achieve a balance between private initiatives and state intervention, between economic prosperity and political sovereignty? In Wright's view, "Newman never relinquished his deep, formative commitment to the fundamentals of the postwar liberal consensus in North America, including laissez-faire capitalism, anticommunism, and fiscal conservatism. Thus even at the height of his nationalist piety in the 1970s, he continued to work toward some kind of reconciliation of these two deeply ingrained ideological impulses, however uneasily."

Dimitry Anastakis' essay in this collection also explores the relationships between nationalism and continentalism, between protectionism and free trade, in the postwar years. In his examination of Canada's negotiations with nonstate actors such as America's major car producers, Anastakis uses the 1965 Auto Pact as a case study through which to view a range of possible postwar trading relationships: multilateralism, economic nationalism, and bilateral free trade. He argues that "all three strains of postwar Canadian trade policy" could be found in the Auto Pact. In the long run, the Auto Pact contributed to continentalization and the integration of the North American market. Anastakis' essay thus helps us to understand the political decisions that structured, to a certain degree, postwar prosperity and adds to our comprehension of the broader economic history of the postwar period.

Automobiles had implications for national trade policy, but they also shaped urban planning, work, leisure, relationships among individuals, and relationships between these individuals and their communities. The imagined community explored in Steve Penfold's essay is "a drive-thru nation" structured by ties of commerce rather than by national sentiment. The new fast food restaurants that began to dot the Canadian landscape in the 1960s and 1970s created a new mental map of the country and new signposts along the freeways and strip malls that linked communities and munici-palities. However, the market created for fast food was continental, even global, rather than strictly national: McDonald's, for instance, became the symbol "of an increasingly homogenized, global mass culture." Fast food restaurants thus integrated Canadian consumers into a North American market and, perhaps, a North American "community." Penfold insists, how-ever, that in practice this market was not entirely homogeneous and that fast food could be delivered in ways that took into account the local and the regional. The "early history of fast food," he proposes, "was not really a 'national' story, except insofar as fringe populations in metropolitan and urban centres shared some broad economic and social developments."

Diversity and Dissent

The essays in the second part of this collection insist on the diversity of Canadian experiences in the postwar years and on the ways that these years witnessed various forms of dissent despite (or because of) the pressures for conformity, for which the early postwar years, at least, are well known. By "diversity," we mean differences structured by politics and ideology, social class and occupation, gender and sexuality, race and ethnicity, language, and region. The dissent discussed here includes the well-known rebellions and revolutions of the "Sixties," which were played out on the nightly news, on university campuses, in downtown coffeehouses, and in "the bedrooms of the nation," to borrow Trudeau's well-worn phrase. We also insist, how-ever, on the lesser-known currents of dissent present throughout the late 1940s and 1950s: debates around Cold War politics, around conformity, and around domesticity.

Michael Dawson's essay, "Leisure, Consumption, and the Public Sphere: Postwar Debates over Shopping Regulations in Vancouver and Victoria dur-ing the Cold War," shows how an international Cold War vocabulary of free enterprise, democracy, and dictatorship was deployed in local battles around store openings and closings in postwar Vancouver and Victoria. Dawson points out that Cold War rhetoric, while politically useful, was also "mal-leable" and could be appropriated by actors with competing visions. He insists, moreover, that while Cold War concerns were important, they were not the sole influence on public debate in postwar Canada. Furthermore, contrary to the received wisdom, Cold War politics did not always shut down debate – in the story told here, they fuelled it. As Dawson writes, "postwar debates over consumerism and leisure show the public sphere to have been more dynamic and vibrant than the existing literature on the Cold War period would suggest."

Postwar debates over questions of consumerism and leisure are also evident in Becki Ross' contribution to this collection, "Men Behind the Marquee: Greasing the Wheels of Vansterdam's Professional Striptease Scene, 1950-75." Ross demonstrates that early postwar emphases on domesticity and conformity co-existed with, and were challenged by, other postwar realities. Vancouver's professional striptease scene promoted an explicit sexuality, discretionary spending, and an urbanity far removed from the postwar bedroom suburbs. Ross' essay also introduces us to a diversity of historical actors largely absent from most postwar histories: women employed as exotic dancers, for instance, alongside entrepreneurial businessmen – often first- or second-generation Canadians or men of colour – involved in industries considered by many citizens to be far from respectable. Finally, Ross shows us a Vancouver starkly divided along lines of class, race, and norms of acceptable behaviour. "There is little doubt," she writes, "that the East End cabarets pushed hardest against the limits of postwar Anglo Vancouver's 'community standards.'"

Robert Rutherdale's essay in this anthology underlines the centrality of breadwinning to fatherhood and to masculinity in the 1950s. Yet his pan-Canadian study also allows us to see the ways that experiences of fatherhood differed according to class, ethnicity, and region. He argues that breadwinning as an economic function transformed the "faces" of postwar fathers. They became, in broader terms, *providers* for families who saw them navigating the threshold between public and private life. "The return to normalcy, so eagerly sought by younger couples raising children during Canada's baby boom," Rutherdale concludes in a study that draws on both oral histories and life-writing, "revived and reconfigured the father's central role as provider within families that strove for security through income, consumption, and demonstrated social status." His essay presents various portraits of fathers as providers to explore how all family members conceived of fatherly breadwinning as a complex activity that linked family life to work outside the home.

Like Rutherdale, Karen Dubinsky addresses the question of postwar families. However, her essay, "'We Adopted a Negro': Interracial Adoption and the Hybrid Baby in 1960s Canada," departs considerably from the home-centred literature that we now know quite well. Rather, her study of the adoption of black babies by white, primarily anglophone couples in postwar Montreal interrogates the ways that children have been and continue to be "used as markers of racial and national boundaries." As Dubinsky suggests, "All adoptive parents in this era were in the curious position of reconciling essentialist notions of blood, heredity, and familial sameness and security – mainstays of North American culture in the mid-twentieth century – with the practice of introducing complete genetic strangers into their lives forever." Transracial adoptions were even more destabilizing in that they crossed "the apparently secure biological borders of race." Like Christabelle Sethna's essay on the sexual revolution as seen in the pages of the University of British Columbia's campus newspaper, Dubinsky's essay evokes the impact of social activism. The interracial adoptions examined here took place in the context of the American civil rights movement, decolonization movements, and the activism of parent groups such as Montreal's Open Door Society. Sethna's analysis, however, reminds us that "revolutions" do not always mean social justice for all. She provides evidence, the sexual revolution notwithstanding, that the sexist portrayal of single female students in the pages of *The Ubyssey* waned only when the women's liberation movement, or "second-wave" feminism, influenced the discussion of sex in the student newspaper and challenged its "traditional masculinist bias."

Sethna's study of postwar youth cultures and a "New Morality" addresses themes also found in Marcel Martel's discussion of reactions to illegal drug use in 1960s Canada. Like Sethna's analysis of student sexuality and Éric Bédard's examination of *felquiste* thought, Martel's essay points to the importance of 1960s countercultures, particularly among younger Canadians and Quebecers and perhaps especially in urban centres. Martel demonstrates the range of opinions that existed in 1960s Canada on the use of drugs such as marijuana and LSD. He focuses particularly on the opinions of two powerful interest groups: law enforcement agencies and the medical community. The liberalism of many members of the medical profession reflected a new tolerance of drug use, as users increasingly came from the middle class and from the student population. However, the medical profession was itself divided over the question of drug use, a situation that allowed the views of its more liberal members to be defeated by law enforcement agencies, which were united against the liberalization of drug laws. Because of internal divisions within the medical community, Martel argues, law enforcement officers ultimately "won the battle over the orientation and goals of public drug policy." What Martel, following Kenneth J. Meier, calls "morality politics" was far from new in the postwar decades. The ways that such politics were received, however, may well have been changing in a period when the very idea of social "norms" appeared to be under attack from a variety of directions.

By the mid-1970s many of the markers of the postwar "Golden Age" no longer seemed quite as evident. Seemingly boundless prosperity had given way to stagflation; the postwar settlement and welfare-state thinking had disintegrated, to be replaced by neo-liberalism and worries about deficit reduction; collective quests for liberation appeared to have ceded to the "Me Generation."[52] The coherence of the period 1945-75 is perhaps most visible in retrospect, at a moment when some of what was built in the postwar period has been dismantled or called into question. As historian Eric

Hobsbawm noted recently, "private lives are embedded in the wider circumstances of history. The most powerful of these was the unexpected good fortune of the age. It crept up on my generation and took us unawares, especially the socialists among us who were unprepared to welcome an era of spectacular capitalist success. By the early 1960s it became hard not to notice it. I cannot say that we recognized it as what I have called 'The Golden Age' in my *Age of Extremes*. That became possible only after 1973, when it was over."[53] The essays in this collection provide new perspectives on what we might call Canada's *"trente glorieuses,"* on the three postwar decades that are only now coming into focus as a distinct historical moment. They reveal the ways that citizens imagined and reimagined their communities – national and otherwise – during these years, and they insist on the diversity of Canadian experiences and on the important currents of dissent that ran through the postwar era.

Acknowledgments
We would like to thank Dimitry Anastakis, Steven High, Christabelle Sethna, and the two anonymous reviewers for their careful reading of this "Introduction" and their helpful suggestions.

Notes
1 See especially Reg Whitaker and Gary Marcuse, *Cold War Canada: The Making of a National Insecurity State, 1945-1957* (Toronto: University of Toronto Press, 1994); and Richard Cavell, ed., *Love, Hate, and Fear in Canada's Cold War* (Toronto: University of Toronto Press, 2004).
2 Marlene Epp, Franca Iacovetta, and Frances Swyripa, eds., *Sisters or Strangers? Immigrant, Ethnic, and Racialized Women in Canadian History* (Toronto: University of Toronto Press, 2004), 6, 15.
3 Nancy Christie and Michael Gauvreau, eds., *Cultures of Citizenship in Post-War Canada, 1940-1955* (Montreal and Kingston: McGill-Queen's University Press, 2003); Jean Fourastié, *Les trente glorieuses, ou La Révolution invisible de 1946 à 1975* (Paris: Fayard, 1979); Eric Hobsbawm, *Age of Extremes: The Short Twentieth Century, 1914-1991* (London: Abacus, 1995), 1-2, 258.
4 Christie and Gauvreau, eds., *Cultures of Citizenship;* Magda Fahrni, *Household Politics: Montreal Families and Postwar Reconstruction* (Toronto: University of Toronto Press, 2005). Christie and Gauvreau usefully point to the British historiography, which typically considers the Attlee years and the "Age of Austerity" to be a discrete historical period.
5 See François Ricard, *La génération lyrique: Essai sur la vie et l'oeuvre des premiers-nés du baby-boom* (Montreal: Boréal, 1992); Yves Bélanger et al., eds., *La Révolution tranquille: 40 ans plus tard – Un bilan* (Montreal: VLB Éditeur, 2000); Myrna Kostash, *Long Way from Home: The Sixties Generation in Canada* (Toronto: J. Lorimer, 1980). On the "Sixties" in Canada, see also Dimitry Anastakis, ed., *The Sixties: Style and Substance* (Montreal and Kingston: McGill-Queen's University Press, forthcoming).
6 James Struthers, *The Limits of Affluence: Welfare in Ontario, 1920-1970* (Toronto: University of Toronto Press, 1994).
7 On Canada's cautious postwar consumption patterns, see Joy Parr, *Domestic Goods: The Material, the Moral, and the Economic in the Postwar Years* (Toronto: University of Toronto Press, 1999).
8 On Canada's postwar economy, see Kenneth Norrie and Douglas Owram, *A History of the Canadian Economy* (Toronto: Harcourt Brace Jovanovich, 1991), Chapters 20-21; Paul Phillips and Stephen Watson, "From Mobilization to Continentalism: The Canadian Economy in the Post-Depression Period," in Michael S. Cross and Gregory S. Kealey, eds., *Readings in*

Canadian Social History, vol. 5, *Modern Canada, 1930-1980s* (Toronto: McClelland and Stewart, 1984); David A. Wolfe, "The Rise and Demise of the Keynesian Era in Canada: Economic Policy, 1930-1982," in ibid.

9   See http://www.statcan.ca/english/freepub/11-516-XIE/sectiona/sectiona.htm.

10 On postwar immigration, see Freda Hawkins, *Canada and Immigration: Public Policy and Public Concern* (Montreal and Kingston: McGill-Queen's University Press and the Institute of Public Administration of Canada, 1972).

11 Norrie and Owram, *A History of the Canadian Economy,* 581-84.

12 Gilles Paquet, "Les années 1950 au Québec," *Bulletin d'histoire politique* 3, 1 (Fall 1994): 15-18 at 15.

13 Richard Harris, *Creeping Conformity: How Canada Became Suburban, 1900-1960* (Toronto: University of Toronto Press, 2004), 7.

14 Paul Rutherford, *When Television Was Young: Primetime Canada, 1952-1967* (Toronto: University of Toronto Press, 1990).

15 Robert Bothwell, Ian Drummond, and John English, *Canada since 1945: Power, Politics, and Provincialism,* rev. ed. (Toronto: University of Toronto Press, 1989), 7.

16 In addition to Christie's and Gauvreau's *Cultures of Citizenship in Post-War Canada,* we might point to Donald Avery's and Roger Hall's collection of previously published essays *Coming of Age: Readings in Canadian History since World War II* (Toronto: Harcourt Brace Canada, 1996). Designed for classroom use, the collection acknowledges the extensive production of social history during the past thirty years but also "unashamedly resurrect[s] politics" (3). Diversity, the editors argue, is their "chief narrative theme" (2) – a theme that is also central to the present collection.

17 Creighton's synthesis of the years between 1939 and 1957 (the beginning of the Second World War and the end of twenty-two years of Liberal power in Ottawa) is focused largely, although not exclusively, on formal politics. One of the principal narrative thrusts of Creighton's *The Forked Road: Canada, 1939-1957* (Toronto: McClelland and Stewart, 1976) is condemnation of what he calls "the obsequious Liberal acceptance of American economic control and political influence" (289).

18 Bothwell et al., *Canada since 1945,* 3, xi, 4.

19 Alvin Finkel, *Our Lives: Canada after 1945* (Toronto: J. Lorimer, 1997).

20 Denis Smith, *Diplomacy of Fear: Canada and the Cold War, 1941-1948* (Toronto: University of Toronto Press, 1988), 5.

21 Whitaker and Marcuse, *Cold War Canada;* Joseph T. Jockel, *No Boundaries Upstairs: Canada, the United States, and the Origins of North American Air Defence, 1945-1958* (Vancouver: UBC Press, 1987); Bruce Muirhead, *The Development of Postwar Canadian Trade Policy: The Failure of the Anglo-European Option* (Montreal and Kingston: McGill-Queen's University Press, 1992); Merrily Weisbord, *The Strangest Dream: Canadian Communists, the Spy Trials, and the Cold War,* 2nd ed. (Montreal: Véhicule Press, 1994).

22 Lizabeth Cohen, *A Consumer's Republic: The Politics of Mass Consumption in Postwar America* (New York: Alfred A. Knopf, 2003), 8. For similar cautions, see Parr, *Domestic Goods;* and Christie and Gauvreau, eds., *Cultures of Citizenship.*

23 Struthers, *Limits of Affluence.*

24 J.L. Granatstein, *The Ottawa Men: The Civil Service Mandarins, 1935-1957* (Toronto: Oxford University Press, 1982); Doug Owram, *The Government Generation: Canadian Intellectuals and the State, 1900-1945* (Toronto: University of Toronto Press, 1986).

25 James Struthers, *No Fault of Their Own: Unemployment and the Canadian Welfare State, 1914-1941* (Toronto: University of Toronto Press, 1983); Dominique Marshall, *Aux origines sociales de l'État-providence: Familles québécoises, obligation scolaire et allocations familiales, 1940-1955* (Montreal: Presses de l'Université de Montréal, 1998); Peter Neary and J.L. Granatstein, eds., *The Veterans' Charter and Post-World War II Canada* (Montreal and Kingston: McGill-Queen's University Press, 1998).

26 Ruth Roach Pierson, "Gender and the Unemployment Insurance Debates in Canada, 1934-1940," *Labour/Le Travail* 25 (Spring 1990): 77-103; Nancy Christie, *Engendering the State: Family, Work, and Welfare in Canada* (Toronto: University of Toronto Press, 2000); Ann

Porter, *Gendered States: Women, Unemployment Insurance, and the Political Economy of the Welfare State in Canada, 1945-1997* (Toronto: University of Toronto Press, 2003).

27 Yves Vaillancourt, *L'évolution des politiques sociales au Québec, 1940-1960* (Montreal: Presses de l'Université de Montréal, 1988); Marshall, *Aux origines sociales;* P.E. Bryden, *Planners and Politicians: Liberal Politics and Social Policy, 1957-1968* (Montreal and Kingston: McGill-Queen's University Press, 1997).

28 Shirley Tillotson, *The Public at Play: Gender and the Politics of Recreation in Post-War Ontario* (Toronto: University of Toronto Press, 2000).

29 John Richards and Larry Pratt, *Prairie Capitalism: Power and Influence in the New West* (Toronto: McClelland and Stewart, 1979).

30 Ronald Rudin, *Making History in Twentieth-Century Quebec* (Toronto: University of Toronto Press, 1997); Gérard Bouchard, *Genèse des nations et cultures du Nouveau Monde: Essai d'histoire comparée,* 2nd ed. (Montreal: Boréal Compact, 2001).

31 See, for example, the two volumes of Paul-André Linteau et al., eds., *Histoire du Québec contemporain* (Montreal: Boréal Compact, 1989).

32 See Paul-André Linteau, "Un débat historiographique: L'entrée du Québec dans la modernité et la signification de la Révolution tranquille," in Bélanger et al., eds., *La Révolution tranquille,* 21-41.

33 Michael D. Behiels, *Prelude to Quebec's Quiet Revolution: Liberalism versus Neo-Nationalism, 1945-1960* (Montreal and Kingston: McGill-Queen's University Press, 1985); Jacques Rouillard, *Histoire du syndicalisme québécois* (Montreal: Boréal, 1989); Jean-Pierre Collin, *La Ligue ouvrière catholique canadienne, 1938-1954* (Montreal: Boréal, 1996); Nicole Neatby, *Carabins ou activistes? L'idéalisme et la radicalisation de la pensée étudiante à l'Université de Montréal au temps du duplessisme* (Montreal and Kingston: McGill-Queen's University Press, 1997); Lucie Piché, *Femmes et changement social au Québec: L'apport de la Jeunesse ouvrière catholique féminine, 1931-1966* (Quebec: Presses de l'Université Laval, 2003); Louise Bienvenue, *Quand la jeunesse entre en scène: L'action catholique avant la Révolution tranquille* (Montreal: Boréal, 2003).

34 Lucia Ferretti, *Brève histoire de l'Église catholique au Québec* (Montreal: Boréal, 1999); Jean Hamelin, *Histoire du catholicisme québécois: Le XXe siècle,* vol. 2, *De 1940 à nos jours,* ed. Nive Voisine (Montreal: Boréal Express, 1984); Michael Gauvreau, *The Catholic Origins of Quebec's Quiet Revolution, 1931-1970* (Montreal and Kingston: McGill-Queen's University Press, 2005).

35 Doug Owram, *Born at the Right Time: A History of the Baby-Boom Generation* (Toronto: University of Toronto Press, 1996); Ricard, *La génération lyrique.*

36 Elaine Tyler May, *Homeward Bound: American Families in the Cold War Era* (New York: Basic Books, 1988).

37 Joanne Meyerowitz, ed., *Not June Cleaver: Women and Gender in Postwar America, 1945-1960* (Philadelphia: Temple University Press, 1994); Sylvie Murray, *The Progressive Housewife: Community Activism in Suburban Queens, 1945-1965* (Philadelphia: University of Pennsylvania Press, 2003).

38 The expression "doldrum years" is from Dorothy Sue Cobble, "Lost Visions of Equality: The Labor Origins of the Next Women's Movement," *Labor's Heritage* 12, 1 (Winter/Spring 2003): 6-23 at 7.

39 Mary Louise Adams, *The Trouble with Normal: Postwar Youth and the Making of Heterosexuality* (Toronto: University of Toronto Press, 1997); Mona Gleason, *Normalizing the Ideal: Psychology, Schooling, and the Family in Postwar Canada* (Toronto: University of Toronto Press, 1999).

40 Veronica Strong-Boag, "Home Dreams: Women and the Suburban Experiment in Canada, 1945-60," *Canadian Historical Review* 72, 4 (1991): 471-504; Valerie J. Korinek, *Roughing It in the Suburbs: Reading* Chatelaine *Magazine in the Fifties and Sixties* (Toronto: University of Toronto Press, 2000); Joan Sangster, *Earning Respect: The Lives of Working Women in Small-Town Ontario, 1920-1960* (Toronto: University of Toronto Press, 1995); Franca Iacovetta, *Such Hardworking People: Italian Immigrants in Postwar Toronto* (Montreal and Kingston: McGill-Queen's University Press, 1992).

41 Joy Parr, ed., *A Diversity of Women: Ontario, 1945-1980* (Toronto: University of Toronto Press, 1995), 7, 5.
42 Epp, Iacovetta, and Swyripa, eds., *Sisters or Strangers?*
43 See, for example, Robert Rutherdale, "Fatherhood and the Social Construction of Memory: Breadwinning and Male Parenting on a Job Frontier, 1945-1966," in Joy Parr and Mark Rosenfeld, eds., *Gender and History in Canada* (Toronto: Copp Clark, 1996); Chris Dummitt, "Finding a Place for Father: Selling the Barbecue in Postwar Canada," *Journal of the Canadian Historical Association* 9 (1998): 209-23; Vincent Duhaime, "'Les pères ont ici leur devoir': Le discours du mouvement familial québécois et la construction de la paternité dans l'après-guerre, 1945-1960," *Revue d'histoire de l'Amérique française* 57, 4 (Spring 2004): 535-66.
44 Cohen, *Consumer's Republic*, 403.
45 Parr, *Domestic Goods*, 10.
46 Magda Fahrni, "Counting the Costs of Living: Gender, Citizenship, and a Politics of Prices in 1940s Montreal," *Canadian Historical Review* 83, 4 (December 2002): 483-504; Donica Belisle, "Exploring Postwar Consumption: The Campaign to Unionize Eaton's in Toronto, 1948-1952," *Canadian Historical Review* 86, 4 (December 2005): 641-72.
47 On this debate, see Parr, *Domestic Goods*, 9-10.
48 As Benedict Anderson writes in *Imagined Communities: Reflections on the Origin and Spread of Nationalism*, rev. ed. (London: Verso, 1991), 6: "Communities are to be distinguished, not by their falsity/genuineness, but by the style in which they are imagined."
49 See also E.-Martin Meunier and Jean-Philippe Warren, "De la question sociale à la question nationale: La revue *Cité Libre* (1950-1963)," *Recherches sociographiques* 39, 2-3 (1998): 291-316.
50 J.L. Granatstein, *How Britain's Weakness Forced Canada into the Arms of the United States* (Toronto: University of Toronto Press, 1989); José E. Igartua, *The Other Quiet Revolution: National Identities in English Canada, 1945-71* (Vancouver: UBC Press, 2006).
51 George Grant, *Lament for a Nation: The Defeat of Canadian Nationalism* (Toronto: McClelland and Stewart, 1965).
52 See, for example, Nicole F. Bernier, *Le désengagement de l'État providence* (Montreal: Presses de l'Université de Montréal, 2003). According to Norrie and Owram, *A History of the Canadian Economy*, 541, 600, and to Phillips and Watson, "From Mobilization to Continentalism," 33, the end of postwar prosperity can be traced to 1973, a year characterized by oil crises and by stagflation.
53 Eric Hobsbawm, *Interesting Times: A Twentieth-Century Life* (London: Abacus, 2002), 222.

Part 1
Imagining Postwar Communities

1
Constructing the "Eskimo" Wife: White Women's Travel Writing, Colonialism, and the Canadian North, 1940-60

Joan Sangster

In her travel narrative describing her trip to Povungnetuk, Baffin Island, in 1946 to become the wife of a Hudson's Bay Company (HBC) trader, Wanda Tolboom recounts her anticipation of her perfect wedding, with bouquet, cake, and ceremony, in the land of ice and snow. "There were few couples like us," she noted, who could boast that their wedding was "attended by every white couple within 600 miles."[1] The promotion of these white weddings as romantic "firsts" in an uncharted, empty land – captured visually in *The Beaver* photograph of a Pangnirtung wedding – was symbolic of changes in the Arctic in the post-Second World War period. More white women were travelling north to work as professionals or as partners of male traders, missionaries, and officials; at the same time, the Canadian state and religious missions believed that it was important to impart to Inuit women the same education, domestic life, and moral outlook that these white women supposedly brought with them.

The images of Inuit life created through white women's travel narratives published from the 1940s to the 1960s are the subject of this chapter. Women's sojourning narratives were part of a well-established, popular form of writing extending back to nineteenth-century settler accounts of life in the "wilds" of Upper Canada. Women's accounts of the twentieth-century Arctic, published within Canada and internationally, offered powerful portrayals of cultural encounter and difference at a critical point in the history of the Canadian North. We need to ask what the "reciprocal relationship" between the "political and textual practices"[2] of colonialism was in this travel literature: what were the likely readings, and thus political and social consequences, of the "knowledge" that circulated in women's travel narratives? Even if the images of the Inuit in these books bore little resemblance to the identity of the Inuit themselves, their potential power as an arbiter of public opinion was important, particularly because they were published as the Canadian state extended its control over the Arctic and as Canadian society revealed a renewed, popular fascination with the "North."[3] These sojourners' portraits of Inuit life,[4] consumed as authentic accounts of exotic peoples, thus created the cultural landscape on which political and economic decisions could be rationalized.

Sojourners' renditions of their encounters with the Inuit of the eastern Arctic stressed themes of racial and cultural difference, often arguing for understanding and tolerance between whites and Indigenous peoples. Yet this cultural relativism could also operate as a form of anticonquest,[5] articulating liberal tolerance while nonetheless reaffirming Euro-Canadian cultural and social hegemony. Writers employed a variety of techniques of colonial discourse, surveying, classifying, sometimes even idealizing their Inuit neighbours.[6] Contemplating the strange behaviour of the "other" – the Eskimo – sojourners' accounts ultimately suggested dichotomized images of civilized and primitive, modern and premodern. In doing so, they became part of Canada's distinct history of internal colonialism, sustaining unequal relations of gender, race, and class by sanctioning a story of the inevitability of white settlement and "progress" coupled with the transformation/displacement of more "primitive" Aboriginal ways.

By illuminating the dominant constructions of the imaginary Inuit North, we can also uncover prevailing cultural images of the postwar "South," however overly simplistic this term may be, for colonial visions often imagined the metropolis as the "antithesis of the colony."[7] At the time, most Canadians presumed that peace, order, and progress moved in one direction – northward – but in fact a dialectical relationship was created through this image: by constructing the Inuit North as primitive and untouched, the predominantly Euro-Canadian "South" became the very epitome of progress and development. Postwar images of Canada's economic progress, its embrace of modernity, its celebration of consumption, were also the mirror image of the Inuit North, the land, we learned in the incredulous language of our school texts, where people still lived in igloos and rode on dog sleds.

Gender, Race, and Colonialism in Canada's North

Looking primarily at women's narratives foregrounds the question posed in recent writing on women, travel, and imperialism: what was the role, rationale, and meaning of white women's participation in colonial ventures, their "investment" in the racial hierarchies of colonialism?[8] The risk in overvalorizing a singular binary of race or colonialism within this query, however, may be the erasure of other axes of power, such as class, age, and gender, and thus a denial of the complexities of gender relations as they were lived out in colonial contexts. Women's travel accounts were to some extent shaped by their writers' gender, and they are useful texts precisely because women were especially curious about Inuit women, notably their work and family life. At the same time, women's responses were also shaped by age, race, and social position. For instance, although white women so-journing in the North were less likely to adopt the masculine persona of the "bold hero adventurer,"[9] their narratives sometimes overlapped with those of male northern travellers, revealing a colonial, superior surveillance of Inuit ways.

This superiority has much to do with "orientalist" ways of seeing. The white person's Inuit was manufactured using discursive strategies such as disregarding, essentializing, and generalizing about their cultures; as a consequence, their subject position was largely erased, and they remained curious objects of colonial scrutiny, often counterpoints to whites' self-portrayal as modern, rational, progressive, and scientifically superior. Hugh Brody put it well: the "Eskimo are seen by whites *only as* Eskimo," never as individuals. Drawing on stock, repeated stories, whites construct tales depicting the true, original essence in all Eskimo people, often doing so by pointing to the bizarre in their culture: "they are *illustrations*."[10] Orientalism was also gendered. White women played an active role in constructing orientalist discourses through cultural forms such as travel writing, while Aboriginal, nonwhite women were often sexualized and rendered the passive objects of masculine as well as colonial fantasy.

One inherent problem with our focus on colonial *representations* is the way that we too might lose sight of the *subjective* position and experiences of Inuit men and women, ironically making them, again, the objects of our inquiry rather than active subjects. I offer no definitive solution to this conundrum, although we can also read these accounts against the grain, paying attention to the silences and subtle articulations of displeasure or disagreement expressed by the Inuit and reported on by white observers, an indication that their views were not shared by the Inuit themselves.

Moreover, our explorations of the cultural "contact zone" of colonialism should not ignore the historically specific and economically and socially structured inequalities of colonialism. An analysis of travel narratives must also *historicize*, linking them to the prevailing politics, social relations, state practices, and labour regimes.[11] Most eastern Arctic Inuit communities at this time were facing a rapidly changing social and economic context, shaped not only by continuing missionization but also by the changing intentions of capital (not limited to the Hudson's Bay Company) and of the Canadian state. The accounts discussed here were published precisely as the North was being invoked by political visionaries and economic leaders as Canada's last frontier to be developed and as the government strove to reassert Canadian sovereignty/property rights in the paranoid atmosphere of Cold War international politics.[12] In the eastern Arctic especially, the Inuit economy was also in precarious shape due in part to drastic fluctuations in the fur trade.

By the later 1950s the state abandoned hope that "benign neglect" would allow traditional economies to survive; its interventionist approach now attempted to integrate the Inuit into the dominant economic order and a wage economy, creating new services for the Inuit by centralizing and relocating them. This strategy, shaped by the state's penchant for economy as well as paternalism, inevitably undermined existing social, cultural, and economic links between individuals, families, and communities, the most infamous of which was a coerced, highly contentious relocation of some Inuit to the high Arctic.[13] The provision of new services was imagined by the state as an aid to the Inuit's assimilation into the "equal citizenship" of the welfare state, and this was encouraged by experts like anthropologist Diamond Jenness, who portrayed the Inuit as a primitive group, unintentionally undermined by the forces of modernity, now in need of "wise" federal policies reflecting Ottawa's "moral responsibility" for its Inuit.[14] In the midst of these changes, portrayals of the Inuit as stubborn adherents to a premodern culture could only reinforce existing power relations, perpetuating Canada's distinctive brand of internal colonialism, which involved not only "geographical incursion" but also the *ideological* construction of a hierarchy of white progress, culture, and history.[15]

Impressions of an Alien Environment

White women's travel accounts varied considerably in style and mode of presentation. Some used conventions of the autobiography and the exploration narrative; others utilized anecdote, irony, and "humour"; one author recounted immense scientific and environmental data; and some were more openly pedagogical in nature.[16] Commonalities were nonetheless evident. Most women stressed that they were anomalies in a land inhabited by few whites: Wanda Tolboom remembers being inspected as a curiosity on her arrival, claiming the Inuit women "fingered her clothing, touched her hair and pointed to her rings."[17] However, this rhetorical technique of self-effacing reversal, as Mary Louise Pratt argues, can also mask as much as undo relations of power and hegemony.[18] Women's sense of difference was also relayed in the language of exploration and conquest as they stressed their presence in an empty, silent, unknown land, a technique that tended to negate the Inuit human presence.

Women writers identified their travels with the histories of famous white explorers, and their accounts proclaimed their place as "firsts": the first white woman on a particular island, the first white woman to negotiate a particular journey, or the "most northerly wedding."[19] Even accounting for language differences, when white women spoke initially of loneliness, they usually longed for the company of other white women. Yet, as Mena Orford recounted in her *Journey North*, the same longing was not true for children;

hers quickly made Inuit friends, with whom they chatted and played, frequently visiting them in their homes.

White women saw themselves bonded by their common isolation, and they often claimed that divisions of class or female rivalry were not a part of their northern experience. In part, this may have been their autobiographical reluctance to reveal uncomplimentary views of themselves and others, although the northern (western) autobiography of HBC trader's wife Jean Godsell is replete with tales of hostile, nasty, competitive, and class-conscious white women.[20] Many of the Arctic sojourners discussed in this chapter, of course, came from similar backgrounds: most were Anglo-Saxon Protestants from farm or middle-class families with high school or university educations. Manning was a graduate nurse trained in Halifax and working in Montreal, Marjorie Hines a British-born welfare teacher, and Katherine Scherman a scientist from the United States. Miriam MacMillan, much younger than her explorer husband, came from a cultured, middle-class New England family. Orford, too, came from a comfortable prairie family who saw her marriage to a poor, rural doctor husband as something of a decline in status. Elsie Gillis, who had attended university, actually joked that she was a "spoiled city girl"[21] whose farthest travels had been to New York City, while Tolboom, although she came from rural Manitoba, was also educated and middle-class in outlook.

Their cultural distance from Inuit women was accentuated by the fact that the latter were often employed by them as domestic servants, thus making the racial simultaneously a class relation. White women embraced the use of paid help in a domestic environment in which they found it overwhelmingly difficult, if not impossible, to survive. Manning's ability to survive entirely on her acquired skills was seen as extremely unusual and "courageous" by local HBC traders, who dubbed her a veritable "white Eskimo."[22] More common was the experience of Mena Orford, who was told upon her arrival, in the language of household effects, that her maid, Nukinga, "went with the house."[23] Faced with unending dishes, Gillis looked around the settlement for an Inuit woman who might "have some vague idea of white man's ways." "I would be glad to have Inooyuk as my maid," she told her husband, who then had the HBC trader strike the "bargain" for Inooyuk by paying her in HBC credit.[24] Most sojourners, publishing in the 1940s and 1950s, would not have portrayed *themselves* as imperious employers; rather, they tried to employ humour and anecdote to describe their cultural estrangement from their hired help, although this too often revealed a clear sense of hierarchy.[25]

White women were also understood to be a potential liability due to their inability to weather the physical surroundings. As a result, their narratives were characterized by ambivalence, awkwardness, and a need to justify their presence, dissimilar to the tales of many men. Of course, unlike nineteenth-century middle-class women travellers, these modern sojourners had citizenship rights, participated in the professions, and had recently been exalted during the war for their equal embrace of male labour. Even the professional women, however, commented on the difficulties that they encountered. "It's a man's country," was the recurring theme that Hines found when she applied for jobs in the North: "had I been a man it would have been fairly easy to find a job in Arctic Canada at that time ... Nursing and teaching had been undertaken by [female] missionaries – but neither missions nor matrimony attracted me!"[26] Manning, who accompanied her husband on his geodetic surveys, had trouble persuading the government to make her an assistant on the second expedition, nor could she find a pilot with the Royal Canadian Air Force who would fly both of them into the North. The idea was greeted with a "burst of laughter," and only a strategy of immense persistence worked. While Hines and Manning could position themselves as adventurous, path-breaking explorers, those who went as wives often cast themselves as reluctant or intrepid partners in their husbands' Arctic ventures.

Women were considered potential problems in an environment associated with hostile natural forces, danger, masculine bravery, and contact with "primitives." Writing of her earlier travels before the Second World War, MacMillan described how she had to prove herself relentlessly, taking on task after task to prepare for her husband's expeditions and, when she was finally allowed on board, also taking her night watch like the men. Despite her husband's claim that the "crew would not want a woman on board,"[27] the crew eventually produced a petition calling for "Lady Mac's" participation in the trip. Women also found their distinct space by stressing their feminine roles and attributes. In *North Pole Boarding House*, Gillis, like some other narrators, became a social, domestic focus of the all-male community, a surrogate mother or sister to other local white, single men, helping to celebrate birthdays, provide domestic rituals, and organize Christmas celebrations.

Moreover, in the post-Second World War period, white women were increasingly welcomed in the North, both in feminized professions (as nurses and teachers) and as wives of fur traders. The earlier HBC practice of traders marrying Indigenous women was now discouraged, and every effort was made to make the white HBC wife comfortable with chesterfields, canned food, and appliances. Not surprisingly, these white HBC wives often portrayed liaisons between white men and Inuit women as undesirable or unworkable. Some depicted Inuit-white liaisons as a remnant of the whalers' (irresponsible) past, although others, drawing on nineteenth-century racial theory, implied that their mixed-blood progeny might produce a "superior" type of Eskimo.[28] A man from white "civilization" who married "an Eskimo woman," an RCMP constable told scientist Scherman, "would be dragged down."[29] Gillis related an incident in which a young white man at their weather station was teased about the attention that he was receiving from an older Inuit woman. He then received a warning: "an Eskimo woman's skin, so I was told, looks very brown to a white man during his first year in the Arctic. In the second year, it may not look so brown. If, in the third, it looks white, then it's high time for a man to get out. He's in danger of becoming bushed."[30] While Hines was less critical of interracial marriage, she was scathing about white men's sexual use of Inuit women, and she suspected that the fascination with wife-trading tales of the "Eskimo" had much to do with the predatory voyeurism of white males.

Women, then, were conscious of their status as precarious outsiders even though they were favoured as partners for white men. Like white men, they were preoccupied with physical survival in an environment that was equated with danger: the North was described as physically inhospitable, frightening, literally at the end of the universe. Both men and women invested considerable detail in discussions of the making and wearing of Arctic dress, travel by *komatik,* the building of snow houses, hunting for food, and the preparation of skins and meat afterward. Their detailed descriptions of daily survival became a form of anthropological and scientific classification,[31] a technique that carried with it an air of authorial certainty.

Women, however, were more self-deprecating about their own uselessness and vulnerability. When she first arrived, Manning imagined the Inuit women thinking – with justification – who is this useless woman who knows nothing about preparing skins and clothing?[32] On the other hand, some of the wives informed their readers that their white husbands became such skilled, masculine outdoorsmen that they were almost "Eskimo" and respected for their survival skills. Some also waxed eloquent about their husbands' paternal kindness to the Inuit. "He loved these simple people," said MacMillan of her husband, and according to her, they revered him.

Ice and snow were not the only dangers described. More than one woman recounted the tale of an RCMP wife "torn to pieces by husky dogs."[33] Since this *one* incident took place in the 1920s and was still being recounted in the late 1940s, it had clearly become an Arctic myth symbolizing the vulnerability of white women in the North. The Inuit might also be a potentially menacing presence. Despite the dominant picture of the passive, jolly "Eskimo," many narratives included at least one tale of a vicious murder and/or cannibalism, suggesting that the Inuit might lack an evolved sense of humane compassion. Since many women had read standard Arctic travellers' accounts, they called up incidents from these works reinforcing this point of view – sometimes citing the very same cannibalistic "event" from Peter Freuchen's book.[34] These descriptions of death in the Arctic often lack intensive knowledge of the Inuit culture; they might also dwell on the gruesome details of death, perhaps included consciously as a means of inciting the reader's interest in the narrative.

Nor was theirs a picture only of male violence. Hines recounted a much-repeated story of a woman in her community who, years before, had participated in a religion-crazed, cold-blooded murder of some of her family, sending them out to the ice floes. On one of their ship's stopovers north, Gillis' husband was commandeered onto a makeshift jury trial for an Inuit woman accused of murdering her husband. Gillis characterized her as a woman without remorse, creating an image of an amoral primitive: "Her beady brown eyes looked unconcernedly at us and her face broke into a happy grin. This is really serious business, I thought, shocked at her deportment ... Then I remembered that here was a daughter out of another era, a child out of the stone age, suddenly thrust among people thousands of years distant from her ... Obviously she was completely unable to understand all this colour and ceremony to teach white man's ways to her and her people."[35] Even a quick glance at Gillis' account suggests a more complex situation: the woman, pressed into a marriage she did not want, claimed that she was abused and threatened with a knife; a signed "confession" in syllabic was produced even though she did not write, and the trial was undertaken in English, which she did not speak. Gillis, a newcomer to the North, ventured that her sentence of banishment was *desired* by the woman as a mark of prestige, further proof of the need to impose new values on those who could so cold-bloodedly take a human life. Since the interwar period, the state had slowly tried to impose its superior legal norms on the Indigenous peoples of the North. Travellers' accounts could only reinforce support for this project since they evoked a sense of fear about the occasional but unpredictable violence of the Inuit.[36]

The more preponderant image of the Inuit was that of a people who were primitive and simple, happy and good-natured, a cultural motif often replayed in popular magazines like *The Beaver,* which featured photos of "The Cheerful Eskimo."[37] Descriptions of these "stone age" peoples in women's narratives were so numerous that one cannot begin to recount them. Katharine Scherman's first impressions will suffice: titling her opening chapter "back to the ice age," she describes the Inuit as "exotic gnomes" with oriental eyes, men of the "stone age" who had the "simplicity and directness of children" and who taught her scientific party what it was like to be "uncivilized" again. Describing Idlouk, the guide who sustained their expedition to Bylot Island, Scherman's use of temporal metaphors stressed the "caveman" image: "he was cut off from us by a barrier of many thousands of years of progressive civilization, the counterpart of our Asian ancestors who drifted east and west out of an unknown, faintly remembered Garden of Eden."[38] While Scherman was there to study birds, her stature as scientist also endowed her observations of the Inuit with the force of veracity.

In their descriptions of Inuit society, writers utilized orientalist techniques, such as generalizing and essentializing, to create an image of a stone age people on a collision course with modernity. Scherman's book recounted many Inuit stories, collected by the local HBC trader from elders; these myths, she explains, with their animalistic spirits, were not abstract or symbolic, as in more developed cultures; they were merely full of "magic."[39] Other writers claimed that the Inuit had no real forms of governance, only hunting leaders, that they embraced superstitious fantasies, especially about the spirits of the dead, and that they even "drilled holes in the heads" of those who appeared insane.[40] Although some women also wrote of Inuit "intelligence," even this was dependent on white assessment. MacMillan, for example, cites her expert husband: "they appear to be as intelligent as the educated persons of a civilized world"; indeed, her husband had "definite proof of this."[41] This repeated language of "primitiveness" inevitably had a cumulative ideological impact. "Primitive" denotes "barbaric, savage, prehistoric, crude," designating someone less technologically and intellectually advanced and without a complex social organization, cultural world, or history. Denying non-Western Indigenous peoples a history, as David Spurr argues, is one of the key rhetorical means of denying them humanity.[42]

The trope of the noble savage was also used by some writers. Manning noted that she found the interior Inuit "poor but gentle," their character proof that those Inuit with "the least contact with whites were the finest."[43] The Inuit were presented as a communal people lacking in individualistic selfishness, an image that idealized, but also essentialized, in its simplicity.[44] Some northern travellers saw themselves escaping the pressures and spiritual vacuum of modernity, claiming that the simple Inuit had not yet absorbed the bad traits of a materialist society: "Eskimos," Gillis related, "never stole even when they were hungry."[45] Hines had little use for such romanticization, noting that there were "good and bad" in all peoples and that Inuit could certainly steal, including from her: "when Eskimos know the English language well enough to read what has been written about them," she concluded sardonically on this score, "they'll get enough laughs to last a life-time."[46]

Despite immense respect for Inuit environmental skills, whites were still portrayed as those in leadership roles, with the best interests of the Native in mind, a view also reflected in some progressive, social democratic attempts to improve the lives of northern Native peoples at this time.[47] Utilizing the language of British imperialism, authors described the Inuit as "children" and whites as their paternal protectors. While fur trade history does suggest relations of some reciprocity,[48] HBC sojourning wives tended to portray the company as paternalism incarnate, emphasizing instances of credit, food, and medicine humanely extended. When families faced "hunger and hardship" and men came to the post destitute, Tolboom explained, they were given old clothes, and their biscuits were spread "thick with lard" (the company ration) to help them out.[49]

Like the traders, the RCMP were also benevolent and fair. Gillis noted that McKeand, a retired chief of the Eastern Arctic Government Patrol, was a "great white father" to the Inuit, while Scherman reassured her readers that the northern RCMP were good men who "really want to do something for the Eskimo, not just exploit them."[50] Because the Inuit did not understand what was best for their children, writers explained, payment of family allowances was overseen by the RCMP. Without this humane check, Inuit parents might have purchased useless luxuries rather than the pablum that they required. These paternal metaphors are ironic given the way that the Inuit saw whites. Describing the early RCMP on Baffin Island, elders remember that "they were just like kids ... like children," as they had to have everything done for them – clothes made for them, posts cared for, igloos built, and even their tea mugs held in the cold![51]

Not all accounts, however, described religious missions and residential schools favourably. Reflecting a more secular age after the Second World War, authors like Scherman noted that judgmental, moralistic missionaries had destructively disparaged Inuit traditions. Other writers did praise the missionary work of whites in the North (usually referring to a few heroic individuals), but overall women writers were less adamant about the need for Inuit conversion than nineteenth-century writers had been.

Many sojourners' accounts debated the pros and cons of whites' incursions into the North; although framed within relativist terms, these did not always reflect a true "reciprocity"[52] of equals as much as a subtle paternalism premised on some of the same sentiments as missionization. Furthermore, the image of a less materialistic people, living a "timeless gypsy life,"[53] was used not only to idealize but also to suggest Inuit lack of initiative, shiftlessness, and a premodern fatalism. Recounting the three most noteworthy things about the Inuit (who, ironically, had been indispensable to their expedition), Scherman lists: "no sense of time, laziness and unending sociability."[54] In Orford's account, her doctor husband becomes exasperated, if not enraged, because he claims that the Inuit won't save food and plan for the future. As a result, families are starving: "they are just too bloody fatalistic and improvident to provide for tomorrow."[55] Yet most whites learned how to cache food under rocks from the Inuit, and material goods always had a different meaning for hunters who had to carry things with them. Like the poor, blamed for their own unemployment, the Inuit were viewed as architects of their own fate. Inuit "fatalism" explained why the Inuit were starving, rather than trade conditions, the depletion of resources, or social dislocation. Conservation by the Inuit, Manning wrote, was completely inadequate due to their lack of modern understanding of firearms.

Citing her husband as expert, she claimed that the Inuit fired "wantonly" on seals and needed whites to oversee the walrus hunt in order to protect this species.[56] Hines' harsh judgments about Inuit relocation are especially salient: those who were relocated "were supplied with everything necessary for the undertaking ... Inertia on their part was the cause of poor return ... now that there is a good market for Eskimo handicraft there is no need for any Eskimo to be penniless."[57]

Inuit culture was thus celebrated as a remnant of a nobler, simpler past but impugned for its primitive, fatalistic ways. The image of the Inuk woman as "post-Native" made this clear: she *should* become civilized, but she could never really be so. Inuit women might "act white" but never embrace whiteness.[58] Inuit labour was essential for northern whites, yet sojourners warned of the danger of "post-Natives" becoming "spoiled," as they wanted the same luxuries without working for them. Describing a woman working as a servant for the HBC, Scherman noted that "Makpa was one of the few examples I had seen of Eskimos ruined by coddling. They were easy to spoil, being adaptable and lazy ... It was obvious that this elegant, neat, lazy girl could never again live the life of her people ... She was no longer a true Eskimo but neither was she anywhere near being a woman of our civilization."[59] Since it was children who were normally spoiled, this language suggested the infantilization of the Inuit in the eyes of their white "parents."

Family, Sexuality, Consumption

One of the signs noted by many writers of the "spoiled Eskimo" was her taste for the dress and make-up of white women. Women sojourners' narratives offered detailed descriptions of Inuit women's dress, work, family life, domesticity, and consumption, categories of particular fascination because Inuit women were portrayed as highly valued for their work but nonetheless as subordinate members of patriarchal households. Authors often equated primitive with patriarchal, referring to a recent past of Inuit men fighting violently for women, of female infanticide, or of arranged marriages. There was some interest in the notion of "wife trading" too, although this was more often discussed in men's accounts of their lives in the North.[60] Ignoring anthropological evidence of egalitarian relations between Inuit men and women, white narratives adhered to the image of their own social order as more progressive, egalitarian, and fair to women. Although white women were sometimes equated with vulnerability, they also became symbols of modernity, particularly in discussions of sexuality, family, and consumption. As in other colonial situations, the imposition of "superior" white norms, especially relating to domesticity, was accomplished *not* by direct coercion but by repeated example, image, and subtle ideological persuasion.[61]

Inuit childbirth was often endowed with notions of the primitive, being portrayed as easily accomplished and as occasioning less pain and disruption than was experienced by white women.[62] Writers noted how soon Inuit women were back at their work, although this may have been a necessity, as it was for some working-class women. While there is some evidence that white nurses in the North were trying to relate Inuit practices to new ideas of "natural" childbirth,[63] many sojourners' accounts still invoked images of primitive reproduction. Manning's one example was telling: "The [woman] was too lazy to do more than she had to do any time, but I did think she would make something ready. As an Eskimo baby's layette consists of a single garment, a hood, there is little sewing to be done ... there wasn't even a hood ready, and as soon as the baby was wiped – with her hands – she snatched the filthy rag of a hood that Lizzie had made for her doll. Neither did asepsis have any place in the whole procedure."[64] Manning may well have been unaware of an Inuk taboo about making clothing for an unborn child.[65] Mena Orford was horrified to find out that her young daughters had witnessed an Inuit home birth and didn't want them to give her curious husband a description (especially at the dinner table), fearing the children might be "damaged" by witnessing this primal scene. Pressed on by the doctor, who had not yet seen a Native birth, their description convinced him that Inuit midwives were ignorant, as they did not tie the cord properly, causing women's deaths. The most modern northern birth of Mena's own child, in contrast, took place in the hospital, while she was under anaesthetic, "out like a light."[66]

Rituals such as marriage became markers of domestic difference. Bouquet, dress, and bridesmaid all had to be in place for Tolboom's wedding, and although she is gently self-mocking in her description of her vigilance to custom, it is clear that this symbolized the proper standards of marriage. That a white wedding denoted a virginal one was made clear with contrasts to Native weddings. When the Anglican minister made a visit to Povungnetuk, Tolboom recounts, he was perturbed to find a Native couple who had their child baptized, then announced they wanted to be married. Facing an "impatient and annoyed" minister, the "couple grinned foolishly," and in response to his lecture about the proper place of marriage, they explained that "we forgot."[67] Some women's accounts also lauded the existence of long-lasting Inuit unions – particularly to counter accounts of wife trading – but the underlying sense was still that marriage might be taken less seriously by the Inuit.

Nowhere was the difference between the primitive and the modern more evocatively symbolized than in descriptions of food and dress. Consumption defined white domesticity, indicated by the pantries of white women, often provisioned for a full year by the visit of the *Nascopie* (or other ships after its sinking in 1947). Describing the arduous work of unpacking,

One of a number of northern "white weddings" was displayed in the HBC's magazine, *The Beaver*. The caption read: "The wedding party in Pangnirtung in the Fall of 1942. Pictured left to right: Rev. H.A. Turner, Rt. Rev. (Bishop) A.L. Fleming, Mr. and Mrs. (Alan and Gwen) Ross, Miss (Nurse) Reeves (bridesmaid), James Thom (best man). Sandra Thom on extreme left. Photographer: Norman Ross."
Hudson's Bay Company Archives, Archives of Manitoba, HBCA 1987/205/1156

Tolboom notes that her shelves included everything from "staples" to "shredded coconut, olives and strawberries ... and cases of fresh potatoes, eggs and oranges."[68] Gillis' shelves were so full after ship time that they "looked like a full grocery store." Referring to ready-made ingredients, she describes their desserts alone of "canned fruit, pies, cakes, puddings, jello ... Apple pie, raisin, dried apricot, pumpkin, caramel, chocolate, butterscotch, lemon."[69] The contrast with the "biscuits covered in lard" that were served to the Inuit is striking. On a visit to a local tent, Tolboom realized that her garbage was being recycled as household items; her table scraps went to Inuit families. Gillis told of charitably sending her rotten eggs and potatoes to thankful families.[70] For white women, now accustomed to consuming rather than producing food, the thought of losing ship provisions was disastrous. The 900 pounds of meat sent north for Gillis' boarding house never made it, resulting in her images of "starvation" and her incessant "public complaints" about the loss – the latter so embarrassed her husband that he became publicly enraged with her.[71] Some women, however, also came to value Inuit food, especially the meat provided by local hunters, and Hines was understandably critical of both the introduction of infant formula and the government's attempts to tell Inuit women how to preserve game![72]

Household items and dress also marked out the "modern." Many white women wanted to create familiar domestic space, importing everything from wallpaper to crystal, silver and china, and a full closet of clothes. Sojourners had to have winter clothing made for them by Inuit women – otherwise, they would have frozen – yet white fashions, from nail polish to stockings, remained a symbol of social prestige, as the Inuit's baggy "shift" was disparaged. Some writers portrayed the advent of catalogues, the harbinger of consumption, as a ray of hope for the untidy Inuit women, dressed in "shapeless, long, ugly cotton skirts," admittedly a Christian mission influence.[73] Immediately after Gillis accused her maid of being spoiled by proximity to whites, she explained how she had acted as a role model in terms of fashion and manners: "on Sundays, of course, I always wore one of my best silk dresses [for dinner]. On Inooyuk's first Sunday with me [as an extra maid] she came dressed as usual. She did not again make that error."[74]

Yet, when Inuit women imitated white dress, they were often ridiculed. Appearing for Christmas incongruously mixing white and Native costume, the maid Kowtah wore a "lady's maroon felt ribbon trimmed hat, over her black braids ... a wine-coloured coat, draped with a huge fur collar. On her feet were ladies fur trimmed velvet overshoes. In her ears were ear-rings, and her lips and finger-tips were daubed with bright red ... It was all I could do to keep the smile from becoming a shout of laughter. Kowtah imagined herself a fashion plate straight out of one of the magazines she had seen at Jimmy's. Her Fifth Avenue costume had no doubt come out of some missionary bale."[75] Reviewers of these books clearly found such accounts amusing.[76] Could these descriptions of Native women dressed up as whites be characterized as colonial mimicry? Perhaps they were for Inuit women, although those with the discursive power in this case were white women whose texts reinforced mocking colonialist images rather than subverting them with "hybridity."[77]

Women offered detailed descriptions of Christmas celebrations as they tried to recreate "home" in an alien environment. Christmas also became a means of establishing new modes of consumption and cultural practice. Women transported Christmas trees, candles, decorations, serviettes, and other paraphernalia to celebrate properly amidst the "Natives." At their celebration for the Inuit, the Tolbooms offered up "party favours" (unsold HBC items from the trading post), games, and refreshments: "what a party we had ... into the office and waiting room porch crowded 87 men, women and children. Never since have I seen so many joyful, perspiring Eskimo faces." The HBC couple distributing the party favours were impeccably dressed "parents," imperial in image: "I felt gala in my red woolen dress, high heels and nylon stockings. Perfume, nail polish and a little corsage of evergreen and holly berries provided special touches. [Wulf] wore his good suit ... Oh, but we did feel like the Lord and Lady of the Manor."[78]

That Inuit women's bodies were objects of merriment in these descriptions bore some similarity – but also difference – to earlier accounts of southern First Nations women.[79] The equation of whiteness with cleanliness, whereas Indigenous women were "dirty, greasy," and unkempt, was found in both sets of racist discourse. However, Inuit women were not sexualized as degenerate or promiscuous temptresses in quite the same manner as First Nations women, perhaps because nudity was equated with sexuality, and Inuit women's layers of dress precluded this, or perhaps because the Inuit people were imagined as "primitive" more than "savage." Inuit women were rendered more childlike than voluptuous, with Inuit men cast in the caveman role of sexual possessors – a stereotype, argues Brody, reflecting white sexual desires/anxieties more than anything else.[80] Nonetheless, Inuit women's sexual *availability* was implied, with references to their easy liaisons with whalers, their acceptance of past polygamy, their lack of inhibitions concerning privacy in one-room homes, and their supposedly seasonal sexual coupling. "In early summer in every Eskimo encampment," wrote Tolboom, "Sex rears its head. But here it is not an ugly one. It is looked on as ... the changing of the seasons. It is accepted as simply as the matings of all wild things in this Land."[81]

Inuit women's domestic labour, especially their provision of food and dress, however, was vigorously extolled, as readers were offered many examples of Inuit aid without which whites would have perished. Writers nonetheless absorbed the reigning anthropological and popular images of a patriarchal Inuit culture, with male hunting at the pinnacle of prestige and power. Since many sojourners saw men trapping, trading furs, and acting as guides and saw women doing "inside" labour such as sewing and childcare (deemed feminine and valued less in their own culture), it was assumed that the gendered division of labour reflected the power of men. This assumption was not necessarily shared by a few writers who spent more time immersed in Inuit culture and who spoke the language; one HBC fur trader stressed the co-operative partnerships of Inuit husbands and wives as well as women's crucial role in directing decisions about extramarital liaisons.[82] Although women sojourners were sometimes critical of the *sexual* status of Inuit women, they easily accepted the gendered division of labour; some even recommended more and better domestic training for Inuit girls.

Some women's narratives also became tales of increased respect for the Inuit over time. In one small incident, Tolboom's favourite dog had to be shot, and her husband warned her that the skin *had* to be used by locals, who were in desperate straits, for warm mitts. Initially upset, she came to understand that the careful use of all resources for daily life was a positive part of Inuit life. When Gillis first saw her maid polishing the glasses by spitting on them, she recounts, "I was just sick with disgust."[83] But after a discussion with her husband, she admitted that in a culture where so much of women's work involved chewing, this was simply a logical use of a "tool."

Discussions of childrearing were used most notably by Mena Orford to symbolize her transformation from critic to acolyte of Inuit culture. Many accounts lamented the lack of discipline for Inuit children but then lauded the good behaviour of children and the intense love of parents for their offspring. Mena Orford's first impression of her Inuit helper, Nukinga, literally betrayed physical disgust, yet this was followed by a quick revelation of her children's different response: "A churning started in the pit of my stomach ... as I watched this gross woman with the dark-skinned perspiring face encircle my two in her wide arms and in turn, rub each of their noses with her own ... but as [the children] left, their faces shone with a contentment and happiness I hadn't seen for some time."[84] More dramatic was her realization that the Inuit aversion to the physical discipline of children was perhaps more compassionate than her own belief in spanking. When she hit one of her children in front of her two Inuit helpers, she encountered pure horror in their eyes. She began to question her superior knowledge, acknowledging that the Inuit make "a pretty good job" of childrearing.[85]

The Political Implications of Travel Writing
Inuit women were often portrayed as docile in descriptions of the Arctic, but the refusal of Orford's helpers to accept her methods of childrearing indicates otherwise. If they disagreed with the white women for whom they worked, they might simply stop coming or indicate, without words, their disapproval. White women often took silence for approval, yet Inuit women were likely showing *ilira*, a deference to intimidating individuals that "reflected the subtle but pervasive result of inequality."[86] Scherman, among others, also noted instances where Inuit women and men seemed to simply disregard advice or orders; clearly, even those Inuit working for whites maintained a strong sense of their own needs, values, and judgments. Hines was more likely than some authors to endow her Inuit neighbours with complex reactions and agency, and she too noted instances in which Inuit would simply not comply with orders if they judged something to be unsafe or unwise, no matter how insistent whites were.

In some instances, then, travel narratives might be read against the grain, indicating not the "jolly, docile" Inuit woman but a far more complex human being, one coping with rapid social change and sometimes less enamoured with Euro-Canadian incursion than whites understood. However, assessing the *dominant* messages behind these sojourning narratives is still important. How would the Inuit have been imagined by readers in postwar Canada? On one level, there were messages of tolerance, respect for Inuit skills, and compassion for other human beings. One night as Mena Orford went to have tea and chat with her Inuit neighbour, she saw her neighbour's son mauled by a dog; her autobiography reveals her immense distress with the memory of this event, and there is no doubt that Orford felt compassion for this devastated mother, a woman whom she would come to call her friend.

But tolerance and compassion can co-exist with paternalism, also a theme in many narratives. The image of a primitive and fatalistic culture facing the painful fact of inevitable adaption appeared repeatedly, along with the notion that whites were well placed to oversee the difficult, uphill path to modernization. Rhetorical and discursive strategies of colonial representation – superior surveillance, scientific classification, modernist idealization and eroticization – were all woven into sojourners' accounts. As a result, the non-Indigenous "South" was portrayed, in the light of modernization theories of the time, as more progressive, modern, urban, and industrial, the repository of knowledge that might allow the Inuit to develop socially and economically.[87]

These images were also deeply political, especially in an era when the North was an increasingly important economic frontier and military concern and when government intervention in Inuit lives was increasing. The fate of northern Indigenous residents was being debated by popular writers, with some extolling the North for its resource potential and others offering exposés of starving Indigenous peoples abandoned by a callous government.[88] Whether the racism and poverty that engulfed the lives of southern Aboriginals would be replicated in the North became a point of repeated, concerned debate.

In one sense, sojourners' respect for Inuit environmental survival skills and their hopes for positive Inuit adaption to "modern" ways endowed the women's narratives with a tone of liberal tolerance and relativism. Writing on the northern Inuit did not simply replicate writing on the southern First Nations; within colonialist discourse, there was some distinction between a language of northern Inuit "primitivism" and the language of First Nations "savagism," with the latter arguably being even more pessimistic and negative in character. Nonetheless, both perspectives ultimately reflected broader patterns of colonialist thinking on history, white settlement, and "modern" development; both were apt metaphors for a tradition of internal colonialism within Canada.

As cultural producers of sojourning narratives that juxtaposed "primitive" Inuit peoples with the encroachment of more progressive, modern Canada, women authors played an active, constitutive role in the creation of colonial texts. The cultural images created by white women sojourners with direct or "scientific" knowledge of Inuit life were undoubtedly endowed with the weight of a certain veracity, authenticity, and memorability: it was assumed that actual experience living in the "wild" gave them more immediate insight into their Indigenous neighbours. The tone of superior surveillance of Inuit life assumed by many women writers thus had much in common with works authored by men, although women's less confident relation to the "wild" North – particularly if they came as helpmates – and their more detailed descriptions of women's lives, domesticity, and con-sumption also made their narratives distinct. Perhaps most important, sojourners' admissions that Inuit women and men retained views and val-ues different from those of whites, sometimes disagreeing with them, also suggested that paternalist traditions were not unchallenged in the North. Inuit efforts to sustain their culture and to organize the defence of their lands indicated that the culture of colonialism was never monolithic or unassailable.

Acknowledgments
I wish to thank Shelagh Grant, Janet McGrath, and Caroline Langill for their comments and suggestions on this research.

Notes
1   Wanda N. Tolboom, *Arctic Bride* (New York: William Morrow and Co., 1956), 37.
2   Deidre David, *Rule Britannia: Women, Empire and Victorian Writing* (Ithaca: Cornell Univer-sity Press, 1995), 5. Women's travel narratives were a popular form of writing extending back to Upper Canada; see, for example, Anna B. Jameson, *Winter Studies and Summer Ram-bles* (Toronto: McClelland and Stewart, 1965); Georgina Binnie-Clark, *Wheat and Woman* (Toronto: University of Toronto Press, 1979); Agnes Deans Cameron, *The New North: An Account of a Woman's 1908 Journey through Canada to the Arctic* (Saskatoon: Western Pro-ducer Prairie Books, 1986). For analysis, see Marian Fowler, *The Embroidered Tent: Five Gen-tlewomen in Early Canada* (Toronto: Anansi Press, 1982); Jennifer Henderson, *Settler Feminism and Race Making in Canada* (Toronto: University of Toronto Press, 2003); Barbara Kelcey, *Alone in Silence: European Women in the Canadian North before 1940* (Montreal and Kingston: McGill-Queen's University Press, 2001).
3   The "North" had long exercised an important role in the imaginary construction of the Canadian nation, although renewed interest was evidenced in postwar Canada by accounts like Pierre Berton's *The Mysterious North* (Toronto: McClelland and Stewart, 1957) and by numerous articles in magazines like *Maclean's* and *Saturday Night*. For some discussion of the imaginary North, see Shelagh Grant, "Arctic Wilderness and Other Mythologies," *Jour-nal of Canadian Studies* 32, 2 (1998): 27-42; Janice Cavell, "The Second Frontier: The North in English-Canadian Historical Writing," *Canadian Historical Review* 83, 3 (2002): 364-89; Carl Berger, *The Sense of Power* (Toronto: University of Toronto Press, 1970); David Heinimann, "Latitude Rising: Historical Continuity in Canadian Nordicity," *Journal of Can-adian Studies* 28, 3 (1993): 134-39; Sherrill Grace, *Canada and the Idea of the North* (Montreal and Kingston: McGill-Queen's University Press, 2001); and Sherrill Grace, "Gendering North-ern Narratives," in John Moss, ed., *Echoing Silence: Essays on Arctic Narratives* (Ottawa: Uni-versity of Ottawa Press, 1997), 163-82.
4   Although the "North" is a contested concept referring to geographical, environmental, social, and even cultural boundaries, I have concentrated on seven texts published after 1940 about the eastern sub-Arctic and Arctic, although a broader sample of northern travel writing has been consulted. Many of these seven texts were reviewed positively in Canad-ian magazines and journals. They include Marjorie Hines, *School House in the Arctic* (Lon-don: Geoffrey Bles, 1958); Katherine Scherman, *Spring on an Arctic Island* (Boston: Little Brown and Co., 1956); Mrs. Tom Manning, *A Summer on Hudson Bay* (London: Hodder and Stoughton, 1949); Mrs. Tom Manning, *Igloo for a Night* (University of Toronto Press, 1946);

Elsie Gillis, with Eugenie Myles, *North Pole Boarding House* (Toronto: Ryerson Press, 1951); Mena Orford, *Journey North* (Toronto: McClelland and Stewart, 1957); and Miriam MacMillan, *Green Seas and White Ice* (New York: Dodd, Mead and Co., 1948). Others consulted include Eva Alvey Richards, *Arctic Mood* (Caldwell, ID: The Caxton Publishers, 1949); Constance and Harmon Helmricks, *We Live in the Arctic* (New York: Little Brown and Co., 1947); Jean Godsell, *I Was No Lady: I Followed the Call of the Wild* (Toronto: Ryerson Press, 1959); Doug Wilkinson, *Land of the Long Day* (Toronto: Clarke Irwin and Co., 1955); Ritchie Calder, *Men against the Frozen North* (London: George Allen and Unwin, 1957); Frank Illingworth, *Highway to the North* (New York: Philosophical Library, 1955); Joseph P. Moody, *Arctic Doctor* (New York: Dodd Mead and Co., 1953); Duncan Pryde, *Nunaga: Ten Years of Eskimo Life* (New York: Walker and Company, 1971); and one travel narrative of northern Ontario, Gordon Langley Hall, *Me Papoose Sitter* (New York: Thomas Crowell, 1955).

5 Mary Louise Pratt, *Imperial Eyes: Travel Writing and Transculturation* (London: Routledge, 1992), 7. Other works include Inderpal Grewal, *Home and Harem* (Durham: Duke University Press, 1996); Sara Mills, *Discourses of Difference* (London: Routlege, 1991); Dea Birkett, *Spinsters Abroad* (Oxford: Blackwell, 1989); Alison Blunt, *Travel, Gender and Imperialism: Mary Kingsley and West Africa* (New York: Guildford Press, 1994); Helen Callaway, *Gender, Culture and Empire* (London: Macmillan 1987); Antoinette Burton, *Burdens of History* (Chapel Hill: University of North Carolina Press, 1994); Ellen Jacobs, "Eileen Power's Asian Journey, 1920-21: History, Narrative and Subjectivity," *Women's History Review* 7, 3 (1998): 295-319; Laura Donaldson, *Decolonizing Feminisms: Race, Gender and Empire Building* (Chapel Hill: University of Northern Carolina Press, 1992); Karen Dubinsky, *The Second Greatest Disappointment: Honeymooning and Tourism at Niagara Falls* (Toronto: Between the Lines, 1999), 55-85; Antoinette Burton, ed., *Gender, Sexuality and Colonial Modernities* (London: Routledge, 1999); Clare Midgley, ed., *Gender and Imperialism* (Manchester: Manchester University Press, 1998); Anne McClintock, *Imperial Leather: Race, Gender and Sexuality in the Colonial Context* (London: Routledge, 1995); and Ann L. Stoler, *Race and the Education of Desire: Foucault's History of Sexuality and the Colonial Order of Things* (Durham: Duke University Press, 1995).

6 David Spurr, *The Rhetoric of Empire: Colonial Discourse in Journalism, Travel Writing and Imperial Administration* (Durham: Duke University Press, 1993).

7 Antoinette Burton, "Rules of Thumb: British History and 'Imperial Culture' in Nineteenth- and Twentieth-Century Britain," *Women's History Review* 3, 4 (1994): 483-500 at 483.

8 Ann Stoler, "Making Empire Respectable: The Politics of Race and Sexual Morality in 20th Century Colonial Cultures," *American Ethnologist* 16, 4 (1989): 634-59 at 636; Ruth R. Pierson and N. Chaudhur, "Introduction," in Ruth R. Pierson and N. Chaudhuri, eds., *Nation, Empire, Colony: Historicizing Gender and Race* (Bloomington: Indiana University Press, 1998), 4; Jane Haggis, "Gendering Colonialism or Colonizing Gender: Recent Women's Studies Approaches to White Women and the History of British Colonialism," *Women's Studies International Forum* 13, 1 (1990): 105-15; Angela Woollacott, "'All This Is the Empire, I Told Myself': Australian Women's Voyages 'Home' and the Articulation of Colonial Whiteness, *American Historical Review* 102, 4 (October 1997): 1003-29.

9 Mills, *Discourses of Difference*, 22.

10 Hugh Brody, *The People's Land* (London: Penguin Books, 1975), 79, original emphasis. On orientalism, see Edward Said, *Orientalism* (New York: Vintage Books, 1979); and Reina Lewis, *Gendering Orientalism: Race, Femininity and Representation* (London: Routledge, 1996).

11 I draw here on authors who offer more materialist critiques of postcolonial theories, including Himani Bannerji, "Politics and the Writing of History," in Pierson and Chaudhuri, eds., *Nation, Empire, Colony*; Arif Dirlik, "The Post-Colonial Aura: Third World Criticism in the Age of Global Capitalism," *Critical Inquiry* 20 (Winter 1994): 328-56; Ella Shohat, "Notes on the Post-Colonial," *Social Text* 31, 32 (1992): 99-113; and Aijaz Ahmad, *In Theory: Classes, Nations, Literatures* (Verso: London, 1992).

12 Shelagh Grant, *Sovereignty or Security? Government Policy in the Canadian North, 1936-50* (Vancouver: UBC Press, 1988).

13 Peter Kulchyski and Frank Tester, *Tammarniit (Mistakes): Inuit Relocation in the Eastern Arctic, 1939-63* (Vancouver: UBC Press, 1994).

14 Diamond Jenness, "Enter the European," *The Beaver* (Winter 1954): 23-38 at 30.

15 James Frideres, *Native People in Canada: Contemporary Conflicts,* 2nd ed. (Scarborough: Prentice-Hall Canada, 1993), 295.
16 Some had precise descriptions of northern flora and birds (Manning), others offered more direct opinions (Hines), while some attempted a more "light-hearted" description of northern life (Gillis). Differences were also apparent in men's accounts, with one unusual one being English author Gordon Langley Hall's *Me Papoose Sitter.* Despite the terrible title, his portraits of his northern neighbours sometimes resembled a collection of characters reminiscent of some eccentric British village.
17 Tolboom, *Arctic Bride,* 59.
18 Pratt, *Imperial Eyes,* 84.
19 Gillis, with Myles, *North Pole,* 10, 124.
20 Godsell, *I Was No Lady.* Manning, *Summer,* 53, refers briefly to such conflicts.
21 Gillis, *North Pole,* 6.
22 Provincial Archives of Manitoba (PAM), Hudson's Bay Company Papers, Wolstoneholme Post Journal, B 397/a/9, January 1940.
23 Orford, *Journey North,* 17.
24 Gillis, *North Pole,* 88.
25 Again, Godsell, *I Was No Lady,* 45, was different, discussing attempts to teach the servants "who was master."
26 Hines, *School House,* 15.
27 MacMillan, *Green Seas,* 75.
28 Scherman, *Spring,* 105.
29 Ibid., 188.
30 Gillis, *North Pole,* 165.
31 Spurr, *Rhetoric of Empire,* 61-75.
32 E. Wallace Manning, "Explorer's Wife," *The Beaver* (September 1942): 12-15 at 12.
33 Gillis, *North Pole,* 15. The incident is also mentioned in men's narratives; see Moody, *Arctic Doctor,* 9.
34 Peter Freuchen, *I Sailed with Rasmussen* (New York: Julian Messner, 1959). On the themes of death, mystery, and violence in popular narratives, see Grace, "Gendering Northern Narratives," 179.
35 Gillis, *North Pole,* 48.
36 Shelagh Grant, *Arctic Justice: On Trial for Murder, Pond Inlet, 1923* (Montreal and Kingston: McGill-Queen's University Press, 2002).
37 "The Cheerful Eskimo," *The Beaver* (March 1952): 7-14. For a discussion of images of the Inuit in *The Beaver,* see Joan Sangster, "*The Beaver* as Ideology: Constructing Images of Native and Inuit Life in Postwar Canada," *Anthropologica* 49, 2 (2007): 191-210.
38 Scherman, *Spring,* 229.
39 Ibid., 180.
40 Ibid., 138.
41 MacMillan, *Green Seas,* 158.
42 Spurr, *Rhetoric of Empire,* 167.
43 Manning, *Summer,* 26.
44 Ibid., 127.
45 Gillis, *North Pole,* 184.
46 Hines, *School House,* 161.
47 David M. Quiring, *CCF Colonialism in Northern Saskatchewan: Battling Parish Priests, Bootleggers, and Fur Sharks* (Vancouver: UBC Press, 2004).
48 Arthur Ray, *The Canadian Fur Trade in the Industrial Age* (Toronto: University of Toronto Press, 1990).
49 Tolboom, *Arctic Bride,* 173.
50 Gillis, *North Pole,* 9; Scherman, *Spring,* 192.
51 Timothy Kadloo and Sam Arnakallak (Pond Inlet), quoted in Grant, *Arctic Justice,* 232.
52 Pratt, *Imperial Eyes,* 84.
53 Scherman, *Spring,* 117.

54 Ibid., 138.
55 Orford, *Journey North,* 95.
56 Manning, *Summer,* 140.
57 Hines, *School House,* 154-55.
58 This would echo some of Homi Bhabha's characterizations of hybridity. The Native might be "anglicized but could never be 'English'"; see Bart Moore-Gilbert, *Postcolonial Theory* (London: Verso, 1997), 120.
59 Scherman, *Spring,* 189.
60 Of note is Duncan Pryde's description of his own participation in spouse swapping in *Nunaga.*
61 Notions of proper domesticity were central to many other colonial projects; see Jean Comaroff and John Comaroff, *Ethnography and the Historical Imagination* (Boulder: Westview Press, 1992); and K. Hansen, ed., *African Encounters with Domesticity* (New Brunswick, NJ: Rutgers University Press, 1992).
62 Patricia Jasen, "Race, Culture and the Colonization of Childbirth in Northern Canada," in V. Strong-Boag, M. Gleason, and A. Perry, eds., *Rethinking Canada: The Promise of Women's History* (Toronto: Oxford University Press, 2002), 353-66.
63 Judith Bender Zelmanovitz, "Midwife Preferred: Maternity Care in Outport Nursing Stations in Northern Canada," in Georgina Feldberg et al., eds., *Women, Health and Nation: Canada and the United States since 1945* (Montreal and Kingston: McGill-Queen's University Press, 2003), 161-95.
64 Manning, *Igloo,* 55.
65 My thanks to Janet McGrath for pointing this out to me.
66 Orford, *Northern Journey,* 113.
67 Tolboom, *Arctic Bride,* 102. Since these women did not discuss their own sexuality, one can only infer their belief in sex only after marriage from other vague references to their pre-marital "shyness." That their sexuality was not mentioned, unlike that of Inuit women, again placed the latter in the category of more sexualized "other."
68 Tolboom, *Arctic Bride,* 62.
69 Gillis, *North Pole,* 57, 75.
70 Ibid., 151.
71 This may not have been in response to their proximity to less affluent Inuit but because, after a radio message home, he worried that everyone knew their business: "If you ever mention food again ... I'll kill you." Was the author aware of how negative a view she presented of her husband? See Gillis, *North Pole,* 62, 75.
72 Hines, *School House;* Kulchyski and Tester, *Tammarniit,* 85.
73 Manning, *Igloo,* 21.
74 Gillis, *North Pole,* 95.
75 Ibid., 137.
76 A review by anthropologist Douglas Leechman of Gillis' book in *Canadian Geographic Journal,* February 1952, ix, notes that her description of the "oddities" of the Inuit made it an entertaining book.
77 As Grace, *Canada,* 100, points out, "mimicry is unstable and uncontrollable; it can also backfire on the mimics." For discussion of differences between feminist characterizations of mimicry as "dissent" and the characterization provided by Bhabha, see Diana Fuss, "Interior Colonies: Franz Fanon and the Politics of Identification," *Diacritics* 24 (1994): 20-42.
78 Tolboom, *Arctic Bride,* 93.
79 For earlier images, see Sarah Carter, *Capturing Women: The Manipulation of Cultural Imagery in Canada's Prairie West* (Montreal and Kingston: McGill-Queen's University Press, 1997). On twentieth-century images of "Indians," see Gail Guthrie Valaskakis, *Indian Country: Essays on Contemporary Native Culture* (Waterloo: Wilfrid Laurier University Press, 2005); and Daniel Francis, *The Imaginary Indian: The Image of the Indian in Canadian Culture* (Vancouver: Arsenal Pulp Press, 1992).
80 Hugh Brody, *The Other Side of Eden* (Toronto: Douglas and McIntyre, 2000), 263.

81 Tolboom, *Arctic Bride,* 225.
82 Pryde, *Nunaga.*
83 Gillis, *North Pole,* 90.
84 Orford, *Journey North,* 20.
85 Ibid., 70-72.
86 Brody, quoted in Grant, *Arctic Justice,* 17.
87 Catherine Scott, *Gender and Development: Rethinking Modernization and Dependency Theory* (London: Routledge, 1996).
88 Farley Mowat, *The People of the Deer* (Boston: Little Brown, 1952).

2
The Intellectual Origins of the October Crisis
Éric Bédard

Future historians, writing at a greater distance from the 1960s than us, will no doubt view the decade as the theatre of an unprecedented cultural revolution. Youth embarked on a radical contestation of traditional norms and of the institutions that had until then held authority.[1] Among these institutions was the Catholic Church, which despite its efforts at reform through Vatican II, was considered by most baby boomers to be an archaic, outdated institution. In the era of the consumer society and an infinite quest for freedom, of structuralism and the birth control pill, the Catholic Church, even reformed, seemed to offer no satisfactory responses to those who sought to take up the challenges of modern life. Thus in all Catholic countries, churches were increasingly empty, fewer and fewer priests were ordained, and many clerics returned to civil life.[2] We must not, however, be misled by this cultural break with religion. If the church, as an institution, no longer seemed to respond to the expectations of the population, did this necessarily mean the disappearance of the sacred? Or should we instead see the 1960s, as philosopher Marcel Gauchet has argued,[3] as a period in which the sacred was transferred to other spheres, as a "revolution in faith"? Did spiritual expectations disappear, or were they invested in other goals? The study of the most radical Quebec nationalism of the 1960s, situated in its context, can provide several avenues of reflection on this question.

Quebec's Quiet Revolution and Its Consequences
The coming to power of Jean Lesage's Liberals marked the beginning of Quebec's Quiet Revolution. This period of dramatic political change brought about highly important reforms ranging from the nationalization of Quebec's private hydro-electric power utilities to the establishment of a Ministry of Education. Quebec's late transformation into a welfare state – some fifteen years after most other Western societies – was due largely to conservative resistance within the Union nationale government,[4] which had been in office since 1944, and to the dominance of the Catholic Church,

which staffed and operated a large part of the school network and most institutions responsible for the care of the ill and the needy. Together, these conservative powers had long persuaded a majority of French Canadians to put their trust in the laws of the free market and the social teachings of the church. By the end of the 1950s, however, their views no longer seemed to convince much of the Quebec electorate. On the one hand – as the Laurendeau-Dunton Commission showed in 1968 – the economic lot of French Canadians remained glaringly inferior despite thirty years of exceptional prosperity following the Second World War. On the other hand, owing to the breakdown of the tradition of mutual support within the extended family, institutions of social welfare could no longer keep up with growing needs.[5] In June 1960, under new influences spread mostly by television, a majority of French Canadians decided to support a political party that proposed to make the Quebec state the engine of economic recovery for French Canadians as well as the instrument of a new form of social solidarity.

These economic and social transformations brought about the development of a new Québécois nationalism that was distinct from the type of nationalism traditionally espoused by the Union nationale and the Catholic Church. In the new nationalist way of seeing and labelling things, the idea of "Quebec" as a nation gradually came to replace the notion of "French Canada" as an ethnic community. The new Québécois nation now defined itself by reference to territory rather than culture and claimed to be more inclusive since belonging to Quebec no longer depended on one's ethnicity or religion. Followers of this new nationalism practically all came around to supporting the goal of Quebec independence. Their particular paths varied considerably, however. Some, like René Lévesque and Jacques Parizeau, became *souverainistes* because they wished to see the state in charge of all the tools required for the full development of the Quebec nation. These "reform" nationalists who launched the Parti Québécois in 1968 were mostly born before the Second World War, belonged to a new middle class whose outlook was shaped by the study of the social sciences, and were opposed to the Union nationale regime in their youthful twenties. Others, referred to as *indépendantistes* rather than *souverainistes*, believed in an independent Quebec for altogether different reasons. For the *indépendantistes*, the struggle to be waged by the Québécois was akin to the struggles of the Algerians, Vietnamese, or Afro-Americans against the forces of colonialism. Children of the baby boom, a number of these noisy young *indépendantistes* held that, since the British Conquest in 1760, the Québécois – the "White Niggers of America" to borrow the notorious phrase of the leftist activist Pierre Vallières – constituted a people colonized, economically and politically. To put an end to this domination, some advocated resorting to the same violent methods as the Front de libération nationale (FLN), which after a long war of attrition against the French Army, had succeeded in securing independence for Algeria in 1962. It is therefore not by mere coincidence that the following year a handful of Quebec *indépendantistes* set up the Front de libération du Québec (FLQ), a clandestine organization that fully expected to overthrow Anglo-Saxon colonialism through tried and true revolutionary methods.

Between 1963 and 1970 FLQ actions often attracted public attention. In the beginning the clandestine group would mostly set off bombs at night in Montreal locations symbolizing the Canadian government (e.g., mailboxes) or big "Anglo-Saxon" capital (e.g., the Stock Exchange). In 1970 the FLQ's most dramatic actions sparked what has become known as the October Crisis. The crisis was set off when a British diplomat was kidnapped and held in confinement for two months and Quebec's vice premier assassinated by FLQ kidnappers. To end the crisis, the Canadian government, headed by Pierre Elliott Trudeau, invoked the War Measures Act, temporarily suspending the rights and freedoms of citizens. During the troubled weeks of the October Crisis, armoured vehicles of the Canadian army patrolled Montreal streets in order, it was said, to ensure the security of the people. The police proceeded, without warrants, to arrest over 500 persons, all on the grounds of their alleged association with the *indépendantiste* movement. Even today, the exact number of Québécois who belonged to the FLQ is difficult to tally since, as a clandestine association, the FLQ did not keep up-to-date membership lists. At most, a few hundred activists and around a thousand sympathizers were involved in this underground organization.

The events of the 1970 October Crisis deeply marked the Québécois and Canadian psyches. In Quebec literature and cinema, there are countless references to these few troubled days. Among the most prominent *felquistes*,[6] as well as among those who sought to track them down,[7] several have borne witness. Furthermore, both levels of government published important enquiry reports offering a better grasp of what really happened.[8] Despite what the authorities of the day may have let the public believe, one of the things that stands out in all this testimony and these investigations is the improvised nature of the FLQ's actions. Contrary to other revolutionary movements, the FLQ of October 1970 did not have an "armed branch" at its disposal, nor did it even benefit from a very strong organization. Why, then, move into action at that particular moment?

To answer this difficult question, it is most helpful to read *La Cognée* attentively.[9] Published at regular intervals between 1963 and 1967, this newspaper is a very rich source. Beyond tracing the many ups and downs of FLQ activists, it enables us to follow their assessment of the Quebec situation at the time, to analyze their proposed means of improving the lot of the people, and to understand the dilemmas that they faced when the time came to act. Published with insignificant means, this tiny voice was in no way designed to formulate some new doctrine of social action nor indeed to win over a wide public. *La Cognée* was published twice a month. At the beginning 100 copies of each issue were printed. By the mid-1960s around 3,000 copies of each issue were printed.[10] First and foremost, *La Cognée* was a liaison bulletin aimed at ensuring that activists were informed of the movement's directives. Even so, it is no less valuable a resource inasmuch as clandestine and violent activism was a new phenomenon in French Canada's history. The activists wrote up this bulletin in the heat of action, with little concern for coherence. Its purpose was mainly to galvanize energies, not to build a thought system. The identities of the contributors to *La Cognée* are still unknown. All of the newspaper's writers published under pseudonyms and took great care not to reveal any information that might have allowed the police to identify them.[11]

A glance at *La Cognée* shows that, even if the *felquistes* used the same idiom as the *indépendantistes* concerning the need to decolonize Quebec, two waves can be identified within the FLQ. The first, which dominated until the mid-1960s, set revolutionary action in the context of the long term: the individual strove to be faceless within the group, the structure, the "Party." A servant of the "Cause," he practised obedience to the movement's enlightened hierarchy. In such a context, life counted little when measured against the success of the "Final Struggle," a grand victory that would be made possible only by methodical preparatory work to bring together the "objective conditions" for the "Revolution." The second wave, which imposed itself in the end, is termed *spontanéiste*. Inspired by Latin American guerrillas and the heroic action of Che Guevera, the *spontanéistes* were in greater haste to commit acts that would strike the imagination. In their eyes, every spectacular deed would be another call to revolutionary action. Spontaneity put the valiant activist in the forefront: only the most courageous are capable of the great deeds that success requires. The high spirit of a courageous activist, or even that of a cell imbued with a sense of history, sets an example of bravery to be followed in resisting bourgeois and colonial forces.

The exploratory hypothesis outlined in the following pages is that, while the first wave of the FLQ was moved by a millennialist spirit, the second came closer to, or even blended in with, the countercultural landscape of the late 1960s. If militant FLQ activists moved into action in October 1970, it is because they were more committed to the *spontanéiste* view. This hypothesis is empirically fragile because the first wave seems to have been composed of activists more inclined to reflect and to write, while adherents of spontaneous action seem to have preferred handling explosives to wielding the pen.

The First FLQ: The Millennialist Wave

At first glance, a quick reading of *La Cognée* would lead us to believe that its ideology was breaking with the past, in tune with the era launched in 1964 by *Parti pris*, Quebec's first truly *indépendantiste*, socialist, and secular review. Like most radical activists in the 1960s, it nurtured violent resentment toward the Catholic Church. Far more than in its portrayal of Duplessis, the late authoritarian leader of the Union nationale whose name it rarely mentioned, *Parti pris* depicted parish priests as the true "*rois nègres*"[12] responsible for keeping the French Canadian folk in the dark. Here, one easily recognizes the vulgate of *la grande noirceur*, or "great darkness," which had wide currency at the time and consisted of describing the period prior to 1960 as one of gloom and reaction.

These activists felt that, thanks to Marxism, they – more than anyone else – had in hand a most potent analytical tool. Masters of a new truth, they judged older clerics severely for preaching a life away from politics: as for themselves, they had no fear of conflict. The days of resignation were definitely over. "Never has a generation been so thoroughly politicized," wrote the earliest FLQ leaders. Never, they believed, had a generation better understood the dynamics of colonial exploitation and, hence, the need to act. Referring to the action of the new *indépendantiste* parties who accepted the rules laid down by the democratic regime, one activist wrote: "The new generation knows full well what to make of this silliness. It has figured out that it isn't through banquets and debates that one will kick the ass of the dispensers of patronage, throw them out and take their places."[13] This view, with its vindictive, fearless tone and sharp complaints about the church's role, seemed to show that the *felquistes* were breaking with French Canada's religious past. Indeed, by trashing its religious heritage, they were putting forward an ideology of "rupture." Their analysis of the situation opened new vistas focused on the future. Resolutely modern, the ideology of the FLQ served to prove that all things religious had been left behind.

This first-level reading doesn't quite enable one to grasp the full mystical intensity of earlier *felquiste* commitment, however. Indeed, upon closer inspection of their language, we quickly see that these activists were drawing from the mythological universe of millenialism, specifically Judaeo-Christian eschatology, according to which History has an absolute finality and time is slipping away irreversibly. In this view, according to the Book of Revelation, after an age of oppression during which Evil will reign as master, Liberation will follow. Before this can occur, however, a prophet will renew the hope of the downtrodden. He will give meaning to the death of many martyrs, victims of the forces of Evil. On the day of Liberation, the martyrs will all rise from the dead and Peace will settle upon Earth for a thousand years. From this narrative, which the Roman Church swiftly declared heretical, the earlier *felquistes* retained the idea of a *wait*. Radical dissatisfaction with the world is a harbinger of a period of intense revolt. When experienced as sacrifice and filled with faith in happier tomorrows, the *wait* is rewarded by the arrival of a golden era. For the believer, salvation will not necessarily come during his own lifetime but as a result of the achievement of a new earthly order in which peace and justice will reign.[14] Earlier sacrifices will then be recognized: the *wait* will not have been in vain.

Scattered throughout the first pages of *La Cognée* was the millennialist hope, harboured by *felquiste* activists, of a new Quebec freed of its oppressors and harmoniously united in a classless world celebrating its courageous prophets. We are a long way, here, from the combative, albeit good-natured, eagerness of the old Catholic Action activists.[15] This organization was violently rejected, and the crudest possible language was used to indict those seen as having persistently kept the people in the dark. If the prose was different, however, and if action took other, far more extreme forms, existential angst was no less acute, determination to create a radically new world no less sincere. One could go even further. Because they were wagering all by planting bombs and committing other illegal acts, FLQ activists of the first wave needed to give very strong meaning to their deeds. They had to believe their Cause to be that of the people, their deeds so many acts of love, their sacrifices the best they had to offer for the salvation of *la patrie*. That said, we must be careful not to confuse terms. Although the first *felquistes* experienced the need to believe, it would be a mistake to think that they invented some secular religion. As Alain Besançon argues, "underlying faith-based religions, there is awareness of things unknown."[16] At the end of the day, Christians and Muslims alike rely on a Greater Power and acknowledge their inability to understand some of society's inner workings. By contrast, those who hold an ideology to be true – and such was the case of the earlier *felquistes* – feel they know all they need to transform society.

As was seen in the early years of *La Cognée,* while the first wave of the FLQ did not borrow from traditional religious speech, here and there one detects elements of a variety of millennialism new to French Canada. I have identified a few: the relationship to the past and to the future, the role of learning and knowledge in the march of History, the place of the individual in relation to the group.

Although harsh toward the bourgeois and clerical elite, FLQ activists of the first wave seldom used the expression *"grande noirceur."* While believing themselves entrusted with a new mission, and considering themselves more enlightened about the true meaning of the course run by the Québécois, they didn't see themselves as having been generated spontaneously, like titans coming out of the earth, to save a debased people. This was hardly a complete and definitive break with the past: on the contrary, the new activism sought to respond to a new perspective on the past. During its early years *La Cognée* insisted repeatedly on carrying forward the "ancestral combat" and recalled "the struggle of our fathers" to give better meaning to the battle in progress. In its first issue announcing the program of the Front de libération du Québec, one can read: "We are struggling in memory as much of Asbestos, Murdochville, and Louiseville, as of conscription in 1917 and 1943, Saint-Eustache and the Plains of Abraham."[17] One was therefore not required to start from scratch and sweep away the past. Quebec's history teems with heroic battles, courageous personalities of distinction, resolute characters. Accordingly, respect was owed to the heroes of the Plains of Abraham and to the courageous forefathers who died, pitchfork at the ready, in the 1837 Rebellions because, before anyone else and despite their era, they had understood the true direction of History. On the other hand, those who consistently blocked "the path of progress" were traitors. Here, the notion of progress was of paramount importance, referring, as it did, to a linear and teleological view of History. Indeed, history was spelled with a capital "H," being the History of people making their way toward liberation. Great movements were those able to discern the right time to move into action so that History could achieve its true destiny.

While History moves in a certain direction, it is not fatalistic. Unlike their forefathers, the new activists had at hand a scientific method enabling them to move forward with the great advances of progress. Indeed, this is how they distinguished themselves from the heroes of yesteryear. The latter were not aware of the History they were shaping, whereas, better equipped, today's activists had learned the lessons of the past. History had taught them the path to follow.[18] Inspired by such teachings, the task of FLQ activists was now to bring together "objective conditions" for revolution. Circulated to FLQ activists, *La Cognée* insisted repeatedly on "the necessity of proceeding scientifically." Paul Lemoyne called upon the *felquistes* "never to play with insurrection."[19] Inspired by revolutionary deeds in several Third World countries, the guiding lights of the journal believed that effective action required rigorous methods. Revolution invariably followed four steps: organizational preparation; training, agitation, and propaganda; a test of strength; then seizure of power.[20] Here and there the role of the agitator was explained,[21] "the technical use of bombs" was taught,[22] and the case was made that a real war is always "subject to scientific laws," that revolution has its own "techniques."[23] Only insofar as all these teachings were correctly understood and incorporated into FLQ praxis could *le Grand Soir* be brought within reach.[24]

It was easy to figure out, however, that it was not enough to know the laws of History and to have at hand the techniques required to bring about Revolution. Unquestioning faith in science would never suffice to cause the new Québécois to break out of his shell. National liberation would be possible only if Quebec's most courageous sons agreed to sacrifice their lives for the salvation of all. Before there could be a harmonious synthesis of new beginnings, the enemy would have to be conquered physically, in hand-to-hand combat, never to rise again. In their 1963 program, the *felquistes* highlighted the following from Chénier: "Some of ours will be killed; you will pick up their guns."[25] Later, *La Cognée* returned again and again to this idea of the possibility of sacrifice and the unavoidable death even of brothers, insisting that at times the honour of *la patrie* is the daughter of tragic necessity. Accordingly, life counted for little measured against the collective work to be accomplished, and its sacrifice could even prove useful to the victory of the Nation. Thus the FLQ was not a movement of Romantic adventurers in pursuit of powerful emotions: it presumed to embody the people as a whole, and all its members were meant to take a backseat to the common cause. Those who agreed to sacrifice everything – freedom, life – would some day enter the pantheon of the liberators of the people. Recollection of their heroic deeds would be their highest reward.

In response to those who accused the FLQ of being a terrorist group, *La Cognée* replied that it was not FLQ activists who were terrorizing the people but those who had taken advantage of them ever since the Conquest. FLQ terrorism introduced itself as a new form of humanism, "a vast front of love and fraternity."[26] Conquering one's fears and resorting to violence to follow the course of revolutionary logic were made necessary by love for a group of men and women so alienated that they had come to mistake their material and political inferiority for moral superiority. The salvation of the group, and it alone, would enable individual members to unshackle themselves from their chains.

One could say, without much exaggeration, that the early ideological discourse of *La Cognée* is rather closely related to the millennialist ideas described by Yves Couture in his work on radical nationalist rhetoric in the 1960s.[27] First, one senses among these earlier *felquiste* activists a radical dissatisfaction with their society. Hence they were living in the expectation of a liberated Quebec and in the hope as well of radical renewal, of a change of life for the Quebec people, for after this collective life of misery and shrinkage, the sun was to rise on a new day: that of independence. "On that day," wrote *La Cognée*, "our people will cease surviving and begin simply to live, as does any free nation where justice reigns."[28] Here, one recognizes Judaeo-Christian eschatology. This new beginning is in fact the ultimate end of Quebec History.

These earlier FLQ activists seemed to be saying that the wait for *le Grand Soir* would be a long one. Before ridding Quebec of its clique of exploiters, there would have to be much sacrifice, a few martyrs, and many setbacks. While the wait would be long, difficult, and filled with traps, triumph would be all the more glorious for the enlightened vanguard that had anticipated Liberation. This millennialist variety of *felquiste* rhetoric illustrates very well how misleading it is to view the Quiet Revolution as marking a definitive break with all things religious. A new gnosis emerged to fit new premises. Some, the reformers, shifted their focus toward the state,[29] while others, the radicals, pinned their hopes on a nation freed from its perceived exploiters. The first wave of the FLQ is an interesting case in point. Inspired by Third World ideologies of decolonization mentioned above, the earlier *felquistes* communed in a millennialist hope of a new kind.

The Second-Wave FLQ: Countercultural Spontaneity?

The patience needed to wait for *le Grand Soir,* a sense of anonymous sacrifice, and faith in History were not to everybody's liking. Here and there, somewhat different noises were heard about the actions required, the future of the movement, and the meaning of daily struggle. Those uttering these divergent opinions were hardly preoccupied with mastering the science of revolution. They had little use for laws of History and wanted nothing to do with objective conditions: all they sought was to act, to strike at those who were keeping the people alienated. It was through spontaneous action that the masses would recognize their true defenders, not in obscure theories about Marxism.[30] If the end seemed the same, namely to free Quebec from perceived colonial oppression, there was a change in the nature of the means to achieve it. At first glance, it is clear that this new praxis coincided with a new way of conceiving revolutionary action, or so at least the last few issues of *La Cognée* (published before it disappeared in 1967) would seem to indicate. This transformation had less to do, however, with some new philosophy, matured at length, than with a context in which a therapeutic view of society had attracted numerous followers among the French Canadian elite of the 1960s.[31] In light of the 1966 and 1970 election results, many FLQ activists concluded that the wait had lasted long enough. In 1966, after six years of Quiet Revolution, the Union nationale regained power. Four years later, the Liberal Party returned to office, while the Parti Québécois, which ran candidates for the first time in its history, managed to elect only seven members despite gathering 23 percent of ballots cast. It was obvious that many *indépendantistes* were greatly disappointed with the outcome and felt that the Québécois feared real change. According to some, the time had come, after the early days of millenialist mysticism, to apply real shock therapy to this people unaware of its true alienation. In order to understand this, it is necessary to draw on the rich context of protest of the late 1960s.

Less given to reflection than the activists of the millennialist sort, the second wave, labelled *spontanéiste,* was rather anti-intellectual. Deeply hostile toward the guiding spirits of *Parti pris,* whom they accused of preferring poetry to revolutionary action, the *spontanéistes* could not stand these youths who "waste their time in idle chatter."[32] According to them, the activist's abundant energy did not need to be intellectualized in order to yield real results. Moreover, theories about revolutionary action were often ephemeral and contradictory, whereas actions themselves left a deep imprint on the mind. Exactly four days before the October Crisis, they wrote that "any doctrine can be, and is, virtually overtaken."[33]

Without doubt, 1966 was a turning point for nationalist activists of the revolutionary left. In their eyes, the election in June of the Union nationale was a distinct step backward, even a return to the Duplessis years. During the election campaign, Daniel Johnson, leader of the Union nationale, had severely criticized the expansion of the Quebec state for contributing to the dissolution of "intermediate bodies" (e.g., family, church). For many, the victory of the Union nationale marked a return in strength of the clericalism of yore, a significant "flip-flop" from the preceding years.[34] This "clerical reaction" was perceived as a crisis of the Quebec conscience. There could be no revolution, however, without real secularism. Some of the guiding lights of *Parti pris* asked themselves whether before changing society, before proposing new structures, it might not perhaps first be necessary to change Man. To achieve a socialist and independent society, might it not be necessary to reeducate the Québécois, to instil in them a new conscience? To get there, *Parti pris* proposed stressing cultural leadership at the grassroots level. The disalienation of a nation comes, at first, from the reform of consciences, not from the transformation of structures that constitute society's framework.

The election of the Union nationale affected FLQ activists in like fashion. This return to the past supplied munitions to proponents of immediate, direct action. Not only did the "objective conditions" of revolution seem out of reach, but one also had the feeling of witnessing the retrogression of national awareness. The confluence of these circumstances was all that was needed to intensify the sense of urgency of the *spontanéistes*. The people were more alienated than had even been imagined and had to be awakened to reality. Following the election of 5 June, an activist described "the growing uneasiness in Quebec."[35] As he saw it, agricultural stagnation, labour discontent, student dissatisfaction, and the crisis in the political system were all signs of an imminent breakdown. The FLQ had to move into action and fulfil its vanguard role. The last issues of *La Cognée* stated the urgency of doing so in many ways. In December 1966 it condemned "the prodigious mess of the Estates General"[36] of French Canada, which it likened to yet another exercise in largely useless "chatter" and "palaver." Only force and direct action would enable the Québécois to escape from this dead-end. In the next-to-last issue of *La Cognée* available to us (dated 15 January 1967), FLQ activists vowed to carry on "clandestine combat" and "political agitation" throughout 1967. Most of all, warned one FLQ activist, "don't expect fantastic explosions or spectacular D-Days ... it's quite sure we aren't relying on a reserve army of 100,000 guerilla fighters in secret camps to act." Above all, it was necessary to set up an "authentic organization" capable of moving into action swiftly. *La Cognée* published its last issue on 15 April 1967.[37] It is therefore not possible to follow the evolution of the ideas of the *spontanéistes* beyond this point, a sign perhaps that, from then on, FLQ activists were staking everything on direct action. As well, we now know how drastic their actions would be and what mark they would leave on the national imagination of the Québécois.

While from April 1967 onward there are no written traces whatsoever of the evolution of FLQ *spontanéisme*, the context of the late 1960s offers the view of a clear convergence toward direct action. There is every reason to believe the *felquistes* of the *spontanéiste* school saw this as confirming their predictions. The student leaders of the day also seemed weary of "idle chatter." Following the October 1968 walkouts, the wind of radicalization blew away everything in its path. At the beginning of 1969 the leaders of the Association générale des étudiants de l'Université de Montréal (AGEUM) decided to scuttle their association. Among the reasons put forward was a concern to return to their roots, a way of "fostering the development of a responsible man's conscience within everyone."[38] Almost at the same time, the same thing occurred at the Union générale des étudiants du Québec (UGEQ). At a final stormy convention, the UGEQ also decided to dissolve itself after students opted for the most radical of courses. Proponents of this view reckoned that the UGEQ was duplicating the elitist structure prevailing in Quebec. But, the activists insisted, it was important for them to return to their roots. Before defending their own wellbeing, student activists had a duty to concern themselves with "politicizing the masses" and "setting up a self-managing revolutionary society."[39]

Ideas such as "returning to grassroots," "politicizing the masses," and "developing revolutionary awareness" gave rise to new organizations typical of the times. Political action committees (*comités d'action politique,* or CAPs), whose mission was to support workers striving to break free, appeared in Montreal working-class neighbourhoods. Associations of the same nature (e.g., the Travailleurs étudiants du Québec, or Quebec Student Workers, and the Front de libération populaire, or People's Liberation Front) proliferated. The Mouvement syndical politique (Political Movement of Trade Unions, or MSP) was born at the young Université du Québec à Montréal (UQAM), which opened in September 1969. These activists and would-be revolutionaries saw themselves as a seminal group – a *"minorité agissante"* to borrow a term that enjoyed wide circulation at the time. In no way did the MSP intend to replace the UGEQ, for it was "at the grassroots that the real work is done."[40]

The feverishness of this energetic militancy – in many respects unprecedented – fed *spontanéiste* action. FLQ activists who wished to move into action saw their sense of urgency justified by student activists eager to move things forward in a hurry. "To challenge," wrote one MSP activist, "is not to 'criticize,' it is to 'demolish'; to challenge is not to 'reform': it is to tear down, to revolutionize. To challenge is not to build together in order to do better, it is to eliminate the worst ... We no longer want your society of rot and fraud with conscience at rest."[41] This rhetoric for spreading revolt was rather at odds with the millenialist rhetoric outlined above. A patient wait for some golden era to come had been replaced by appetite for action, frenzy for disorder, fascination with violence. Revolution had yielded to revolt; the sacrifice of some for the salvation of all had given way to a glory trip. Yesterday's institutions (e.g., AGEUM, UGEQ) were cast aside for immediate revolutionary activism. Ties to a past that no longer had anything to offer were severed; the time had come to jump into action. From hope in human renewal, revolutionary militancy seemed to have become an end in itself, no longer embedded in the long march of History. One felt justified in behaving this way because the past had crippled the alienated people. The task of healing minds, a mission of the vanguards and *minorités agissantes*, was far beyond their means. Still, it was necessary to seize the opportunity, capture the imagination, and shake the prevailing torpor.

Against this background, to liken the FLQ's October 1970 action to shock therapy is no exaggeration. After the April electoral victory of Robert Bourassa's Liberals and the very disappointing results obtained by the Parti Québécois, the FLQ felt the need to strike a sharp blow. In the summer that followed, a few activists organized a kidnapping plan, although it didn't secure unanimous approval among *felquistes*. Nevertheless, on 5 October 1970 the Libération cell went into action and kidnapped commercial attaché James Richard Cross of the British Consulate General in Montreal from his Westmount home. The members of the Chénier cell learned of the news over the radio on their way back from the United States. In *Pour en finir avec Octobre*, Francis Simard recalls the disappointment that he felt at the time.[42] He, the Rose brothers, and Bernard Lortie totally improvised an attack of their own by kidnapping Quebec's vice premier, Pierre Laporte, whom they assassinated a few days later. The events that followed are well known. Incapable of following these improvised acts coherently, the FLQ was rapidly neutralized and its leaders jailed or sent to Cuba.

Weary of theoretical discussions and tiny isolated bombs that no longer stirred anyone, several *felquistes* decided that the waiting had lasted long enough. Yet they could rely only on a handful of activists, had no influence over any large media, and could call upon no organized armed group. In this context, how could they expect to win? "We weren't really ready in terms of organization to deal with events like that," said Paul Rose in an interview that he gave several years later. "It was suicidal, after all, to come and do kidnappings, just like that, and then not be able to follow up with others."[43] Charles Gagnon, active in the FLQ from the movement's very beginning and a leader of Quebec's Marxist-Leninist left during the 1970s, explained in a recent text that might be seen as a kind of testament, "the FLQ remained a movement that was essentially *spontanéiste*, in which one mythologized immediate, direct action, rather than political reflection and strategic thinking ... Rebellious youth ... didn't want anything to do with debates about the path of socialism, about strategy, about objective and subjective conditions, etc. Young people wanted action, they acted, and they collided headfirst with the established order."[44]

The evolution in the thought and actions of FLQ activists during the 1960s tends to confirm the intuitive observations made by François Ricard in 1984, at a point when the *souverainiste* movement was at its lowest. Having determined that many activists, full of enthusiasm for the cause not long before, now seemed to have withdrawn into private life, Ricard wondered whether the drift in *souverainiste* ideals might not be due to its basically "narcissistic" inspiration. In the 1960s, he argued, the *indépendantiste* ideal had undergone a "vast turnaround in meaning." The restless humanism of predecessors like Hubert Aquin and Gaston Miron, and of the journals *Liberté* and *Parti pris*, might have yielded its place to a "new spirit," to "the expression of undiluted yearning for liberation without object," to a "vague taste for Quebec." According to Ricard, the seriousness of the first *indépendantistes*, their earnestness in the face of the collective effort to be marshalled, had been replaced by an overflowing lyricism in which activism had become a huge narcissistic *trip*. From a scheme to provide French Canadians with a structure to overcome their cultural fatigue, independence had been transformed into a massive celebration, a big party.[45] In short, said Ricard, as preached by the Parti Québécois, sovereignty had been stripped of its sacred character. Defended in the beginning by a handful of committed activists willing to sacrifice their own lives to bring about *le Grand Soir*, the *indépendantiste* ideal had, little by little, become "laid-back."

Because there are too few indicators to support the idea, it would be imprudent to confirm the hypothesis that the *spontanéistes* were narcissistic. Likewise, it would be a mistake to draw parallels between the *souverainisme* of the Parti Québécois in 1968 and the radical *indépendantisme* of the FLQ. Yet, like Ricard, we can observe a "turnaround in meaning" of 1960s FLQ militancy and share his impression that the 1963 activists did not give the same meaning to their actions as would, later on, the activists of 1970. Without knowing it, early FLQ activists practised the three mythical virtues described by Jean-Marc Piotte, namely devotion, faith in a new ideal, and hope for a radically new world to come. Piotte's hypothesis was that the new type of activists were seeking to reconstitute the "original community" – the village – held together by stability, warmth of affection, sharing, and some constraints.[46] Later activists, however, did not seem cut from the same cloth. Their action was not designed for the long term and their determination to do something seemed to have overtaken their determination to succeed. At the origin of this transformation was a feeling of urgency fired up, or so it would seem, by a therapeutic conception of society. For FLQ activists, the "politicization of the masses," or the freeing-up of their awareness, called for a particular kind of therapy. After two general elections – those of 1966 and 1970 – the people needed an electroshock of sorts. The effects of such therapy were unimportant: before anything else, what was needed was to act, to shake this sick body in order, at long last, to awaken it.

The discovery of the corpse of Pierre Laporte would have extraordinary reverberations. It would indeed seize the imagination of many. Although it remains noteworthy, the event did not bring about the expected effect. On the contrary, it marked the end of *spontanéisme* and of a certain revolutionary romanticism.

Acknowledgments
A much earlier version of this essay appeared in French in the *Journal of Canadian Studies – Revue d'études canadiennes* 37, 2 (Summer 2002): 33-46. The author wishes to thank Professor Magda Fahrni for her judicious comments and helpful suggestions as well as Pierre Joncas and Alysha Trinka for their translation.

Notes
1 Doug Owram, *Born at the Right Time: A History of the Baby-Boom Generation* (Toronto: University of Toronto Press, 1996), 159-215.
2 Denis Pelletier, *La crise catholique: Religion, société, politique en France (1965-1978)* (Paris: Payot, 2002), 52, 59.
3 Marcel Gauchet, *La religion dans la démocratie* (Paris: Gallimard, 1998).
4 Translators' note: For idiomatic reasons in some cases and because of particular connotations in others, a few terms in this chapter have been kept in the original French. The Union nationale was the political party created by Maurice Duplessis in the mid-1930s out of the remnants of the old provincial Conservative Party and discontented nationalistic provincial Liberals. "National Union," while it would have been correct, has gradually fallen into disuse and is virtually forgotten nowadays. The Parti Québécois never gave itself an English name: it and the abbreviation PQ have always been used in both languages. While those who advocated Quebec secession in the early 1960s quite naturally called themselves separatists *(séparatistes)*, they later preferred to style themselves *indépendantistes* and *souverainistes*. These terms – which are neologisms in French – have been retained as a reminder of the evolution in sovereigntist vocabulary. *Felquiste,* a popular neologism, and the more academic *spontanéisme,* have also been retained. *Patrie* could have been translated as "fatherland," "motherland," or "homeland," but to avoid misleading connotations ("fatherland" might suggest the Third Reich, "motherland" seems a bit soft, and "homeland" brings to mind current conditions in the US), the less loaded *patrie* has been retained. *Grand Soir* could have been translated "Revolution" (as in "Come the Revolution"), but as it would have lost some of its mystical baggage in the process, the original French was retained. Note finally that English versions of quotations from French sources are our translations.
5 On this subject, see Daniel Fournier, "Que s'est-il passé au Québec? La fin du Canada français," *Société* 20, 21 (Summer 1999): 57-93.

6 Louise Lanctôt, *Une sorcière comme les autres* (Montreal: Québec/Amérique, 1981); François Schirm, *Personne ne voudra savoir ton nom* (Montreal: Quinze, 1982); Francis Simard, *Pour en finir avec Octobre* (Montreal: Stanké, 1982); Pierre Vallières, *Nègres blancs d'Amérique* (Montreal: Parti pris, 1969).

7 Robert Côté, *Ma guerre contre le FLQ* (Montreal: Trait-d'Union, 2003); Carole DeVault, *Toute ma vérité* (Montreal: Stanké, 1981); Gérard Pelletier, *La crise d'Octobre* (Montreal: Les Éditions du Jour, 1971).

8 Jean-François Duchaîne, *Rapport sur les événements d'Octobre* (Quebec: Gouvernement du Québec, ministère de la Justice, 1981); Jean Keable et al., *Rapport de la commission d'enquête sur des opérations policières en territoire québécois* (Quebec: Gouvernement du Québec, ministère de la Justice, 1981); D.C. Macdonald et al., *Royal Commission of Inquiry into Certain Activities of the RCMP,* vol. 1 (Ottawa, 1981).

9 *La Cognée* translates as "The Hatchet."

10 Louis Fournier, *FLQ – Histoire d'un mouvement clandestin* (Montreal: Lanctôt éditeur, 1998), 55.

11 Ibid., 58.

12 Literally, "negro kings," a concept introduced in "La théorie du roi nègre" (*Le Devoir,* 4 July 1958) by André Laurendeau, the journalist and intellectual (and later co-chairman of the B&B Commission), to describe the servile attitude of Maurice Duplessis toward Anglo-American suppliers of capital. The term carries much the same connotations as "Uncle Tom" and "puppet ruler."

13 *La Cognée,* February 1964.

14 Yves Couture, *La terre promise* (Montreal: Liber, 1994), 44.

15 FLQ activists didn't seem at all influenced by the spirit of social Catholicism or by Personalism. In *La Cognée* there are no positive references to a religious heritage. "Personalism" is but a reference to the very negative idea of the individual seeking to embody the revolution heroically. We are dealing here with people of the *Parti pris* generation for whom it isn't the Great Depression of the 1930s that really matters but the Quiet Revolution. For these people, the church played a strictly negative role in Quebec, collaborating, as it did, with the enemy.

16 Alain Besançon, *Les origines intellectuelles du léninisme* (Paris: Gallimard, 1977), 15.

17 *La Cognée,* October 1963.

18 *La Cognée,* December 1963.

19 *La Cognée,* 15 April 1964.

20 *La Cognée,* 30 April 1964.

21 *La Cognée,* 31 August 1964.

22 *La Cognée,* University issue, 1965.

23 *La Cognée,* 1 October 1965. The whole issue was devoted to the techniques of revolution.

24 *Le Grand Soir* is the night when the liberation of the Québécois would finally be celebrated.

25 *La Cognée,* October 1963.

26 *La Cognée,* 31 May 1964.

27 Couture, *La terre promise.*

28 *La Cognée,* October 1963.

29 On this subject, see E.-Martin Meunier and Jean-Philippe Warren, *Sortir de la "Grande noirceur": L'horizon personnaliste de la Révolution tranquille* (Sillery: Septentrion, 2002).

30 The *spontanéiste* FLQ current had no intellectual masters to guide it. There were no serious references in *La Cognée* to accredit the theory of this kind of praxis. This leads one to believe that *spontanéisme* was a frenzy for direct action in tune with late-1960s radicalization. According to some testimony, there is reason to believe that this was the kind of social action preferred by less well-educated activists. It has also been noted that this current asserts the highly masculine nature of social engagement: action would betoken virility, while reflective thinking would signify coyness and weakness.

31 Stéphane Kelly, "La critique du clérico-nationalisme: La veine teutonne," *Société* 20, 21 (Summer 1999): 189-212.

32 *La Cognée,* 24 February 1964.

33 Ibid.
34 André J. Bélanger, *Ruptures et constances* (Montreal: Hurtubise, 1977), 182.
35 *La Cognée,* 16 June 1966.
36 *La Cognée,* 10 December 1966.
37 This is confirmed by Louis Fournier, *FLQ: Histoire d'un mouvement clandestin* (Montreal: Québec/Amérique, 1982), 59.
38 Aldéï Darveau, "La dissolution: Hara-kiri ou mort naturelle," *Quartier latin,* 18 February 1969, 7.
39 François Béland, "L'anti-congrès," *Recherches sociographiques* 13, 3 (September-December 1972): 380-91 at 383.
40 *Bulletin de liaison du MSP* 2, 1 (August 1969).
41 Ibid.
42 Simard, *Pour en finir avec Octobre.*
43 Marc Laurendeau, *Les Québécois violents* (Montreal: Boréal, 1990), 62.
44 Charles Gagnon, "Il était une fois ... Conte à l'adresse de la jeunesse de mon pays," *Bulletin d'histoire politique* 13, 1 (Fall 2004): 43-56 at 45-46.
45 François Ricard, "Quelques hypothèses à propos d'une dépression," *Liberté* 153 (June-July 1984): 40-48. This reading is strongly influenced by Christopher Lasch, *The Culture of Narcissism* (New York: Norton, 1977).
46 Jean-Marc Piotte, *La communauté perdue* (Montreal: VLB Éditeur, 1987).

3
Acadian New Brunswick's Ambivalent Leap into the Canadian Liberal Order
Joel Belliveau

Acadians. For many Canadians, the word evokes either colonial times or, at the very least, tightly knit communities shrouded in tradition. A reader would be hard pressed to find much information on the contemporary existence of this ethno-linguistic group in books on Canadian history since references to them in the national historiography are relatively rare.[1] As for "national" English-language or even "Québécois" media, they rarely focus their attention on today's Acadian community, and when they do, they are just as likely to perpetuate romantic myths as to shed any light on the subject.[2]

The relative absence of "Acadia" from Canadian contemporary history and media coverage can be partially excused. After all, Acadians – defined here as French-speaking Maritimers – number only 280,000 or so,[3] representing a little less than 1 percent of the Canadian population. Still, the recent history of Acadians is worth discovering, for it is rich in teachings on Canada's postwar linguistic and cultural transformations. This is not the story of a group forever entrenched behind the high walls of a static heritage, with little or no interaction with the rest of the nation. Rather, this is the story of a community that, enthralled by the optimism of the postwar period, embraced the ideas of "modernity" and "progress," profoundly redefining its collective identity in the process. It is the story of the most geographically concentrated French-language minority in the country, which rejected its relative isolation and gave up its hard-earned indigenous institutions in order to participate fully in state affairs and which, in the process, was largely responsible for bringing the modern welfare state to New Brunswick. Acadians also influenced the Canadian conception of official bilingualism and played no small part in the federation's attempts to accommodate modern Quebec's aspirations, a "role" that did not prevent them from mimicking Québécois separatism for a time. It is also the story of a group who, with their English-speaking neighbours, ended up developing an indigenous form of linguistic accommodation. The latter is a hybrid system, pragmatically Canadian perhaps, that lies somewhere between total integration and Belgian-style institutional and territorial autonomy.

To be sure, the community has also known failures during this period. For example, neither state intervention nor entrepreneurial initiatives have succeeded in meeting the challenge of economic development in the Acadian heartland.[4] And hard-fought policies and compromises on the linguistic front have not eliminated the menace of assimilation, which is still turning francophones into anglophones at an average rate of almost 9 percent per generation in the province (13 percent in cities and linguistically mixed regions).[5]

What follows is a chronicle of the transformations in New Brunswick's Acadian community during Canada's "*trente glorieuses.*"[6] Attention will be given to this evolution's internal dynamic, but also to the ways that Canadian historical benchmarks – postwar social programs and economic prosperity, the Massey and Laurendeau-Dunton Commissions, Trudeau's doctrine – influenced Acadians and were influenced by them. We will see that like Québécois separatism, First Nations affirmations, and multicultural awakenings, the "Acadian question" has represented a cultural challenge to contemporary Canada's evolving, liberal model of citizen integration.

Yearning for Participation

A Cultural and Ideological Crossroads

Halfway through the twentieth century Acadia came to an invisible crossroads. The large-scale socio-economic transformations of the 1940s and 1950s – the war economy and the postwar boom, government infrastructure expenditures and the first programs of the Canadian welfare state – deepened Acadian New Brunswick's integration into the North American market economy, of which it had long been – officially – suspicious. This integration had a dizzying number of effects: work for wages became the norm, traditional occupational structures were destabilized, rural exodus intensified, the family's function as a unit of production declined as extra revenue permitted increasing consumption of modern commodities, and fishing and farming became full-fledged professional activities demanding important investments.[7] Briefly stated, economic and political circumstances tugged at a peripheral, culturally distinct Acadian community and aligned it with wider continental trends. Acadians' average income, however, remained well under the Canadian mean.

All of these changes represented very real challenges for thousands of individuals. But they also posed an ideological challenge for the Acadian elite and its "national" ideology. This discourse, which traces its origins to large "national conventions" held at the end of the nineteenth century, was one of "withdrawal," relatively devoid of demands toward the political system. It did not aim to give Acadians, as individuals, equal rights within the province or country but to develop an autonomous, almost autarkic sphere of Acadian life. This ideology was akin and related to the French Canadian ideology of *"survivance"* (but distinct in its ideological symbols and geographic attachment) and was not devoid of messianic interpretations:[8] Acadia was to be a simpler, rural, agricultural society, isolated from the evils of urbanization and capitalism as well as from the dangers of Protestantism.

This nationalist discourse had never actually been an accurate reflection of reality. Despite its relative isolation, some distinct cultural practices, and its collective identity, the Acadian ethno-linguistic community had always been influenced by outside cultural, economic, and political logics,[9] but nationalist discourse served as a filter, denying these outside realities and creating an "imagined community"[10] in which, it was believed, "l'Acadie" had an autonomous existence. However, in the face of the transformations of the 1940s and 1950s, this discourse's credibility was wearing increasingly thin.

At the beginning of the 1950s New Brunswick's large (and still growing) Acadian community was therefore one of paradox. In its practices, especially its economic practices, it was increasingly liberal. But its dominant conception of the world and of its place in it was resolutely aliberal. If one were to wholly believe the national ideology, Acadians formed a self-sufficient, rural community living on the fringes of North America and were proud of it. Such a dissonance between reality and discourse could not last forever. Acadian collective identity would need to change or risk disappearance due to irrelevance.

The Early Years, 1950-59
Since the beginning of the century, the Acadian elite had produced permanent political organizations. Network-type patriotic associations linked nationalist leaders with notables from every village and town of importance.[11] Throughout the first half of the twentieth century, these nationalist networks worked relentlessly – if discreetly – for the advancement of Acadian and French Canadian causes. At first, the spirit of self-reliance that was put forth in the national ideology was applied in this indigenous – or parallel – political sphere. If any interaction with the state was to occur, it was done through discreet, personal appeals to politicians and decision makers. But for the most part, Acadians' goals would be accomplished by Acadian – or at least French Canadian – means. This was done through vast private "subscription campaigns" (or fundraisers), which were organized on the regional or pan-Canadian level to accomplish specific social, educational, or cultural goals chosen from among the ethno-linguistic group's priorities. The

sums thus collected went to support French-language institutions such as newspapers and radio stations, hospitals, and schools or colleges. For example, a national campaign raised $106,000 in 1943-44 in order to permit *L'Évangéline* to become the first Acadian daily newspaper.[12]

But now, in the progress-obsessed, booming postwar years, these communitarian means seemed insufficient to more and more Acadian leaders. Across the Western world, social and economic progress was increasingly seen as something that could result only from state planning and intervention. The state was growing; so were its resources. Shouldn't the Acadians get out there and get their fair share? Wasn't this especially true given that even if they didn't turn toward the state, the state was coming to them? In this era of bureaucratization, the state was increasingly regulating spheres in which the elite had managed to carve out pockets of autonomy, such as education and colonization. For this reason, since the 1930s, Acadian institutions had reluctantly, almost timidly, started to intervene a bit more in state affairs.[13]

After the war, despite their autonomy-oriented official discourse, progressive members of the elite were slowly coming to the realization that increased participation in provincial and national political affairs could be beneficial to Acadian society, and the content of the nationalist discourse began to change. One important factor that contributed to this change in attitude toward the state is without a doubt demographic growth. Acadians as a group represented only 16% of the New Brunswick population in 1871. By 1951 they comprised almost 40%. During this time span, the province's French-language population increased by 340%, compared to 30% for the population of British origin.[14] This ever-increasing demographic and electoral weight no doubt reassured would-be Acadian lobbyists that their messages would not fall on deaf ears should they venture into the provincial – or even federal – arena.

Other factors, linked to the evolution of the Acadian community's internal dynamic, also played a role. With or without demographic change, the elite felt the need to make adjustments. For one thing, the need was felt to modify a "national" ideology that was less and less seen as a credible reflection of reality and that was losing the masses' favour. But the new orientation also reflected the Acadian elite members' changing goals and aspirations. The increasing availability of government positions and functions slowly convinced the elite that a further integration into the wider environment was desirable not only for the community as a whole, but also for themselves. Seeing their traditional base of power being gradually eroded, the elite chose to invest themselves in the state and its functions; they would henceforth be a "relay class" occupying a position between the Acadian population and the political powers.[15]

The illusion of autonomy could therefore not go on forever. But how could Acadians let go of their national ideology without losing their sense of collective identity? How could they find a balance between the community's traditional autonomist stance and increased integration in the economy and the state? The Acadian elite of the 1950s spent a good deal of time trying to solve this conundrum.

A good example of this ideological tightrope act can be found in the organization of the Acadian Deportation's 200th anniversary commemorations. Some of the most prominent members of the elite, made up of leaders from L'Assomption, *L'Évangéline*, and the Université Saint Joseph (USJ), started planning the event seriously in 1953.[16] The celebrations would be spread out over a whole year and incorporate many religious, historical, artistic, and patriotic activities. But what message would be diffused, ideologically speaking?

The result was a monument to paradox and conciliation. For starters, the events were funded through both a French Canadian "subscription campaign"[17] and government contributions,[18] something decidedly new for Acadian patriotic events. These public contributions were agreed to because, according to all involved, the celebrations were meant to promote Acadian identity but *not* to revive old wounds or rancour toward English Maritimers or the Crown.[19] To do this, the emphasis would be squarely placed on Acadian society's "Renaissance," or rebirth, and on its future. The past would be invoked mostly with regard to tradition, folklore, and faith, while the Deportation – the pretext for the whole event – would ironically be pushed to the sidelines. By omitting aspects of the traditional ideology, the organizers hoped to help Acadians make peace with the Deportation, abandon the idea of a providential destiny, and adhere to a vision in which Acadian society could take its future in its own hands while working with its anglophone neighbours.[20] The Acadians must participate more fully in New Brunswick and Canadian society: such was the subtext that the organizing committee gave to the celebrations.

The organizers conceived this event as a stepping stone to a more modern Acadia. And they fully expected to contribute to its realization. During the subscription campaign, potential donors – including the formally solicited Quebec government of Maurice Duplessis – were told that proceeds would go not only toward the festivities but also to the establishment of a "permanent secretariat" for the newly revived Société nationale acadienne (SNA). This was done in 1958.[21] The opening was presented as a historic occasion, and in many ways it was. With it, the Acadian national movement moved out of the shadows and put on a public face. The institution was to act as an official mouthpiece for the ethno-linguistic group; it was to do research, build dossiers, establish formal relationships, and most important, intervene in the public and governmental spheres to defend Acadian interests.[22] Today, the establishment of a "national" representational structure might not seem like an act of particular "openness," but in the Maritimes of the 1950s it was a sure sign that Acadian leadership wanted to participate more fully in ambient society.

Other signs of increasing political, social, and cultural integration abounded during the 1950s. The 1952 election had been a windfall for New Brunswick Acadians, whose long and remarkable demographic climb was starting to produce results. Four French-speaking Conservatives had been elected – a first – in Hugh John Fleming's government, two of whom were named ministers. Ten of the sixteen Liberal opposition members seated across the floor were Acadian.[23] Among them was a newly elected, twenty-six-year-old lawyer named Louis Robichaud.

Acadian politicians and nationalist leaders had always formed overlapping but separate spheres. This remained true in the 1950s, but with a growing Acadian presence in the Legislature, nationalist elements were optimistic that a more equitable sharing of state resources and power was close at hand. Slowly and surely, the number of requests of a linguistic nature that were made to the state started to rise, such as limited official recognition of French, the establishment of a "bilingual" teacher's college, and a greater share of public employment. Results were, however, rare and infrequent and far from spectacular.[24]

The young Robichaud incorporated many political currents found in 1950s Acadia. As a member of the Ordre-de-Jacques-Cartier, he knew the traditional Acadian leadership, ideology, and methods.[25] But he was also from a long-time Liberal family, and his studies at Laval's Faculté des Sciences sociales – along with his conversations with the "Father of the Quiet Revolution," Georges-Henri Lévesque – had amplified his liberal philosophy and turned him into an unflinching partisan of social justice and state intervention.[26]

The 1950s were also the decade of the federal Royal Commission on National Development in the Arts, Letters and Sciences, presided over by Vincent Massey. Laval's Father Lévesque was a prominent member of the commission. In fact, many Quebecers mistakenly believed that he was its co-president. At this juncture, Acadians, like other Canadians, turned to the state to fulfil their cultural needs. In the 1940s French Canadians had held a subscription campaign to give French speakers in Manitoba their own radio station.[27] In the 1950s, when progressive Acadian leaders decided that French-language radio was necessary to stem assimilation, they did not even consider this option. Father Clément Cormier, Université Saint Joseph's president and a member of the Congregation of the Holy Cross, took the leadership in this cause. As another one of Father Lévesque's former Acadian students, he had no trouble gaining the Massey Commission's attention. With a handful of acolytes, he successfully lobbied the federal government into granting the region its first Radio-Canada radio (1954) and then television (1959) stations.[28]

Cormier was an active reformer in his field as well. During his stint as founding director of the Université Saint Joseph's École des Sciences sociales and then as University president, he worked tirelessly to modernize the institution. New programs were instituted in the fields of commerce, the sciences, engineering, and the social sciences, making the USJ the first among Acadian colleges to distance itself from the "classical course" model.[29] The modest university even attracted many youth from Quebec bent on specialization in "modern" disciplines, still rare in French Canadian colleges.

In this quest for educational and scientific modernization, the state was once again called upon. The USJ played a leading role, along with Mount Allison University, in the fight that was put up by "private" colleges for financial assistance from the New Brunswick government.[30] The situation was very partially redressed in 1952, but in 1959 the University of New Brunswick still received almost seven times as much money per student as the average confessional university.[31]

Nonetheless, Cormier was bent on creating a modern French-language university in New Brunswick. For this progressive cleric, this centre of higher learning had to be in the city, where one found a critical mass of services and of potential students. His administration began a gradual transfer of the college's activities from the village of Memramcook to the City of Moncton, about twenty-five kilometres down the road. This consolidated – some would say confirmed – a fifty-year trend among French-language institutions. Despite the agriculturalist national ideology, Moncton had become the nonofficial Acadian "capital," where were concentrated major institutions such as the Archbishopric, L'Assomption, *L'Évangéline*, Radio-Canada, the SNA, and now the largest and most modern of Acadian colleges. It seemed that the city, just like the state, was increasingly accepted as a "normal" part of the Acadian community's realm. The era of isolationism was definitely coming to an end.

It is through this nonstop toiling on the part of the elite's most progressive fringe – present in the colleges, in the provincial capital, at *L'Évangéline*, and in "national" associations – that the ideal of liberalism was thrust into the Acadian psyche.[32] Slowly and surely, a new discourse based on the ideas of "participation" and "integration" took form during the 1950s. Participation in the political and economic spheres, co-operation with English-speaking neighbours and integration into the state apparatus became the new political ideal. This ideal was firmly liberal in its philosophy since the only thing it expected from the state (and the only thing believed to be necessary in order to achieve equality for all) was an identical treatment of all citizens, without any attention being paid to their particularities – cultural or otherwise. "After having almost denied the existence of the Other in its discourse, or at the least having insisted on the fundamental differences that separate the two societies, the ideologues are brought to recognize their cohabitation in the Maritimes and to privilege that which unites them with anglophone society."[33]

During this time, the dominant idea of the elite's function also gradually changed. It was no longer seen as the guardian and administrator of wholly Acadian institutions. Rather, it was now its members' role to take their rightful place in the provincial (and even Canadian) power structures. In doing so, it was said, they were not only assuming their responsibilities as full-fledged citizens, but also ensuring that the needs of Acadians would be well represented. The Acadian elite thus finally succumbed to the Western world's postwar faith in rational – even "scientific" – governance.[34]

During this important shift, the elite tried hard to avoid any open schism with the traditional nationalist ideology. Tactics used to this end included syncretism and total dissociation of the cultural and the political realms.[35] However, the rising "integrationist" and modernist ideological elements quickly became dominant.[36] This is especially true after Louis Robichaud's Liberal Party surprised everyone and formed the government in June 1960, one week after Jean Lesage's Liberals did the same in Quebec.[37]

The Triumph of Political and Economic Participation, 1960-66

If the 1952 election had been a windfall for Acadians, the 1960 election was an earthquake. It was the first time in the province's (almost) two-hundred-year history that an Acadian was elected premier.[38] Furthermore, few had given Robichaud much chance of winning just seven weeks earlier, when a confident Hugh John Fleming had called the election.[39]

Some observers therefore did not know quite what to expect from this young Liberal. Would he lead a campaign of retribution on the part of the important but long-marginalized French minority? Had he not talked, not so long ago, about the need for religion in public schools?[40] Had he not just recently expressed strong support for Acadian nationalists' main request – the building of a French normal school? Had his electoral platform's main promise – the suppression of hospital premiums and the financing of hospital insurance through general revenues – not pitted rural against urban and French against English citizens?[41] And now, to top everything off, was his Cabinet not composed of six francophones and six anglophones, yet another first in the province's history?

However, it would soon become clear enough that the new man in office was above all a proponent of administrative, economic, and political modernization. During the election campaign, the Liberal Party – and even the Acadian elite, now completely enthralled with the idea of "participation" – had gone out of its way to present ethno-linguistic origins as being irrelevant. The politician, for his part, mostly ignored the topic and stressed that he wanted to be "premier of all New Brunswickers,"[42] and he presented all his policies in terms of their contribution to the "greater good" and "progress."[43] Once in office, he made it very clear to all lobbyists, and particularly to the Acadian associations, that their priorities could not be imposed on him.[44] But most of all, it was the content of his agenda that was reassuring. Listening to Robichaud talk about building canals, attracting new industry, replacing antiquated liquor laws, improving the education system, and even maritime (political) union, one knew that he was not simply a political hired gun.

Even reforms and public investments favourable to the Acadian community were done in the context of larger, broader reforms that were ostensibly for the good of all. The creation of the Université de Moncton in 1963 is a case in point. With it, Acadians finally gained access to a modern, equitably funded, French-language university.[45] This new institution, however, was only one of a host of recommendations made by the Royal Commission on Post-Secondary Education.[46] Its creation came simultaneously with the extension of equal financing to English-language denominational universities *and* the creation of a new English university campus in Saint John. Finally, overall funding per student for postsecondary education was increased. Thus the arrival of the Université de Moncton was simply part of a wider modernization of the province's postsecondary educational system, and it was presented as such.[47]

Robichaud's most profound reform, dubbed Programme of Equal Opportunity (PEO), also fitted into this pattern. With this reform, which required the abrogation of some 40 laws and the proclamation of 130 new ones, the provincial government would henceforth be solely responsible for taxation,[48] health, education, social services, and justice.[49] County councils would be eliminated, but on the other hand, rural regions would benefit from a uniformization of taxation and of public services. PEO did benefit the Acadians, but this was for the simple reason that many of their communities were situated in rural, economically depressed counties that were unable to finance decent public services. Many English-dominated regions benefited as well, and the reforms rationalized the provincial state's structures – to the point that debates on the subject, although heated, did not provoke polarization along ethnic lines.[50]

During the first half of the 1960s, the bicultural society that is New Brunswick, whose political life had until then "sought its legitimacy in its local and decentralized nature,"[51] was suddenly permeated by the state's logic and functions. On the Acadian side, the church was made to abandon its many social functions. The overwhelming popular support that these reforms garnered among the Acadian population demonstrates to what point the ideology of participation had become dominant. The quasi-unanimous support for the Robichaud reforms should not, however, lead us to forget that a mere ten or fifteen years earlier, they would have been practically unthinkable. The change was stupendous: in a few short years, Acadian society, whose elite had long wished for autonomy, had accepted – and even cheered on – the integration of its most important institutions into the bureaucratic controls of the provincial government.[52] A few denounced the "expropriation" of hospitals, colleges, and county governments, but the majority celebrated the coming of a new era of modern public services. During the same period, the Ordre-de-Jacques-Cartier disbanded[53] and L'Assomption Fraternal Society became Assomption-Vie, a mutual insurance company responding first and foremost to the imperatives of financial viability and profitability.[54] The Association Acadienne d'Éducation, which considered equality in education now to be a done deal, also put an end to its activities.[55] In ten short years, the Acadian elite's traditional institutional structure had disappeared, leaving in its place what seemed like a new society.

The ideal of participation and "equal opportunity" was on everyone's lips and was little – if at all – contested during the first half of the 1960s. Even the emerging, rebellious student movement at the Université de Moncton adhered, although unwittingly, and one could say somewhat aggressively, to the dominant discourse of "participation." In fact, they pushed the ideology further than any of the official nationalist organizations. The latter, although they now pinned their hopes on the state, made efforts to remain loyal to Acadian nationalism's traditional symbols, historical legacy, and noteworthy personalities. But there would be no such compromise for the students, for whom everything "old" had to go. In their newspaper and in public forums, they constantly derided the SNA for not having prepared the Acadians for modern life[56] and for having failed to explain the Acadians' pitiful situation to the province's English speakers.[57] They criticized the Robichaud government for not giving Acadians all the means that they needed to succeed fast enough. They shunned other Acadian student associations – based at colleges affiliated with the Université de Moncton – and created new organizations with students from the province's English universities. The new generation would succeed where the old ones had failed, and the incomprehension between linguistic groups was but one of the evils that would quickly disappear under its modern, rational, and democratic watch.[58]

Finally, in 1966, during a youth conference organized by the SNA – which was hoping to recruit a few junior members – the Moncton students heavily influenced the assembly and convinced it to adopt many iconoclastic resolutions, criticizing just about every Acadian institution. The final – and most symbolic – resolution to come out of the Ralliement de la jeunesse acadienne recommended that "all patriotic symbols, such as the flag, the patron saint and the national holiday be conserved in Acadia's folklore but cease to be invoked as symbols of national identity."[59] Even the *word* Acadian seemed

Acadian students in synch with their North American colleagues: protest against the Vietnam War in Moncton, November 1967.
With permission from the Centre d'études acadiennes

good for the wastebasket, as the youth again and again preferred the generic – and relatively new – term "francophones," which seemed devoid of ethnic and religious connotations. Decidedly, in Acadian New Brunswick the years 1960-66 were all about breaking with the isolationist past and becoming full-fledged New Brunswickers and Canadians.

The buzzwords of integration and participation were also applied to the field of the economy. Acadians cheered as the Robichaud government stimulated, incited, and pushed forward dozens of industrial development projects in the fields of pulp and paper, mines, hydro-electricity, and even chemicals.[60] A new wave of industrialization would raise the regional per capita income to the Canadian average, or so it was hoped. Acadian support was also initially strong for the federal-provincial joint efforts on the front of regional development.[61] Robichaud recruited modernity-minded members of the Acadian elite as agents in the implementation of these policies,[62] which, it was hoped, would bring prosperity to the most rural regions of the province.

Foreign investments and state intervention were not, however, seen as the only ways forward. The 1960s also witnessed a breakthrough for a liberal-capitalist economic discourse in Acadia. The more familiar co-operative model of economic development, which had until then been celebrated by the elite as a communitarian alternative to "Protestant" capitalist practices, was more or less pushed to the background as professors at the Université de Moncton's new Faculty of Commerce spread the gospel of capitalist development and entrepreneurial culture in the classroom as well as through a magazine that they founded, *La Revue Économique:*

> We must constantly remember the fact that even the French element of the province lives in a North American economy. The latter knows only dynamism, optimism and an unshakeable faith in the future. It is a progressive economy, always on the lookout for opportunities to perfect itself. This type of economic activity has such a strong hold [on society], even in socialist countries, that it would be inconceivable, if not impossible, to build, on the North American continent, an exclusive economy corresponding to the aspirations of a particular group. This is why I consider it urgent, for us, to build inside of the established economic structure. Our economic development will thus be easier, and I do not believe that it will prejudice our national character.[63]

The adherence of many to a capitalist ethos that would have seemed foreign not long before was another sure sign that participation in the wider world was the dominant ideal in 1960s Acadian New Brunswick.

During the 1950s and 1960s a liberal discourse of participation and integration was developed in Acadian New Brunswick. It was put forth cautiously at first, then with increasing force. By the first half of the 1960s, Acadian nationalism was almost completely negated. Louis Robichaud's election as premier was seen by many as living proof that Acadians *could* participate successfully in the wider public sphere and even have an important influence on provincial and national politics. This did not apply merely to members of Robichaud's Cabinet and deputation; many Acadian notables from all parts of the province invested in the state in many different ways, thus participating in the rationalization of the state's relation with local communities.[64] What was happening was not so much the state being "Acadianized" as the Acadian community being integrated into the state apparatus and the maritime market economy. Many must have thought, as they were entering the Canadian Centennial year, that the "Acadian question" would soon be history. They were in for a surprise.

The Emergence of Ideological Pluralism

The Appearance of Dissenting Voices, 1967-69

Between 1967 and 1969 the participation discourse was shattered and fundamentally called into question. Many elements played a role in this unexpected ideological twist, but no preponderant individual or principal group can be said to have been the main proponent of the changes. The new discourse that was starting to appear and was contesting "participation's" domination was prepared by no school of thought and by no lobby. The change was brought forth by many small incidents and seemed to take everyone by surprise. By the time anyone could reflect on the events, the linguistic situation in New Brunswick had changed considerably. Participation had lost the almost unanimous acceptance and appeal that it had enjoyed since the turn of the decade. What would later be called "neo-nationalism" was born.

One of the roots of change lay in a growing disenchantment with "statism." The idea that increased state planning and intervention would lead to better-off communities was starting to be questioned. Robichaud's government had certainly improved the state of educational and public services province-wide, but the overall socio-economic situation of Acadian regions had changed little since 1960. The promise of government-initiated foreign investments remained just that. It was also becoming clear that northern New Brunswick's mineral boom would never fully materialize, despite heavy provincial involvement. The early signs of a university-nurtured entrepreneurial culture only seemed to create jobs in or around cities. And especially, regional-development efforts seemed to be making no difference and were becoming increasingly intrusive, as they were now trying to convince families to move to regional "growth centres."

The most visible symbol of Acadian rural communities' frustration with state-sponsored development schemes remains the expropriation of 215 homes on New Brunswick's eastern coast in 1969 to create the new Kouchibouguac National Park. The residents, although relatively impoverished, resisted – politically, legally, and sometimes physically – the efforts to move them and their homes. And their leader, Jackie Vautour, became a martyr of sorts for the cause of rural resistance.[65] To more and more rural Acadians, state economic intervention seemed insensitive and disrespectful of local realities and culture. As for the market economy, it seemed to promise only subservience, just like the fish merchants and lumber barons of old.

These economic problems did not touch the growing urban "francophone" population directly. But trouble was brewing on the side of linguistic issues as well. Acadians had embraced participation, but they expected in return the tools and the respect that were needed to participate on an equal footing. Some events, however, gave the impression that equal conditions of participation were not so close at hand. As early as 1965 a few incidents had ruffled the feathers of the *"bonne entente"* that was reputed to prevail between the linguistic groups. The contents of the celebrations marking the seventy-fifth anniversary of Moncton's incorporation had annoyed quite a few Acadians. Not a word of French was spoken during the ceremonies, nor was the important Acadian presence in the city acknowledged. To top it all off, the Union Jack and Red Ensign were thrown about generously as decorations, but there was no sign of the newly adopted Canadian flag. The year also saw the Fredericton School incident. The city's education board refused parents' request for a local French school even though it was serving the provincial capital. What would happen to the children of French-speaking bureaucrats and politicians?[66] The optics were bad.

Some cynically remarked that the Fredericton defeat didn't matter much since the proportion of Acadians in the higher levels of public administration wasn't growing as fast as they'd hoped anyway. In the eyes of many, the provincial government's record was not squeaky clean either. It had, for example, taken *seven* years for it to deliver on the promise of a French teachers' college, mostly because of the opposition of the "provincial" normal school, situated in Fredericton. This was particularly irritating for the partisans of participation since the elevation of Acadians' general educational level – which required teachers qualified to teach in French – was one of their highest priorities.

Up to this point, however, although some were occasionally disgruntled, the idea of participation was not really called into question. This was to change starting in 1967, partly due to what could be called the "de Gaulle spark." During the summer of 1967 officials from four important Acadian institutions[67] were invited to meet the French president to discuss Franco-Acadian cultural co-operation. The news started spreading a mere month or two after the French president's infamous "Vive le Québec libre!" speech, and many members of the local and national English-language press, along with many important public figures, cried scandal. Many Acadians were annoyed or hurt that their English neighbours regarded the donation of books to a new university, the establishment of scholarships to study abroad, and the gift of a new printing press for *L'Évangéline* as "cultural imperialism" or "interference with Canadian sovereignty." The returning delegation invoked English-language precedents such as the Commonwealth and the Rhodes scholarships,[68] and the controversy slowly died out. But it left behind a newly heightened state of linguistic tension.

This tension spilt over into yet another growing language debate, making it more and more acrimonious. In school District 15, situated in Moncton, a half-dozen French-language schools were administered along with numerous English-language schools. The existence of a distinct French curriculum had finally been legally recognized a few years back, but all was not well. Teachers and parents were increasingly critical, claiming that since French board members were perpetually in a minority position, their schools were regularly neglected during the allocation of budgets and equipment as well as during the setting of priorities. To top everything off, the district board's meetings were held in English only, even if the structure was technically "bilingual."[69] During the first months of 1967, many had started demanding the creation of a distinct French-language district, which would

Demonstrating for equal opportunity in a modern world: Université de Moncton students crowding the rectoı's office (and the campus' chief of security) during the lead-up to the January 1969 week-long occupation of the campus' administrative building and Faculty of Science.
Centre d'études acadiennes, UM001987-A

give the francophone community control over "its own" schools.[70] The tension became so severe that two of the better-known French-speaking board members resigned in protest in May. These demands in favour of overlapping, language-defined, but publicly funded structures was something resolutely new in New Brunswick. And it was squarely incompatible with the ideal of participation, which implied shared public institutions.

This new logic, albeit still only vaguely articulated, instantly seduced students at the Université de Moncton. For one thing, both the university's professors' association and the Student Union had been quick to give their public support to the District 15 "secessionists." But in the fall, still reeling from Mayor Leonard Jones' reaction to the De Gaulle invitation and still excited by an early April appearance by Hubert Aquin – a prominent member of Quebec's Rassemblement pour l'indépendance nationale (RIN) and a well-known author – the students started applying a communitarian logic to their own demands. Facing the prospects of yet another tuition hike, they turned the issue of university funding into a linguistic one, at least partially. The Acadian formed a linguistic and cultural community, they argued, a community that has the right to its own public institutions, which should be of comparable quality to those of the linguistic majority. This philosophy was used to justify large demonstrations held by the students in

February 1968 and January 1969.[71] Taking aim at the province, they invoked the Acadian community's *particular* situation and the *special* needs of its only university. Since Acadians represent 40% of the population, they argued, "their" sole institution should receive 40% of the province's university funding, even if it served only 25% of the province's students.[72] Universities were all of a sudden considered *community* institutions – rather than provincial ones – which did not correspond to legal realities.

The District 15 controversy and the radicalization of the Université de Moncton student movement point to the reappearance of the concepts of "collectivity" ("collective needs," "collective rights") and of "cultural specificity" in the Acadian political discourse. What was happening at the end of the 1960s was that students, educators, and a growing segment of the Acadian population were starting to call into question the liberal idea according to which the identical treatment of all citizens – without regard for any particular group identities – could lead to real equality. This represented a challenge to the liberal political model of participation.

But the strong postwar liberal current in Acadian society had not said its last word; it was not about to give way without a fight. In order to stem a further slide toward communitarianism, the now embattled Louis Robichaud government, along with its allies, brought out the ultimate linguistic concession that they could make without straying from their fundamentally liberal worldview. This concession was official bilingualism.

The timing was ripe for a move toward the adoption of French as the nation's second official language. Across the country, there was a sense that "something had to be done" to stem Québécois separatism. In October 1967 René Lévesque had left the Quebec Liberal Party to devote himself to the "indépendantiste" cause. A month later, a large French Canadian conference, Les États Généraux du Canada Français, had confirmed the progress of separatism among the Québécois political class (or at least of "go-it-alone-ism").[73] Mere days later, the divergences between the Quebec government[74] and the "rest of Canada" had been highlighted during the "Confederation of tomorrow" conference.[75] Finally, the federal Royal Commission on Bilingualism and Biculturalism issued its first report a week later. It illustrated the very real inequalities that persisted between anglophones and francophones, and the commissioners (who included Father Clément Cormier)[76] recommended, among other things, that the federal, Ontario, and New Brunswick governments become officially bilingual.[77]

Now that the Canadian national agenda was pointing toward linguistic accommodation, Robichaud's Liberal government could easily present the adoption of official bilingualism both as an act of fairness toward the Acadian population *and* as New Brunswick's contribution to national unity.[78] Thus in March of 1968 Robichaud presented a motion to the Legislature announcing the government's intention to proceed with official bilingualism, and in April 1969 the change was made into law by the adoption of an Official Languages Act partly inspired by the new federal law of the same name.[79]

The adoption of French as an official language both in Ottawa and in Fredericton was an event of high symbolic importance, and a large majority of Acadians, like many French Canadians both outside and inside Quebec, were delighted. In Acadian New Brunswick these events kept all minds – including the new, young, and (re)emerging nationalist forces – partly focused on issues of common participation in shared public structures. They kept alive the dream of two "nations" working in harmony in one country. The Moncton student movement, for example, while it demanded a special status for its university, also led a direct and public confrontation with Moncton's Mayor Jones in the hopes of bringing about a more inclusive – that is, bilingual – municipality. This battle would be followed by a broad-based, SNA-sponsored Comité pour le bilinguisme à Moncton until 1974, without avail.[80] Nonetheless, bilingualism – and the idea of equal chances of participation in public affairs regardless of language – would remain (and remains today) a central theme in Acadian political discourse.

Neo-Nationalism and the Rise of a New Ideal, 1970-75

The idea of participation – notably through institutional bilingualism – was here to stay. But this did not mean that it was to go unchallenged. Relative unanimity such as that displayed by the Acadian population during much of its history – vis-à-vis traditional, church-laced nationalism until 1960 and vis-à-vis the Robichaud program during the first half of the 1960s – was now a thing of the past. And the deep fissures that cracked the ideology of participation were slowly spawning new discourses of their own.

Bilingualism, as a political project, was weakened by the skepticism of many. Would the anglophone majority, in fact, profoundly change its ways? Could the province be trusted? Many sections of the Official Languages Act were scheduled to be proclaimed only in the mid- to late 1970s! And many of the first requests that were made to the province for actual bilingual services had been turned down. For example, the requests of Moncton students that their trial be held in their language were repeatedly refused, albeit with apologies.[81] Skepticism over the provincial state's will or capacity to change favoured the development of two relatively different movements supporting Acadian autonomy.

Territorial Autonomy

The most openly autonomist and most structured of these two movements had strong regionalist overtones and had its base in north-eastern New Brunswick. Its unofficial beginning came on 1 December 1971, dubbed "Black Wednesday" in this region. On this day three of the region's largest employers announced layoffs totalling 1,700 employees. Still more layoffs followed.

The news triggered a wave of protests orchestrated by unions and the Conseil régional d'aménagement du Nord (CRAN).

The CRAN was a federally funded regional-development council. Its young, university-educated field workers (or "social animators") had become increasingly radical during the late 1960s, acting less and less like government planners and more and more like spokespersons for the rural population. These radical elements had gained control of the organization's board in the spring of 1970 and had been actively spreading a somewhat romantic, back-to-the-earth gospel of self-development ever since.[82]

The events of January of 1972 not only mobilized thousands of protesters and created a strong feeling of regional solidarity, but also reinforced links between the CRAN and students and faculty from the Collège de Bathurst. Some young professors there had been quietly developing what they called "neo-nationalist" ideas during the past few years. Now, feeling that the timing was right, they and recruits from the CRAN seized the moment to launch and organize a brand new political party: le Parti Acadien (PA).[83]

The founders of the PA borrowed from many existing ideas and ideologies. The idea of socialism, or at least that of a fair distribution of wealth, was very present. Capitalism was rejected for having allowed the persistence of deep economic disparities, of which many Acadian regions were

Communitarian and romantic backlash: The rise of the autonomist Parti Acadien. Seen here is the executive elected during the party's first annual congress in December 1973. Seated: Euclide Chiasson (president), Yvon Babineau, Germaine Moreault (treasurer), Jean-Marie Nadeau (candidate), and Louis Boudreau. Standing: Gilles Thériault (fisher union organizer and candidate), Walter Giachino, Léon Thériault (historian and councillor), and Ronald Robichaud.
Centre d'études acadiennes, collection de L'Évangéline, E18818

victims. The party claimed that, in the face of big business' shameful domination, it wanted to represent "ordinary" Acadians like workers and small producers. Its ideal, although rarely well defined, was the creation of a renewed rural society in northern and eastern New Brunswick. To attain this end, it advocated the local control of natural resources and an egalitarian redistribution of land, among other things. Later, decentralization of the provincial state's powers and even the creation of an Acadian province would also become central issues.[84]

The PA scorned "traditional" political formations, centrally planned regional-development efforts, and even urbanization and industrialization. It knew that it could not form the government but hoped to obtain the balance of power, thereby giving the Acadian regions a "real" voice in the Legislature. But this was not to be. During the three elections in which it took part (1974, 1978, and 1982), its candidates never received more than 8 percent of the votes in all the ridings that they contested, although a few came very close to being elected.[85]

Rural socialism and territorial autonomy thus never represented a seriously considered option for New Brunswick's Acadian electors. However, the social and political unrest in northern New Brunswick made it clear that these electors could no longer be taken for granted. And during its ten years of existence, the PA exerted a constant pressure on Richard Hatfield's government (elected in 1970), whose Conservative Party – historically based in Protestant, English New Brunswick – was determined to make a historic break into the Acadian electorate. It also, somewhat unwittingly, served as an ally of sorts to existing nationalist Acadian organizations, who used the pressures exerted by the PA as leverage for their own demands. These demands, while presented as more "reasonable" than the PA's territorial yearnings, nonetheless represented an affirmation of communitarianism that was a bold break from the "participation" ideal.

The Idea of Duality
During the first half of the 1970s, "traditional" Moncton-based Acadian mouthpieces such as the SNA and *L'Évangéline* were the foyers of another, more linguistic form of neo-nationalism. Its central, motivating idea was *institutional duality*. Assuming that territorial autonomy was neither practical nor desirable, and unwilling to ignore the ever-growing urban francophone population, most Acadian institutions more or less ignored the PA's platform and chose, instead, to exert increasing pressures for institutional autonomy. What was requested, in effect, was the creation of French-language administrative units within the state in certain, select spheres of activity. While proponents of duality agreed to share *most* public institutions with the English-speaking majority, they also insisted that *some* public institutions – especially those linked to education and culture – should be operated *by* the French

community, *for* the French community. Of course, the relative marginalization of the PA in Acadian circles did not prevent the SNA and others from presenting "duality" to the government as an efficient way to win over the ebullient French-speaking population of northern New Brunswick.

The first case where this idea was put forward, made explicit, and developed was of course the ongoing District 15 confrontation. The pressure in this affair kept mounting, and more and more Acadian groups and French-language organizations kept diving into the fray, until, in 1971, Hatfield announced that Moncton's French-language schools would be integrated into District 15, a district catering to a neighbouring francophone region.[86]

By now, war had been declared on all supposedly "bilingual" districts and schools,[87] the latter being seen as important foyers of assimilation.[88] The Moncton victory was seen by the SNA as a mere stepping stone toward a completely "dual" educational system. This organization had been revitalized during the past few years, many members from the "Robichaud generation" having left and much new, young blood having joined the fold. Its new general secretary, Hector Cormier, was one of the leaders in the District 15 fight and a symbol for the new, more affirmative Acadian militancy. Even the ebullient students had a newfound respect for the SNA under his leadership.[89]

Early 1972 was a tension-filled period on the "linguistic border" in southeastern New Brunswick, just as it was in the regionalist, predominantly Acadian north shore. On 8 January, Radio-Canada television broadcast *L'Acadie, l'Acadie!?!* – a documentary by two prominent Quebec filmmakers depicting the Université de Moncton students' large demonstrations of 1968-69 and their struggle for municipal bilingualism. Mayor Jones' ice-cold and paternalist handling of the students, depicted in black and white, shocked audiences nation-wide and set off a new round of demonstrations in Moncton. Jones himself added oil to the fire a few weeks later by refusing to put up a French-language plaque offered by the SNA to match the English one already hanging on the new Moncton City Hall complex.[90]

This latest, local failure of the bilingualism ideal gave added resolve to the proponents of linguistic duality. The following August the SNA submitted a memorandum to the province in which it formally asked for the establishment of full duality in the sphere of education, which meant purely and simply a total split of the province's Department of Education. *L'Évangeline* followed up with numerous favourable editorials,[91] and again a chorus of Acadian voices – individuals, organizations, and associations of all types – joined in support. Such near-unanimity in the Acadian community had not been seen since Louis Robichaud's Programme of Equal Opportunity. Was duality becoming the new, nonofficial national ideology? Was participation dead in the water? Was all this, as a few claimed, inexorably leading to an Acadian independence movement?

Conclusion: A Delicate Balance between Integration and Autonomy

In the end, the fight for educational duality was a last, ephemeral moment of relative unanimity for Acadian New Brunswick. The conditions of geographic and cultural isolation that were the causes of Acadians' bloc positions of old had long disappeared. Modernity, so wished for by the elite of Robichaud's generation, had caught up to the community and given it the bittersweet gift of internal diversity.

The Parti Acadien would keep up its partisan fight for a while, but the real change in 1970s electoral politics was the disappearance of the Liberal Party's near-automatic hold on the "Acadian ethnic vote."[92] The Conservatives have Richard Hatfield (as well as his so-called "French lieutenant," Jean-Maurice Simard) to thank for this, as his government ably, slowly, but surely earned the trust of tens of thousands of Acadians, including many soft neo-nationalists (most of whom were estranged from the Liberals, perceived as the "Establishment"). This was done thanks to carefully chosen symbolic gestures and significant compromises, the most important of which were duality in the field of education (granted in 1974 with the sole reservation that both linguistic sections would fall under the same minister)[93] and the establishment, with federal help, of French cultural and educational community centres in cities where Acadians constituted a small minority (Fredericton, Saint John, and the Miramichi).[94]

Although no one could have predicted it in 1975, after these important gains the ideal of duality would more or less stall. Neither Acadian nationalist associations nor the Parti Acadien would be able to present it convincingly as a necessity in any other sphere of activity, with the exception of culture. (The latter, however, was not enough to bring people to the barricades.) This can be seen as liberalism's tranquil revenge. Reassured that education was in competent and familiar francophone hands, Acadians began to feel relatively comfortable sharing all other public institutions with the anglophone majority, and they would continue to do so. The autonomist bubble, it seems, was contained.

What the neo-nationalist wave of the 1970s *did* manage to provoke, however, was an explosion of cultural and artistic production. Its romantic, somewhat antimodernist streak encouraged a "rediscovery" of Acadia's folkloric treasures and their adaptation for a modern popular market. Acadian singers and musicians blended traditional and rock music, and many had success in Quebec and even in France. Large music festivals were organized. A French-language publishing house opened, and Acadian poetry – highly influenced by the vernacular – flourished. Documentaries were produced locally. Professional theatre companies appeared.[95] These developments, all of which represented "firsts," were significant because they created a renewed appreciation for a cultural heritage that had been deemed irrelevant – or even archaic – just a few years back. This creative wave, however, did not content itself with a reinvention of tradition. It also inspired a healthy production of contemporary art and literature. And despite numerous nationalist overtones, much of the new cultural production lent its voice to the "little people" in Acadian society – fishermen, truckers, women on social assistance, disempowered and slang-speaking youth, and the like – sometimes to the dismay of the more traditionalist, Radio-Canada-based cultural elite. If the 1960s were a decade of modernization and political integration, the 1970s, for their part, were one of cultural revival, artistic development, and renewed "national" pride.

Despite this new popular appreciation for all things Acadian, the SNA – and its new provincial offshoot, the Société des Acadiens du Nouveau-Brunswick (SANB) – while more vocal than ever, would be seen less and less as incarnations of "the elite" and more and more as "the linguistic lobby" during the 1970s. The switch is subtle but important: the idea of an Acadian autonomous sphere, overseen by a kind of paternal "parallel government," was finally, definitely dead. Adding to this relative devaluation of Acadian associations' weight was the constant increase in their numbers. Indeed, the days when the SNA could claim to be the linguistic group's sole – or "official" – mouthpiece were over. Now, not only were there three provincial Acadian associations,[96] but there was also a growing trend toward the creation of multiple "sectorial" French-language associations,[97] many of which had regular contacts with both levels of government. However, contrary to the Acadian elite of old, they acted more like para-governmental watchdogs than real partners in governance. Logically, given its more modest status, this new, government-sponsored version of the Acadian leadership had less ascendancy among the population than the bygone elite. Acadians were increasingly urbanized, educated, and media-exposed, and they were growing increasingly diverse in their interests and allegiances.

During the *trente glorieuses,* New Brunswick's Acadian community experienced two important paradigm shifts in quick succession. It first rushed headlong into commerce-driven, state-planned modernity, trading in – without guarantees – their hard-earned, long-established networks of institutions for the right to participate fully in the provincial and Canadian public spheres. Then, hardly a decade later, it experienced a short-lived but intense romantic and nationalist backlash during which the dream of an autonomous Acadian society lived once more. However, the province's political system, under the improbable leadership of the Conservative Party, was able to recuperate this wave of protest with a few reforms that were both symbolic and significant.

The two waves of change represented different strategies of entry into the modern world that could be adopted by a minority group: integration and differentiation. Both models were initially presented in relatively pure form, but pragmatism ended up ruling the day, and by the mid-1970s accommodation between New Brunswick's linguistic groups rested upon a mix of liberal and communitarian logics. This situation has changed little since 1975.[98] Acadian civil society, which is more institutionally complex than ever, essentially acts as a watchdog, denouncing insufficiencies in bilingualism here and asking for greater autonomy there.[99] However, mass rallies are now mostly a thing of the past, and more important, no new paradigm of linguistic accommodation seems set to appear on the horizon. Acadians in New Brunswick, it seems, are destined to live in a state of permanent tension between the imperatives of community and the facility of integration. Their existence constitutes a test for the capacity of ethno-linguistic groups to maintain their specificity in the modern world without the benefit of a state of their own.

Acknowledgments
The author would like to thank Michèle Dagenais, Joseph Yvon Thériault, and Magda Fahrni for having kindly agreed to read and comment on an earlier version of this text.

Notes
1 Jacques-Paul Couturier, "L'Acadie, c'est un détail: Les représentations de l'Acadie dans le récit national canadien," *Acadiensis* 29, 2 (2000): 102-19.
2 See, for example, "Survival of the Most Spirited," *Maclean's,* 24 March 2003.
3 Statistics Canada, "Language Composition of Canada: Highlight Tables, 2001 Census," in *2001 Census Standard Data Products,* http://www.statcan.ca/start_f.html.
4 The average annual revenue of francophones in northern New Brunswick was only 67% of the Canadian average in 1991, versus 80% for their anglophone neighbours and 100% for their French-speaking cousins in the more urbanized south of the province; see Maurice Beaudin, "Les Acadiens des Maritimes et l'économie," in Joseph Yvon Thériault, ed., *Francophonies minoritaires au Canada – L'état des lieux* (Moncton: Éditions d'Acadie and RUFHQ, 1999), 247.
5 These numbers are calculated by dividing the number of people whose day-to-day language is French from those whose mother language is French; see Marc Johnson and Isabelle McKee-Allain, "La société et l'identité de l'Acadie contemporaine," in Thériault, ed., *Francophonies minoritaires,* 213-17.
6 The term, coined by French economist Jean Fourastier, refers to the 30-year span of uninterrupted growth between 1945 and 1975. Eric Hobsbawm named the period the "Golden Age" in his *Age of Extremes: The Short Twentieth Century* (London: Abacus, 1995), 1-2, 258.
7 Derek Johnson, "Merchants, the State and the Household: Continuity and Change in a 20th Century Acadian Fishing Village," *Acadiensis* 29, 1 (1999): 57-76 at 67-69.
8 Camille Richard, "Le discours idéologique des conventions nationales et les origines du nationalisme acadien: réflexions sur la question nationale," *Les Cahiers de la Société historique acadienne* 17, 3 (1986): 73-87.
9 See, in particular, Joseph Yvon Thériault, *L'Identité à l'épreuve de la modernité: Écrits politiques sur l'Acadie et les francophonies canadiennes minoritaires* (Moncton: Éditions d'Acadie, 1995), Chapter 1; Jacques-Paul Couturier, "Perception et pratique de la justice dans la société acadienne, 1870-1900," in Jacques-Paul Couturier and Phyllis LeBlanc, eds., *Économie et société en Acadie, 1850-1950* (Moncton: Éditions d'Acadie, 1996), 73-75; Joseph Yvon Thériault, "Développement dépendant et pénétration coopérative," *Revue de l'Université de Moncton* 13, 1-2 (1980): 7-23; and Johnson, "Merchants," 63.
10 The expression is borrowed from Benedict Anderson, *Imagined Communities: Reflections on the Origins and Spread of Nationalism* (London: Verso, 1983).

11 First came La Société fraternelle de l'Assomption, a properly Acadian organization created in 1903. Its first goal was mutual economic relief for families in need, but it very quickly became a political forum as well. It was joined in the 1920s by a new French Canadian secret society, L'Ordre-de-Jacques-Cartier, which had thirty *"commanderies"* – or local committees – in New Brunswick by the 1950s. Le Conseil de la vie française en Amérique was its public incarnation. See Marcel Martel, *Le deuil d'un pays imaginé: Rêves, luttes et déroutes du Canada français – Les rapports entre le Québec et la francophonie canadienne (1867-1975)* (Ottawa: Presses de l'Université d'Ottawa, 1997); and Gabriel Bertrand, "L'Ordre de Jacques Cartier et les minorités francophones," in Gratien Allaire and Anne Gilbert, eds., *Francophonies plurielles* (Sudbury: Institut franco-ontarien, 1998), 13-58.

12 The transition to a daily was completed only in 1949; see Martel, *Le deuil d'un pays imaginé*, 46-51; and Gérard Beaulieu, "L'Évangéline," journal des institutions acadiennes, 1944-1982," in Gérard Beaulieu, ed., *L'Évangéline, 1887-1982: Entre l'élite et le peuple* (Moncton: Éditions d'Acadie, 1997), 82-83.

13 Joseph Yvon Thériault, "Le moment Robichaud et la politique en Acadie," in *L'ère Louis J. Robichaud, 1960-70: Actes du colloque* (Moncton: Institut canadien de recherche sur le développement régional, 2001), 47; Louis F. Cimino, "Ethnic Nationalism among the Acadians of New Brunswick: An Analysis of Ethnic Political Development" (PhD thesis, Duke University, 1977), 64-67; Jean-Roch Cyr, "La colonisation dans le nord du Nouveau-Brunswick durant la crise économique des années 30," in Couturier and LeBlanc, eds., *Économie et société*, 123-25.

14 Thériault, "Le moment Robichaud," 42.

15 Cimino, *Ethnic Nationalism*, 13-14.

16 They were Calixte Savoie and Gilbert Finn, the two highest figures in L'Assomption Society; Father Clément Cormier, rector of the Université Saint-Joseph; Emery LeBlanc and Euclide Daigle, the director and the editor of *L'Évangéline*, respectively; and judge Adrien Cormier. See Sasha Richard, "Commémoration et idéologie nationale en Acadie: Les fêtes du bicentenaire de la Déportation acadienne," *Mens: Revue d'histoire intellectuelle de l'Amérique française* 3, 1 (2002): 27-59 at 31-35.

17 It was operated by the Conseil de la vie française en Amérique and raised $40,000; see Martel, *Le deuil d'un pays imaginé*, 90.

18 Hugh John Fleming's Conservative government in New Brunswick agreed to contribute $20,000 to the festivities; see Richard Wilbur, *The Rise of French New Brunswick* (Halifax: Formac, 1989), 185.

19 In fact, the Queen was even invited, to the great surprise of the British high commissioner; see Richard, "Commémoration et idéologie," 35-38.

20 The head organizer, a young, well-known lawyer named Adélard Savoie, told *L'Évangéline* that the festivities "should not give people the idea of a State within the State"; quoted in Richard, "Commémoration et idéologie," 44.

21 Until this moment, it had been called Société nationale l'Assomption. This association was theoretically the public face of Acadian nationalism, but it had been moribund since 1937, the Société fraternelle l'Assomption (the future Mutual Life company) and the Ordre-de-Jacques-Cartier (OJC) having taken over the task of political representation.

22 Bernard Poirier, "La nouvelle structure," editorial, *Évangéline*, 20-21 January 1964, 4; Jean-Paul Hautecoeur, *L'Acadie du discours: Pour une sociologie de la culture acadienne* (Sainte-Foy: Presses universitaires de Laval, 1975), 92-101; Richard, "Commémoration et idéologie," 44.

23 Wilbur, *Rise of French New Brunswick*, 182-83.

24 Ibid., 191; Martel, *Le deuil d'un pays imaginé*, 79-81.

25 Robichaud left the secret society in 1958, upon his election as party leader; see Michel Cormier, *Louis J. Robichaud: Une révolution si peu tranquille* (Moncton: Éditions de la Francophonie, ca. 2004), 101. This title has also been translated to English by Jonathan Kaplansky under the title *Louis J. Robichaud: A not so quiet revolution* (Lévis, QC: Faye Editions, 2004).

26 Ibid., 35-40.

27 Martel, *Le deuil d'un pays imaginé*, 51-55.

28 Nicolas Landry and Nicole Lang, *Histoire de l'Acadie* (Sillery, QC: Septentrion, 2001), 289; Robert Pichette, "'Longtemps l'Acadie a attendu un chef': Clément C. Cormier, c.s.c. (1910-1987)," *Les Cahiers de la Société historique acadienne* 30, 4 (1999): 235-56 at 242-43.

29 The following document is an eloquent testament to Father Cormier's drive: "Développement de l'USJ à Moncton – préparation d'un document," Fonds Clément Cormier 177.1865, Centre d'Études Acadiennes (Moncton). See also Jacques-Paul Couturier, *Construire un savoir: L'enseignement supérieur au Madawaska, 1946-1974* (Moncton: Éditions d'Acadie, 1999), 135-36.

30 Until the end of the 1940s, confessional colleges in New Brunswick received absolutely no financing from the government, an exception in Canada.

31 Couturier, *Construire un savoir*, 127-30.

32 Ian McKay suggests that the history of Canada is essentially that of a perpetually progressing "liberal project" that overcomes all resistance in its path – be it traditional, communitarian, socialist, or other; see Ian McKay, "The Liberal Order Framework: A Prospectus for a Reconnaissance of Canadian History," *Canadian Historical Review* 80, 4 (2000): 617-45.

33 Hautecoeur, *L'Acadie du discours*, 167, my translation.

34 Cimino, *Ethnic Nationalism*; Joseph Yvon Thériault, "Domination et protestation: Le sens de l'acadianité," *Anthropologica* 23, 1 (1981): 60-68 at 56-57.

35 For a crystal-clear illustration, see Father Clément Cormier's speech during the "national convention" of 1960, "Les Acadiens en 1960: Besoins et perspectives," in *XIIIe Congrès général des Acadiens* (Pointe-de-l'Église, NS: SNA, 1960), 32-34.

36 Thériault, "Domination et protestation," 56; Hautecoeur, *L'Acadie du discours*, 30-31.

37 Many similarities between the socio-political changes in Quebec and Acadian New Brunswick could be identified and discussed, too many for the space allowed here. For a comparative exercise, see Joel Belliveau and Frédéric Boily, "Deux Révolutions tranquilles? Expériences néo-brunswickoise et québécoise comparées," *Recherches sociographiques* 46, 1 (2005): 11-34.

38 Peter Veniot, born Pierre Vienneau, replaced his predecessor as premier for a time, only to be defeated in 1925 in a nasty campaign during which letters allegedly from the Ku Klux Klan circulated in the province; see E.R. Forbes and D.A. Muise, *The Atlantic Provinces in Confederation* (Toronto and Fredericton: University of Toronto Press and Acadiensis Press, 1993), 268.

39 Cormier, *Louis J. Robichaud*, 98.

40 The context of McCarthyism, however, rendered this request more palatable to many.

41 Wilbur, *Rise of French New Brunswick*, 186, 191, 195; Pichette, "'Longtemps l'Acadie,'" 246.

42 Thériault, "Le moment Robichaud," 49; Della Stanley, *Louis Robichaud: A Decade of Power* (Halifax: Nimbus, 1984), 53.

43 Cormier, *Louis J. Robichaud*, 103.

44 Ibid., 117-21, 127.

45 This university would federate all existing French postsecondary institutions, which would become "affiliated colleges." The university as such would alleviate shortcomings in the existing network by offering programs that had thus far not been offered in French in New Brunswick.

46 The commission was under the chairmanship of Dr. John Deutsch, vice-principal of Queen's University; see Couturier, *Construire un savoir*, 131-47; Stanley, *Louis Robichaud*, 65-66; John Deutsch, *Report of the Royal Commission on Higher Education in New Brunswick* (Fredericton, NB: Province of New Brunswick, 1962).

47 In fact, the imperative of "non-ethnicity" had such force that at first the new university in Moncton was described by Father Clément Cormier, its first rector, as "a university that is French in culture but bilingual for all practical purposes"; quoted in *L'Évangéline* and the *Moncton Times*, 28 February 1966.

48 As an exception, municipalities conserved the capacity to tax real property.

49 Robert Young, "The Programme of Equal Opportunity: An Overview," in *The Robichaud Era, 1960-70: Colloquium Proceedings* (Moncton: Canadian Institute for Research on Regional Development, 2001), 23-35.

50   Stanley, *Louis Robichaud,* 143-53; Cormier, *Louis J. Robichaud,* 211-23.

51   Thériault, "Le moment Robichaud," 47, my translation.

52   Thériault, "Domination et protestation," 57.

53   Martel, *Le deuil d'un pays imaginé,* 145-47.

54   E. Daigle, *Petite histoire d'une grande idée: Assomption, compagnie mutuelle d'assurance-vie, 1903-1978* (Moncton: Imprimerie acadienne, 1978).

55   Cimino, *Ethnic Nationalism,* 120.

56   *Liaisons,* April 1964, 1, 5, 9.

57   *Liaisons,* February 1964, 2.

58   Joel Belliveau, "Naissance d'un discours discordant: Identité et mobilisations étudiantes à l'Université de Moncton avant *L'Acadie, l'Acadie!?!* (1960-1967)," in André Magord, ed., *Adaptation et innovation: Expériences acadiennes* (Bruxelles: P.I.E.-Peter Lang, 2006), 51-75.

59   "La jeunesse acadienne réclame de nouveaux symboles d'identité acadienne," *L'Évangéline,* 4 April 1966, 1. See also Hautecoeur, *L'Acadie du discours,* 202.

60   Beaudin, "Les Acadiens des Maritimes," 98-101.

61   Robert A. Young, "L'édification de l'État provincial et le développement régional au Nouveau-Brunswick," *Égalité* 13-14 (double issue) (1984): 125-52; Donald J. Savoie, *La lutte pour le développement: Le cas du Nord-Est* (Sillery, QC/Moncton: Presses de l'Université du Québec/Institut canadien de recherche sur le développement régional, Université de Moncton, 1988).

62   For example, the very influential Martin Légère, director of the twenty-eight-branch co-operative Fédération des caisses populaires acadiennes, was named director of the regional Industrial Development Board for north-eastern New Brunswick by Louis Robichaud in 1960. Five years later, when the structure was transformed into the Conseil régional d'aménagement du Nord-est, he stayed at the head of the organization; see Wilbur, *Rise of French New Brunswick,* 226.

63   Jean Cadieux, quoting Aurèle Young, another professor at the Université de Moncton, in "L'Acadie économique," *Revue de l'Université de Moncton* (September 1968): 45-48 at 47, my translation. (*La Revue économique* became *La Revue de l'Université de Moncton* in 1968.)

64   Thériault, "Domination et protestation," 56-57.

65   Roger Frappier, *Kouchibouguac* (NFB-ONF, 1978); Greg Allain, "Chronologie des événements entourant la création du parc national Kouchibougouac," *Égalité* 7 (1982): 185-91.

66   Louis Robichaud's own children would never be as comfortable in French as in English, something that the ex-premier says is one of his life's greatest regrets; see Cormier, *Louis J. Robichaud,* 125. The situation was fully redressed only in 1978, when a K-12 French-language school and community centre opened its doors in the city. This was thanks to federal funding and Conservative premier Richard Hatfield's continued support for the project in face of strong opposition from some elements of the English community, including Fredericton Municipal Council, the English-Speaking League, the Fredericton Council of Women, and the Fredericton Heritage Trust, as well as from the local newspaper, the *Daily Gleaner;* see Greg Allain and Maurice Basque, *Une présence qui s'affirme: La communauté acadienne et francophone de Fredericton, Nouveau-Brunswick* (Moncton: Éditions de la Francophonie, 2003), 163-73, 207-10.

67   They were Adélard Savoie, the Université de Moncton president; Gilbert Finn, CEO of the Société mutuelle Assomption; Dr. Léon Richard, president of the SNA; and Euclide Daigle, vice president of the Association Acadienne d'Éducation.

68   Cormier, *Louis J. Robichaud,* 255-65.

69   The term had a singular signification in New Brunswick before 1969. It mostly meant that the institution thus described catered (totally or in part) to a French-speaking public. For example, there were "regular" and "bilingual" schools. Although a certain level of service was implied by the denomination, it was by no means guaranteed.

70   "L'Association du Foyer-école demande la creation d'un nouveau district scolaire ... ," *L'Évangéline,* 16 March 1967, 1; "Les professeurs de l'Université de Moncton recommandent la creation de deux unites administratives égales," *L'Évangéline,* 30 March 1967, 3. See also Hector Cormier, *La scission du district scolaire no 15: L'histoire d'une lutte, mais surtout d'une victoire* (Moncton: Éditions du Sorbier, 2000).

71 Joel Belliveau, "Contributions estudiantines à la 'Révolution tranquille' acadienne," in Madeleine Frédéric and Serge Jaumain, eds., *Regards croisés sur l'histoire et la littérature acadiennes* (Bruxelles: P.I.E.-Peter Lang, 2006), 169-90; Hautecoeur, *L'Acadie du discours,* 276-85. The demonstrations were also caught vividly on film by a National Film Board crew; see Pierre Perreault and Michel Brault, *L'Acadie, l'Acadie!?!* (NFB-ONF, 1971).

72 Furthermore, the small number of students attending their university, relatively speaking, is taken by the students to be a direct consequence of the French-speaking population's economic inferiority, which is a further argument, according to them, for a new distribution of the provincial funds. Finally, the youth of the university is also evoked as an argument. These arguments would receive national coverage; see "5 jours de révolution à Moncton: L'Acadie, c'est fini," *Le Magazine Maclean,* April 1968, 1.

73 Martel, *Le deuil d'un pays imaginé,* 148-71.

74 The government was now formed by Daniel Johnson's Union nationale.

75 Stanley, *Louis Robichaud,* 176-78.

76 For an analysis of Cormier's positions in the commission, see Frédérique Fournier, "The Conceptions of Linguistic and Political Development in a Fragmented Society, the Society of New Brunswick: Father Clément Cormier's Role within the Royal Commission on Bilingualism and Biculturalism from 1963 to 1971" (MA thesis, Université de Poitiers and University of New Brunswick, 2000).

77 Léon Dion, *La révolution déroutée, 1960-1976* (Montreal: Boréal, 1998), 194-220.

78 "Thus, it is the view of my government that this province must now accept a special role within a new Canada-wide effort to deepen national unity in this country of two basic cultures. You will be asked, therefore, to support measures by which New Brunswick will become officially and practically a province of two official languages – English and French – within the context of a new national regime in this regard"; extract of throne speech, 27 February 1968, in New Brunswick Legislative Assembly, *Synoptic Report of the Proceedings,* vol 2 (1968), 4.

79 Stanley, *Louis Robichaud,* 182-89; Pichette, "'Longtemps l'Acadie,'" 244-45.

80 Sasha Richard, *Fighting for Rights in the "City with a Heart,"* paper presented at the Canadian Historical Association's annual congress, Halifax, May 2003, 10-16. Moncton would finally become officially bilingual only in 2002. To the city's credit, it must be said that it then became the first officially bilingual city in Canada, although many others also offer a wide range of services in both official languages.

81 Stanley, *Louis Robichaud,* 182, 189.

82 Wilbur, *Rise of French New Brunswick,* 235-47; Greg Allain, "The State and Regional Development Organizations in New Brunswick, Canada (1960-1990): A Social Control Perspective" (PhD thesis, University of California at Santa Barbara, 1998); Greg Allain and Serge Côté, "Le développement régional, l'État et la participation de la population: La vie courte et mouvementée des Conseils régionaux d'aménagement du Nouveau-Brunswick (1964-1980)," *Égalité* 13-14 (1984-85): 187-215.

83 For a partisan but up-close and lively account of these heady days, see Pierre Godin, *Les révoltés d'Acadie* (Montreal: Éditions Québécoises, 1972), 35-99.

84 Roger Ouellette, *Le Parti acadien: De la fondation à la disparition, 1972-1982* (Moncton: CEA and Université de Moncton, 1992), 57-74, 79-83; *Le Parti acadien* (Petit Rocher, NB: 1974). The latter is a kind of collaboratively written manifesto.

85 Ouellette, *Le Parti acadien,* 87-97.

86 "Regroupement des francophones des districts 13 et 15," *L'Évangéline,* 12 February 1971, 1; "Le nouveau district scolaire ... représente une grande victoire pour les francophones ...," *L'Évangéline,* 9 August 1971, 2.

87 The last of the bilingual schools would disappear only at the end of the 1970s.

88 The 1961 and 1966 censuses had clearly demonstrated that New Brunswick francophones' demographic climb had come to a halt due to out-migration, lower fertility, and increasingly, assimilation. Contrary to a widely held belief of the early 1960s, Acadians would probably never be a majority in New Brunswick.

89 "S.N.A. – Rencontre avec Hector Cormier," *L'Embryon* (Université de Moncton student paper), vol. 1, no. 2, January 1971, 3; Pierre Godin, *Les révoltés d'Acadie* ([Montreal]: Éditions Québécoises, 1972), 119-58.

90 Wilbur, *Rise of French New Brunswick*, 249; Richard, *Fighting for Rights*, 13.
91 *L'Évangéline*, 19 October 1972, 31 January 1973, 2 February 1973, and 23, 26, and 30 March 1973, among others.
92 Jean-Guy Finn, "Développement et persistance du vote ethnique: Les acadiens du Nouveau-Brunswick" (MA thesis, University of Ottawa, 1972).
93 Some core administrative functions would also be shared.
94 Jacques Poitras, *The Right Fight: Bernard Lord and the Conservative Dilemma* (Fredericton: Goose Lane, 2004), 37-81; Richard Starr, *Richard Hatfield: The Seventeen Year Saga* (Halifax: Formac, 1987), 125-31; Achile Michaud and Michel Cormier, *Richard Hatfield: Un dernier train pour Hartland* (Montreal: Libre Éxpression, 1991), 156-75.
95 Patrick Condon Laurette, "Aspects historiques de l'art en Acadie," in Jean Daigle, ed., *L'Acadie des Maritimes: Etudes thématiques des débuts à nos jours* (Moncton: Chaire d'études acadiennes, Université de Moncton, 1993), 789-844. This collective work was also published in English under the title *Acadia of the Maritimes: Thematic Studies from the Beginning to the Present* (Moncton: Chaire d'études acadiennes, Université de Moncton, 1995).
96 The Société Saint-Thomas d'Aquin, in Prince Edward Island, is the eldest of the three, having existed since the early 1900s. The Fédération des Acadiens de la Nouvelle-Écosse (FANE) and the Société des Acadiens du Nouveau-Brunswick (SANB) were created in 1968 and 1973 respectively, mostly due to the federal State Secretariat's preference for dealing with provincial bodies. The responsibility for official languages has since been given to the Department of Canadian Heritage.
97 Today, New Brunswick is home to French-language associations organizing groups such as jurists, municipalities, youth, senior citizens, artists, teachers, women, and businesses, to name but a few.
98 An exception is Law 88, adopted in 1981, which recognizes "the equality of New Brunswick's two linguistic communities." It is a mostly symbolic law, and it has not been tested by jurisprudence, but it nonetheless reinforces the logic of duality in the province. A somewhat watered-down version of the law was included in the Canadian Charter of Rights and Freedoms in 1993.
99 For a statistical (demographic, linguistic, economic, etc.) overview of today's Acadian New Brunswickers, see the "profile" published by the Fédération des communautés francophones et acadiennes du Canada (FCFA) in 2004, available at http://fcfa.ca/uploads/profil_NB_e.pdf.

4

The "Narcissism of Small Differences": The Invention of Canadian English, 1951-67

Steven High

Nationalism is a "quintessentially homogenizing, differentiating, or classifying discourse."[1] Ever since the emergence of the modern state in the sixteenth century, and certainly since the American Revolution of 1776, nation-states have sought to distinguish themselves from their linguistic and geographic neighbours.[2] Noah Webster, for example, advocated abandoning his country's linguistic ties to Great Britain in the immediate aftermath of the American Revolution. "As an independent nation," Webster wrote, "our honor requires us to have a system of our own, in language as well as in government."[3] Webster's spelling book of 1783 and his dictionaries of 1806, 1828, and 1840 prescribed changes to American spelling, including the conversion of *-our* and *-re* endings to *-or* and *-er*. Henceforth, his countrymen claimed to speak "American English."[4]

Collective identities rely, historian Peter Burke notes, "on what Freud once called, in a famous phrase, 'the narcissism of small differences,' exaggerating whatever makes one community distinct from others."[5] Such was the case in Canada in the decades following the Second World War. Between the release of the final report of the Royal Commission on National Development in the Arts, Letters and Sciences, chaired by Vincent Massey, in 1951 and Canada's Centenary in 1967, the idea of "Canada" came to take on new meaning. The heady anti-Americanism of these decades was, in part, a reaction to the perceived economic and cultural invasion of Canada by the United States.[6] Nationalist sentiment ran particularly deep in the lead up to 1967, when English-speaking nationalists (see Robert Wright's essay on Peter C. Newman in this volume) set out to Canadianize the country's economy, culture, and universities.[7] The desire to differentiate Canada from Great Britain and the United States led to the invention of "Canadian English."[8]

Unlike French-speaking Canadians, whose language set them apart from the rest of North America, English-speaking Canadians shared the same language as Americans. Or, at least, so it seemed. A band of lexicographers in the Canadian Linguistics Association (CLA) set out to show that Canadians did, in fact, speak English with a distinctly Canadian accent. This "dictionary movement" produced a series of Canadian dictionaries, culminating in 1967.[9] First, lexicographers at the Université de Montréal, headed by Jean-Paul Vinay and underwritten by the Toronto publishing house McClelland and Stewart, produced Canada's first bilingual dictionary in 1962. *The Canadian Dictionary/Le dictionnaire canadien* sought to bridge Canada's own linguistic divide between "Canadian French" and "Canadian English." Next, a team of dictionary makers led by Walter Avis and Matthew Harry Scargill, in co-operation with another Toronto publisher, W.J. Gage, produced *The Dictionary of Canadian English,* a set of three graded school dictionaries between 1962 and 1967. The fourth volume of this series, *The Dictionary of Canadianisms on Historical Principles,* the "national lynchpin" of Gage's lexicographical efforts, provided a comprehensive record of words invented or used in Canada.[10] The Canadian media heralded the *Dictionary of Canadianisms* as a fitting tribute to Canada on its Centenary. These dictionaries – materializing as they did in a remarkably short five-year time span – established "Canadian English" in the minds of Canadians. The national differences in vocabulary, spelling, pronunciation, and grammatical structure were all recognized and celebrated.

The dictionaries of Canadian English appeared at a time of tremendous lexicographical activity the world over. In the United States the four-volume *Dictionary of American English on Historical Principles,* completed in 1944, recorded any word that had a "real connection" to the history of the country and its people.[11] This was followed by Mitford M. Mathews' 1951 book *A Dictionary of Americanisms on Historical Principles,* which recorded only those words originating in the United States.[12] Many English-speaking countries followed suit, including Jamaica (1967), South Africa (1978), the Bahamas (1982), and Australia (1981).[13] In each instance, a national dictionary was seen as "one of the rare objects that can materialize the existence of a language, and hence a nation, acting as a symbol of the unification of a community."[14] It represented, then, much more than a reference book for words and their meanings; it was an assertion of a linguistic community. Canada was thus part of a postcolonial rush to compile national dictionaries.[15]

Ultimately, the Canadian English dictionary movement aspired to help unify the country. This wish might seem paradoxical given that Canada is a country of English and French speakers. However, the movement tried to reconcile Canadian English with Canada's history of ethnic and linguistic pluralism by highlighting the historical influence of French Canadians and Canada's First Nations on the development of Canadian English and by minimizing the influence of Great Britain and the United States. What made Canadian English unique and different, linguists argued, was its prolonged contact with Canada's northern environment and its other founding peoples.

In sharp contrast to linguistic nationalism in Europe, which emphasized language purity, dictionaries of Canadian English emphasized language change and diversity. A study of Canadian English reveals that the cultural politics of language paralleled and intersected with the politics of Canadian nationalisms in the post-Second World War era.

The Birth of a Dictionary Movement in Canada

Those linguists who have journeyed back in time to explore the origins of Canadian English usually go no further than the American Revolution.[16] The great influx of political refugees, or Loyalists, into what remained of British North America ensured that Canadians spoke with a distinctly North American accent. The wave of immigrants from Great Britain that followed the War of 1812 did little to change this linguistic pattern. These newcomers, however, created a duality that has become a fundamental feature of Canadian English. Not without difficulty, British and American English have co-existed in Canada ever since. Linguist J.K. Chambers, for example, has shown how these early linguistic tensions surfaced in the writings of Susanna Moodie and Anna Jameson, two British women who were horrified by Canadian speech. In *Roughing It in the Bush* (1854), Moodie disapprovingly comments on the use of "pritters," which was "vulgar Canadian for potatoes."[17] An 1857 speech to the Canadian Club by the Reverend A.C. Geikie – credited with the first recorded mention of Canadian English as a linguistic category – looms especially large in the historical imagination of linguists. Like Moodie and Jameson, Geikie was appalled by the "degradation" of the English spoken here.[18] He condemned it as "expressive of corrupt dialect growing up amongst our population, and gradually finding access to our periodical literature, until it threatens to produce a language as unlike our noble mother tongue as the negro patua or the Chinese pidgeon English."[19] For these early writers, anything but the Queen's English was coarse and uncouth.

Canadian English, it seems, has a long and ignoble tradition in Canada. But as Eric Hobsbawm has observed, traditions that appear old are often of recent vintage.[20] Much the same can be said of language or dialect. While the English language has been spoken in Canada since the earliest settlement of Newfoundland, Canadian English as a recognized national language, distinct from British and American varieties, is a recent innovation. Linguists discovered Canadian English in the mid-1950s, and through their prodigious efforts, Canadians were made aware of its existence in the 1960s.

Until this happened, however, the prevailing wisdom was that Canadians and Americans spoke with the same North American accent. Canada's leading linguist of the day, Henry Alexander of Queen's University, wrote an influential essay on "The English Language in Canada" for the Massey Commission in 1951. At no point in the paper does he mention "Canadian

English." Instead, in his expert opinion, there were no significant linguistic differences between Canada and the United States. Where there was mixed usage, such as the use of British and American spellings, he called on Canadian schools to adopt the American standard. In his mind, there was no indigenous aspect to the English language in Canada. "Let Canada keep her North American accent," he declared in 1951.[21]

The notion that Canadians spoke with a strongly North American accent was repeated four years later when CBC radio invited two linguists to speak on the subject. Raven I. McDavid, the American author of the *Linguistic Atlas of the United States and Canada,* told listeners that the number of purely Canadian words was "very small." Those Canadianisms found in Ontario, he argued, could be counted on one hand. As a result, there was no linguistic border between the two countries to speak of, as there had been "linguistic free trade" for centuries.[22] In the second address, Henry Alexander contended that Canadians did not have their own national language. The English spoken in Canada, he said, was simply an amalgam of "North American English" and "British English," with a strong leaning toward the former.[23] Canadians thus spoke of candy, trucks, and elevators instead of sweets, lorries, and lifts. This American influence was hardly surprising to Alexander: "We read American comic strips, we listen to American comedians on the radio, and we see and hear them in the movies and television. And it must be admitted that there is an exciting and infectious quality about much American slang that is perhaps not so evident in the more conservative informal language of Britain."[24] Wanting to cut Canada's colonial ties to Great Britain, Alexander emphasized what Canadians and Americans shared linguistically, not what differentiated them.

Yet an effort was already underway to recognize Canadian English as one of Canada's two national languages. In a pioneering article appearing in *Saturday Night* magazine in 1956, boldly entitled "Canadians Speak Canadian," Calgary-based linguist M.H. Scargill challenged those who would deny the existence of Canadian English: "Other matters Canadian are now considered worthy of study: literature, politics, history, resources. Why not Canadian English?"[25] He then related a story of a speaker in Montreal who was taken to task for the mere suggestion that Canadians had developed a variety of English. "What a narrow view," he declared. "Who discovered insulin, pray, and named it from the Latin? Who experimented with and named the splake? And since when have Americans or British freely discussed Clear Grits, Digby Chickens, Socreds, the Land of Little Sticks, separate schools, nitchies, longlinermen?"[26] To convince the nay-sayers, he called for an authoritative dictionary of Canadian English. Without this, he lamented, Canadian English teachers used "books based on British or American usage."[27] To prove to Canadians that Canadian English existed as a distinct variety of English, he added, "we must show not that it shares features with both but that it differs from each of them."[28]

Others shared Harry Scargill's passion. There were a sufficient number of linguists active in the emerging field of Canadian English that his colleague, Walter Avis, could refer to the existence of a "dictionary movement" in 1957. The movement had as its immediate objective the production of a series of dictionaries "appropriate to this country."[29]

The Canadian dictionary movement began with the formation of the Canadian Linguistics Association in 1954. At its founding meeting in Winnipeg, ten linguists discussed the need for a dictionary of Canadian English. Three years later a lexicographical committee of the CLA was formed. The committee was composed of the first generation of Canadian linguists, most of whom were foreign-born. Naturally, the first chairperson of the committee was Harry Scargill. Born in Yorkshire, England, in 1916, Scargill married a Canadian woman during the war and relocated to Canada in 1948. He was joined on the committee by Walter Avis, who was an English professor at Kingston's Royal Military College. Canadian-born, Avis had completed his doctoral studies at the University of Michigan at a time when it was a world centre in linguistics.[30] In an oral-history interview, Jack Chambers remembers Avis as "larger than life." Everything about this "lumber jack" of a man was big: his body, his voice, even his white beard. "He made a large impression," Chambers recalled. "When he entered a room, people tended to look."[31]

Other important founding members of the committee included French-born J.P. Vinay and the head of translation for the federal government, P. Daviault, who focused their attention on a made-in-Canada translation dictionary. Finally, there were Charles Julien Lovell, an American; Robert J. Gregg, originally from Ireland; and even Henry Alexander, who would shortly return to England.[32] The CLA became a rallying point for scholars interested in seeing Canadian English recognized as a unique variety of the language.[33]

Much as Noah Webster had done in the United States, this pioneering generation of linguists felt it more important to cut Canada's linguistic ties to Great Britain than to the United States. Briticisms were associated with Canada's colonial past as well as with upper-class pretence. The antipathy for the British accent, Walter Avis noted, represented a "rejection by a former colonial people of British attitudes after a century and a half of domination of Canada by Britishers whose condescending ways and superior airs have come to be associated connotatively with British speech and mannerisms."[34] Strong words, indeed.

It was only slightly less important for this generation of linguists to distinguish Canadian English from American English. In 1957 Walter Avis appealed to Canadians to become aware of their linguistic identity as a nation:

"We have been satisfied to look across the ocean or across the border for guidance. The time has come to look to ourselves, for Canada has grown from colony to nation. In searching for a sense of national identity we must not neglect our language, for our manner of speech, at least within the English-speaking community, binds us securely together."[35] The *New York Times* reported in 1959 that Canadians were "becoming aware that they speak and write English in a distinctive way. They are discovering what some go so far as to call the Canadian language – a unique conglomeration of spelling, pronunciation and vocabulary."[36] Avis and Scargill attempted to dispel the perception that Canadian English was a mere mish-mash of the British and American varieties of English.[37] For these linguists, Canadian English was neither American nor British but a home-grown variety of English in its own right. The search for national difference drove early linguistic research in Canada.[38]

The Canadian (Bilingual) Dictionary

Most great countries possessed dictionaries that contained a "record of their national languages."[39] Yet Canada had no such dictionary. During the Second World War a bilingual military dictionary had been rushed into print for use by Canada's armed forces. Translation problems in the postwar era were exacerbated by the absence of a single standard, while European translation dictionaries proved incapable of handling the distinctiveness of Canadian French and Canadian English.

By the mid-1950s a French-English bilingual dictionary had become an immediate need. "Did you ever realize," commented one Edmonton radio announcer, "that Canada is the only great country in the world which does not have a dictionary of its own language? Probably not, and yet, like the lack of a national flag and a national anthem, this is one of the series of deficiencies in our Canadian culture."[40] To fill this void, McClelland and Stewart approached one of Canada's leading linguists, Jean-Paul Vinay, at the Université de Montréal in December 1954 and proposed a made-in-Canada bilingual dictionary.[41] After seven years of effort the *Canadian Dictionary/Le dictionnaire canadien* appeared in 1962.[42]

The dictionary was published at a fortuitous moment in Canadian history: Liberal leader Lester B. Pearson pledged himself and his party that year to a bilingual vision of the country. The rise of bilingualism offered Canadians the "promise of uniqueness vis-à-vis the Americans and an expansive future for French Canada."[43] Previous to this time, there were only two linguistic departments in the country, and both were in Quebec. This situation soon changed as the Canadian government invested huge sums in bilingual services and translation. The bilingual dictionary project thus symbolized the new Canada taking shape.

Thanks to Webster's spelling reforms in the United States, conflicting spelling practices have been the rule in English-speaking Canada. The editors of the *Canadian Dictionary* noted that in both English spelling and usage, "Canadians sometimes follow the British example, sometimes the American, and in rare cases neither." Nonetheless, the dictionary's editors decided to retain many British spellings: double *ll* spellings for traveller (traveler), -*our* endings for colour (color), use of -*ae* in aesthetic, and -*re* endings such as centre (center), not to mention employee (employe), grey (gray), programme (program), moustache (mustache), and cheque (check).[44] Yet the dictionary adopted the American spelling of theater (theatre), recognize (recognise), and defence (defense).[45] Linguist Robert J. Gregg, another founding member of the CLA, noted that the decision to privilege British -*our* endings would meet resistance in Canada, where American -*or* endings were in the ascendancy. Shortly thereafter, the *Windsor Star* took issue with the British slant of the dictionary, suggesting that many British spellings were fast becoming "archaic."[46]

Despite this criticism, Canada's first bilingual dictionary was unveiled to great fanfare at the Canadian Conference on Education held in Montreal. The editors of the *Toronto Daily Star* wrote: "Here is the Canadian language, both French and English."[47] It was a "dictionary for Canada," Robert Fulford agreed. It would, he added, make Canadian bilingualism "less of a myth and more of a reality."[48] The *Globe and Mail* held out similar hopes: "No amount of smiles or handshakes in the past have done as much for Canadian unity as the new dictionary will in future. Armed with the book, we can communicate."[49] Naturally, the *Canadian Dictionary* was also heralded as a sign of Canada's nationhood.[50] A review published in *The Canadian Reader* made this connection explicit: "Without definition, our language remained only half-recognized dialects of the versions used in the metropolitan countries. This was, somehow, a serious omission in our march to nationhood. The Oxford English Dictionary stabilized the language of the United Kingdom. Webster contributed to his nation's nineteenth-century nationalism by producing an American dictionary ... Now, at last, Canada has a comparable authority for its own national languages."[51] With the help of Canada's news media, the dictionary sold well in English-speaking Canada, and the Book-of-the-Month Club even recommended the dictionary as a bonus to Canadian subscribers.[52] By 1975, 200,000 copies of the dictionary had been sold.[53]

Despite these sales, the bilingual dictionary fell victim to a changing political climate in Quebec, wherein the provincial government increasingly played the role of language guardian, defender of the purity of the French language.[54] Many Québécois now felt that some anglicized words used in everyday Canadian French should not have been included in the dictionary.[55] The move toward a "purer" form of French and away from slang or *joual* meant that the *Canadian Dictionary* was seen as substandard. Jack McClelland later recalled: "While the original *Dictionary* did well by normal yardsticks ... it was hampered by two factors. First, because of a change in the political climate in the Province of Quebec and their attitude towards the French language in Quebec City, the *Dictionary* was not in that version acceptable in Quebec. Sales there were minimal."[56] Thus, in the context of Quebec's Quiet Revolution, the inclusion of anglicisms associated with language loss and assimilation in *The Canadian Dictionary* made it unacceptable to the Quebec government for use in provincial schools.

Efforts to revise the *Canadian Dictionary* began soon after the appearance of the first edition. With the financial support of McClelland and Stewart and the federal government, Vinay's team (now based at the University of Victoria) struggled to expand the dictionary and revise its content to make it acceptable to Quebec's language guardians.[57] The proposed elimination of anglicisms from Canadian French represented a major change in editorial direction.[58] Jean Paul Vinay reported that "in the case of French Canadian terms that have been widely accepted or received the official blessing of the Office de la Langue Française we will give an indication to this effect. Those which have not attained official recognition will be starred or otherwise identified so that we will not be open to criticism that we are helping to propagate sub-standard forms of the language."[59] The dictionary's name was also reconsidered to make it more marketable in the United States.[60] Despite almost twenty years of additional effort, and tens of thousands of dollars in advance payments by McClelland and Stewart, Vinay failed to produce a second edition of *The Canadian Dictionary*. The appearance of the Robert and Collins bilingual dictionary from France killed the project in 1979.[61]

The Dictionary of Canadian English: Beginning, Intermediate, and Senior

By comparison, the production of Canadian English school dictionaries proved to be far more successful. The Ontario Ministry of Education announced in April 1959 its intention to replace imported school dictionaries with Canadian ones.[62] Foreign dictionaries, the department declared, were not doing the job. To make the point, the government's spokesperson cited a laughably inept British dictionary definition of hockey as a "game played with a ball and a stick."

With public interest in Canadian English aroused, and a ready market guaranteed, the publishing house of W.J. Gage Limited of Toronto, Canada's premier textbook publisher of the day, agreed to sponsor *The Dictionary of Canadian English* for Canadian schools. Patrick Drysdale, originally from Ireland, was hired as Gage's chief lexicographer. There were actually three graded dictionaries: *The Beginning Dictionary* (1962) for students in grades four and five, *The Intermediate Dictionary* (1963) for grades six to nine, and

The Senior Dictionary (1967) for high school students and adults. While these dictionaries were based on the American *E.L. Thorndike and Clarence L. Barnhart Dictionary,* each one was customized for the Canadian market. One enthusiastic writer for the Winnipeg-based armed forces newspaper *Voxair* called the dictionaries the most significant contribution to "Canadian letters in the past 300 years. At last we have a language and a fascinating one!"[63]

Journalists across the country were thrilled by the discovery that Canadians had their own way of saying things. Many commentators noted that the *Senior Dictionary* had put to rest any lingering doubt about the existence of Canadian English. The *Brockville Recorder and Times,* for example, told its readers that the dictionary's editors had successfully shown "the richness and variety of the particularly Canadian element in our vocabulary."[64] The *Windsor Star* likewise noted that the "average modest Canadian" would be pleasantly surprised to see this book "seriously declaring itself to be 'Canadian English.'"[65] The journalists at the *Vancouver Sun* even had some fun with the new language: "You're standing on the permafrost in your mukluks, eating CPR strawberries wondering how you've wound up in a moose pasture. You may be miserable. But ... you're pure Canadian."[66] Others spoke of "Calgary Red-eye." Calgary Red-eye (mixture of beer and tomato juice), CPR strawberries (prunes), moose pastures (unproven mining claims): the Canadian media were delighted.[67]

The dictionary was similarly read by the news media as a sign of the nation's coming of age and as a "refreshing assertion of Canada's growing national character."[68] Canadian newspapers such as the *Albertan* celebrated the dictionary's publication as "an event worthy of Centennial Year."[69] The *Charlottetown Patriot,* in turn, noted that the dictionary helped "the nation in our search for a Canadian identity."[70] A Gage spokesperson confirmed the timeliness of the dictionaries: "Most nations are known for their languages, but nobody has previously identified the Canadian language. We are identifying it for the first time and that to me is the really significant reason that this is a good centennial project. In fact, if you accept the premise that a nation is known by its language, to me our project is the most important one on the whole list" of Centennial projects.[71] Several commentators even hoped that the dictionary would dispel Canada's inferiority complex.

Virtually all columnists and book reviewers concluded by saying that the *Senior Dictionary* should be in the homes, offices, and classrooms of every Canadian. The *Victoria Daily Colonist,* for its part, urged its readers to buy the dictionary: "This is a Canadian book for Canadians and one every Canadian home will be proud to own and proud to use."[72] Other journalists were equally effusive in their praise. "At last, a dictionary we can call our own," trumpeted the *North Bay Nugget.*[73] Clearly, "Canadian" was the selling word of the day.[74] As a result, British and American varieties of English appeared increasingly foreign.[75]

But how Canadian was this national dictionary? Its origins in the *E.L. Thorndike and Clarence L. Barnhart Dictionary* from the United States rarely surfaced in media reports. To do so would have brought into question the Canadianness of the dictionary. When it was mentioned, the media were careful to emphasize its many Canadian features. The *Lindsay Post,* for example, reported that "the original work has been carefully blended with Canadian words and expressions."[76] The retention of the original illustrations, however, resulted in some awkwardness. For example, the caption under a US marine read: "Marine: Canada has no marines."[77]

The spelling principles adopted by the editors of *The Dictionary of Canadian English* have been preserved in the personal papers of Walter Avis, housed at Queen's University in Kingston. His files reveal that the dictionary editors opted for American spelling (see Table 4.1). Thus where *-or* (labor) competed with *-our,* the editors favoured the American spelling. The same was true of *-m* (program), *-dgm* (judgment), *-l* (enrol), *-ize* (realize), and *-ce* (defence). However, British spelling was retained in the cases of *-ette* (cigarette), *-re* (theatre), *-ie* (cookie), and *-yse* (analyse).[78] Either way, British and American spellings were cross-listed and alternative spellings sold as another distinctly Canadian feature of the dictionary.

At the outset, Canadian newspapers generally lauded the dictionary makers' decision to include both British and American spellings. The *Northern Daily News* of Kirkland Lake, Ontario, for example, praised it as a sign of Canadian independence and lack of rigidity.[79] This reaction was predictable, as Canadian newspapers relied on the *Canadian Press Style Guide,* which had recommended American spellings since 1947.[80] Although it sometimes led to confusion, the hybrid nature of Canadian spelling represented a style that was all our own.[81]

By contrast, the prescription of American spelling received a mixed reaction from Canadian teachers. The *BC Teachers* newsletter, for its part, heralded

Table 4.1

Spelling choice in *The Dictionary of Canadian English*

British	American	Word choice
-our (labour)	*-or* (labor)	*-or* (labor)
-mme (programme)	*-m* (program)	*-m* (program)
-dgem (judgement)	*-dgm* (judgment)	*-dgm* (judgment)
-ll (enroll)	*-l* (enrol)	*-l* (enrol)
-ise (realise)	*-ize* (realize)	*-ize* (realize)
-se (defense)	*-ce* (defence)	*-ce* (defence)
-ette (cigarette)	*-et* (cigaret)	*-ette* (cigarette)
-re (theatre)	*-er* (theater)	*-re* (theatre)
-yse (analyse)	*-yze* (analyze)	*-yse* (analyse)

the dual usages included in the dictionary as sensibly Canadian: "that is, it is not overpoweringly 'British,' nor is it infuriatingly 'American.'"[82] There were, however, storm clouds on the horizon. At an early point in the dictionary's production, Walter Avis expressed concern that even his nine-year-old son refused to accept the shorter American spellings that "we are advocating."[83] Apparently, his son's teachers, and therefore Ontario's curriculum, advocated British forms for the most part. Avis realized that the dictionary makers risked dampening teachers' interest in their project if they went too far in recommending US spellings.

The tenacity with which Canadian educators clung to British spelling traditions, bolstered by the nationalism of the time, was not to be reasoned with. Just as the bilingual dictionary fell victim to the changing political winds in Quebec, the *Dictionary of Canadian English* soon found itself under attack for recommending American spelling. Given the growing unpopularity of America's war in Vietnam, the desire to differentiate Canada from the United States intensified. In linguistic terms, this trend could be seen in the push to expunge American spelling from Canadian English. Gage's decision to recommend American spelling thus proved to be increasingly controversial. D.L. Berg, a specialist librarian at the Ontario Institute for Studies in Education (OISE), for example, questioned the editorial decision to use American spellings in an October 1969 letter to the publisher.[84] He also noted that his concern was shared by many other educators.

One of the most vocal critics of the Gage dictionaries was Thomas M. Paikeday, the editor of the rival *Webster's Dictionary of Canadian English* (1969).[85] Writing in *Quill & Quire* in 1975, Paikeday labelled Gage's preference for American forms a "dubious choice."[86] His own decision to privilege British spellings in Webster's was justified, he said, by recent language usage studies conducted in Canada. Thus, under "labor," the reader of Paikeday's dictionary is directed to "see LABOUR"; the opposite was true in Gage. In his preface, Paikeday advised his readers that "spelling differences are in conformity with the current styles approved by Departments of Education and educational publishers generally rather than those of the news media. From our questionnaires we found that spellings such as 'labour,' 'grey,' 'paralleled,' and 'bettor' (one who bets) are more acceptable than 'labor,' 'gray,' 'parallelled,' and 'better.'"[87] The two school dictionaries also differed in their treatment of pronunciations such as lieutenant. Whereas Winston's privileged the British "f" sound, Gage noted that the American "u" sound was most common. In the most explicit terms possible, Paikeday dismissed the Gage *Senior Dictionary* as not truly Canadian. Lost in the nationalist rhetoric, however, was the simple fact that both publishing houses were American-owned.

The war of words spilled over into the daily newspapers. One journalist, after speaking to Harry Scargill, defended the inclusion of American and

British spellings: "There are some Canadian nationalists – mostly academics – who insist that every time we write 'color' instead of 'colour' we are losing our national identity because of American cultural dominance."[88] A dictionary should, Scargill told the press, describe common usage, not prescribe another. Yet the times were changing. Whereas the dictionary movement of the 1950s and 1960s sought to distance Canada from British and American varieties of English, the 1970s saw a larger emphasis on the differences with American English. The yearbook of Queen's Alma Mater Society changed its name from *Tricolor* to *Tricolour* in 1978. Others followed. Once provincial school boards began to insist on British spellings as a sign of Canadianness, dictionary publishers had no choice but to follow suit.[89] Gage abandoned its increasingly vulnerable position in the mid-1990s and switched to British spellings "in light of current trends."[90] With this reversal, linguistic nationalism overcame and surpassed the founders of the dictionary movement that had given it life.

The Dictionary of Canadianisms

The publication of the fourth volume in the Gage series, *The Dictionary of Canadianisms*, was nothing less than an "iconic event" for Jack Chambers.[91] The very idea of publishing a comprehensive historical record of Canadianisms spoken in Canada gave Chambers a "wonderful liberating kind of feeling" as a young graduate student.[92] C.J. Lovell, an American, was invited by Toronto publisher W.J. Gage Limited to prepare the dictionary from materials that he had already collected as a research associate for the *Dictionary of Americanisms*. In fact, he had assembled 50,000 quotations "illustrating the development of Canadian English."[93] Before he could begin, however, Lovell died in March 1960. But the dictionary project did not die with him. Gage purchased Lovell's entire lexicographical collection and convinced two linguists, Walter Avis and Harry Scargill, to proceed with the project.

The content of the *Dictionary of Canadianisms* came from five major sources. In addition to the nucleus of words originating in Lovell's original collection, there were sizeable donations of linguistic material from Walter Avis (mainly Ontario materials), Douglas Leechman (mainly related to Canada's Northwest), and Charles Brandel Crate, a teacher in Quesnel, British Columbia. The fifth source of data originated in new materials gathered by Scargill's Lexicographical Centre. Volunteers from across Canada sent in citation slips on which they wrote the word to be illustrated, a quotation, and its source.[94] Taking advantage of government Centennial grants, the editors were able to advance the date of publication from 1970 to 1967.[95]

The term Canadianism was defined specifically for this project. The editors initially considered limiting the dictionary to words originating in Canada. However, there were not a sufficient number to warrant a dictionary. Moreover, Scargill noted, such a narrow definition would have excluded many words that were "certainly Canadian" but that originated elsewhere. A Canadianism was thus defined as a "word, expression, or meaning which is native to Canada or which is distinctively characteristic of Canadian usage though not necessarily exclusive to Canada." This definition proved more expansive than its equivalent in the *Dictionary of Americanisms*.

What did the editors of the *Dictionary of Canadianisms* hope to achieve? Harry Scargill attempted to answer this very question in a March 1967 speech at York University. For him, the dictionary was much more than a record of changing spellings, pronunciations, and meanings. Indeed, language was the "best record available of the forces and events that have shaped a nation." It was our distinctive language, he argued, that made us uniquely Canadian: "The Canadian may drive a car engineered in Detroit and wear a suit of British wool; but many of the things he talks about give him an identity which is neither British nor American."[96] The linkage between language and national identity was paramount in Scargill's eyes: "Don't wave the flag, speak Canadian to prove you are one." By encouraging Canadians to identify with Canadianisms, the dictionary thus set Canada apart from other English-speaking nations.[97]

Each entry in the *Dictionary of Canadianisms* was supported by dated quotations from printed sources such as published travel diaries, novels, music lyrics, periodicals, and newspapers. The quotations provided were usually the earliest and most recent quotations on file: "With extensive files based on writings over a long period from all parts of the country, it will give the history of a given word, show whether or not it has become obsolete and list its various meanings and spellings at different periods. It will thus show what is distinctive about the English language in Canada."[98] However, quotations that provided fuller descriptive detail were sometimes selected, as were those that stood out for their interpretative or entertainment value. Oral evidence was not included.

The entries can be grouped into several subheadings. Words describing geographical features including flora and fauna are most frequent. Words of Native origin also appear in abundance. French terms such as *Aboiteau* – Acadian for dike, dam, or sluice gate – appear in large numbers alongside everyday slang phrases such as "main drag," defined as "the principal street of a village or town; the main street of a city."[99] Canada's rich political history is on display with words such as "acclamation" and "advance poll" and with party names such as "Clear Grits" and "Socreds." Words associated with the fur trade, mining, logging, farming, and the railway also make their appearance. Sports-related vocabulary, particularly those words associated with hockey, such as "deke" (a fake shot or movement), pepper the dictionary. A few Canadianisms for consumer items are identified. The word chesterfield, Canadian for couch or sofa, for example, loomed large in the linguistic imagination. Walter Avis was particularly fond of telling the story of a Canadian in an American department store who asks to see the chester-fields only to be shown the cigarette counter. The chesterfield story served as a linguistic marker, or shibboleth, that told Canadians that there was such a thing as Canadian English.

Each entry provided Canadians with a short course in Canadian history and literature. For example, the entry for "shanty" provides two meanings. First, it referred to "a crude hut used as a dwelling by lumbermen in the bush." Or it referred to "a specially designed log bunkhouse used by a gang of loggers." The origins of the word are explained by the dictionary's edi-tors: "Although the most probable source of shanty is Cdn F [Canadian French] chantier, especially in lumbering contexts, the possibility remains that a similar word, derived from Irish Gaelic sean tig hut, may have been introduced by Irish immigrants into Upper Canada, where the term seems first to have enjoyed currency; it may well be, therefore, that two different words of similar form contributed to the generalization of this term and its derivatives in Canada during the nineteenth century."[100]

The entry for "shanty" cites several published examples dating back to 1822. For its part, the *Victoria Daily Colonist* noted that only in Canada was "a banker both a man who handles finances and a fisherman who works the Grand Banks off the Newfoundland coast."[101] For the *Ottawa Journal*, "Most Canadians have been aware that Canadian English had its own idi-osyncrasies – words and phrases and meanings not found in British or Ameri-can English."[102] The borrowings from Native and French languages thus differentiated Canadian English from other varieties.[103] The staggering number of entries for words of French or Native origin stand as a testament to the inclusiveness of the language spoken here. In fact, their sheer number is arguably out of all proportion to current or past usage.

In effect, the *Dictionary of Canadianisms* played down the country's impe-rial connection to Great Britain in favour of a made-in-Canada language. The secrets of a people's identity, *Canadian Business* wrote approvingly, "can be found in its vocabulary."[104] The Canada that emerges in the citations included with each entry is one of exploration and settlement, the fur trade and farming, railways, logging, and mining. Writing in *Saturday Night*, Mavor Moore stated that this was "no mere word museum" but a "vivid historical theatre."[105] Largely left off stage, however, are words derived from urban Canada, from immigrant groups (such as Yiddish-speaking Canadians) other than the French and English, and from industry or the working-class experience.

The active invention of a national language, one of two official languages after 1969, was obscured, however, by the claim that Canadian English had existed for generations. Nationalists often invoke their nation's "primordial essence."[106] In this regard, Canadian dictionaries called forth Canada's pio-neering past: the age of European discovery, the fur trade, and the British

Loyalist migration. Given the emphasis placed on the roots of language, the place of etymology in these Canadian dictionaries was critically important. According to American historian Kenneth Cmiel, "etymology told citizens that they were one, that their roots, quite literally, were the same."[107] This process of linguistic invention, however, was presented as a simple act of discovery, recovery, or recognition.

Nationalist vocabulary, it seems, has a lengthy history in Canada. "All-Canadian," defined here as "situated wholly within Canada's borders" or alternatively as "consisting entirely of Canadian people, talents, resources," seemed to be in wide circulation during the 1950s. Canada's relationship with the United States also makes its appearance in entries for "across the border" and "across the line." The social construction of national difference surfaces again in the entry for "Canadian football." Here, the editors note that the Canadian game differed from American football but not to the degree that it differed from English rugby. *The Dictionary of Canadianisms* made every effort to differentiate Canada from both Great Britain and the United States but conceded that Canadian English shared much with the American variety. In this respect, the dictionary mirrored the American orientation of the other school dictionaries.

Drawing Conclusions

The crest of the wave of Canadian English lexicography broke in the late 1960s. The first generation of linguistic nationalists had run out of steam, and the second generation was more interested in syntax and pronunciation than in collecting Canadianisms.[108] Jack Chambers remembers the early 1970s as a time of change within the Canadian Linguistics Association. His own work on the Canadian accent, particularly his 1973 paper on "Canadian raising," generated debate and discussion about changing speech patterns. This study and the many others that followed established Chambers as Canada's foremost linguist in the field. His work has shown that the traditional tolerance for linguistic variance (the double standard) in Canada is fast disappearing. American pronunciation has largely supplanted British pronunciations of words such as "leisure" and "schedule." Even the use of "chesterfield" is on the wane.[109] The decline of Briticisms thus mirrors Canada's progressive abandonment of old imperial symbols, such as "God Save the Queen," in the postwar era.[110]

If Briticisms are dying out in the spoken language of Canadians, it has proven easier to impose and maintain British norms in spelling. The resurgence of British spelling in most parts of Canada is striking.[111] Book publishers such as UBC Press, the publisher of this volume, now demand that writers use "British/Canadian spelling." Even the Canadian Press has reverted to British spellings. Canadians also continue to use the British "zed" over the American "zee" overwhelmingly.[112] The appearance of the *Canadian Oxford*

Dictionary in 1998 is further evidence that Canadians have come to claim British spelling as their own.[113]

By emphasizing its indigenous roots and minimizing its British ones, the dictionary movement of the 1950s and 1960s sought to demonstrate that Canadian English was truly our own. As Harry Scargill once said, "Canadian English is not a mongrel mixture of British with American English, it exists in its own right and owes its existence to the Canadians who made it what it is."[114] By the end of the 1960s, however, the perceived threat of American cultural and economic dominance overshadowed any previous concern over British influences. To differentiate themselves from American English, Canadians made British spellings their own. Even so, one is struck not so much by the differences between American and Canadian English today as by the similarities. The differences between the two dialects are "neither many nor large."[115] Yet not so very long ago, these linguistic differences loomed larger than life. One can conclude only that these small differences were exaggerated to serve as markers of national distinctiveness at a time of intense national anxiety and nation building.

Acknowledgments

I would like to thank Jack Chambers, Peter Cook, Barbara Lorenzkowski, John Walsh, Krissy O'Hare, the participants of the "Cultural Approaches to Canadian Nationalism" conference at Nipissing University, the participants of the "The Sixties: Style and Substance" conference at the McCord Museum in Montreal, and the archivists at Queen's University, the University of Victoria, and McMaster University. Funding for this chapter was provided by Nipissing University.

Notes

1   Katherine Verdery, "Whither 'Nation' and 'Nationalism'?" in Gopal Balakrishnan and Benedict Anderson, eds., *Mapping the Nation* (London: Verso, 1996), 109.
2   Anthony D. Smith, quoted in Stephen Barbour, "Nationalism, Language, Europe," in Stephen Barbour and Cathie Carmichael, eds., *Language and Nationalism in Europe* (Oxford: Oxford University Press, 2000), 4, and see also 15; Alon Confino, *The Nation as Local Metaphor: Wurttemberg, Imperial Germany, and National Memory, 1871-1918* (Chapel Hill: University of North Carolina Press, 1997), 3. German philosopher Johann Gottfried von Herder even declared language to be the "essential defining characteristic of nation"; see Johann Gottfried von Herder, *Outlines of a Philosophy of the History of Man* (1784; reprint, New York, 1966).
3   Noah Webster, quoted in Henri Bejoint, *Tradition and Innovation in Modern English Dictionaries* (Oxford: Clarendon Press, 1994), 138.
4   Kenneth Cmiel, "'A Broad and Fluid Language of Democracy': Discovering the American Idiom," *Journal of American History* 78, 3 (December 1992): 913-36 at 913. There are many other examples. Sweden embraced old vowels in order to exaggerate the distinctiveness of the Swedish language, which had been heavily influenced by Danish; see Lars S. Vikor, "Northern Europe: Languages as Prime Markers of Ethnic and National Identity," in Barbour and Carmichael, eds., *Language and Nationalism,* 109-10; Stephen Barbour, "Germany, Austria, Switzerland, Luxemburg: The Total Coincidence of Nations and Speech Communities?" in Barbour and Carmichael, eds., *Language and Nationalism,* 162-64. This process was repeated in German-speaking Luxemburg and Austria after the Second World War. Not wanting to be associated with the crimes of the Third Reich, Luxemburg insisted that its speech represented a "distinct language," and Austrian leaders promoted an Austrian identity, including "distinct Austrian forms of German."

5   Peter Burke, *The Art of Conversation* (Ithaca: Cornell University Press, 1993), 67-68.
6   The Massey Commission warned of the Americanization of the country; see Paul Litt, "The Massey Commission, Americanization and Canadian Cultural Nationalism," *Queen's Quarterly* 98, 2 (1991): 375-87 at 375. For an excellent summary of Canadians' mixed feelings for the United States during the 1950s, see J.M. Bumsted, "Canada and American Culture in the 1950s," in J.M. Bumsted, ed., *Interpreting Canada's Past: After Confederation* (Don Mills, ON: Oxford University Press, 1986), 398-411.
7   There is a considerable scholarship on this movement. See Stephen Azzi, *Walter Gordon and the Rise of Canadian Nationalism* (Montreal and Kingston: McGill-Queen's University Press, 1999); Sylvia Bashevkin, *True Patriot Love: The Politics of Canadian Nationalism* (Toronto: Oxford University Press, 1991); John Bullen, "The Ontario Waffle and the Struggle for an Independent Socialist Canada: Conflict within the NDP," *Canadian Historical Review* 64, 2 (1983): 188-215; Robert A. Wright, "'Dream, Comfort, Memory, Despair': Canadian Popular Musicians and the Dilemma of Nationalism, 1968-1972," *Journal of Canadian Studies* 22, 4 (1987-88): 27-42; Steven High, "'I'll Wrap the F*#@ Canadian Flag around Me': A Nationalist Response to Plant Shutdowns, 1969-1984," *Journal of the Canadian Historical Association* 12 (2001): 199-226.
8   The notion of invention is used in this chapter in the same sense used by Anthony D. Smith, as something more than nationalist fabrication: "a novel recombination of existing elements." See Anthony D. Smith, "Nationalism and the Historians," in Balakrishnan and Anderson, eds., *Mapping the Nation*, 109.
9   The Canadian English dictionary projects were part of a much larger effort to help Canadians understand their national identity. Other nationalist projects among historians included the *Historical Atlas of Canada*, the *Dictionary of Canadian Biography* (first volume published in 1966) and the *Centenary Series of Historical Works* (1955-88). The theme of unification underlay all three projects. For analyses of these projects, see Graeme Wynn, "Maps and Dreams of Nationhood: A (Re)View of the Historical Atlas of Canada," *Canadian Historical Review* 76, 3 (September 1995): 482-87; P.B. Waite, "Journeys through Thirteen Volumes: The Dictionary of Canadian Biography," *Canadian Historical Review* 76, 3 (September 1995): 464-81; Lyle Dick, "'A Growing Necessity for Canada': W.L. Morton's Centenary Series and the Forms of National History, 1955-80," *Canadian Historical Review* 82, 2 (June 2001): 223-52.
10 G.M. Story, "The Role of the Dictionary in Canadian English," in W.C. Lougheed, ed., *In Search of the Standard in Canadian English*, Strathy Language Unit Occasional Paper No. 1 (Kingston: Strathy Language Unit, 1986), 2-3.
11 Sir William A. Craigie and James R. Hulbert, eds., *A Dictionary of American English on Historical Principles* (Chicago: University of Chicago Press, 1938), v. The stated purpose of the dictionary was to distinguish American English from that of England and the rest of the English-speaking world. See also A.J. Aitken, "The Period Dictionaries," in Robert Burchfield, ed., *Studies in Lexicography* (Oxford: Clarendon Press, 1987), 101.
12 The melting pot idea permeates the dictionary's preface: "The student of American English has always to keep in mind the important fact that many people of many tongues took part in shaping the language of the United States. There are many linguistic phenomena in American English that cannot be intelligently explained within the limits of the English language." See Mitford M. Mathews, ed., *A Dictionary of Americanisms on Historical Principles* (Chicago: University of Chicago Press, 1951), vii.
13 *Dictionary of Jamaican English* (Cambridge: Cambridge University Press, 1967); *Dictionary of Bahamian English* (Hyde Park, NY: Lexic House, 1982); *A Dictionary of South African English on Historical Principles* (Oxford: Oxford University Press, 1978); Arthur Delbidge, *The Macquarie Dictionary of Australian English* (Sydney: Macquarie Library, 1981).
14 Ibid., 138.
15 However, there were differences. Whereas the South African and Australian national dictionaries were derived from British dictionaries, *The Dictionary of Canadian English* was a revised version of the American *E.L. Thorndike and Clarence L. Barnhart Dictionary;* see Bejoint, *Tradition and Innovation*, 79-80. Even the *Dictionary of Canadianisms* was "firmly modeled" on the *Dictionary of American English;* see Aitken, "Period Dictionaries," in Burchfield, ed., *Studies in Lexicography*, 104.

16   J.K. Chambers, "'Lawless and Vulgar Innovations': Victorian Views of Canadian English," in Sandra Clarke, ed., *Focus on Canada* (Amsterdam: John Benjamin, 1993), 1-26; M.H. Scargill, "The Growth of Canadian English," in Carl F. Klinck, ed., *Literary History of Canada: Canadian Literature in English,* vol. 1 (Toronto: University of Toronto Press, 1976).

17   Susanna Moodie, quoted in Chambers, "'Lawless and Vulgar Innovations,'" 6-7; J.K. Chambers, interviewed by Steven High, Toronto, June 2003, audio cassettes in possession of the author.

18   J.K. Chambers, ed., *Canadian English: Origins and Structures* (Toronto: Macmillan, 1975), vii.

19   Reverend A. Constable Geikie, quoted in J.K. Chambers, "'Canadian Dainty': The Rise and Decline of Briticisms in Canada," in Raymond Hickey, ed., *The Legacy of Colonial English: Studies in Transported Dialects* (Cambridge: Cambridge University Press, 2003). My thanks to Jack Chambers for showing me an advance copy of the chapter.

20   Eric Hobsbawm, "Introduction: Inventing Traditions," in Eric Hobsbawm and Terence Ranger, eds., *The Invention of Tradition* (Cambridge: Cambridge University Press, 1983).

21   Henry Alexander, "The English Language in Canada," *Royal Commission Studies: A Selection of Essays Prepared for the Royal Commission on National Development in the Arts, Letters and Sciences* (Ottawa: Edmond Cloutier, 1951), 13-24 at 21.

22   Dr. Raven I. McDavid, "Why Do We Talk That Way," *CBC Times,* [no month] 1955, 1991-041, 1.15, University of Victoria Archives (hereafter UVIC).

23   Henry Alexander, "Is there a Canadian Language?" *CBC Times,* 27 February-5 March 1955, 2-3.

24   Ibid.

25   M.H. Scargill, "Canadians Speak Canadian," *Saturday Night,* 8 December 1956, 16-17.

26   Ibid.

27   Ibid.

28   Ibid.

29   Walter Avis, "Canadian Lexicon in the Making," *CBC Times,* 14 April 1957. There are several recent books that explore nationalism and professionalization in Canada. See, for example, the study of the Canadian Sociology and Anthropology Association in Jeffrey Cormier, *The Canadianization Movement: Emergence, Survival and Success* (Toronto: University of Toronto Press, 2004); and more generally, Gillian Creese, *Contracting Masculinity: Gender, Class and Race in a White-Collar Union, 1944-1994* (Don Mills: Oxford University Press, 1999).

30   Raven I. McDavid, Jr., "Webster, Mencken and Avis: Spokesmen for Linguistic Autonomy," *Canadian Journal of Linguistics* 26, 1 (1981): 118-25.

31   J.K. Chambers, interviewed by Steven High, Toronto, June 2003, audio cassettes in possession of the author.

32   This description of early events comes from the preface written by M.H. Scargill, in *Dictionary of Canadian English: A Dictionary of Canadianisms on Historical Principles* (Toronto: W.J. Gage, 1967), vi. Henry Alexander's early contribution to the movement should not be underestimated. Not only did he write an essay on the subject for the Massey Commission, but he also edited *The Winston Dictionary for Canadian Schools* (Toronto: John C. Winston, 1955). This American dictionary had been Canadianized to some extent by the inclusion of British spellings (labour) and the addition of Canadian appendices (lists of prime ministers, etc.).

33   Walter S. Avis, "Problems in the Study of Canadian English (1965)" in *Essays and Articles* (Kingston: Royal Military College of Canada Occasional Papers of the Department of English, 1978), 11.

34   Walter Avis, "The English Language: A Report," [1970?], file 2-16, box 1, ser. 1: Subject Files, Walter Avis, 3711.1, Queen's University Archives.

35   Walter Avis, "Canadian Lexicon in the Making," *CBC Times,* 14 April 1957.

36   "A 'New' Language: Canadian English," *New York Times,* 29 November 1959, 148.

37   "Canada Month," *Canada Month,* 13-14 December 1961, 13.

38   The first issues of the *Journal of the CLA* (later renamed the *Journal of Canadian Linguistics*) were dedicated almost entirely to dialect geography and lexicography.

39 "A Canadian Bilingual Dictionary," [1954?], File: "Dictionary – Early Records," McClelland and Stewart Collection, McMaster University Archives. Most famously, British English was enshrined in the monumental twelve-volume *Oxford English Dictionary (OED)*, published in instalments – one letter at a time – by Clarendon Press between 1884 and 1928. The *OED* was initiated by the Philological Society of London in 1857. According to the mover of the resolution, the dictionary would "capture the very lettered soul of this proud nation preparing to define itself by its history, literature, and scientific spirit." The *OED* thus relied on "the great imaginary library" of British arts and letters. Quoted in John Willinsky, *Empire of Words: The Reign of the Oxford English Dictionary* (Princeton: Princeton University Press, 1994), 27.

40 "Tentative Script for Delivery over Station CKFA Edmonton by Staff Announcer," [1961?], File: "Dictionary – Early Records," McClelland and Stewart Collection, McMaster University Archives.

41 Professor H. Alexander, "The Search for a National Dictionary," n.d., File: "Dictionary – Early Records," McClelland and Stewart Collection, McMaster University Archives. This need was also recognized by the Canadian Linguistics Association at its founding meeting in 1954; see J.P. Vinay and P. Daviault, "Dictionnaires canadiens I: Les Dictionnaires bilingues," *Translators' Journal* 3, 3 (July-September 1958): 109-13. The study of Canadian French was much more advanced than the study of Canadian English; J. Bélisle's *Dictionnaire général de la langue française au Canada* was published in 1954 (Quebec: Bélisle Éditeur).

42 Jean-Paul Vinay, Pierre Daviault, and Henry Alexander, eds., *The Canadian Dictionary/ Dictionnaire canadien* (Toronto: McClelland and Stewart, 1962).

43 Donald J. Horton, *André Laurendeau: French Canadian Nationalist, 1912-1968* (Toronto: Oxford University Press, 1992), 205. Once in power, Pearson named André Laurendeau to the Bilingualism and Biculturalism Commission, which culminated in the Official Languages Act of 1969.

44 Vinay, Daviault, and Alexander, eds., *Canadian Dictionary/Dictionnaire canadien*, ix.

45 Robert J. Gregg, "Canadian Lexicography," *Canadian Literature* 14 (Autumn 1962): 68.

46 "Canadian Dictionary," *Windsor Star*, 17 April 1962.

47 "A Dictionary for Canada," editorial, *Toronto Daily Star*, 10 March 1962.

48 Robert Fulford, *Toronto Star*, 23 March 1962.

49 "New Canadian Bilingual Dictionary in Two Years," *Globe and Mail*, 13 April 1957.

50 Peter Martin, "Review," *The Canadian Reader*, April 1962. There is an extensive secondary literature on Quebec's Quiet Revolution; see, for example, Kenneth McRoberts, *Quebec: Social Change and Political Crisis*, 3rd ed. (Toronto: McClelland and Stewart, 1988); and Paul-André Linteau et al., eds., *Quebec since 1930: A History* (Toronto: Lorimer, 1991).

51 Martin, "Review." These hopes and dreams were shared by the dictionary's editor; see Vinay and Daviault, "Dictionnaires canadiens I."

52 J.G. [Jack] McClelland to Leon Lortie, Secretary General, University of Montreal, 11 September 1964, McClelland and Stewart Collection, File: "Editorial Canadian Dictionary, 1958-63," McMaster University Archives.

53 Jack McClelland to Howard Petch, President of the University of Victoria, 16 July 1975, LRC 1991-041, 1.7, UVIC.

54 Nationalist leaders in Quebec had taken a dim view of Canadian French. André Laurendeau, editor of *Le Devoir* and future head of the Bilingualism and Biculturalism Commission, stated in October 1959 that the speech of Québécois was merely "joual talk"; quoted in Sophia Preisman, "Canadian French Is a Language," *Canadian Library* 19, 1 (July 1962): 15-16 at 16.

55 Hand-written note, [1963?], McClelland and Stewart Collection, File: "Editorial Canadian Dictionary, 1958-63," McMaster University Archives.

56 Jack McClelland to Howard Petch, President of the University of Victoria, 16 July 1975, LRC 1991-041, 1.7, UVIC.

57 One of the major criticisms of the first edition was that it did not contain many everyday words; see M.J. Savage, Editor at McClelland and Stewart, to Editorial Board, Memorandum

of 13 February 1965 Meeting in Montreal, LRC 1991-041, 1.5, UVIC. The dictionary was half the size of the competing bilingual dictionaries from Harrap, Larousse, and Cassell; see Jean-Paul Vinay, "Suggestions Concerning Possible Changes to the Concise Edition of the C.D.," 4 February 1963, McClelland and Stewart Collection, File: "Editorial Canadian Dictionary, 1958-63," McMaster University Archives.

58 M.J. Savage to J.P. Vinay, 9 December 1965, LRC 1991-041, 1.5, UVIC.

59 J.P. Vinay to Jack McClelland, 12 March 1973, LRC 1991-041, 1.6, UVIC.

60 Alberta linguistic consultant B.H. Smeaton noted that the title of the first edition may have been appropriate to the nationalistic 1960s but that it needed to be changed to make it marketable in the United States. Indeed, the "most serious disadvantage of all of giving a dictionary a national label, of course, is that to do so tends to restrict its marketability to the country designated (even the British version of CD1 has 'with special reference to Canadian usage' as its subtitle); and if that country has a comparatively small population, it follows that only a small number of copies of the work will be sold. In the present case one is left with the paradox that the most patriotic thing to do, really, is to see to it that, in all major respects, one's product is palatable to the American market, if one proposes to invade it (as, heaven knows, the Americans have invaded ours in the publishing field, with no thought as to whether it was patriotic to do so or not)"; see B.H. Smeaton, Department of Linguistics, University of Calgary, to Jean-Paul Vinay, 7 April 1974, "Progress Report on revision and enlargement of *The Canadian Dictionary/Dictionnaire canadien*," 1, LRC 1991-041, 1.3, UVIC.

61 J.P. Vinay to Jack McClelland, 5 January 1979, LRC 1991-041, 1.7, UVIC. However, the dream of a comprehensive bilingual Canadian dictionary did not die. The Canadian Bilingual Dictionary Project is now coming to completion at the University of Ottawa. As one of its directors, Roda Roberts, noted, "every self-respecting country has its own dictionary ... Canada, with two official languages, owes itself at least one, don't you think?"; quoted in Kelly Egan, "Bilingual Dictionary a Labour of Love," *Ottawa Citizen*, 9 March 1999.

62 "Canadian Dictionary Gets Cool Reception," *Halifax Chronicle-Herald*, 24 April 1959, 28.

63 "Centennial Reader," *Winnipeg Voxair*, 2 January 1968.

64 "Book Proves There Is 'Canadian English,'" *Brockville Recorder and Times*, 13 March 1967.

65 "Canadian English," *Windsor Star*, 22 April 1967.

66 "Linguist Takes a Slangshot," *Vancouver Sun*, 24 August 1967.

67 A sample of the headlines makes this evident: "Nobody but a Canadian calls a tavern a 'beer parlour,'" *Alberta Country Life*, 7 October 1967; "Canadians Have Own Words," *Winnipeg Free Press*, 7 October 1967; "Genuine Canadian Words Found in New Dictionary," *Rouyn-Noranda Press*, 12 October 1967.

68 "Canada Month," *Canada Month*, 13-14 December 1961, 13.

69 "Coming of Age Etymologically in First Canadian Dictionary," *Albertan*, 18 March 1967.

70 Wallace Ward, "Canadians get a new identity," *Charlottetown Patriot*, 13 March 1967.

71 W.R. Wees, vice president of publishing, W.J. Gage Ltd., quoted in *Monetary Times*, December 1966.

72 Alec Merriman, "Special Dictionary for Canadians," *Victoria Daily Colonist*, 25 March 1967.

73 "At last, a dictionary we can call our own," *North Bay Nugget*, 8 March 1967.

74 H. Rex Wilson, "It's broader than beer parlour and baby bonus," *Globe Magazine*, 8 April 1967, 19.

75 Fergus Cronin, "Do you speak Canadian?" *Canadian Weekly*, 7 February-5 March 1965. This shift in perception could be seen in the ready dismissal of American dictionaries. The Canada Council, for example, noted in 1962 that foreign dictionaries failed "to give a satisfactory account of the language spoken in Canada"; quoted in "Speaking as a Canadian," *Canada Council Bulletin* 13 (Autumn 1962): 1-5.

76 "New Senior Dictionary deserves a place in every home," *Lindsay Post*, 17 April 1967.

77 H. Rex Wilson, "It's broader than beer parlour and baby bonus," *Globe Magazine*, 8 April 1967, 19.

78 "Summary of Spelling Principles for the Dictionary of Canadian English Series," File: "Jack Chambers, 1974-76," box 1, ser. 1: Correspondence Files, 3726.3, Walter Avis Collection, Queen's University Archives.

79 "New Dictionary Features 'Canadian' Words, Phrases," *Kirkland Lake Northern Daily News,* 7 March 1967.

80 J.K. Chambers, "Three Kinds of Standard in Canadian English," in *In Search of the Standard in Canadian English,* ed. W.C. Lougheed (Kingston: Strathy Language Unit, 1986), 5-6.

81 "A Woman's World for New Books," *Red Deer Advocate,* 29 March 1967.

82 "Reference," *BC Teachers,* December 1967.

83 Walter Avis to Canadian Linguistics Association, 25 February 1959, box 1, ser. 1: Correspondence Files, 3726.3, Walter Avis Collection, Queen's University Archives.

84 D.L. Berg, Specialist Librarian, OISE, 2 October 1969, box 1, ser. 1: Correspondence Files, 3726.3, Walter Avis Collection, Queen's University Archives.

85 Webster's was one of several US dictionary makers to produce a Canadian edition in the 1960s and 1970s. Thomas Paikeday's remarkable life story is sketched out by Robert Fulford. He was originally from Southern India and came to Canada to work – initially – for Gage's *Dictionary of Canadian History.* See Robert Fulford, "What Higgins Taught Eliza," *Toronto Daily Star,* 28 April 1966.

86 Thomas M. Paikeday, "Do We Have a Canadian Dictionary?" *Quill & Quire,* April 1975, 4-5.

87 Thomas Paikeday, quoted in P.W. Rogers, "Review Article: Unlocking the Canadian Word Hoard," *Queen's Quarterly* 77, 1 (Spring 1970): 111-23 at 116.

88 "Canadians find 'colour' in language controversy," *Victoria Express,* 12 January 1974, 13.

89 A study of how provincial departments of education (especially Ontario's) promoted British spelling is needed. Such a study could also examine school textbooks as well as elementary and high school curricula.

90 This news was welcomed by journalists; see Michael Valpy, "Over the hedge words: A look at Canadian English," *Globe and Mail,* 21 November 1996, A19.

91 J.K. Chambers, interviewed by Steven High, Toronto, June 2003, audio cassettes in possession of the author.

92 Ibid.; *Dictionary of Canadian English: A Dictionary of Canadianisms on Historical Principles.*

93 "Speaking as a Canadian," *Canada Council Bulletin* 13 (Autumn 1962): 1-5.

94 One source indicated that there were 500,000 completed slips mailed in. Unfortunately, this claim could not be verified. See "Speaking Notes," 10 May 1966, LRC 1991-041, 1.15, UVIC.

95 Walter Avis noted that the reason for moving up the publication date was two-fold. First, it would ensure that the dictionary would ride the wave of nationalist euphoria. Second, the project could be funded as an official Centennial project. See File: "Problems of Editing a Dictionary of Canadianisms on Historical Principles," 2-15, box 2, 3711.1, Walter Avis Collection, Queen's University Archives.

96 Dr. M.H. Scargill, Conference Speech at York University, 6 March 1967, LRC 1991-041, 1.15, UVIC.

97 Language was a product of history and, as such, set a people apart from the rest of humanity; see W.R. Wees, "Preface," in *Dictionary of Canadian English: A Dictionary of Canadianisms on Historical Principles,* v.

98 Fergus Cronin, "Do You Speak Canadian?" *Canadian Weekly,* 7 February-5 March 1965, 16-17.

99 *Dictionary of Canadian English: A Dictionary of Canadianisms on Historical Principles,* 1, 457.

100 Ibid., 682.

101 "12,000 Entries in New Dictionary," *Victoria Daily Colonist,* 22 March 1966.

102 "From Abatteau to Zombie: A Dictionary of Canadianisms," *Ottawa Journal,* 9 December 1967.

103 Joan Finnigan, "Only Canada has beer parlours," *The Canadian,* 28 January 1967, 7.

104 "Canadian Identity Discovered," *Canadian Business,* December 1967, 1.

105 Mavor Moore, "How We Talk Canadian," *Saturday Night,* November 1967.

106 David A. Bell, *The Cult of the Nation in France: Inventing Nationalism, 1680-1800* (Cambridge, MA: Harvard University Press, 2001), 3.

107 Cmiel, "'Broad and Fluid Language,'" 931.

108 Change to format used above: J.K. Chambers, interviewed by Steven High, Toronto, June 2003, audio cassettes in possession of the author. Language usage surveys proliferated during the 1970s and 1980s. The explosion of scholarly interest in the field could be seen in

two bibliographies of Canadian English. Walter Avis' 1965 bibliography of Canadian English contained only 168 items. Ten years later, another 455 entries were added. See McDavid, Jr., "Webster, Mencken and Avis," 125.

109   The word "chesterfield" originated in Victorian Britain for a particular brand of stuffed leather sofa and made its way to Canada, where it became a standard term for sofas of any kind. A survey by Walter Avis in 1950 found that 88.8 percent of Canadians used the term. This was no longer the case by the early 1990s, when J.K. Chambers surveyed 935 people in Ontario's Golden Horseshoe region and 80 Americans in the adjoining area of Niagara Falls-Buffalo, New York. Age was the determining factor. Whereas few informants over the age of fifty used "couch," over 80 percent of those under thirty did; see J.K. Chambers, "Social Embedding of Changes in Progress," *Journal of English Linguistics* 26, 1 (March 1998): 5-36 at 7-8. The same pattern of decline can be seen in a handful of other markers of Canadian linguistic identity. Examples cited by Chambers include several hallmarks of Canadian pronunciation such as "Canadian raising" (the difference in how we pronounce wife and wives) and "yod-dropping," which occurs when Canadians abandon the "u" sound in news for the American "nooz" (17-19).

110   Chambers, "'Canadian Dainty.'"

111   Chambers, "Three Kinds of Standard," 7-8.

112   J.K. Chambers, interviewed by Steven High, Toronto, June 2003, audio cassettes in possession of the author.

113   Katherine Barber, "Preface," *Canadian Oxford Dictionary* (Don Mills: Oxford University Press, 1998).

114   Scargill, "Growth of Canadian English," 7.

115   Charles Boberg, "Geolinguistic Diffusion and the U.S.-Canada Border," *Language Variation and Change* 12 (2000): 1-24 at 4.

5
From Liberalism to Nationalism: Peter C. Newman's Discovery of Canada

Robert Wright

In the foreword to his 1973 book *Home Country: People, Places, and Power Politics*, veteran journalist and author Peter C. Newman described his "love affair with Canada" as follows: "Perhaps my real ideological swing has been away from a blind acceptance of the 'small-l' liberalism of the Fifties to a strongly-felt nationalism. In retrospect, it seems to me that liberalism perhaps never really had that much hold on the Canadian consciousness; it was more an American ideal, enshrined within the U.S. constitution and unwittingly imported into Canada during the period when we were entranced with the American dream."[1] As a bestselling author, as a founding member of the Committee for an Independent Canada (CIC), and especially as editor of *Maclean's* magazine, Newman was at the centre of a seismic shift in English Canadians' sense of themselves and their nation in the Trudeau era. His was one of many prominent nationalist voices in Canada in these years, but unlike the Waffle and others on the Left who sought to graft nationalism root-and-branch onto socialism, Newman came directly out of the dominant liberal tradition in Canada and never lost his faith in what he called Canadians' "cautiously progressive, tenaciously pragmatic individualism."[2] Indeed, even as he was positioning himself as a leading "investment nationalist" in the 1970s and arguing for state regulation of foreign investment in Canada, he continued to write with unbridled enthusiasm about the achievements of the Canadian business elite in enormously popular books like *The Canadian Establishment* (1975).[3]

The purpose of this chapter is to revisit Peter C. Newman's claim about his transition from liberalism to nationalism in the 1960s not only in the light of his five-decade writing career but also in the context of the resurgence of continentalism as the predominant economic paradigm in post-Free Trade Agreement (FTA) North America and the concomitant rise of neo-liberalism as its ideological handmaiden. Although I have no doubt that Newman understood his own ideological evolution to have been a true metamorphosis, I want to argue that he overstated his "blind acceptance" of postwar liberalism and, hence, that his transition to a "strongly-felt na-tionalism" was neither as momentous nor as categorical as he suggested. What emerges from my reading of Newman is not a portrait of a man con-verted. Rather, I see him as a forceful, complex thinker given not only to bold declarations of conviction but also to careful study and revision, a man open to nuance, ambiguity, and contradiction. In my view, Newman never relinquished his deep, formative commitment to the fundamentals of the postwar liberal consensus in North America, including laissez-faire capitalism, anticommunism, and fiscal conservatism. Thus even at the height of his nationalist piety in the 1970s, he continued to work toward some kind of reconciliation of these two deeply ingrained ideological impulses, however uneasily.

To date, Newman has been of almost no interest to Canadian scholars, except perhaps as a competitor. Several general observations about his work as an author should therefore be ventured at the outset. The first is that Newman has been uncommonly prolific. By my count he had by 2005 writ-ten twenty-four books (excluding reprints bearing titles different from the original); his articles and columns, on subjects ranging from business and politics to sailing and jazz, number in the thousands. In 1999 Newman estimated that he had written two million words for *Maclean's* alone.[4] The second is that he has been extraordinarily successful. In 1995 Newman's lifetime book sales were estimated to be in the range of two million units, making him one of Canada's all-time bestselling nonfiction writers.[5] The conversion of his books into television fare has been, if anything, even more popular – the CBC's series on *The Canadian Establishment*, for example, was said to have drawn "a staggering 14 million Canadian viewers over three airings."[6] The third is that Newman has enjoyed unprecedented access to the rich and powerful in Canada, so much so that some observers have compared "a written profile by Newman" with a Karsh portrait: "it's thought by many subjects to be a testament to their importance."[7] The fourth is that he has, in the blunt words of the late Sandra Gwyn, "elevate[d] auto-plagiarism into a modus operandi"[8] by continually recycling his own prose – an indict-ment on which he appears never to have commented publicly. The fifth is that he has occasionally incurred the wrath of academics who accuse him of playing "fast and loose" with historical evidence, a charge to which he has replied: "I'm not writing history. I'm just a storyteller."[9]

Newman's critics have also suggested, some of them in no uncertain terms, that his record of publication has been uneven. There is some truth to this. Particularly with respect to his later works, *The Canadian Revolution* (1995) and *Defining Moments* (1997) most notably,[10] reviewers have accused Newman of patching together books from his vast archive of columns and articles, a technique that "prevent[s] him from saying anything coherent or even con-sistent about his stated subject."[11] It is probably fair to say that his best work came at mid-career, in the 1960s and 1970s, and that *Renegade in Power: The Diefenbaker Years* (1963) remains his finest book.[12] But it is also true that as a columnist – not only in those decades, when his name was a household word, but right up to the present – the combination of insight, poignancy, and passion with which Newman has contemplated all things Canadian has been unrivalled. Judged not only by longevity but by perspicacity, his contribution to the "national conversation" in Canada has had few equals, and it will almost certainly never be surpassed.

Brumal Blankness

Peter C. Newman (Peta Karel Neuman) was born in Vienna in 1929 and spent his boyhood in Czechoslovakia, where his father worked as "an industrialist and economic advisor to the government."[13] In 1940 his family fled Nazism, an experience Newman has cited as having been formative for himself as a Jew and also as a Canadian patriot. In 1999 he reflected: "Since my family and I landed here, escaping the Nazi terrors of wartime Europe in 1940, the credo that has animated my own life is that Canada happens to be the most fortunate country on Earth. Most Canadians don't subscribe to that notion, preferring to bellyache and curse their destiny. That's wrong. To be a citizen of this country – with all its faults and unrealized potential – imposes an obligation not to take its many freedoms and privileges for granted."[14] Newman's flight from Nazi-occupied Prague to Canada was without question traumatic. "There was nothing on God's earth worse than being a refugee," he reflected, "nothing. You are homeless and dispossessed, a target for anybody to shoot at, driftwood without roots or recourse."[15] Newman has described his family as having endured a dangerous passage through Europe to the port of Biarritz, France, where "wing-mounted [German] machine-guns us[ed] us for target practice."[16] From there they sailed to England and then directly on to Canada. How much in the way of liquid assets his parents managed to carry with them is not something that Newman has ever discussed publicly. That his father was able to enrol him as a boarder at prestigious Upper Canada College (UCC) in 1944 suggests, however, not only that his family retained a good deal of its former wealth but also that, by virtue of this wealth, their passage as Jewish refugees into wartime Canada was comparatively easy.[17]

Newman's critics have commonly asserted that his fascination with Canada's corporate elite began at UCC, but at least one observer has noted that his father had been grooming him since childhood for a career in business.[18] That he went on to the University of Toronto and obtained a master's degree "specializing in economics"[19] suggests that there was far more to his nascent interest in the North American economy than mere infatuation with its leading tycoons – as does the fact that he started his journalistic career at the no-nonsense *Financial Post* in the 1950s. Even so, as Newman himself has admitted, his first encounters with the scions of what he later called the Canadian "Establishment" were coloured by his own considerable sense of awe. Certainly, the enormous popularity of his books owed more than a little to his gossipy, lifestyles-of-the-rich-and-famous treatment of their lives. ("One of [Bud] McDougald's more relaxing hobbies," Newman would write in *The Canadian Establishment*, "is showing visitors his collection of classic automobiles. The temperature-controlled garages of Green Meadows house thirty cars.")[20] As late as 1971, at the height of his conversion to nationalism, Newman was by his own admission so "excited about the possibility of doing an article on E.P. Taylor" that he struck the following bargain: "If he would agree to see me, to discuss both his present preoccupations and his views as to what has been happening in Canada, I can guarantee that we would publish a most favorable story."[21]

The person who almost single-handedly inspired the nationalist movement in postwar Canada was Walter Gordon, a man whose influence on Newman's thinking was both formative and of long duration. Born in 1906 and educated at Upper Canada College and Royal Military College (RMC), Gordon was, by pedigree if not by temperament, an unlikely iconoclast. In 1935 he became a partner in the accounting firm of Clarkson Gordon, and during the Second World War he served in the federal Ministry of Finance, even chairing a little-known 1946 royal commission on the reorganization of the public service. In the mid-1950s Gordon chaired the Royal Commission on Canada's Economic Prospects, which launched his three-decade-long public obsession with what he called "the sell-out of [Canadian] resources and business enterprises to Americans and other enterprising foreigners."[22] In 1963 he became Lester Pearson's minister of finance, tabling a budget that included a tax on foreign takeovers of Canadian firms. After enduring the concerted wrath of the business community and a personal dressing-down by Montreal Stock Exchange president Eric Kierans, Gordon withdrew the contentious tax provision, causing himself and the government, as he later put it, "great damage."[23] He resigned from the Cabinet in 1965, only to return as president of the Privy Council in 1967 in order to launch yet another task force on "the foreign investment issue," headed by economist Mel Watkins.[24] Gordon left politics for good in 1968, co-founding the nonpartisan CIC two years later.

In the 1960s Newman described Walter Gordon as a man who looked "overprivileged, the very model of an upper-middle-class WASP in pin-striped suit and regimental tie," a characterization with which his later biographers have mostly concurred.[25] Aloof, sober, devoid of the kind of media-friendly charisma that might have turned his obsession with foreign investment into a public crusade, Gordon's was indeed a voice that seemed doomed to cry in the wilderness. Newman appears instinctively to have understood that Gordon was a victim of his own staid public persona, perhaps because he was himself hamstrung by a similar combination of intellectual passion and public reticence. Long-time acquaintances have said of Newman that he has always been "both painfully shy and terribly intense," a man who "rarely managed to be anything but awkward and uncomfortable in the presence of other people."[26] There appears to have been more than a little autobiography, then, in Newman's colourful description of Gordon:

> He never did conquer the Canadian people, in part because the kind of man he really was tended always to be obscured by the kind of man he seemed to be ... He liked good food, fine wines, paintings, antiques, travel, and the company of his peers. He could be warm and amusing with close friends, but remained an intensely private person who abhorred the little arts of popularity that are the touchstones of politics in western democracies. His language was that of his class – cool, reasonable, passionless. He could never transform himself from an ideologue into a revolutionary and in the conduct of his nationalistic crusades he remained a sort of Garibaldi without a horse. Even his books, with their revolutionary implications for Canadian society, read like dry texts on bee-keeping.[27]

Like Walter Gordon, Peter C. Newman would be the gentlest of patriots.

However much Newman's public persona might have had in common with Gordon's, it could never be said that his prose was dry. Indeed, in the late 1950s, when the nationalist strains in Newman's thought were germinating, his florid prose style owed more to the likes of Ayn Rand than to any Canadian accountant. Rand, whose bestselling novel *Atlas Shrugged* took the North American literary world by storm in 1957, openly celebrated the virtues of self-interest, rugged individualism, and laissez-faire capitalism. And she did so in an epic prose style perfectly suited to the hyper-patriotism of the early Cold War era. Newman's first book, *Flame of Power* (1959), venerated in similar language the handful of venture capitalists whose courage, vision, and determination had "made [Canada] the sixth-largest industrial and fourth-greatest trading nation on earth." Theirs, wrote Newman, was a "remarkable achievement": "The businessmen in this book transformed Canada from a community of traders and land tillers into one of the world's economically most animated nations. They changed the history and the face of their country. They raised private armies and overthrew ministries. They stabbed the hump of mine headframes against the brumal blankness of the north. They erected the angular silhouette of factories across the urban twilight."[28]

The ideological effect of Newman's spirited celebration of Canada's entrepreneurial pioneers in *Flame of Power* was to subordinate nationalism thoroughly and unabashedly to liberalism. He wrote enthusiastically of "national destiny" but only in the context of a capitalist ethos that demanded the "subjugation" of Canada's vast untapped resources and promised "immense personal rewards" to "those who master the organizational, financial, and technical skills" of the new industrial era. "Before the stirrings of their ambition turned the thoughts of this book's entrepreneurs westward, the Prairies were generally regarded as uninhabitable wilderness," wrote Newman. "The inheritors of financial grandeur in Canada will be the men who first realize, on a sufficiently magnificent scale, that our north can shed a similar stigma, in a taming like that already achieved by Russia." He addressed the question of foreign investment that the *Gordon Report* had flagged just two years earlier, but he did so only tangentially and in such a manner as to temper mounting fears in Canada that American investment signalled a calculated erosion of national sovereignty:

> Accompanying our postwar population growth and the resultant burgeoning of business opportunities has come an unprecedented influx of American and other capital, which has given Canada more foreign investment within its borders than any other country in the world ... The Americans have not come here in the tradition of the sixteenth-century conquistadors. In the process of their profit-ferreting, they have underwritten the development risks, reducing from generations to years the time required for Canadians to attain their current standard of living. But if this country hopes to retain long-term control of its economic destiny, Canadian businessmen must recapture at least part of these industrial and mineral assets, reverting the profits they yield to domestic command.[29]

Here in *Flame of Power* were the first inklings of the ambivalence with which Newman would view US investment in Canada over the next three decades. As a 1950s-era liberal, he maintained that American investment had been critically important to the success of the Canadian economy, but as a budding 1960s-era nationalist, he had to concede that this success had come at the expense of Canadian economic sovereignty.

Renegade in Power
So wedded had Newman become to the heroic narrative style of *Flame of Power* that he adopted it for use in his political writing – a dubious choice of genre given that the subjects close at hand were not devil-may-care mavericks but the "indecisive" John Diefenbaker and the "bland, uninspiring" Lester B. Pearson.[30] Like Pierre Berton and so many other popular chroniclers of Canadian history, Newman seemed incapable of resisting the archetype of Canada as a vast northern wilderness to be tamed under entrepreneurial, technological, and political domination. While this schema may have allowed him to lionize the myriad "adventurers" who made his books exciting and accessible, and indeed to make Canada itself seem heroic, it also

accounts for his occasionally patronizing attitude toward ordinary Canadians – "the overwhelming majority of the nation's citizens who never venture farther north than their summer cottages."[31]

These tensions were apparent in Newman's second book, *Renegade in Power: The Diefenbaker Years* (1963), the work that cemented his status as the country's leading political commentator and one of its bestselling authors. *Renegade* has been called "groundbreaking," and to the extent that it "helped to change the way both journalists and ordinary Canadians thought about national leaders," this praise is warranted.[32] But there were striking ambiguities in the book, nowhere more so than in Newman's attempt to reconcile his personal affinity for Diefenbaker's nationalist "Vision" with his decidedly liberal critique of the prime minister's policies. Decades later Newman would acknowledge that "many of the failings I ascribed to Diefenbaker should, more fairly, be blamed on the dreadfully difficult situation in which he found himself."[33] Written as it was in the white heat of the moment, however, with Newman literally documenting the day-to-day trajectory of Diefenbaker's political rise and fall between 1957 and 1963, *Renegade in Power* never managed to reconcile the competing claims of inspiration and disillusionment in his estimation of the prime minister. Diefenbaker thus appeared in the book as a delusional figure, a man of great vision hobbled by his own sloganeering, part political opportunist and part false prophet.

There is no question that Newman had, like many Canadians, been inspired by Diefenbaker's nationalist oratory as it took shape in 1957 and 1958. Adopting the epic tone of *Flame of Power,* and even recycling some of its most memorable turns of phrase, *Renegade in Power* captured Diefenbaker's magnetic appeal: "Throughout his 1958 campaign, the Conservative leader expanded and emphasized his Vision. The voters were caught up in the imagined pageant of Diefenbaker's new 'Canada of the NORTH.' To stab the hump of mine headframes against the brumal blankness of the Arctic twilight; to erect lavish plastic bubble settlements in a hinterland that had previously abided silent and inaccessible; to tame the wilderness that had always whispered to the nation's adventurers – these things seemed a noble and compelling mission to mid-twentieth-century Canadians."[34] Here, in this earnest, unselfconscious fusion of Diefenbaker's campaign rhetoric with his own romantic idea of the Canadian North, Newman's affinity for the prime minister's nationalist vision was unmistakable. His disappointment was all the more bitter, then, when apart from the occasional symbolic gesture, the prime minister seemed incapable of doing anything "to further the cause of Canadian nationalism" while in power.[35] Asked in 1963 why *Renegade* was such an angry book, Newman replied: "Because [Diefenbaker] did such irreparable harm to our economic culture and social future, as Canadians. Because there isn't a country in the world he didn't insult one way or another. Because somebody has to explain what happened to turn such great expectations into failure."[36]

When *Renegade in Power* was published, Newman's idea of Canada's "economic culture," if not its "social future," remained decidedly liberal; thus it was Diefenbaker's betrayal of liberalism to which he took the greatest exception. On his economic policies, for example, Newman wrote approvingly of the prime minister's commitment to a "more egalitarian society" but fell in squarely behind those who said that he had violated the laissez-faire ethos of Canadian business: "It became obvious very early in the Diefenbaker years that his was a Conservative government in name only. Instead of moving to promote and strengthen the country's financial community, Diefenbaker rushed in the opposite direction – harassing, curbing, and discouraging free enterprise at every turn. In the privacy of their clubs, dismayed executives clucked their disapproval of Diefenbaker and all his works as a fundamentally disruptive force. The right-wing *Fort Erie Letter Review* condemned Diefenbaker's concept of social justice for being 'as revolutionary as Marxism, but perhaps a better name for it would be Robin Hoodism.'"[37] As deeply rooted in postwar North American liberalism was Newman's critique of Tory foreign policy, whose authorship he attributed as much to Howard Green, Diefenbaker's minister of external affairs, as to the prime minister himself. Green's "Kiwanian approach to world problems," wrote Newman sardonically, was the direct result of his naive belief in Canada's "moral superiority" – a view that "exasperated the cynical professionals at the United States State Department." The government's refusal to fall in behind President Kennedy during the Cuban Missile Crisis in October 1962 came in for particularly harsh treatment in *Renegade*. "Severe obstacles were placed in the way of the United States in its attempts to provide effective North American air defence," wrote Newman of Diefenbaker's refusal to allow the US to deploy nuclear-armed planes and missiles in Canada. Such posturing, he concluded, "demonstrated to the Canadian public that the Diefenbaker government's indecision had isolated their country among the Western family of nations in failing to offer immediate moral support for the anti-communist stand of the American President."[38]

In its tacit defence of "free enterprise," anticommunism, and continental defence imperatives, *Renegade in Power* revealed Newman's continuing commitment to the postwar liberal consensus in North America. The book's unprecedented popularity – it sold 30,000 copies in its first ten weeks in print[39] – suggests that it had captured the zeitgeist of the Diefenbaker era, but it was not without its critics. Tory strategist Dalton Camp, for example, a man who would become famous for his role in deposing Diefenbaker, noted that the book had brought "a generous supply of tar and feathers" to its subject.[40] Without question, however, the most perceptive critic of *Renegade*'s liberal bias was George Grant, philosopher, religious studies professor, and author of the seminal *Lament for a Nation: The Defeat of Canadian National-ism* (1965).[41] Indeed, if *Renegade in Power* may be said to have had any en-during impact on the national conversation in Canada, it was as *agent provocateur* for Grant and the many 1960s-era left-nationalists who came to accept his contention that Canadian nationalism and liberalism were fundamentally incompatible.

Much might be said about the relationship of *Renegade in Power* to *Lament for a Nation*, but for the purposes of this chapter, two broad observations will suffice. The first is the inescapable inference that Grant must have writ-ten the first three of *Lament*'s seven chapters with a copy of *Renegade* at his side.[42] Along with veteran *Maclean's* writer Blair Fraser, "Peter Newman" was the only person named explicitly in *Lament* as a "journalist of the establish-ment" – that is, as one who disparaged Diefenbaker's attempts to assert Canadian autonomy and "rejoice[d] that we have back in office the party of the ruling class," the Liberals.[43] Indeed, Grant's wholesale indictment of the manner in which Canadian journalists eviscerated the prime minister ap-pears to have derived almost entirely from his reading of Newman:

> The "news" now functions to legitimize power, not to convey information. The politics of personalities helps the legitimizers to divert attention from issues that might upset the *status quo*. Huntley and Brinkley are basic to the American way of life. Canadian journalists worked this way in the election of 1963. Their purposes were better served by writing of Diefenbaker's "in-decision," of Diefenbaker's "arrogance," of Diefenbaker's "ambition," than by writing about American-Canadian relations. Indeed, his personality was good copy ... But behind all the stories of arrogance and indecision, there are conflicts – conflicts over principles. The man had a conception of Can-ada that threatened the dominant classes.[44]

The second observation is that, although Grant stressed the British char-acter of English Canadian nationalism in *Lament for a Nation*, he believed that the only practical means of challenging continental liberalism was to push nationalism decidedly to the left. Echoing Walter Gordon, although taking a decidedly more radical approach to the repatriation of the Canad-ian economy, Grant wrote:

> [Diefenbaker] did not accomplish the work of economic nationalism. The "northern vision" was a pleasant extra, but no substitute for national sur-vival. During his years in office, American control grew at a quickening rate. This was the crucial issue in 1957. If Canada was to survive, the corner-stone of its existence was the Great Lakes region. The population in that area was rushing toward cultural and economic integration with the United States. Any hope for a Canadian nation demanded some reversal of the

process, and this could only be achieved through concentrated use of Ottawa's planning and control. After 1940, nationalism had to go hand in hand with some measure of socialism. Only nationalism could provide the political incentive for planning; only planning could restrain the victory of continentalism.[45]

Grant's assertion of a left-nationalist ideal for Canadian economic development would emerge in the late 1960s as a *sine qua non* in a broad debate within the ranks of English Canadian nationalists. On the democratic left, and especially within the Waffle wing of the NDP, *Lament for a Nation* would become something of a sacred text, James Laxer calling it "the most important book I ever read in my life."[46] For other leading nationalists, however, including Walter Gordon and Peter C. Newman, it was precisely *Lament*'s challenge to liberalism that would place it beyond the pale.

Remarkably, there is nothing in the public record to suggest that Newman ever read *Lament for a Nation* or acknowledged Grant's accusation that he served as a spokesperson for the Canadian "ruling class."[47] There is no question, however, that his evolution as a nationalist in the mid-1960s took shape alongside Canadians' changing sense of themselves and their country in these years, a movement that George Grant did a great deal to inspire. Like other leading members of the English Canadian intelligentsia, Newman embraced the "new Nationalism" in these years, becoming one of the "new voices call[ing] for increased sovereignty in economics and culture while popularizing Canadian cultural products and an awareness of Canadiana."[48] By 1968, when his third book, *The Distemper of Our Times,* was published, Newman had evolved from a lukewarm supporter of Walter Gordon to one of his greatest public defenders, emerging as a leading force for economic repatriation in his own right; he had abandoned his unquestioning acceptance of continental defence priorities, a trend that would come to full bloom in the early 1970s, when he became one of Canada's most outspoken critics of the Vietnam War; he had hardened his opposition to continental free trade; and he had become a supporter not only of state subsidies in the realm of culture but also of state regulation of commercial mass media. Most dramatically of all, he had reconceptualized his idea of liberalism itself, questioning what he called "the old Ottawa Establishment credo that governments should limit their function to economic justice and that the duty of the responsible man in public life was to exercise a restraining influence on political risk-taking."[49]

Integrating Ourselves into the US Industrial Machine

The forum in which Newman evinced this intellectual transition in the years between *Renegade in Power* and *The Distemper of Our Times* was his weekly column in the *Toronto Star*. He became the *Star*'s Ottawa editor in

July 1964, at the height of his fame as author of *Renegade*, having served in the same capacity at *Maclean's* since 1957. The decision to join the *Star* was itself a measure of his shifting sensibilities, given that it was then under the stewardship of editor-in-chief (and later publisher) Beland Honderich, a leading Canadian nationalist in his own right. The tone and substance of Newman's published work in these years was still that of a perspicacious Ottawa insider, one who enjoyed privileged (probably unequalled) access to politicians and civil servants as well as a reputation for discretion. He had not yet assumed the role of nationalist spokesperson, a shift that would be cemented only after his move in 1971 back to *Maclean's*. Yet by the time he left the *Star*, what he later described as his "ideological swing" from "the 'small-l' liberalism of the Fifties to a strongly-felt nationalism" was complete. Nothing in the decades that followed – not even the free trade debate of the late 1980s or the globalization debate of the 1990s – would alter his position substantively.

Newman's continuing struggle to balance the claims of liberalism and nationalism was most evident in his ambivalence about the changing international trade environment in which Canada found itself in the 1960s. This was the true era of globalization. The liberalization of international trade and especially the transnationalization of capital were together testing the ability of nation-states to manage their economies, inexorably accelerating the integration of small countries like Canada into larger regional trading blocs. One of the most significant watersheds in this broader trend was the signing of the Canada-US Automotive Products Agreement in 1965. The Auto Pact, as it became known, took the form of a bilateral trade agreement covering passenger cars, trucks, buses, and automotive parts. Under its terms, North American automakers agreed to maintain a fixed production-to-sales ratio in Canada as well as a fixed proportion of value-added "Canadian content." The advantage to Canada of a continentally integrated auto industry, it was argued, would be more efficient production, guaranteed access to well-paying jobs in the auto sector, and lower car prices for consumers; the cost would be the cementing of Canada's status as a subsidiary of the US auto industry, complete with the permanent loss of corporate control and a diminished role in research and development.

The Auto Pact in its final form was an example not of free trade, as many of its later detractors and defenders would claim, but of regulated trade. Peter C. Newman was one observer who understood this crucial distinction. He knew the central importance of the auto industry to the Canadian economy and to the prosperity of thousands of ordinary Canadians; indeed, he found much to praise in the prospect of expanded trade and guaranteed access to the lucrative US market, a point that he made regularly in the *Star*. Yet in the autumn of 1964, when Canadian and American trade officials were known to be negotiating a new deal in the auto sector – "desperately" and behind closed doors – it was rumoured that even the top ministers in the Pearson government were indicating a willingness to abandon Canada's historic protectionism if this was the price of guaranteed access to the US auto market. Newman recognized the historical import of this possibility. Writing in October 1964, he reminded Canadians that the tariff had been the historic guarantor of Canadian autonomy: "The free-trade scheme in automobiles and their parts would channel this important commerce into a north-south direction, and when applied to other trade items, could destroy the east-west backbone of Canada's economy, first fostered by the building of the CPR and Sir John A. Macdonald's National Policy. The new plan's continental approach jettisons the traditional argument that tariffs are the price Canadians must pay for their independence." Newman's inside sources were telling him at this time that "executives of Canadian automobile concerns" were being called to Ottawa for "secret briefings." This fact alone, he argued, cast doubt on whether the Canadian negotiators had a clear sense of the national interest. "The men who speak for the car firms are not really manufacturers representing Canadian interests, but merely the Canadian chiefs of American corporations," he wrote. "Even if they wanted to, they couldn't agree to any scheme which would hurt or even embarrass their parent firms." Newman signed off with an ominous warning: "The outcome of the current automobile talks will do more than set the pattern of our future trade relations with the U.S. It will test the government's determination to guard the remainder of our vanishing economic sovereignty."[50]

How committed Newman himself was to "the traditional argument that tariffs are the price Canadians must pay for their independence" is not clear. Although he deployed the historic language of the National Policy to sensational effect when it came to the Auto Pact, elsewhere Newman argued that freer trade in general – and the reduction of tariffs in particular – would be good for Canada. What can be said for certain is that his litmus test for federal economic policy was increasingly that of the investment nationalist: the question was not one of tariff policy per se but of whether this or that measure fostered Canadian economic and especially political sovereignty. On the Auto Pact, the case was clear: it was bad for Canada because it irrevocably subordinated Canadian manufacturers to their American overseers. On other clear-cut cases of what he called US "interference" in Canadian economic life, Newman was equally firm. He emerged as one of Canada's harshest critics of the American Trading with the Enemy Act in the 1960s, for example, and he regularly criticized US officials who attempted to curtail Canadian trade with Cuba and China by invoking extraterritoriality clauses in US trade statutes.[51] Most strikingly of all, whether the federal minister of finance was worth his salt now boiled down to the question of whether he had the fortitude to stand up to Washington. Commenting in

January 1965 on Mitchell Sharp's first major policy address as minister of finance, Newman wrote bluntly that the new minister seemed weak-willed: "The Sharp speech, significant as it was, failed to answer one question: Does he intend to carry on or drop complete [sic] the economic nationalism of his predecessor? The issue is dismissed with one perfunctory phrase: 'Canadians should finance more of Canada's economic development themselves.' This sounds suspiciously like the kind of limp lip-service that finance ministers who preceded [Walter] Gordon paid to the idea of Canadian economic nationalism, without ever actually intending to follow it up with policies."[52] Newman was thrilled when, one year later, Sharp "exploded" at Securities and Exchange Commission (SEC) chairman Manuel Cohen for nonchalantly remarking that US investment law should apply equally to Canadians and Americans.[53]

Yet when it came to Canada's trade relations generally, Newman remained ever the laissez-faire liberal, embracing freer trade, increased international competition, and lower tariffs. To cite but one important example, in May 1967 Newman devoted several *Star* columns to the "Kennedy round" of negotiations of the General Agreement on Tariffs and Trade (GATT) then taking place in Geneva. He wrote with enthusiasm about the fact that, although the talks mainly concerned Europe and the United States, they might have "momentous implications for Canada, dislocating our traditional industrial patterns, changing the character and quantity of both our imports and exports, and possibly launching us into a period of intensive manufacturing expansion which could become the basis for another economic boom." Newman's sources were reporting from the "secret talks" that tariff reductions in the range of 25 to 35 percent seemed likely. "Even this limited success could have a large impact on Canadian manufacturers and producers of raw and semi-processed materials," he wrote. "It would gain for them much freer entry not only to the rich market of the United States but as an added bonanza, easier access to the 250 million affluent consumers of the European Common Market Countries." Newman acknowledged that some sectors of the Canadian economy would be adversely affected by tariff reductions on this scale, and he insisted that "the most severely hit areas" should be targeted for federal "transitional assistance programs."[54] Otherwise, he approved of the proposed reductions unequivocally.

The most telling aspect of Newman's assessment of the 1967 GATT talks was his sense of the advantage that they might provide Canada in asserting economic autonomy vis-à-vis the United States. Indeed, this was one instance in which the competing claims of liberalism and nationalism appear to have catalyzed a new intensity in his own ideological soul-searching. The Kennedy round, Newman told his *Star* readers, represented "a constructive solution to the trading dilemma" into which Canada had been drifting for a decade. This was because "our economy has tended to become increasingly isolated in a world rearranging itself into powerful trading groups such as the European Common Market. Instead of being able to enjoy the advantages of large-scale production and mass distribution which come with membership in such blocs, most Canadian manufacturers have been hemmed into the small domestic consumer market of 20 million people spread over an immense geography." In stark contrast with his assessment of the *bilateral* Auto Pact, which threatened to sunder the historic linkage of Canadian economic protectionism and national sovereignty, here in the context of liberalizing *global* trade the tariff merely "hemmed" Canadians in. Clearly, Newman was now gravitating toward the view that trade liberalization was desirable for Canada only insofar as it strengthened the country's ability to resist economic domination by the United States. The ideological effect of this shift was to subordinate liberalism to nationalism:

> It is only the Kennedy round – with its multilateral lowering of tariffs – which can provide us with an acceptable compromise between the extremes of becoming a closed, inward-looking economy or having to form a trading block of our own with the United States. Most politicians and economists who have studied these alternatives view them both with alarm. With our standard of living already about twenty-five per cent below that of the United States, any move to isolate our economy (and thus inevitably depress the standard of living) would almost certainly prompt a mass exodus of Canadians to better-paying jobs south of the border. The formation of a free trade area with the United States might have equally drastic, though quite different, effects.

Newman concluded his reflections on the GATT with his now-standard warning: "By integrating ourselves into the U.S. industrial machine in what would, by definition, be an unequal partnership, we would also be hazarding our freedom of political action."[55]

The Distemper of Our Times

By 1967, fully a decade after the *Gordon Report* had been tabled, the debate about foreign investment in Canada had moved from the margins of the national conversation to centre stage. Walter Gordon's was no longer the only voice trumpeting the cause of economic sovereignty, nor were his ideas necessarily any longer in ascendance. As historian Stephen Azzi has shown, Gordon's insistence on the preservation of the tariff was being challenged throughout the ranks of investment nationalists, presaging his increasingly "extreme" views on foreign ownership in the 1970s.[56] For Newman, Gordon remained a touchstone for his own deepening nationalist convictions and would continue to serve as one of his most valuable allies in the era of the CIC. But it was Eric Kierans, a relatively new convert to the nationalist cause

– the same Eric Kierans who had so publicly chastised Walter Gordon over his 1963 budget – who provided Newman with an ideological roadmap that was compatible with his deeply liberal leanings.

Kierans had the kind of intellectual, business, and political pedigree to which Newman has always been attracted. He had been director of the McGill School of Commerce and president of the Montreal Stock Exchange. In the mid-1960s, when he made his greatest impression on Newman, he was serving in Jean Lesage's "Quiet Revolution" Cabinet as minister of revenue (1963-65) and health (1965-66). (Between 1968 and 1971 he would serve as a minister in the Trudeau government, after having tried unsuccessfully for the leadership of the federal Liberal Party.) On the evening of 3 January 1966, as he himself later put it, Kierans "stayed up all night ... to figure out how I could start a national debate" on Canada's new bilateral balance-of-payments agreement with the United States. Having studied the minutiae of the new investment guidelines, he concluded that they represented "the greatest threat to Canadian independence since the War of 1812" because they allowed Washington to limit the terms and extent of US investment abroad. To the consternation of a number of Canadian officials, Kierans then proceeded to write scathing letters of protest directly to US secretary of commerce John Conner and secretary of the treasury Henry Fowler, later telling journalists: "This [agreement] poses serious problems for Canada. We are no longer dealing with the disparate and independent decisions of thousands of businessmen, but with hard government policy."[57]

Newman knew that he had found his nationalist muse in Eric Kierans but not because the minister had pilloried US officials with such abandon. Indeed, Newman seemed taken aback by his incorrigibility. "The Kierans' [sic] initiative may have been crude," Newman wrote. "It certainly was undiplomatic, and it's doubtful if it will have much lasting effect." What did strike Newman forcefully was that Kierans appeared to have found a way around the dilemma that Walter Gordon had posed for investment nationalists like himself. In a passage that speaks volumes about his own ideological evolution, Newman wrote: "It's important to distinguish the Kierans' [sic] approach from Walter Gordon's past attempts to force American firms to yield Canadians minority equity interests. Gordon was concerned with Canadian ownership; Kierans is concerned with Canadian sovereignty. He doesn't care how much of Canada the Americans own, as long as they don't try to run it."[58] The clarity with which Kierans had staked out his position as a liberal-nationalist struck Newman as something of an epiphany. Although Newman would never go so far as to say that it did not matter how much of the Canadian economy Americans owned, the minister's position appeared to demonstrate that one could defend laissez-faire principles and be no less a patriot. "Kierans comes out squarely against socialism," Newman wrote sympathetically, because as the minister himself put it, "socialism is the last hope of societies that do not respond to change or are not concerned with the welfare of their citizens."[59] In Newman's estimation, moreover, Kierans was "one of those rare Canadian politicians who is a convincing and convinced nationalist without being anti-American."[60] After January 1966 Newman seldom missed an opportunity to promote Kierans' views.

In the 1970s Newman would often be asked, as one open-line radio caller put it, "Well, tell us, Mr. Smart-Apple Newman, why are you so anti-American? Eh?"[61] He always replied that his "love" for Canada did not imply anti-Americanism. Yet, as he himself intimated in the foreword to *Home Country*, and as George Grant's *Lament for a Nation* had demonstrated even more forcefully, in Canada virtually any critique of liberalism could be read in some measure as a critique of the United States. The postwar liberal consensus to which most Canadians and Americans had subscribed, Newman foremost among them, assumed a convergence of national economic and strategic interests that was simply taken for granted. This was the ideological import of Canadians' preference for John F. Kennedy over John Diefenbaker in the wake of the Cuban Missile Crisis. By the tumultuous late 1960s, however, when the New Left, the youth counterculture, feminism, the civil rights movement, the "ecology" movement, and especially the antiwar movement had shattered the liberal consensus even within the United States, little remained of its continental counterpart. For Newman and for the growing ranks of Canadian nationalists in the Centennial era, too intimate an economic integration of Canada with the United States inferred a loss of political autonomy; and given the contentious direction in which American policy seemed to be headed, especially US foreign and defence policy, the need to preserve Canada's political independence never seemed more urgent.[62]

Newman's protestations against his presumed anti-Americanism notwithstanding, by the mid-1960s his weekly *Star* column had begun the metamorphosis from straight reportage to openly nationalist advocacy that would reach its apotheosis at *Maclean's*. To cite but one important – and prescient – example, in the spring of 1967 he wrote a lengthy, three-part analysis of the stakes for Canada should it decide to renew the North American Aerospace Defense Command (NORAD) agreement, inaugurated a decade earlier. Newman's editorial position on the changing nature of continental defence in the era of the intercontinental ballistic missile (ICBM) was set out clearly and in uncharacteristically strong language: "If negotiations now under way commit this country to another 10 year term as a partner in the North American Defence Command, we could become involuntary participants in the costliest and kookiest armaments race in history. Should the Americans and Russians decide to proceed with their anti-ballistic missile installations, our NORAD partnership would involve Canada in the outlandish business of trying to stop enemy missiles hurtling down from outer space."[63]

Newman objected in particular to the "anti-ballistic missile network" that had been proposed as part of NORAD since any conceivable scenario for its use would mean that "much of World War III would be fought in the upper atmosphere over Canada, and we would get most of the fallout." Citing US Defence Department statistics on the "obvious" superiority of US nuclear forces over those of the Soviets, he noted sardonically that "efforts by American scientists to find some counter-weapon to the Soviet missiles have reached Buck Rogers proportions."[64] In the final installment of the series, Newman turned to the underlying politics of the defence partnership. He acknowledged not only that pulling Canada out of NORAD was virtually impossible but also that "specifically opting out of any future anti-ballistic missile network" – presumably the policy that he would himself have preferred – had been dismissed by the Canadian military as impractical. Such intractability, he surmised, was a function not merely of Cold War strategy but also of economic self-preservation. The American military had spent $5 billion in Canada since the Second World War, and they continued to spend in the range of $300 million annually. This gave the Americans "great leverage" over Canada, Newman conceded. "The Pentagon had broadly hinted that it would abandon the special concessions we now enjoy under the defence sharing agreement, unless we remain loyal members of NORAD."[65]

The most suggestive element in Newman's *Star* series on continental defence policy, however, was the headline of the second installment: "Suddenly McNamara's a Dove." Just in case his readers missed the allusion, he spelled it out: "It's a paradox of the growing debate over anti-ballistic missiles that the chief American 'dove' is none other than Robert McNamara, the US secretary of defence whom Canadians have come to regard as one of the great 'hawks' of the Viet Nam [sic] war."[66] By 1967 Vietnam had become the catalyst for virtually all Canadian nationalists' disaffection with the United States. Newman would later observe, quite correctly, that "it was the Vietnamization of the United States that finally brought about the Canadianization of Canada. It jolted us out of our bemusement with the external aspects of the American Dream."[67]

Many Canadian observers, especially in the universities, expressed their revulsion for the Vietnam War in no uncertain terms; but within the ranks of the Liberal Cabinet, where caution had been the watchword since Lester Pearson's controversial Temple University speech in 1965, only Walter Gordon had the temerity to speak out openly against American aggression. Speaking in May 1967 at a women's conference, Gordon delivered one of the most controversial speeches of his career. The Vietnam War, he said, "cannot be justified on either moral or strategic grounds." Further, "it might not be any worse for the Vietnamese to be allowed to fight things out among themselves than it is to be bombed, burned and exterminated by a foreign power." Gordon concluded the speech by noting that the conflict held "grave dangers" for Canada, especially if it should escalate into a war between the superpowers. He explicitly urged "Mr. Pearson and Mr. [Paul] Martin ... to do everything in their power to press the Americans to stop the bombing."[68]

Newman described Gordon's speech several days later in almost breathless superlatives. "There's never been a Canadian politician like him," he wrote. "Gordon is one of those rare men who can genuinely claim to be a pivotal figure in the contemporary history of his country." Newman observed that the minister's remarks had come at a particularly sensitive time because "Canada's vaunted status as an impartial mediator" had just been undermined by revelations that Canadian personnel on the International Control Commission (ICC) had been acting as "observers to the Americans." This theme – that Canada's role in Vietnam was to serve as "an American messenger boy" – was one to which Newman would return repeatedly as his revulsion for the conflict increased.[69] For having the courage to defy his Cabinet colleagues and openly state his deepest convictions, Newman offered Gordon the highest of praise: "These are exciting times and it is rebels like Walter Gordon who are the vehicles of change." Thereafter, Newman adopted intact Gordon's critique of Canada's policy on Vietnam, parlaying it into a full-scale indictment of the Canadian tradition of "quiet" diplomacy. "We have been trying to balance a sort of Dale Carnegie approach to world problems with explicit acknowledgment of the fact that we're tied to Washington even in the most minute details of our every initiative," he wrote in late May 1967. "It is high time that we defined our national interest and expressed it in our dealings with other countries."[70] By March 1972 Newman would be advocating nothing less than a wholesale purge of the diplomatic corps in Canada: "Let's superannuate all those External [Affairs] buddies and start recruiting some diplomatic jocks of our own to deal with the Americans."[71]

In 1968 Newman's third book, *The Distemper of Our Times,* was published, in some ways marking the terminus of the intellectual journey that he had begun a decade earlier. *Distemper* borrowed heavily from his work as a *Star* columnist in the five years since *Renegade in Power* had come out. Apropos of its title, it evinced the increasing disquiet that had characterized both Canada and Newman himself in the Centennial era. He claimed in the preface that unlike the period 1957 to 1963, when Canadian politics was "the story of what happened to one gigantic figure, John Diefenbaker," the Pearson years were "dominated by a tumble of events."[72] But this shift in emphasis, from personalities to issues, had less to do with the contours of federal politics than with Newman's evolution as a writer and thinker. Indeed, his characterization in *Distemper* of the ideological struggles confronting Pearson, his Cabinet, and the country at large was transparently autobiographical. The prime minister had "epitomized the quantitative small-l liberalism that dominated the thinking of his Ottawa contemporaries," Newman wrote, but was incapable of making the transition to the "qualitative liberalism that would emerge as an important force during the mid Sixties." As for Canada, it too had foundered: "Lacking the unity of purpose that allows a people to think together on fundamental issues, Canadians became citizens of a country that seemed no longer to believe in itself." Not surprisingly, Walter Gordon emerged as the tragic hero of *Distemper,* a nationalist visionary who had nonetheless also failed to "reconcile the two main strains of Canadian Liberalism: the party's concern over social reform and its barely suppressed desire for economic integration with the United States." Despite his best efforts to reduce foreign investment, Gordon had failed to prevail over Pearson's "firm anti-nationalist" convictions, and he had never been able to persuade "the cabinet's right-wing ministers" that he was anything other than a "tab-collar Castro."[73]

Yet for all of its lamentation, *The Distemper of Our Times* ended on a high note, one that illuminated the ideological denouement at which Newman himself had finally arrived. Walter Gordon may have failed in his patriotic quest, but Canada had not: "The nationalistic fervour that Walter Gordon had never personally been able to stir in Canadians erupted of its own accord during celebrations marking the 1967 centennial year. It was a brief shimmering season in the long wash of history, a mass rite that managed to expose the latent patriotism in even the most cynical Canadians, leaving them a little embarrassed at their sentiment, a little surprised by their tears. It was a wild, happy, crazy year." Like the many visitors who had trekked to Montreal for Expo 67, Peter C. Newman had come to believe "that if this little sub-arctic, self-obsessed country could put on this marvelous show, it could do anything."[74]

Conclusion

Arguably, by 1968 – and certainly no later than 1970 – the intellectual journey that had informed Peter C. Newman's self-proclaimed metamorphosis from a 1950s-era liberal into a 1960s-era nationalist was more or less complete. At the risk of overgeneralizing about the three decades' worth of public commentary that he subsequently produced, it is apparent that although his writing became more polemical and his advocacy more broadly based, Newman's sometimes uneasy reconciliation of liberalism and nationalism would undergo no further radicalization nor any significant revision. Even in the 1990s, the decade in which laissez-faire liberalism returned to hegemony in Canada and throughout the industrialized world, Newman did not recant. The irony could not have been lost on him: in the 1960s he was too liberal for the nationalists, George Grant branding him a puppet of the Liberal "establishment"; yet in the 1990s he was far too nationalist for the neo-liberals. It is telling that a 1995 *Canadian Business* profile of Newman was entitled "The Last Patriot."[75]

Newman's elevation to nationalist spokesperson coincided with his co-founding of the Committee for an Independent Canada and his move from the *Toronto Star* back to *Maclean's*. The CIC was launched in September 1970 as a "moderate" citizens' committee, one that explicitly rejected "the radical solutions called for by the left wing of the NDP," as co-founder Walter Gordon put it.[76] Not surprisingly, Newman sought to impart to the CIC a liberal-reformist ethos. As he had told a group of Toronto high school students the previous spring, "the failure of the Canadian free enterprise system to maintain our economic independence is not in itself proof that large-scale nationalization is the only alternative."[77] Boasting 250,000 members at its peak, the CIC urged the Trudeau Liberals to create a Canadian development corporation as well as an agency to regulate foreign investment in Canada. It also lobbied for state protectionism in the realm of culture, something about which Newman would remain especially passionate. "If Americans play a dominant role in our information media, in television and radio, in record stores, bookstands and movie houses," he told a group of marketing executives in 1971, "we will forget who we are and why we are here."[78] Assuming the post of editor at *Maclean's* the same year, Newman announced that he would "renew and embellish" the magazine's commitment to providing Canada with "a platform that allows the nation to speak to itself."[79] "The Americans are in the process of taking us over not because they want to be our conquerors but because we want to surrender," he wrote. "It's that terrible ingrained uncertainty in us, the absence of knowing who we are and why we are here, that is gradually depriving us of our nationhood. And it's that uncertainty that we must dispel."[80] Newman's transition from observer to provocateur in the great debate on "Canada's survival" was complete.

Having entered the fray in a period of unprecedented nationalist euphoria – the heady days of Expo 67 and Trudeaumania – it was perhaps inevitable that Newman would become disillusioned with the struggle for Canadian independence over the longer run. After the 1976 electoral victory of the Parti Québécois, Newman was still urging that a "new style of nationalism would promote in a thoughtful manner the many practical advantages of Canada's continued existence." He read the separatist threat as a vindication of his own view of the national condition, namely that the "Canadian identity" is "fragile" and in constant need of affirmation. But he also spoke of the "fruitless and sometimes tedious" burden of being a nationalist: "Before [René] Lévesque and his determined disciples took power it was fashionable to take Canada for granted and the few thoughtful men and women who worried about our future were regarded with a kind of benign ridicule, like television preachers or men who devote their lives to collecting rare butterflies."[81] The bitter truth, of course, as events in the 1980s and 1990s would prove, was that Newman and his ilk were already on the wrong side of history. Despite their best efforts, and despite their relatively modest successes in reversing foreign ownership of the Canadian economy, the nationalists would lose the free trade election of 1988 and fail even to raise the ensuing North American Free Trade Agreement (NAFTA) negotiations to the level of a serious national debate.[82] In 2002, by which time the number of Canadians "adamantly opposed" to greater economic integration with the US had dropped to a meagre 5 percent, Newman was still fighting the old fight: "In a sequence of well-timed trial balloons, senior mandarins and cabinet ministers have floated the notion that the Canadian economy be transformed into what would amount to a branch plant of the American dream factory."[83]

How Newman became Canada's leading chronicler of the rich and powerful in the years when he was also one of the country's leading nationalists remains something of a riddle. Without question, he was enamoured of the country's corporate elite and ultimately became one of its most beguiling apologists. Yet, as he acknowledged as early as 1968, Canadian capitalists thought economic nationalism anathema. Walter Gordon's "very name produced a flush of anger in most businessmen," he wrote in *Distemper of Our Times*, "who privately went beyond the socialist label and seriously debated among themselves whether he might not be 'some kind of Commie nut.'"[84] In late 1971 *Maclean's* published a lengthy question-and-answer-styled interview between Newman and media baron Roy Thomson, in which the latter mused, without irony or qualification: "It's inevitable that Canada will gravitate in the direction of a closer partnership with the U.S. My guess would be that we'll probably become one country some years hence – not yet. I think it would be a good thing. It will mean a better standard of living for the people. We're just a carbon copy of America. When people talk about developing a Canadian culture, I can't see that Canadian culture is any different to American."[85] How to account for these extraordinary crosscurrents in Newman's thought?

There appear to be at least three components to this paradox, but admittedly they remain speculative. The first is that despite his claims to the contrary, Newman never made a clean break with liberalism, even at the height of his conversion to nationalism. He has remained a life-long fiscal conservative, for example, insisting on manageable public deficits, cautious investments in the welfare state, and aggressive measures to combat inflation. He articulated this conservatism succinctly in 1967 and has seldom strayed from it since: "The real problem is that governments have tried to do too much at one time. This has partly been due to the opportunism which has made politicians believe they can spend their way into power. Unfortunately, the politicians have not been able to discover or articulate any definable set of national goals, beyond the vague feeling that they should try to make all Canadians prosperous and happy. That's a laudable notion, but it's not precise enough to inspire any set of priorities in the nation's spending patterns."[86] Moreover, Newman's nationalist mentors were not the socialists of the Waffle or *Canadian Dimension* (a famous social-democratic/labour-sympathetic magazine) but men of business like Walter Gordon and especially Eric Kierans, neither of whom would ever come close to sanctioning extensive state ownership of the Canadian economy. Even with some of his closest allies in the cause of reducing foreign investment in Canada – Mel Watkins, for example – Newman agreed to disagree, openly stating his preference for regulation over nationalization. He could never embrace George Grant's dictum that in the Canadian context nationalism and liberalism were incompatible; and given his intimate familiarity with the Canadian corporate elite, he could never accede to Grant's most famous generalization: that "the wealthy lost nothing essential to the principle of their lives in losing their country."[87]

The second element in the paradox follows from the first. Not only was Newman outside the increasingly left-leaning trajectory of mainstream English Canadian nationalism in the 1970s, but as a writer and thinker he refused to embrace any sort of class analysis in his efforts to theorize his own liberal and nationalist inclinations. Nothing in the public record suggests that Newman ever read Philip Resnick's seminal *The Land of Cain* (1977), for example, or grappled with its thesis that it was the "new petty bourgeoisie" who played "*the decisive role* in the eruption of English-Canadian nationalism after 1965."[88] Indeed, Newman seldom acknowledged anywhere in his political or business writing that nationalism was an ideology, at least in the sense that it could be deployed in the interests of certain social groups in their struggles to attain material advantages over others. Nationalism, as Newman understood it, was good for all Canadians – a position that obviously implied his satisfaction with the socio-economic status quo in Canada.

The third element is perhaps the most obvious. George Grant was correct in *Lament for a Nation*: Newman is indeed a "journalist of the establishment." By virtue of his inherited wealth, his privileged education, and his meteoric rise to the highest echelons of Canadian print media, Newman has quite naturally taken his place within the elite strata of Canadian society. As editor of *Maclean's*, one observer noted, he was "the most gossiped-about person in the business."[89] Indeed, at the height of his fame in the 1970s, it was news any time he appeared at an art auction or bought a new yacht. Newman was fascinated by power, even as he wielded it. Yet, much to his credit, he has never become hidebound in the defence of his own social class – unlike, say, a Conrad Black – and even more important, he has regularly skewered its conventional wisdom. To cite but one important example, in 1996 Newman rose to the defence of Canadian liberalism against the onslaught of "neo-con commentators" like David Frum and Andrew Coyne:

According to [their] narrow way of thinking ... Canada's political life ought to be governed by an ideology that holds that everything has a price, that everyone is for sale to the highest bidder and that humanity's highest achievement is to balance your budget – personally, corporately and nationally. Under that harsh protocol, the idea of Canada is reduced to a flag of convenience, to be used or discarded like a moth-eaten T-shirt ... Unlike this reactionary creed, liberalism is mushy and ill-defined, a feeling more than a doctrine, the notion that despite individual strains and weaknesses, people are inherently equal, possessed by the right to pursue their dreams and that the state has a continuing obligation to help the needier among them along the way.[90]

In 1973, not for the last time, Newman waxed nostalgic about his adopted homeland. "During this past most beautiful of summers, on holidays and weekends, I drove with my family across Manitoba and down through the small settlements of southern Saskatchewan, and sailed into various rusty lake ports of eastern Ontario," he told his *Maclean's* readers. "It was a journey I'll always remember as the time when I stopped worrying about the Canadian identity and began to enjoy it."[91]

No such luck. Peter C. Newman has never stopped worrying about this "daily miracle of a country."[92]

Notes

1 Peter C. Newman, *Home Country: People, Places and Power Politics* (Toronto: McClelland and Stewart, 1973), 21-22.
2 Ibid., 21-22.
3 Peter C. Newman, *The Canadian Establishment* (Toronto: McClelland and Stewart, 1975). "Investment nationalism" is Sylvia Bashevkin's term; see her *True Patriot Love: The Politics of Canadian Nationalism* (Toronto: Oxford University Press, 1991).
4 Peter C. Newman, "Au Revoir but Not Goodbye," *Maclean's,* 7 June 1999, 60.
5 Tamsen Tillson, "The Last Patriot," *Canadian Business,* July 1995, 26-30.
6 Ibid., 28.
7 Ibid., 29.
8 Sandra Gwyn, "Recycling Peter Newman," *Globe and Mail,* 14 November 1998.
9 Peter C. Newman, quoted in Tillson, "Last Patriot," 29.
10 Peter C. Newman, *The Canadian Revolution* (Toronto: Viking, 1995); Peter C. Newman, *Defining Moments* (Toronto: Viking, 1997).
11 Ian Malcolm, "Defining Moments: Dispatches from an Unfinished Revolution," *Quill & Quire,* October 1997, 27.
12 Peter C. Newman, *Renegade in Power: The Diefenbaker Years* (1963; reprint, Toronto: McClelland and Stewart, 1989).
13 "Newman," *Toronto Star,* 18 January 1969, 4.
14 Newman, "Au Revoir," 60.
15 Peter C. Newman, "Horrific Reminders of My Days as a Refugee," *Maclean's,* 19 April 1999, 52.
16 Ibid.
17 Irving Abella and Harold Troper describe the attitude of Canadian Immigration Branch officials toward European Jews as implacable by the summer of 1940. To the profound consternation of the Jewish Immigrant Aid Society, for example, even "transitory rights for

most European refugees" had been "peremptorily cancelled" by Ottawa, confirming the general rule that "Canada was determined to barricade herself against all refugees." Abella and Troper recount how three Polish Jews who had made it to France were denied entry to Canada in December 1939, even though they had "combined capital of $120,000." This evidence suggests that successful Jewish entrants to Canada in the early years of the Second World War, including Newman's family, managed to flee Europe only if they possessed substantial (liquid) wealth. See Irving Abella and Harold Troper, *None Is Too Many* (Toronto: Lester and Orpen Dennys, 1982), 70-71.

18 Elspeth Cameron, "Newman, Peter Charles," in *Canadian Encyclopedia,* http://www. thecanadianencyclopedia.com.

19 "Newman," *Toronto Star,* 18 January 1969, 4.

20 Peter C. Newman, *The Canadian Establishment* (Toronto: McClelland and Stewart, 1975), 15.

21 Peter C. Newman, quoted in Tillson, "Last Patriot," 28.

22 Walter Gordon, *A Political Memoir* (Toronto: McClelland and Stewart, 1977), 59.

23 Ibid., 146.

24 Ibid., 264.

25 Peter C. Newman, *The Distemper of Our Times: Canadian Politics in Transition, 1963-1968* (Toronto: McClelland and Stewart, 1968), 214-15. See also Stephen Azzi, *Walter Gordon and the Rise of Canadian Nationalism* (Montreal and Kingston: McGill-Queen's University Press, 1999).

26 Tillson, "Last Patriot," 29.

27 Newman, *Home Country,* 207-9. This description of Gordon first appeared in print in 1965. It later appeared verbatim in Newman, *Distemper,* 214-15.

28 Peter C. Newman, *Flame of Power: Intimate Profiles of Canada's Greatest Businessmen* (New York: Longmans, 1959), 214-15.

29 Ibid., 248-52. By 1959 Newman was asking in *Maclean's,* "Are Canadians just squatters in their own country?"; quoted in Tom Fennell, "*Maclean's* and the 20th Century," *Maclean's,* 26 June 1995, 40-41.

30 Newman, *Distemper,* 81; Newman, *Renegade,* 127.

31 Newman, *Renegade,* 295-97.

32 Tillson, "Last Patriot," 26.

33 Newman, *Renegade,* 17.

34 Ibid., 295-97.

35 Ibid., 255-56.

36 Lotta Dempsey, "Why He Wrote 'That Book,'" *Toronto Star,* 21 November 1963, 49.

37 Newman, *Renegade,* 253.

38 Ibid., 445-46.

39 "Peter C. Newman Joins *The Star* as Ottawa Editor," *Toronto Star,* 11 July 1964, 1.

40 Dalton Camp, "Treacle Trickles through Pearson Biography," *Toronto Star,* 6 April 1964, 7.

41 George Grant, *Lament for a Nation: The Defeat of Canadian Nationalism* (1965; reprint, Toronto: McClelland and Stewart, 1970).

42 No mention of Newman is made in connection with *Lament for a Nation* in William Christian's superb *George Grant: A Biography* (Toronto: University of Toronto Press, 1993).

43 Grant, *Lament for a Nation,* 4-5, 30.

44 Ibid., 7-8.

45 Ibid., 15.

46 James Laxer, quoted in Ryan Edwardson, "'Kicking Uncle Sam out of the Peaceable Kingdom': English-Canadian 'New Nationalism' and Americanization," *Journal of Canadian Studies* 37, 4 (2002): 131-50 at 134.

47 In the foreword to the 1989 reprint of *Renegade in Power,* Newman wrote, somewhat defensively, that he had "no fixed political affiliation" (15) prior to 1957 nor any at the end of Diefenbaker's tenure as prime minister. This was as close as he ever got to a refutation of Grant's intimation that he had served as a Liberal hack.

48 Edwardson, "'Kicking Uncle Sam,'" 134.

49 Newman, *Distemper,* 54-55.

50 Peter C. Newman, "Customs Union with U.S. Could Destroy Our East-West Backbone," *Toronto Star,* 10 October 1964, 8.
51 See, for example, Peter C. Newman, "A Canada-Cuba Deal that Shook Washington," *Toronto Star,* 4 November 1967, 7. See also Newman, *Distemper,* 218-30.
52 Peter C. Newman, "Sharp Hints He'll Say Good-Bye to Co-operative Federalism Idea," *Toronto Star,* 4 January 1966, 7.
53 Peter C. Newman, "A Meeting Where Canada Spoke Up," *Toronto Star,* 17 March 1966, 7.
54 Peter C. Newman, "What the Kennedy Round Can Mean to Us," *Toronto Star,* 2 May 1967, 7.
55 Ibid. See also Peter C. Newman, "Cheaper Imports and Less Protection," *Toronto Star,* 3 May 1967, 7.
56 See Azzi, *Walter Gordon,* 168.
57 Eric Kierans, quoted in Peter C. Newman, "Why Eric Kierans Wrote Those Letters," *Toronto Star,* 3 February 1966, 7.
58 Ibid.
59 Peter C. Newman, "Kierans' Book May Signal Ottawa's Move," *Toronto Star,* 25 October 1967, 7.
60 Peter C. Newman, "How Did Pearson Keep this Cabinet Working Together?" *Toronto Star,* 6 April 1968, 7.
61 Quoted in Newman, *Home Country,* 229-31.
62 See Robert Wright, *Virtual Sovereignty: Nationalism, Culture and the Canadian Question* (Toronto: Canadian Scholars' Press, 2004), Chapter 2.
63 Peter C. Newman, "Missiles on the Moon?" *Toronto Star,* 10 April 1967, 7.
64 Ibid.
65 Peter C. Newman, "NORAD: The Squeeze Play Is On," *Toronto Star,* 12 April 1967, 7.
66 Peter C. Newman, "Suddenly McNamara's a Dove," *Toronto Star,* 11 April 1967, 7.
67 Peter C. Newman, "Our American Godfather," *Maclean's,* November 1972, 25.
68 Gordon, *Political Memoir,* 280-82.
69 Peter C. Newman, "The Perils of Diplomacy by Good Faith," *Maclean's,* August 1971, 3.
70 Peter C. Newman, "The Liberals' Aching Inertia," *Toronto Star,* 31 May 1967, 7. See also Peter C. Newman, "The Quiet Diplomacy Myth Explodes," *Toronto Star,* 27 May 1967, 7.
71 Peter C. Newman, "Let's Get Some Jocks at External," *Maclean's,* March 1972, 3.
72 Newman, *Distemper,* xiii.
73 Ibid., 54-55, 81, 88, 214-15, 218-30.
74 Ibid., 423-24.
75 Tillson, "Last Patriot."
76 Walter Gordon, paraphrased in "It Needn't Bust Us," editorial, *Toronto Star,* 20 January 1971, 6. See also Walter Stewart, "The Canada Firsters March on Ottawa," *Maclean's,* December 1970, 1-3.
77 Peter C. Newman, quoted in "Independence Top Issue of 70s, Peter Newman Says," *Toronto Star,* 16 April 1970, 4.
78 Peter C. Newman, paraphrased in "Canada Must Fight for Independence, Magazine Editor Says," *Toronto Star,* 27 April 1971, 12.
79 Peter C. Newman, "Why I Believe in *Maclean's* and Why *Maclean's* Believes in Canada," *Maclean's,* May 1971, 3.
80 Peter C. Newman, "Canada and the Psychology of Surrender," *Maclean's,* October 1971, 3.
81 Peter C. Newman, "Canada at Childhood's End," *Maclean's,* 10 January 1977, 10.
82 See Jeffrey M. Ayres, "From National to Popular Sovereignty? The Evolving Globalization of Protest Activity in Canada," *International Journal of Canadian Studies* 16 (Fall 1997): 107-24.
83 Robert Fife, "66% Favour Stronger Ties to U.S.," *National Post,* 21 October 2002; Peter C. Newman, "Beware of Freer Trade," *Maclean's,* 2 December 2002, 46.
84 Newman, *Distemper,* 218-30.
85 Peter C. Newman, "The Table Talk of Roy Thomson," *Maclean's,* December 1971, 41.
86 Peter C. Newman, "Trouble Comes to the Pearson Camp," *Toronto Star,* 28 October 1967, 7. See also "We Are Not Reckless Welfare Spenders," editorial, *Toronto Star,* 6 November 1967, 3.

87   Grant, *Lament for a Nation*, 47.
88   Philip Resnick, *The Land of Cain: Class and Nationalism in English Canada, 1945-1975* (Vancouver: New Star Books, 1977), 167, original emphasis.
89   Tillson, "Last Patriot," 29.
90   Peter C. Newman, "Liberalism's Long Shadow Lingers On," *Maclean's,* 5 February 1996, 42.
91   Peter C. Newman, "A Strong Land, Born of Rejection," *Maclean's,* October 1973, 3.
92   Newman, "Canada at Childhood's End," 10.

6

Multilateralism, Nationalism, and Bilateral Free Trade: Competing Visions of Canadian Economic and Trade Policy, 1945-70

Dimitry Anastakis

Canada, it seemed, had sold its soul to the devil. Writing from his vantage point in the early 1970s, the arch-conservative historian Donald Creighton described the course of Canadian history in the postwar period as having taken the wrong turn in "a forked road." The country had abandoned its British traditions and heritage to embrace increasingly American political and cultural influences. Creighton's famous turn of phrase was particularly aimed at Canadian economic policy and trade policy. After all, for Canadians – so dependent on trade for their prosperity, then as now – trade policy was economic policy, and it was clear to Creighton that after the Second World War, Canada had "sold out" to the Americans.[1]

Yet Canada's economic fate was not so clear or certain in the two and a half decades after 1945. While an obvious American influence was undeniably seen through growing Canada-US economic ties – links whose strength seemed even more dominant in view of the dramatic decline of British ties to her senior dominion – there were more forces at play in Canadian policy making than a simple surrender to the continental pull. Trade multilateralism, as shaped by internationalist postwar organizations such as the 1949 General Agreement on Tariffs and Trade (GATT), encouraged Canada's desire to sometimes counterbalance the American influence by looking outside of North America. At the same time, a reborn and vibrant economic nationalism also provoked Canadians to think of a future that broke from both its traditional British heritage and from the allure of America.

Nonetheless, while others have challenged Creighton's prevailing view that Prime Minister Mackenzie King and his Liberals had sold the country out, Creighton's condemnation of Canada's seeming embrace of the American colossus left an indelible impression on the writing of postwar economic and trade history. This problem has been exacerbated by generally declining interest in such matters – an oversight, given the important questions surrounding Canada's place in an increasingly globalized and simultaneously uni-polar world. Whereas Canadian economic and trade policy and foreign relations were once the mainstay of many history departments, these issues no longer capture the imagination of most historians. Instead, practitioners, trade specialists, and political scientists have largely filled the void, providing their particular disciplinary views on the development of Canadian economic policy.[2]

This chapter provides an opportunity to briefly re-examine the policy options facing Canadians following the Second World War. It argues that instead of choosing one path along the forked road, Canadians simultaneously explored three alternative routes for much of the postwar period. Multilateralism, economic nationalism, and bilateral free trade all held out both challenges and opportunities for Canadians. Somewhat surprisingly, while each policy option developed distinctively, all three streams reconnected in the mid-1960s to determine Canada's trade fate. These competing currents came together in the creation of the 1965 Canada-US Automotive Trade Products Agreement (or Auto Pact), which, while it sprang from an outburst of economic nationalism and was imbued with a dose of multilateralism, ultimately set Canada upon a path of continental free trade. The Auto Pact is a touchstone for all these trends and provides both a case study and a framework for understanding the competing strains of thought that shaped postwar Canadian trade and economic policy.

Multilateralism Ascendant

If Canada ever had a "multilateral moment," surely it was during the first few years after the Second World War. In the decade after 1945 Canadians were everywhere – helping to establish a new world body at the United Nations (UN), playing a pivotal role in Western security through the forging of the North Atlantic Treaty Organization (NATO), and leading the creation of novel trade regimes at the International Trade Organization (ITO) and the GATT. By way of this alphabet soup of acronyms, Canadians came to see themselves on the international stage as helpful fixers, competent and studious "functionalists" whose judicious use of Canada's considerable postwar credibility provided the backdrop for what many considered a "Golden Age" in Canadian diplomacy.[3]

During this period Canadians also created an image of themselves as committed trade multilateralists, determined to be leaders in the internationalism that had been forged in the fires of war. At the ITO – the third plank of the postwar order, along with the UN and the International Monetary Fund and World Bank – Canadians had played a key role, as they had at the UN. As the ITO's enabling initiative, the GATT had made positive, tentative first steps in efforts to lower trade barriers among its original twenty-three signatories. While it had been meant only as a temporary body, intended to be eventually superseded by the ITO, the GATT became the locus of trade expansion as the world rebuilt.[4]

At the head of Canada's GATT delegation stood Dana Wilgress, the capable former deputy trade minister who became an effective chairman for the international body. Wilgress personified Canadians' efforts at multilateral trade liberalization, just as Lester Pearson had come to represent Canada's place at the UN. But it was not only the shining stars of Canada's diplomatic corps who came to define Canadian foreign, trade, and economic policy in the postwar period. Behind every Wilgress and Pearson was a veritable army of diplomats and policy makers who formed the backbone of the Canadian civil service for the next few decades. This cohort of (virtually all) men was present at the creation of the UN, cut its teeth at rounds of ITO and GATT meetings, and became the plumber of Canada's postwar policies as surely as the diplomatic "stars" took their place in the Canadian political firmament.[5]

Like the "government generation" that had gone to Ottawa with a particular view of the role of government in society before 1945, many of these postwar civil servants shared a similar ethos when it came to the state's interaction with the economy. While they were all "nationalists" in the sense that they were public employees seeking to serve Canada the best way that they could, they were decidedly not old-style National Policy protectionists. Nearly all of them had gained some experience at the GATT talks prior to 1963 or would at some point in their careers represent their country at this international body.[6] Eschewing the protectionist policies of the past, they believed that trade liberalization was the key to fostering interdependence among nations, which would reduce the possibility of bloodshed on the scale that they had personally witnessed.[7]

At the same time, these public servants were also comfortable with an interventionist state. During the war they had seen and experienced the immense potential of government as Canada had marshalled its human resources and reorganized its economy. They were comfortable with this Keynesianist approach and brought these lessons to the fore as they instituted economic plans, including in the field of industrial development, such as the auto industry.[8]

S.S. (Simon) Reisman, who was among the most important players in the creation of postwar Canadian economic policy, was typical of this group. When the Second World War broke out, he was studying economics at McGill. During the war Reisman served as a gunner, after which he joined the government. Reisman was part of Canada's first delegation to the GATT and represented the country at all successive sessions of the international body until 1954. By 1958 he was well established in the Ministry of Finance when chosen as a lead researcher for Walter Gordon's Royal Commission on Canada's Economic Prospects, and in 1961 he was appointed assistant deputy minister of finance. During his stellar public service career, Reisman was deputy minister of industry and also of finance and, of course, famously led Canada's team during the 1987-88 free trade negotiations with the US.[9]

Other senior civil servants who were key to economic policy making had similar backgrounds. J.H. (Jake) Warren, who became deputy minister of trade and commerce in 1964, also served in the war and joined the civil service shortly thereafter. By the 1960s Warren had accumulated considerable experience as a trade negotiator and was a committed multilateralist: he had served as alternate executive director for Canada both to the International Bank for Reconstruction and Development and to the International Monetary Fund, and he had also represented Canada at the GATT since 1958. D.A. (David) Golden came to government in 1945 following his army discharge. Golden had survived four brutal years as a prisoner of war after being captured in Hong Kong by the Japanese in 1941. Deputy minister of defence production since 1954, he became the first deputy minister of the Ministry of Industry in 1963.[10]

These Canadian foot soldiers of multilateralism were among a vanguard that toiled to create a brave new world of nondiscrimination. Heartened by an American willingness to turn its back on prewar isolationism and protectionism and to embrace multilateral institutions, Canadians were keen to join and partake in these efforts. Canada's postwar multilateral trade policies were shaped by a number of determining factors. First, Canadians primarily needed markets for their natural goods and foodstuffs. Second, Canada was dependent on two markets for its exports: a declining UK market and a rapidly growing US market. Third, Canadian policy making in this period would be determined by developments outside of Canada's control: if the UK changed its policies on keeping its Commonwealth preferences (a lower tariff rate for its former colonies, which remained from before the war and which the US was determined to end) or if the US turned inward again, Canada would have to govern itself accordingly.[11]

The initial ITO and GATT discussions went swimmingly well. In Havana a new international trade architecture was created, and the US and the UK seemed to have resolved their differences over British preferences. In Geneva important steps were taken to erode tariff protection and nullify other nontariff barriers to trade. At the end of the first GATT negotiating "round," held in 1947, Canada negotiated a number of reductions with the US, which, given that the US was its most important trading partner, meant that these concessions would be passed along to other countries on a most-favoured-nation basis.[12]

Notwithstanding these bold efforts, by the early 1950s it was becoming clear that multilateralism in trade would not fulfil its earlier promise. The overly ambitious ITO, while signed by more than fifty nations but ratified by few, awaited for American approval that never came. With the growing realization of a Cold War upon them, increasingly ideological American views became hardened toward internationalism. A resurgence of skepticism about the utility of such a treaty in a progressively more protectionist Congress, exacerbated by a dearth of trade champions as senior American administration officials shifted out of the scene, meant that the ITO languished until it had been consigned to the scrap heap.[13]

Disappointed Canadians instead focused their efforts on the still-viable GATT, which did not require Congressional approval – as it was not an "official" treaty and had afforded the administration a limited ability to unilaterally reduce tariffs – and which had made such promising strides in 1947. But the next two rounds of negotiations, in France and England in 1949 and 1950-51, were less successful. As the organization added more members, countries became less willing to expose their economies to the increased competition generated by lower tariffs. More exceptions to tariff reductions were demanded, and as the US increasingly signalled an unwillingness to engage in further trade liberalization, the multilateral effort quickly lost momentum. The Canadians had invited the GATT to come to Toronto in 1952 for another round of meetings, but the failure of the US administration to secure further negotiating authority rendered the invitation pointless. There was no Toronto meeting, and it seemed that the efforts for further multilateral trade reductions remained uncertain.[14]

With multilateralism seemingly delayed, Canadian trade was increasingly moving in a north-south direction. The GATT negotiations had opened many segments of Canada-US trade, while Canada's European options remained stymied by continued currency controls and slow economic rebuilding on the continent. By the mid-1950s, Canada's American trade was booming, bringing the two countries' economies ever closer.[15] As historian Bruce Muirhead has argued effectively, "given the failure of these efforts [at the GATT and ITO], it seemed that the only option was increasing continentalization. Canadian policy was multilateral and non-discriminatory by preference, but manifestly North American by default."[16]

In the end, by the mid-1960s Canadian multilateralism was shaped less by the GATT's uncertain future or by whether Britain's weakness forced Canada into the arms of the United States than by the growing realities of the continental marketplace, which beckoned so alluringly. Despite Canada's best efforts to advance multilateral trade in the postwar world, a stunning shift of Canadian trade toward the US market was becoming more apparent with each passing year.[17] Yet, while 200 million customers waited just across the border, a century of tariff walls and a reborn defensive nationalism challenged any notion of the inevitability of a continental destiny for Canada.

Nationalism Resplendent

Old policies die hard. This was particularly true of the nationalism of the National Policy of tariff protection, which remained the core foundation of

Canadian economic and trade policy, even into a postwar world where multilateralism was in such apparent ascendance. Having survived generations of political wrangling, two bitterly fought national campaigns over the issue in 1891 and 1911, and decades of nominally pro-free trade Liberal government, by mid-century the National Policy was something of an electrical "third rail" in Canadian political lore: even the most fearless politician did not dare touch the policy directly for fear of facing certain electoral electrocution. Never fearless, but certainly the wiliest politician of them all, Liberal William Lyon Mackenzie King had spent decades scheming to lower tariffs, to little effect. As we shall see, when a chance came in 1948 to dismantle the National Policy for once and for all, ever-cautious "Rex" turned his back on the opportunity, fearful that abandoning the old policy meant abandoning the flag and losing his place in history, not to mention his party's next election. The third rail retained its electricity.

Notwithstanding this resilience, it was clear that the old policy was facing fresh challenges borne of a new worldview. The Great Depression of the 1930s and the Second World War had left policy makers on both sides of the Atlantic with the lesson that perhaps high tariffs had played some role in these traumatic experiences. America's punishing Smoot-Hawley tariff of 1930 and a British decision to increase tariffs in 1931-32 had signalled protectionism's zenith. Many of the new internationalists reasoned that these high tariffs had been in part responsible for the breakdown in foreign relations in the 1930s, producing an environment where, without trade links, war was made more easily.

This belief had sapped some of protectionism's potency, but while Canadian trade representatives could quietly go about their business in exotic locales such as Havana, studiously but slowly whittling away at the fringes of this protectionist legacy, most Canadians remained happily oblivious and unaffected by these changes. Even after the first few rounds of GATT negotiations, large swathes of Canadian economic output retained much of their tariff protection. This was especially true in the manufacturing field. For example, the automotive industry, which was quickly becoming the most high-profile and visible aspect of postwar industrialism, essentially continued to be governed until the mid-1960s by a creaking nineteenth-century tariff structure originally designed for horse-drawn carriages.[18]

Of course, there still remained a great reservoir of support for protectionism, the bastion of which continued to be the Conservative Party of John A. Macdonald. In the 1930s Conservative prime minister R.B. Bennett had promised to use tariffs to "blast a way" to foreign markets, but the only detonation had been within the Tory party, which after Bennett's disastrous tenure, lost five straight elections between 1935 and 1957. The National Policy's electric third rail brushed particularly close for Conservative leaders:

criticism of Macdonald's hallmark was akin to blasphemy, and any Tory who uttered such sacrilege had surely taken leave of his or her senses. Thus, when prairie lawyer John Diefenbaker took the helm of a dispirited Conservative Party in 1956, there was little discussion of dismantling a policy in place since before Diefenbaker's birth. Indeed, when the Auto Pact eventually emerged in 1965, Conservative MPs such as Alfred Hales denounced the agreement in a hail of National Policy rhetoric, claming that the agreement meant that Canada had sold its "birthright."[19]

Instead, Diefenbaker focused his Canadian trade policy in a most nostalgic direction. Following a Commonwealth meeting, Diefenbaker declared to reporters that Canada would henceforth redirect 15 percent of its trade to the mother country, which came as something of a shock to civil servants in Ottawa and London. While it is unclear where "the Chief's" fit of imperial affection came from, the difficulties incumbent to this kind of *dirigisme* were starkly apparent. To divert Canada's external trade so extensively required a breathtaking autarky in the face of well-established market patterns. Moreover, it was unlikely that a still-rebuilding Great Britain could even absorb or pay for such an influx of Canadian goods. When it became apparent that such a diversion was nearly impossible and that Britain's own affections lay with a united Europe rather than with her imperial offspring, the notion was quietly dropped.[20]

Protectionism's new lease on life, however, emerged not so much from the Diefenbaker Tories as from, of all places, a stalwart of the Liberal Party. The latent protectionism built into Canadian economic policy was resurrected in the 1950s and 1960s under a vibrant new form of economic nationalism, led by its unlikely champion, Walter Gordon. Gordon was a Liberal from Toronto at a time when the Queen City remained resolutely Tory and protectionist, as was he. Thus he was seen as something of a traveller in the Liberal Party, which had long been a wellspring for free trade in the Canadian milieu.[21]

Gordon, accomplished accountant to Canada's captains of industry, was a scion of Bay Street. With such longstanding ties to the economic elite and a penchant for public policy, by the mid-1950s Gordon had established himself as the quintessential go-to "organization man" for some of the difficult questions faced by the Canadian polity. As he also had links to the Liberal Party, it made sense, then, to select him to chair the 1955 Royal Commission on Canada's Economic Prospects, which set out to provide some direction as Canada charted its economic future in a quickly changing postwar world.[22]

The commission gave Gordon public stature and a platform to develop some of his long-held beliefs about the Canadian economy. But as a committed protectionist, Gordon disliked some of the harsher remedies being advocated by a few of his research underlings. Most notably, when Canadian-born and Oxford-educated Yale economist John Young was hired to examine the tariff and its impact on Canada, Gordon was unimpressed by Young's classical economic analysis. Young concluded that the tariff was deeply detrimental to the Canadian economy and that in 1956 alone it would cost the country $1 billion. As a solution, Young advocated free trade with the United States.[23]

Gordon, whose protectionist predilections had ensured that the commission's reports reflected his own concern about the massive American direct investment in the country, realized that such a report contradicted his position and tried to convince Young to reconsider. Simon Reisman, Young's sponsor during the commission, was furious with Gordon for attempting to suppress the work. After much arm-twisting, Young eventually agreed to make a few changes, and Gordon made sure that Young's publication *Canadian Commercial Policy* included a unique disclaimer stating that Young's views were not necessarily those of the commission.[24]

Gordon's battle with Young was but the first salvo in a war of ideas that raged unabated in the 1960s. Gordon's seemingly new tenor fitted well with the fears of American economic domination felt by many Canadians, who were already uneasy about the growing US cultural influence in Canada, from television, to fashion, to the emergence of American car culture and US-style suburban living.[25] A lightning rod for a revitalized economic nationalism, Gordon led a rebirth of protectionist appreciation. As a minister of finance in Pearson's first minority government, Gordon created a new Ministry of Industry, advocated punishing taxes on foreign takeovers, and proclaimed the goal of making American-based publicly traded companies in Canada 25 percent Canadian-owned.[26] With Gordon at Canada's economic helm, there would be no "lament for the nation,"[27] no silent surrender.

When some of these initiatives were repulsed and he later martyred himself by leaving, and then returning to, the Pearson Cabinet, Gordon's place in the pantheon of 1960s economic nationalism was secure. Gordon then turned to propagating his ideas through the written word: his musings during the decade included inflammatorily nationalistic tomes such as *Troubled Canada: The Need for New Domestic Policies,* from which sprang virtually an entire publishing industry dedicated to exposing the influence of American capital in Canada and not too subtly calling for a return to more muscular "national" economic policies.[28]

Gordon's clarion call was taken up by a wide range of Canadians. In the universities Kari Levitt, Mel Watkins, Stephen Clarkson, and a host of other newish and leftish academics developed a critique of Canadian political economy that accused Canada of being wholly dependent on the US, a perilous situation requiring remedies just such as those demanded by Gordon.

On the ground, Canadians embraced Gordon's nationalism as a predictable result of the puffed up patriotism that accompanied Expo 67 and the moralistic haughtiness engendered by America's deepening quagmire in Vietnam and burning racial troubles at home. Canadians, it was felt by many, were finally striking out on their own, and the economy was a logical place to start. In the auto industry, nationalistic auto workers called for the strengthening of Canadian content regulations and demanded that the government force American-owned Canadian companies to build an "all-Canadian car" or, failing that, to create a Crown corporation to nationalize the industry.[29]

Gordon's nationalist legacy was multifaceted: the Liberals were torn between, on the one hand, their longstanding commitment to lowering trade barriers and embracing the US influence as a positive one in Canadian economic affairs and, on the other hand, the increasing popularity of Gordon's economic nationalism. This played itself out in the very public tête-à-tête between Gordon and the more continentally inclined Liberal heavyweight Mitchell Sharp when the two men passionately debated the issue during a Liberal convention in 1966.[30] Liberal indecision over which fork in the road to ultimately take was also apparent in the government's policy choices: from the powerfully continentalizing Auto Pact, to advocating a "Third Option" in Canadian foreign policy, to the overtly nationalistic Foreign Investment Review Agency, Liberals and Canadians alike remained uncertain of which path was safest. This uncertainty and ambiguity toward the ultimate direction of Canadian economic policy can also be seen, as Robert Wright has argued, in the work and views of writers such as Peter C. Newman. Newman's efforts to "work toward some kind of reconciliation" between his nationalism and inherent liberalism were reflective of a struggle that many Canadians experienced in this period.[31]

It was a spirited time in the development of Canadian economic policy, and today economic nationalism conjures nothing less than the youthful idealism of what was then a seemingly new and radical impulse in Canada. It harkens back to an era when righteous Canadians seemingly stood up to the American behemoth and fought for an "independent Canada" that was a "just society," differentiated from the winner-take-all barbarism to the south. Yet for all of its zeal in this tumultuous time, economic nationalism was but one option that Canadians considered as they pondered their country's economic and trade future.

Bilateralism Resurgent

In the postwar period free trade was an issue that did not go away. While much history of the period has focused on the growing incidence of American influence in the functioning of the Canadian economy through foreign direct investment and on the nationalistic reaction to this new reality (as opposed to the creation of a formal free trade agreement between the two countries), continental reciprocity nonetheless loomed in the background. As the alternating current of the National Policy, free trade surged dangerously through the third rail of Canadian politics: those who advocated the policy were sure to be burned by the Canadian electorate, just as Sir Wilfrid Laurier had been in the 1911 election. It was a lesson understood well by Laurier's successor, Mackenzie King. Notwithstanding limited tariff-lowering trade agreements with the UK and the US in 1935 and 1938, wholesale abandonment of protectionism – especially in favour of free trade with the United States – remained a dangerous proposition.[32]

Yet in the postwar period continental free trade was a constant and growing presence in Canadian discourse. Notwithstanding the newfound appreciation of multilateralism that dominated much post-1945 thinking, the tight Canada-US co-operation necessitated by the vagaries of war had illustrated to many Canadians (and to many Americans as well) that closer continental coexistence in the economic field was a worthy goal. Wartime arrangements such as the Ogdensburg and Hyde Park Agreements, which continentalized North America for defence, production, and supply purposes, had driven home the utility and sensibility of working together.[33] The two countries had emerged from the war with a new sense of partnership, one that could not help but be strengthened by the relative decline of the British imperial presence in Canadian considerations.

Indeed, Britain's weakness after 1945 sparked hopes by some in both governments that the lessons of wartime economic co-operation could be placed on a more ambitious, and permanent, footing. In 1948 this ambition presented itself to Mackenzie King in the form of a secret comprehensive free-trade agreement worked out by advocates of such a plan in the foreign affairs departments of both countries. The agreement, "ultimate free trade" in Mackenzie King's view, promised to be of "tremendous benefit to Canada." But he had concerns as well: the Americans were looking to announce the agreement quickly – too quickly, King confided to his diary. Moreover, if the agreement was presented as a fait accompli, he knew that the Conservatives would accuse him of being an American "toy" who had always "wanted annexation with the States."[34]

In the end, Mackenzie King retreated. Although the country faced a severe currency crisis that threatened the whole Canadian economy, King took what he saw was the less dangerous road. He feared that joining the Americans in such a permanent manner would be seen as a betrayal of Canada's British connection and could hand the Tories a galvanizing electoral weapon.[35] Lester Pearson and his colleagues were disappointed: "I cannot help but feel," Pearson wrote fellow diplomat Norman Robertson following the termination of negotiations, "that a very great opportunity has been missed ... I think that 'we missed the bus,' even if we have saved the time table!"[36] Only a series of rigid exchange measures after 1947 (such as curtailing purchases of American luxury goods and limits on Canadian travel to the US) and Canadian participation in the Europe-rebuilding US Marshall Plan averted a Canadian crisis.[37] For now, free trade with the US would have to wait.

However, the notion of a bilateral free trade agreement did not die with the end of negotiations in 1948. In fact, the late 1950s and 1960s witnessed a renaissance of interest in continental free trade. The idea percolated with a host of groups and individuals who were determined to see the growing ties between the two countries developed into a beneficial economic arrangement. For instance, the Canadian-American Committee, a cross-border research association dedicated to studying the close relationship between the two countries, was instrumental in kindling the free-trade flame in the 1960s. Soon after its creation in 1957, the committee began publishing studies emphasizing the free-trade option, including a 1963 book that thrust the idea boldly onto the public agenda, *A Canada-US Free Trade Arrangement: Survey of Possible Characteristics*.[38]

The early 1960s also witnessed a renewed academic interest in the concept of free trade. In 1967 University of Western Ontario economist Ronald Wonnacott – who, along with his brother and fellow economist Paul, was among the most outspoken advocates of continental free trade – published a classic study on the issue, *Free Trade between the United States and Canada: The Potential Economic Effects*.[39] University of Alberta commerce dean Hu Harries declared that the formation of a North American trading bloc was a logical move and even cited the auto industry as a perfect example: "Is the Ford motor plant at Oakville any less economic than the one at Dearborn if both were functioning in a North American market?"[40]

Business and labour leaders sounded off regularly about the desirability of free trade. In early 1961 Proctor and Gamble chairman Neil McElroy made front-page news when he argued that economic integration was the only sensible path for the two countries. A few months later, Sherwood Egbert, president of the Studebaker-Packard Corporation, informed a Toronto audience that he too favoured the idea of economic integration. In a 1963 Empire Club speech, Chrysler America president Lynn Townsend called the possibility of North American free trade a "great economic opportunity."[41]

United Auto Workers president Walter Reuther and his Canadian director George Burt were also committed to the idea of free trade. Union leaders argued that if there was to be free movement of labour, which ultimately drove down labour costs to the detriment of working people, there should be free movement of goods and services. Moreover, free trade was a route to achieve wage parity for workers on both sides of the border. Another prominent labour leader, Henry Waisglass of the United Steelworkers, announced in 1963 that he too favoured free trade.[42]

Notwithstanding Walter Gordon's nationalist call to arms, the idea of free trade was taken quite seriously by the Pearson government. The Liberal Party was, after all, the party of free trade and had reaffirmed its historic commitment to the policy at conventions in 1958 and 1960. Even before the Liberals returned to power, the concept was again being considered in governmental circles. In 1961 *Maclean's* journalist Peter C. Newman confidently reported that free trade was increasingly being discussed by high-ranking civil servants in Ottawa. The suggestion of Canada-US free trade had moved from "outlandish" to "serious" because of Britain's intended entry into the European Common Market. The utter failure of Diefenbaker's 15 percent solution had focused attention on more realistic possibilities to solve Canada's economic problems.[43]

Lester Pearson's long diplomatic and political career was entwined with the issue of free trade, especially after the Second World War. In the early part of his career, he was a keen advocate of free trade, a position well known in Canadian diplomatic circles, if not publicly proclaimed. In 1948, when the free trade agreement with the Americans had been reached and Mackenzie King was wavering on the issue, Pearson had unsuccessfully pushed the reluctant prime minister to proceed and, like other civil servants searching for a solution to Canada's postwar economic problems, was disappointed when the agreement was abandoned.[44]

Once in power, Pearson tacitly supported Walter Gordon's nationalistic policies, although he was not an economic nationalist.[45] Pearson remained committed to the idea of free trade, although he believed that the massive dislocation and adjustment required by the Canadian economy if Canada did enter into a free trade agreement with the United States would be too high a price to pay. Michael Hart, the prolific historian of Canadian trade, has argued that by 1953 Pearson was no longer keen on free trade, but he would never blindly rule out any suggestion of a continental idea.[46] In the typical Pearsonian manner, he remained open to any and all options, which reflected not only his personality and manner of dealing with a complex problem, but also many Canadians' contradictory feelings toward free trade during this period.

The opinions of ordinary Canadians on relations with the United States and on the issues of protectionism and trade liberalization illustrated that they were well aware that free trade was a distinct possibility in the 1960s. The number of Canadians supporting free trade with the US actually increased, despite the nationalist rhetoric of the period. By 1968, the year that Mel Watkins published his study decrying the overwhelming influence of the US in the Canadian economy, the number of Canadians in favour of free trade had increased to 56 percent. At mid-decade a majority of Canadians in every section of the country were in favour of freer trade with the United States. A *Maclean's* poll came to identical conclusions.[47]

Keenly aware that Canadians both inside and out of government were not averse to the idea, American policy makers also viewed free trade with Canada in a positive light and actively sought to advance the notion. Free trade was an idea that fitted well within the context of greater trade liberalization, which the US had been pursuing since the end of the war. After 1945 successive US administrations pursued a policy of lowering tariffs through venues both domestic and international, with varying degrees of success. The GATT was first and foremost a creature of American design. The 1962 Trade Expansion Act authorized the president to make sweeping tariff cuts without having to withstand Congressional scrutiny. The creation of the position of the special representative for trade negotiations (STR) that same year created a powerful office to promote the trade liberalization agenda, and during the 1964-67 Kennedy round of the GATT, the Americans were among the most active players in the international trade scene.[48]

From the American viewpoint, Canada was a necessary partner if this long-term project of trade liberalization was to succeed. The unsuccessful free trade proposal of 1948 (and another less developed effort in 1953) had not dissuaded dedicated free-traders such as Undersecretary of State George Ball from pursuing the concept. Furthermore, the election of the Liberals in 1963 rekindled American hopes that free trade could be achieved. William Brubeck, the White House official in charge of Canadian issues, alerted National Security Advisor McGeorge Bundy to the possibility that the Liberals might be interested in such a venture. "A Liberal government," he wrote, "might eventually approach the US and request bilateral talks, aimed at selected free trade between the US and Canada. They would undoubtedly be dismayed should they be refused out of hand."[49]

Just how serious US officials were about free trade became apparent in the spring of 1964 when Ball addressed the American Assembly in New York. His speech, "Interdependence: The Basis of US-Canada Relations," outlined the general thrust of American economic intentions toward their northern neighbour. "There is no doubt," argued Ball, "that Canada and the United States could employ the resources of North America most efficiently by developing the North American continent as a single great market."[50] Clearly, by the mid-1960s free trade was an idea whose time had seemingly arrived. When it finally did emerge, however, it did so in a form that reflected Canadians' enduring attachment to economic nationalism as well as their abiding faith in multilateralism.

Continentalism Triumphant

The three predominant streams of postwar Canadian economic and trade policy – multilateralism, nationalism, and bilateralism – came to a nexus in the mid-1960s as policy makers grappled with the difficulties faced by what was increasingly Canada's most important industrial sector, the auto industry. The 1965 Canada-US Auto Pact, a hybrid treaty that had its genesis in an aggressive economic nationalism, featured a patina of multilateralism over a solid edifice of continental bilateralism. Its shape reflected the disparate nature of policy making in this period and the Canadian desire to take a uniquely middling course in the face of many forks in the trade and economic road.

By the mid-1950s the automotive industry was the exemplar of postwar economic success. At the post-Second World War height of the "American Century," nothing represented American hegemony better than the millions of gleaming chariots built by Detroit – "Motor City, USA." In North America and abroad, these vehicles and the car-oriented culture that they spawned, as historian Steve Penfold illustrates in this volume, epitomized the success and allure of America and its dream. As Europe's and Japan's shattered economies were rebuilt, they depended on the auto industry to pull their countries into the modern industrial age.[51] Around the world, the measure of a country's economic success and industrial standing was found in the vitality of its auto industry. As a result, many emerging economies developed combative relationships with the largely American-based multinational firms that dominated their domestic industries as they sought to gain the benefits of auto production through protectionist measures or outright nationalization.[52]

In the early 1960s Canada's economic wellbeing was also becoming closely entwined with its auto industry, and it too sought to gain a measure of control over a sector dominated by the US "Big Three" of General Motors, Ford, and Chrysler. The Canadian auto industry had grown up as a "creature of the tariff,"[53] yet technological changes, the necessity for greater economies of scale, and the onerous organizational demands of an increasingly complex automotive industry threatened the Canadian sector. Shackled by the nineteenth-century National Policy tariff structure, which had created a branch-plant industry, the Canadian auto industry was heavily dependent on American parts imports (which entered Canada at a lower tariff rate than completed vehicles) and constrained by a small domestic market. Representatives from both the Canadian subsidiaries of the US Big Three and the Canadian arm of the United Auto Workers union began calling for new measures to salvage a terminally ill industry.[54]

Following the report of a royal commission into the industry led by University of Toronto economist Vincent Bladen, the Canadian response to these difficulties emerged in the form of duty-remission plans designed to encourage the Big Three to source more of their parts from Canadian companies. In return for buying more Canadian content for their vehicles, the auto manufacturers would receive duty-free trade in their own cross-border trade of goods and cars. Thus, by holding out the carrot of tariff-free trade, Canadian policy makers hoped to boost exports, thereby increasing employment and ensuring that the Canadian auto industry could achieve the economies of scale necessary to survive. In other words, if General Motors bought more Canadian goods for its Detroit factories, it would avoid paying duties on the cars and parts that it exported to its subsidiary in Canada. This was National Policy tariff making turned on its head: instead of using tariffs to force import substitution in order to create industry for the home market, the plan was to use tariff reduction to boost production for export.[55]

The plan, initiated by the Diefenbaker government in 1962 and expanded by the Pearson government in 1963, worked well. While a primary goal of the scheme was to shore up Canada's ailing auto industry, government officials were also keen to redress a yawning trade gap with the Americans that had emerged in the automotive field. In 1962 Canada's automotive trade deficit with the US reached nearly $500 million, accounting for an astounding 96 percent of Canada's total trade deficit with the US. As expected, the Big Three American assemblers took advantage of the program and boosted their purchases in Canada in an effort to avoid paying duties. By 1964 employment and production in the Canadian sector had increased, and the trade deficit in automotive parts had narrowed.[56]

The American parts industry was unimpressed. They thought the program too clever by half and claimed that Canada was providing an unfair trade subsidy. Much agitation among their Congressional allies on Capitol Hill ensued. When American representatives predictably called for the program's dismantling, the Canadian government was determined not to bend in the face of these threats. A series of joint Cabinet-level meetings between the two governments in 1963 and 1964 resulted only in a hardening of positions. If the Americans carried through with their threat to slap retaliatory duties on Canadian goods, Canada-US trade could grind to a halt, with devastating results on both sides of the border. With the drums of a trade war beating relentlessly, the two sides attempted to come to some resolution.[57]

Canadian policy makers found themselves in a very difficult position. The Canadian auto industry faced the challenges of a small market with short production runs unsuited for the increasingly challenging demands of the modern automotive industry. However, just across the border lay the huge US market, where the safety of greater economies of scale beckoned. If Canada was to continentalize her industry, it could flourish by taking advantage of the largest and most lucrative marketplace on the planet. But moving to a regime that provided duty-free access to the US meant necessarily giving the US access to the Canadian market too. Free trade in autos conceivably meant the end of any Canadian industry, as there would be no need for the US Big Three to maintain their operations in Canada if they could import across the border without penalty (there were no indigenous Canadian assemblers).

At the same time, Canada did not wish to offend its trading partners around the world and at the GATT by entering into a preferential arrangement with the US. The country was still committed to the idea of multilateral trade reductions, and a regional trade deal with the Americans would surely dismay Canada's other trade partners, such as the British. As a remnant of a bygone imperial era, British autos shipped from across the Atlantic entered Canada virtually duty-free, while far more popular American models from just across the Detroit River faced tariff scrutiny.[58] Moreover, even if Canada and the US could work out a bilateral deal, there was no certainty that their trade partners at the GATT would accede to such a measure.

Initially, the Canadian response to the problem was spearheaded by Minister of Finance Walter Gordon and reflected his nationalist tenor. Canadians, Gordon warned the Americans, needed to have some control over their auto industry. They would get this either by holding steady to the controversial duty-remission schemes or, failing that, by taking the most extreme measures that they could – including nationalizing the industry outright, and damn the consequences. If there was indeed to be some solution to the problem promulgated along continental lines, Gordon demanded that Canada must receive her "fair share" of the North American auto market. Backed by his civil servants, Gordon brandished the nationalist threat menacingly enough that the US auto companies were genuinely fearful that Canada would indeed follow the same protectionist path already being taken by countries such as Australia, Mexico, and Brazil.[59]

The threat worked. Prodded by Gordon's nationalist rhetoric, the Americans agreed to parley. But the two sides could still not agree on the shape of the new program: the US hoped that it could take the shape of a free trade agreement, in keeping with its overall trade liberalization strategy, a plan that the Canadians resisted. As chief Canadian negotiator Simon Reisman told the US side, Canada "could not just remove tariffs and let the ball roll where it would" because, although the Canadians "did not think the ball would roll badly, they could not be sure and could not therefore fail to take precautions."[60] Given the prospect of yet another impasse, by the fall of 1964 the situation looked grim.

With the talks stalled, Reisman and his team hit upon an idea: the Big Three US companies themselves could provide the solution. Reisman suggested to his US counterparts that the auto companies might willingly agree to build a guaranteed amount of their product in Canada, in return for being granted duty-free trade across the border. In classic oligopolistic fashion, the manufacturers all agreed to the new plan, which required special agreements between themselves and the Canadian government, as well as to the Canada-US intergovernmental treaty that set out the terms of the new regime. Thus the Canada-US treaty established that in exchange for duty-free trade, the Big Three promised to annually build as many cars and trucks in Canada as they sold and to annually maintain a base amount of Canadian content (about $600 million) in their operations, determined from the 1963-64 model year. Additionally, the Big Three's side agreements with the Canadian government meant that the companies collectively agreed to invest a further $260 million in the Canadian industry over the next three years, the figure that had been expected under the duty-remission plans. While it was not pure free trade, the American government could not stringently object to a plan that the companies themselves felt was the best that they could achieve under the circumstances.[61]

With the US government on side, the arrangement seemed to make winners out of everyone: the Canadians achieved their nationalistic goals of ensuring a viable Canadian auto industry; the Americans avoided a trade war with their closest ally and largest trading partner and established the foundation for a free trade agreement in North America; and the Big Three auto companies escaped the even more onerous protectionist demands that Gordon had threatened, while the new arrangement held out the possibility of merging and rationalizing their Canadian and American operations on a continental scale.[62]

Implausibly, the Auto Pact contained all three strains of postwar Canadian trade policy within the agreement. First, the nationalism of Canadian policy making was reflected in the stringent conditions acceded to by the auto companies. Their Canadian subsidiaries were required to meet Canadian content, production, and investment stipulations, which met all of Gordon's nationalistic demands. At the same time, the Canadian factories were producing for all of North America – it was a form of protectionist continentalism. The Auto Pact's production requirements would prove immensely beneficial to the Canadian industry, as it was soon producing far more vehicles in Canada that it sold to Canadian consumers. In 1960 Canada accounted for barely 5 percent of North American vehicle production; by 1970 the total had increased to over 12 percent. Because of the Auto Pact, Canadians were producing far more than their share of North America's cars. Similarly, by the late 1960s employment in the sector had expanded tremendously, from 60,300 in 1963 to 83,400 by 1968. The agreement had satisfied even the most nationalistic Canadians. By the early 1970s the Canadian United Auto Workers union had become the agreement's chief defender.[63]

Second, the agreement contained an element of multilateralism. To avoid the appearance of developing a preferential agreement with the US and offending their other trading partners around the world, canny Canadian trade negotiators had managed to keep Canada's aspects of the treaty open to countries other than the US. At the GATT the Canadians had ensured

that other countries could take advantage of the new agreement to establish facilities in Canada (although they did not expect countries such as
Japan or Germany to do so any time soon), a factor that the Americans had
grudgingly overlooked in order to get the arrangement quickly passed at
the international trade body. Thus the Auto Pact was an asymmetrical agreement: it had different rules governing the auto trade on either side of the
border. For example, the Volvo plant in Halifax, which opened in 1963,
could import duty-free from Sweden as long as it met the Canadian Auto
Pact's requirements. But American firms could import duty-free only from
Canada. On the face of it, Canadians' multilateral commitments had remained intact.[64]

Finally, the Auto Pact was an overtly continentalizing agreement, one
that reflected the bilateral realities of Canadian economic life. Although
the two countries' economies had been steadily growing closer in the postwar period, the Auto Pact formalized this reality unequivocally. There had
been a few bilateral economic arrangements in the recent past between
Canada and the US, such as a 1941 free trade agreement in farm imple-
ments and the 1958 Defence Production Sharing Agreement (which formalized the ability of Canadian companies to sell to the US military), but
nothing on the scale of the Auto Pact. The auto industry was by far the
largest component of either country's economies and accounted for by far
the largest amount of each country's foreign trade. After 1965 the auto companies rationalized their production so that their Canadian plants could
build for all of North America: whereas once the auto factories of Windsor,
Oshawa, and Oakville had produced only for the stunted Canadian market,
they now produced for all of North America. By the early 1970s Canada's
plants were totally integrated into the Big Three's North American production plans and were soon producing far more than they ever had in their
pre-1965 Canada-only period. In terms of total trade, there was no precedent, and the Auto Pact remained the single most important trade agreement between any two countries in history, until the passage of the 1989
Canada-US free trade agreement.

By signing the Auto Pact, the Pearson government had chosen Canada's
ultimate trade and economic path. The pact merged the two countries' economic fates, and the continentalizing nature of the agreement had a sweeping impact on the operation of the North American economy. Moreover,
with the new arrangement, which rendered a massive amount of Canada-
US trade duty-free, the door was open to further trade liberalization between the two countries and ultimately, many on both sides of the border
hoped, to a comprehensive free trade agreement. As George Ball put it, "the
handling of the automotive problem is a good example of how two nations
can live together rationally on a single continent."[65] The agreement, however, meant much more than this. After the Auto Pact, it would be difficult

to turn back. Canada had irretrievably taken a step down the road of continental bilateralism.

Continentalism Entrenched

In the long expanse of Canadian trade and economic history, it was a curious moment. Certainly, Donald Creighton would be stunned. In the last weeks of the bitterly fought free trade election of 1988, Conservative prime minister Brian Mulroney was taking a final swing through the largely anti-free trade province of Ontario. As the overwhelming issue of the campaign, his plan for a comprehensive free trade agreement (FTA) with the US had come under relentless attack. Here was a Conservative prime minister and government fighting for free trade – the very antithesis of Creighton's conservatism. While Creighton had railed at Liberals Mackenzie King and Louis St. Laurent for selling out the country lock, stock, and barrel, here was the heir to Sir John A. Macdonald actually fighting for a deal with the devil.

Unsurprisingly, protestors had dogged Mulroney nearly every step of the way, and he had endured just about enough. Lashing out at hecklers who were disrupting a speech in Toronto, Mulroney fired back, calling the anti-free-traders "nervous Nellies." He chided the protestors for being the same people who had opposed the Auto Pact two decades earlier – they had been wrong then, and they would be proven wrong again, Mulroney blustered. The Auto Pact, the prime minister declared, in his familiar basso, had been a "bonanza for Ontario" and proved the case that free trade was the correct path for Canada to take.[66] Mulroney pointed out the obvious implication: the Auto Pact was free trade and had worked for the auto industry and for Canada, so free trade would work for the rest of the Canadian economy.

Resorting to a clever rhetorical slight of hand, one widely employed by the Conservative government in their efforts to convince Canadians of the goodness of free trade, Mulroney and his supporters failed to mention the protectionist and multilateral aspects of the auto agreement. Indeed, during the campaign, local candidates highlighted the free trade elements of the Auto Pact,[67] while government literature espousing the FTA portrayed the 1965 automotive agreement as a precursor to general free trade and implied that the new accord was its logical successor: "Autoworkers on both sides of the border have been the beneficiaries of what has been our most important bilateral free trade deal to date – the Auto Pact."[68] The Conservatives were leaving no stones unturned in their campaign to push free trade.

Notwithstanding the Conservatives' somewhat overblown rhetoric, clearly the Auto Pact had been a turning point in Canadian economic fortunes. By 1970 the continentalized industry was booming, with employment and production more than double that of 1960. Moreover, Canada had turned its massive automotive deficit of nearly $500 million into a surplus of over $200 million. By the mid-1980s, when Mulroney launched his free trade crusade, the sector accounted for the largest single portion of Canadian economic output. By 2000 Canada's economy was driven by the auto industry, which employed one in seven Canadians either directly (e.g., auto assembly, parts manufacturing) or indirectly (e.g., retail sales, advertising).[69]

In a trade-dependent country, the auto sector had become king: automotive products dwarfed Canada's other leading exports, including agricultural products and energy resources such as oil and natural gas, accounting for nearly one-quarter of the country's $400 billion in foreign sales in 2000, virtually all to the US. Automotive products were also Canada's leading imports, constituting over one-fifth of Canadian purchases, again nearly all from the US. On balance, Canada boasted an astounding $20 billion trade surplus in automotive products, a far cry from the difficulties that the country had faced in the years before the Auto Pact.[70]

But the auto agreement was clearly not "pure" free trade. As has been shown, the agreement emerged at the confluence of three distinct but intertwined currents of postwar Canadian trade policy. The agreement reflected Canadians' difficult trade choices in this period, and its hybrid nature illustrated a willingness to pick and choose among the range of public-policy choices. Understandably, Mulroney and the other advocates of free trade would have been loathe to admit that economic nationalist Walter Gordon had played no small role in the creation of the automotive agreement, true though this may have been.

Although the auto agreement was a unique response to a unique situation in a unique industry, when the weight of continentalism in the auto sector was brought to bear on the rest of Canada's economic prospects, it enforced a framework for Canadian economic options from which it was difficult to break free. With so much of Canada's wellbeing bound up in such a powerful and visible economic sector, it was almost impossible for policy makers to ignore (if not to manipulate for political reasons) the importance of the continental precedent set by the automotive agreement.

Could Canadians have continued on a more multilateralist or nationalist path even with the continentalist Auto Pact in place? Although the 1970s boasted a host of economically nationalistic initiatives (from the Foreign Investment Review Agency to the National Energy Policy) at a time when the pact was locking Canada's economy tightly into that of the US, this unsteady asymmetry would eventually come to be questioned. Any country would find it difficult to have bilateral continentalism in the largest and most important sector of the economy with the largest and most important economy in the world while the rest of its economic policy remained on the outside of such a domineering imperative.

This is not to say that the Auto Pact made Canada's bilateral fate inevitable, nor is it entirely accurate to say that by 1970 all but the shouting was done as the North American auto industry was integrated along continental lines. But clearly, the Auto Pact had pushed Canada's economic orientation in a particular direction, one whose primacy was recognized by the 1984 Royal Commission on Canada's Economic Union and Development Prospects, which ultimately took the position that free trade with the US was Canada's best option.[71] By then, Brian Mulroney was finally ready to choose the clouded road of which Canadians and their leaders had been so uncertain and which the Auto Pact had done so much to illuminate.

Notes

1 Donald Creighton, *The Forked Road, 1939-1957* (Toronto: University of Toronto Press, 1976). For a good discussion of the "sell-out" thesis, see Bruce Muirhead, *The Development of Postwar Canadian Trade Policy: The Failure of the Anglo-European Option* (Montreal: McGill-Queen's University Press, 1992), "Introduction." See also J.L. Granatstein, *How Britain's Weakness Forced Canada into the Arms of the United States* (Toronto: University of Toronto Press, 1989).

2 The most prolific recent analyst of Canadian trade policy is Michael Hart, a former member of the Ministry of Foreign Affairs. See his *Fifty Years of Canadian Tradecraft: Canada at the GATT, 1947-1997* (Ottawa: Centre for Trade Policy and Law, 1998). Other recent works that have examined Canadian trade and economic policy include those by political scientists Greg Inwood, *Continentalizing Canada: The Politics and Legacy of the Macdonald Royal Commission* (Toronto: University of Toronto Press, 2005), and Stephen Clarkson, *Uncle Sam and Us: Globalization, Neoconservatism, and the Canadian State* (Toronto: University of Toronto Press, 2002), and that by economist William Watson, *Globalization and the Meaning of Canadian Life* (Toronto: University of Toronto Press, 1998).

3 For more on Canadians at the UN and ITO/GATT, see John English, *The Worldly Years: The Life of Lester Pearson,* vol. 2, *1949-1972* (Toronto: Knopf Canada, 1992); J.L. Granatstein, *A Man of Influence: Norman Robertson and Canadian Statecraft, 1929-1968* (Ottawa: Deneau, 1981); Escott Reid, *On Duty: A Canadian at the Making of the United Nations, 1945-1946* (Kent, OH: Kent State University Press, 1983); Clyde Sanger, ed., *Canadians and the United Nations* (Ottawa: External Affairs, 1988). For a good reassessment of Canada's international role in this period, see Adam Chapnick, *The Middle Power Project: Canada and the Founding of the United Nations* (Vancouver: UBC Press, 2005).

4 On the creation of the GATT and the ITO, see Thomas W. Zeiler, *Free Trade, Free World: The Advent of the GATT* (Chapel Hill: University of North Carolina Press, 1999); Susan Ariel Aaronson, *Trade and the American Dream: A Social History of Postwar Trade Policy* (Lexington: University Press of Kentucky, 1996); and Hart, *Fifty Years.*

5 For views on the civil service, see J.L. Granatstein, *The Ottawa Men: The Civil Service Mandarins, 1935-1957* (Toronto: University of Toronto Press, 1982); Douglas Owram, *The Government Generation: Canadian Intellectuals and the State, 1900-1945* (Toronto: University of Toronto Press, 1986); J.E. Hodgetts, *The Canadian Public Service, 1867-1970* (Toronto: University of Toronto Press, 1973).

6 On Canada at the GATT in this period, see Michael Hart, "Canada at the GATT: Twenty Years of Canadian Tradecraft, 1947-1967," *International Journal* 52 (Autumn 1997): 581-608.

7 See, for instance, Lester Pearson's memoirs, *Mike: The Memoirs of the Right Honourable Lester B. Pearson* (Toronto: New American Library, 1972-75).

8 Men such as C.M. Drury, a former soldier and civil servant who became the first minister of industry in 1963, understood the utility of bringing governmental planning to economic policy. After his exemplary service in the war, Drury was appointed chief of the UN Rehabilitation and Relief Administration in Poland and then served as deputy minister of the Ministry of National Defence from 1947 to 1953. See *Canadian Directory of Parliament* (Ottawa: Queen's Printer, 1963); and C.M. Drury's introduction to "The Canadian Department

of Industry," in The Empire Club of Canada, *Addresses, 1963-1964* (Toronto: The Empire Club, 1964).

9   In 1978 Reisman was appointed to head his own royal commission on the auto industry.

10 Like Reisman, both Warren and Golden had very successful careers. In 1971 Warren became Canadian high commissioner to the UK and in 1975 ambassador to the United States. Golden became president and chairman of Telesat Canada. See *Canadian Who's Who*, vol. 35 (Toronto: University of Toronto Press, 2000). This information is also based on my interviews with S.S. Reisman, C.D. Arthur, and J.H. Warren, December 1997 and November 1999.

11 For views on the difficulties faced by the Canadians in this period, see Robert Bothwell and John English, "Canadian Trade Policy in the Age of American Dominance and British Decline, 1943-1947," *Canadian Review of American Studies* 8, 1 (Spring 1977): 54-65.

12 The "most-favoured-nation" (MFN) principle requires that a nation extend to all nations any treatment that it extends to its "most-favoured" trading partner. On Canadian participation in the ITO, see Michael Hart, ed., *Also Present at the Creation: Dana Wilgress at the United Nations Conference on Trade and Employment in Havana* (Ottawa: Centre for Trade Policy and Law, 1995).

13 See, particularly, Thomas W. Zeiler, "The End of Idealism," in *Free Trade, Free World*, 147-64; and Hart, *Fifty Years*, 49-51.

14 See Bruce Muirhead, "The Failure of the Multilateral Option: The GATT, 1945-51," in *Development of Postwar*, 47-75.

15 Along with their growing trade links, Americans continued to invest in Canada massively; see, for instance, Lawrence Aronsen, "An Open Door to the North: The Liberal Government and the Expansion of American Foreign Investment, 1945-1953," *American Review of Canadian Studies* 22, 2 (Summer 1992): 167-97.

16 Muirhead, *Development of Postwar*, 182.

17 By the mid-1950s, 60 percent of Canadian exports went to the US, while over 70 percent of imports came from the US. Exports to Britain, usually one-third of Canadian shipments before the war (and nearly one-quarter of exports as late as 1949), accounted for less than one-sixth of export trade by 1958. Imports from Britain were less than one-tenth of the Canadian total. See Muirhead, *Development of Postwar*, 182-86.

18 Although there had been some tweaking of the automobile tariff in the mid-1920s and again in the 1930s, automobiles were taxed at a 17.5 percent rate, half of what they had been taxed since first designated under the tariff in 1897.

19 Canada, *Debates of the House of Commons*, 5 May 1966, 4759.

20 On the Diefenbaker "15 percent solution," see Michael Hart, *A Trading Nation: Canadian Trade Policy from Colonialism to Globalization* (Vancouver: UBC Press, 2002), 207-8. While some might consider Canada-UK bilateralism another possible path for Canadian economic and trade policy in the postwar world, the Diefenbaker initiative illustrates that this was an unrealistic avenue for serious consideration.

21 See, for instance, Stephen Azzi, "'It Was Walter's View': Lester Pearson, the Liberal Party and Economic Nationalism," in Norman Hillmer, ed., *Pearson: The Unlikely Gladiator* (Montreal: McGill-Queen's University Press, 1999).

22 Canada, *Report of the Royal Commission on Canada's Economic Prospects* (Ottawa: Queen's Printer, 1958).

23 John H. Young, *Canadian Commercial Policy* (Ottawa: Queen's Printer, 1957).

24 The disclaimer at the beginning of Young's *Canadian Commercial Policy* reads, in part: "'Canadian Commercial Policy' ... makes a more abstract case for free trade – and does so more explicitly – than perhaps some people would expect of think justified in a staff study for a Royal Commission. We do not accept responsibility for or necessarily approve the statements and opinions which it contains." The account of this incident is taken from Stephen Azzi, *Walter Gordon and the Rise of Canadian Nationalism* (Montreal and Kingston: McGill-Queen's University Press, 1999), 59-61.

25 For views on US cultural influences on Canada during this period, particularly on the growth of suburban car culture, see Doug Owram, *Born at the Right Time: A History of the*

Baby-Boom Generation (Toronto: University of Toronto Press, 1996); and Richard Harris, *Creeping Conformity: How Canada Became Suburban, 1900-1960* (Toronto: University of Toronto Press, 2004).

26 Many of Gordon's measures were reversed after his disastrous 1963 budget, which was met by a plunge on the Toronto Stock Exchange.

27 See George Grant, *Lament for a Nation: The Defeat of Canadian Nationalism* (Toronto: McClelland and Stewart, 1965).

28 Gordon's own work includes his autobiography, *A Political Memoir* (Toronto: McClelland and Stewart, 1977), and numerous books, such as *Troubled Canada: The Need for New Domestic Policies* (Toronto: McClelland and Stewart, 1961), *A Choice for Canada: Independence or Colonial Status* (Toronto: McClelland and Stewart, 1966), and *Storm Signals: New Economic Policies for Canada* (Toronto: McClelland and Stewart, 1975). Other works on Gordon include Tom Axworthy, "Innovation and the Party System: An Examination of the Career of Walter L. Gordon and the Liberal Party" (MA thesis, Queen's University, 1970); Douglas Fetherling, "The Lion in Winter," *Saturday Night*, May 1983; John Hutcheson, "Walter Gordon," *Canadian Forum*, May 1987; and Denis Smith, *Gentle Patriot: A Political Biography of Walter Gordon* (Edmonton: 1973).

29 For more on this issue, see Dimitry Anastakis, "Between Nationalism and Continentalism: State Auto Industry Policy and the Canadian UAW, 1960-1970," *Labour/Le Travail* 53 (Spring 2004): 87-124.

30 Smith, *Gentle Patriot*, 291-92; Azzi, "'It was Walter's View,'" 113-14.

31 Robert Wright, "From Liberalism to Nationalism: Peter C. Newman's Discovery of Canada," in this volume.

32 For more on the 1935 and 1938 trade agreements, see Frank Stone, *Canada, the GATT and the International Trade System* (Montreal: Institute for Research on Public Policy, 1984), 11-12; and Michael Hart, "War, Depression and Revolution," in *Trading Nation*. More generally on free trade, see J.L. Granatstein, "Free Trade between Canada and the United States: The Issue that Will Not Go Away," in Denis Stairs and Gilbert Winham, eds., *The Politics of Canada's Economic Relationship with the United States* (Toronto: University of Toronto Press, 1985), 11-54.

33 See, for example, R. Cuff and J.L. Granatstein, *Ties that Bind: Canadian-American Relations in Wartime from Great War to Cold War* (Toronto: Hakkert and Co., 1977).

34 Mackenzie King Diary, 22 March 1948, 2, http://king.collectionscanada.ca/EN/default.asp.

35 On the 1947-48 free trade initiative, see Mackenzie King's fascinating diary entries, including 6, 18, and 22 March 1948. In 1953 another effort at bilateral free trade was engaged during meetings between Prime Minister Louis St. Laurent and President Dwight D. Eisenhower. Like the 1948 interchange, these discussions also came to nought.

36 Pearson to Robertson, 22 April 1948, External Affairs Records, unpublished selected documents for 1947, quoted in Michael Hart, "Almost but Not Quite: The 1947-1948 Bilateral Canada-US Negotiations," *American Review of Canadian Studies* 19, 1 (1989): 25-58 at 4; also quoted in R. Cuff and J.L. Granatstein, "The Rise and Fall of American Free Trade, 1947-1948," *Canadian Historical Review* 58 (December 1977): 459-82 at 478-79.

37 Muirhead, *Development of Postwar*, 19-22.

38 The Private Planning Association eventually became the C.D. Howe Institute. See the following studies: Grant L. Reuber, *The Growth and Changing Composition of Trade between Canada and the United States* (Montreal: Canadian-American Committee, 1960); Francis Masson and J.B. Whitely, *Barriers to Trade between Canada and the United States* (Montreal: Canadian-American Committee, 1960); Sperry Lea, *A Canada-US Free Trade Arrangement: Survey of Possible Characteristics* (Montreal: Canadian-American Committee, 1963); and Ronald Anderson, "US-Canada Free Trade Link Possible, Group's Study Shows," *Globe and Mail*, 5 November 1963.

39 For an overview of the committee's activities in this period, see Sperry Lea, "A Historical Perspective," in Robert M. Stern, Philip H. Trezise, and John Walley, eds., *Perspectives on a US-Canadian Free Trade Agreement* (Washington, DC: Brookings Institute, 1987); Canadian-American Committee, *US-Canadian Free Trade: The Potential Impact on the Canadian Economy*

(Washington, DC, and Montreal: Canadian-American Committee, 1965); and Paul Wonnacott and R.J. Wonnacott, *Free Trade between the United States and Canada: The Potential Economic Effects* (Cambridge: Harvard University Press, 1967).

40 Hu Harries, quoted in Edin Bolwell, "Free Trade with US Proposed as Spur to Canadian Industry," *Globe and Mail,* 16 September 1961.

41 "Market Ties Seen for US, Canada: McElroy Calls Customs Union Sure as Interdependence of Two Nations Grows," *New York Times,* 14 February 1961; "Away with the Border?" editorial, *Globe and Mail,* 26 August 1961; Lynn A. Townsend, "A Great Economic Opportunity," in The Empire Club of Canada, *Addresses, 1963-1964* (Toronto: Empire Club, 1964), 256.

42 For Reuther's views on free trade, see Nelson Lichtenstein, *The Most Dangerous Man in Detroit: Walter Reuther and the Fate of American Labour* (New York: Basic Books, 1995). For the Canadian United Auto Workers' submission to the Bladen Commission, see "How Canadians Can Get a Made-in-Canada Car They Want and Can Afford," 5 July 1960, 2, 4, 7, 8, Library and Archives Canada (LAC), RG 33/45, Royal Commission on the Automobile Industry, no. 18, file 33a; and Wilfred List, "Steelworkers Official Presents Plan: Canada Urged to Back Free Trade Area Including US," *Globe and Mail,* 18 February 1963.

43 National Liberal Federation, *Report of the Proceedings of the National Liberal Convention 1958* (Ottawa: 1958). On the Kingston Conference, see Azzi, *Walter Gordon,* 75-79 and Peter C. Newman, "First Signs of a Merger: Now some planners say one way to beat the Americans is to join them," *Maclean's,* 9 June 1961, 80.

44 Pearson, *Mike: The Memoirs,* vol. 1, 292.

45 Stephen Azzi argues effectively that Pearson allowed Gordon free rein in economic matters. Mitchell Sharp stated that Pearson "was not an economic nationalist, to put it mildly." "'It Was Walter's View': Lester Pearson, the Liberal Party and Economic Nationalism," in Norman Hillmer, ed., *Pearson: The Unlikely Gladiator* (Montreal: McGill-Queen's University Press, 1999), 92-116 at 104.

46 Hart, "Almost but Not Quite," 50.

47 The Gallup poll indicated that 69% of Quebecers, 52% of Westerners, and even 51% of respondents in traditionally protectionist Ontario were in favour of freer trade with the Americans. The *Maclean's* poll was commissioned by *Maclean's, Le Magazine Maclean,* CBC television's *Inquiry,* and the Groupe de recherche sociale de Montréal. The sample was 1,042 respondents.

48 See the introduction to Zeiler, *Free Trade, Free World;* William S. Borden, "Defending American Hegemony: American Foreign Economic Policy," in Thomas G. Paterson, ed., *Kennedy's Quest for Victory: American Foreign Policy, 1961-1963* (New York: Oxford University Press, 1989), 69-71; Kenneth C. Mackenzie, *Tariff-Making and Trade Policy in The US and Canada: A Comparative Study* (New York: Praeger, 1969), 35-41.

49 Brubeck to Bundy, 11 April 1963, National Archives and Records Administration (NARA), RG 59, State Department Central Foreign Policy Files, 1963, File: Box 3852, Political 15-Canada Government.

50 George Ball, "Interdependence: The Basis of Canada-US Relations," 26 April 1964, United States Information Service Text, LAC, RG 20, vol. 2052, file 1021-10, part 2. For an interesting view of the speech and Canadian reaction, see George Ball, "The Problem of Nationalism in a Shrinking World," in R.H. Wagenberg, ed., *Canadian-American Interdependence: How Much? Proceedings of the 10th Annual Seminar on Canadian American Relations, 1968* (Windsor: University of Windsor Press, 1970); Bruce Macdonald, "Tension High for Canada-US Meet," *Globe and Mail,* 29 April 1964.

51 On the postwar US auto industry, see Lawrence J. White, *The Automobile Industry since 1945* (Cambridge: Harvard University Press, 1971); John B. Rae, *The American Automobile: A Brief History* (Chicago: University of Chicago Press, 1965); and George Maxcy, *The Multinational Automobile Industry* (New York: St. Martin's Press, 1981).

52 On state interaction with the auto industry, see Douglas C. Bennett and Kenneth E. Sharpe, *Transnational Corporations versus the State: The Political Economy of the Mexican Auto Industry* (Princeton: Princeton University Press, 1985); Kenneth P. Thomas, *Capital beyond Borders: States and Firms in the Auto Industry, 1960-1994* (New York: St. Martin's Press, 1996); Helen

Shapiro, *Engines of Growth: The State and Transnational Companies in Brazil* (Cambridge: Harvard University Press, 1994).

53 Tom Traves, *The State and Enterprise: Canadian Manufacturers and the Federal Government, 1917-1931* (Toronto: University of Toronto Press, 1979), 101.

54 "UAW Proposes Probe of Jobless Causes," *Globe and Mail,* 4 April 1960.

55 Initially, the plan was restricted to the trade in automatic transmissions (which were not being built in Canada at the time) and some engines.

56 John Holmes, "From Three Industries to One: Towards an Integrated North American Automobile Industry," in Maureen Molot, ed., *Driving Continentally: National Policies and the North American Auto Industry* (Ottawa: Carleton University Press, 1993), 27.

57 On the Auto Pact negotiations, see Dimitry Anastakis, *Auto Pact: Creating a Borderless North American Auto Industry* (Toronto: University of Toronto Press, 2005), especially Chapter 3.

58 British autos had been granted duty-free status by Bennett in the 1930s.

59 In Mexico the government had almost expelled the US manufacturers and had instead demanded 100 percent Mexican content requirements. Similar protectionist measures were taken by Brazil and Australia. Canada stipulated a 60 percent content rule.

60 "Free Trade Arrangement for Automobiles and Automotive Products," Memorandum of Conversation, 17 August 1964, NARA, RG 59, Bureau of European Affairs, Country Directory for Canada, Records Relating to Economic Matters, 1956-66, Country Files, Canada, box 1249.

61 Henry Ford II personally intervened with US President Lyndon Johnson to push acceptance of the plan.

62 For a view of the effects of the Auto Pact on a Canadian subsidiary of a Big Three company, see Dimitry Anastakis, "From Independence to Integration: The Corporate Evolution of the Ford Motor Company of Canada, 1904-2004," *Business History Review* 78 (Summer 2004): 213-53.

63 *DesRosiers Automotive Yearbook 2000* (Richmond Hill, ON: DesRosiers Automotive Consultants, 2000), 112; Anastakis, "Between Nationalism and Continentalism," 119-20.

64 For a more detailed examination of the multilateral aspects of the Auto Pact, see Dimitry Anastakis, "The Advent of an International Trade Agreement: The Auto Pact at the GATT, 1964-5," *International Journal* 55 (Autumn 2000): 583-602.

65 George Ball, "The United States and Canada: Common Aims and Common Responsibilities," *Department of State Bulletin* 52, 1347, 19 April 1965, 573-74.

66 Ross Howard, "Mulroney on last swing in Ontario," *Globe and Mail,* 18 November 1988.

67 During a 1988 all-candidates meeting in the riding of Markham, Ontario, for example, the Conservative candidate made significant use of the Auto Pact as an argument in favour of free trade.

68 External Affairs Canada, *The Canada-United States Trade Agreement: Trade – Securing Canada's Future* (Ottawa: Minister of Supply and Services, 1988), 19.

69 Statistics Canada, CANSIM, Tables 228-0001, 228-0002, and 228-0003, http://www.statcan.ca/english/Pgdb/intern.htm; Holmes, "From Three Industries to One," 27.

70 Ibid.

71 Canada, *Royal Commission on the Economic Union and Development Prospects for Canada: Final Report* (Toronto: University of Toronto Press, 1985).

7
Selling by the Carload: The Early Years of Fast Food in Canada
Steve Penfold

On 1 June 1967, as North Americans discovered hippies, as youth geared up for the famous Summer of Love, and as Canadians looked forward to an optimistic season of Centennial celebrations, George Tidball began his summer of hamburgers. A year before, Tidball had left his job as a management consultant rather than accept an unwanted transfer from Vancouver to Cleveland. He had few immediate prospects, but his wife remembered a popular drive-in restaurant from their days in Chicago and suggested that Vancouver needed one. The restaurant was called McDonald's, then an American-wide chain of almost 1,000 outlets, but it was known to Canadians only through American television and the accounts of travellers who had encountered the company's eighteen-cent hamburgers. With a group of partners, Tidball secured a licence from the chain and formed McCan Franchises Ltd. to develop McDonald's restaurants across western Canada.[1]

For their first location, McCan found a lot at No. 3 Road and Bennett Road in Richmond, a burgeoning suburb of Vancouver. Thanks to improved bridges across the Fraser River, No. 3 Road was fast developing into a "transportation artery between the bulk of the residential area of Richmond and the employment and cultural areas in Vancouver," so the new outlet seemed nicely placed to draw traffic from across the area.[2] More strikingly, Richmond was exactly the kind of community that the American parent held in mystical esteem. "McDonald's is set up to serve local families, not highway transients," a company advertisement claimed, "and the ideal location for a McDonald's is a solid, substantial family community with plenty of churches, schools, shopping centers, and residential streets." Brimming with young, middle-class families living in detached houses along quiet suburban streets like Bennett Road, Richmond was the perfect McCommunity.[3]

The residents of Bennett Road seemed less enthusiastic about McDonald's than McDonald's was about them. Six months before the outlet opened, a delegation of nineteen local homeowners implored Town Council to keep

McDonald's out, fearing for the aesthetic and moral peace of their neighbourhood. Residents knew what to expect from a "drive-in" restaurant: all-
night noise, increased traffic, blowing garbage, and worst of all, the "hoodlum
element." Town officials were sympathetic and referred the issue to various
committees, but in the end they were impotent. Planning staff negotiated
an agreement with McCan to alter the parking-lot layout and to close at
11:00 p.m. every night, but they were powerless to refuse a building permit.
"We could have had a far better and more comprehensive business," noted
Reeve Harry Anderson, "but the property was zoned Commercial Service
District and there's nothing we can do about it."[4]

In retrospect, the new outlet on No. 3 Road seemed to mark the first step
in a new fast food order. Over the subsequent decade McDonald's swept to
the top of the Canadian fast food ladder with remarkable speed. In 1977
the chain's 250 outlets spanned the country, and its annual revenues almost equalled the combined sales of its closest three competitors.[5] Five
years later the company proudly announced a distressing indicator of the
new McContinent: 93 percent of Canadian children believed that John A.
Macdonald was the "guy who makes the hamburgers."[6] By that time, in
fact, McDonald's was in the vanguard of an emerging global mass culture.
As the company's first international outlet, McDonald's Richmond location
represented the first step toward the chain's status as a symbol of this new
reality.[7]

Yet McDonald's ultimate triumph should not obscure the fact that, at the
time, its arrival in Richmond seemed a mere continuation of existing trends.
At a significant moment in Canadian business history, Tidball followed the
well-worn strategy of importing American ideas into the Canadian market.
McDonald's came across the border some years behind early innovators like
Dairy Queen ice cream, Dog 'N Suds hot dog stands, A&W Drive-Ins, Red
Barn Hamburgers, Mister Donut, and Kentucky Fried Chicken – American
companies that had been dotting the Canadian roadside since the late 1950s.
Moreover, McDonald's ultimate triumph was hardly obvious in 1967, as the
chain was simply one more company colonizing the Canadian roadside
with quick-service food outlets.

In fact, this was precisely how the residents of Bennett Road viewed the
new McDonald's: as one of many nuisances that they had to confront in
their increasingly hectic suburban lives. Neighbourhood worries about noise,
garbage, and hoodlums suggested that some middle-class families had come
to think of drive-in restaurants as offering not simply a particular mix of
convenience, affordability, and informality, but also an all-too-predictable
social dynamic. From this perspective, the new McDonald's seems a good
lesson in the link between business institutions, social history, and popular
culture. McDonald's and other fast food companies expressed several key

elements of postwar consumption. Their religious commitment to serving middle-income families, their locations on urban fringes, their large parking lots along busy thoroughfares like No. 3 Road, their limited menus of cheap, easy-to-prepare foods, and their informal surroundings spoke to broader trends in postwar Canada. For fast food companies, these trends crystallized into the idea of "selling by the carload," of reaching not just individual consumers but also increasingly mobile, middle-class families. But fast food outlets also became the touchstone for another postwar social dynamic, the generation gap, since all the strategies for selling by the carload – informal surroundings, large parking lots, inexpensive food – attracted young patrons who promised to drive the families away. Although it tapped powerful trends in postwar society, selling by the carload was no easy proposition.

"Families Dashing Off Somewhere Want to Eat in a Hurry"

The term "fast food" was coined in the 1950s, but even when McDonald's arrived in Canada, it was not commonly used. Like residents of Bennett Road, when Canadians talked about what we now call fast food outlets, they usually called them "drive-in restaurants." Nor was "fast food" used precisely or consistently, although it generally referred to some combination of four basic features: limited menu, rigidly defined production system, paper service, and roadside location. At the same time, these specific features were often less important than fast food's overall symbolic impact.

Since the mid-1970s the mission of fast food companies has been to expand their product offerings, but in the early days they specialized in limited menus of easy-to-prepare and easy-to-eat fare, rarely more than a dozen items including sandwiches, fries, and drinks. Hamburgers and chicken were the most common items on fast food menu boards, but secondary products included donuts, fish and chips, roast beef sandwiches, and pizza (see Table 7.1). Up to 1975 these secondary products did not secure wide appeal. The most surprising failure was fish and chips, which had been popular in many markets for several years. In the 1930s, for example, Toronto had so many fish and chips shops that they were listed separately in the city directory; a decade later, Victoria's twelve establishments claimed to serve twenty tons of fish and thirty-six tons of chips every week. But attempts to integrate fish and chips into Canada's fast food revolution left a string of spectacular failures: P.K. Fish and Chips, Davy Jones, H. Salt, Arthur Treacher's, and others.[8]

Whatever their product, fast food outlets were built for speed. In a typical boast, Big Ben's in Burnaby, British Columbia, promised to serve fifteen-cent hamburgers to a family of four within two minutes. "We take the most popular foods [and] put their preparation and serving on an assembly line basis," bragged Red Barn's Harold Shneer, borrowing a popular phrase from McDonald's president Ray Kroc.[9] The claim was more than rhetoric. With various levels of enthusiasm and enforcement, fast food operators defined

Table 7.1

Estimated share of fast food dollar volume by food type, 1970

Food	%
Chicken	32.0
Hamburgers	29.0
Ice cream	23.5
Donuts	4.5
Pizza	3.5
Hot dogs	3.0
Other*	4.5

* Includes fish and chips (2%), pancakes (1.5%), and roast beef (1%).
Source: Canadian Hotel and Restaurant, 15 March 1970, 43-44.

and refined a "system" of production that squeezed speed and efficiency out of even the smallest operations. Cooking procedures were carefully timed, and even simple steps like adding ketchup and mopping floors were regulated and standardized. To describe these innovations, invoking Ford was more symbolically striking than descriptively accurate since few fast food outlets were large enough to accommodate real assembly lines (although a few experimented with automated broilers),[10] and their strategies had much broader genealogies in the development of mass production. In fact, as sociologist Ester Reiter points out, fast food owed much more to Frederick Taylor than to Henry Ford. Back in Ford's time, Taylor had conducted detailed experiments on work, carefully charting workers' movements to improve efficiency, eliminate discretion from labour processes, and codify every task into a series of rules that management could control and enforce. Long after Taylor's death, fast food companies applied his agenda to the hamburger with considerable vigour.[11]

When fast food emerged from this factory-like system, it was passed to the customer in disposable containers. Whatever their product, fast food outlets dispensed with plates and utensils, serving in bags, boxes, cartons, cardboard buckets, and foil wrappers. From the operator's standpoint, paper service meant no dishes to wash and no money lost to "breakage." From a broader perspective, paper service entailed a different relationship to neighbourhood and customer. When Bennett Road residents worried that McDonald's would turn the area into a "great big garbage dump," they echoed standard complaints from across the country. "Drive-in restaurants are an abomination," Scarborough, Ontario, resident David Steward told his Town Council in 1967, "a dog's playground covered with chicken bones and paper napkins."[12] Managing garbage was not a trivial concern: journalists often noticed the size of the garbage bins as much as the food, so companies tried to enforce strict standards of cleanliness. For operators unwilling to clean up, city councils often stepped in to force the issue. In 1966 Winnipeg passed a strict new antilitter law, which required businesses offering paper service to clean their garbage off public and private property within 100 yards of the outlet.[13]

Paper service also entailed a different notion of serving the consumer, one that links to the fourth characteristic of fast food. Customers were expected to eat in the relative privacy of their cars, so they could have easily driven off with plates and utensils. In the early days, everything about fast food outlets – architecture, signage, products, and service – seemed designed to grab fast-moving automobiles. Few companies sought out downtown locations until the mid-1970s, preferring roadside sites on metropolitan and urban fringes. Along the roadside, pylon signs were designed for maximum efficiency in attracting motoring customers: they were tall, brightly lit, and displayed a minimum number of words and were often spinning or surrounded by flashing lights, all meant to attract attention at forty miles an hour. Red Barn required outlets to be visible from 500 feet away since customers needed time to see the sign, slow down, and pull in. Once they stopped, consumers found enormous parking lots. Companies often looked for an acre of land, but the buildings themselves were small, typically between 1,200 and 1,600 square feet, including the production area. Inside the outlet, interior seating space was limited, if it existed at all. As we'll see, some prewar roadside restaurants (like Nat Bailey's Vancouver-area White Spot) eventually expanded to include tables, counters, and dining rooms, but until the late 1960s fast food chains typically expected customers to eat in their cars or take their food home. Red Barn's early outlets had twelve seats, but their design – moulded chairs with small, attached half-desks painfully familiar to anyone who has suffered through an undergraduate lecture – were hardly meant to encourage lingering. When it arrived in Canada, McDonald's had no seats at all.[14]

Serving the car took many forms. At industry-leading A&W and numerous independent operations, carloads of customers were served by "carhops," usually young women, who brought orders out to cars. Labour costs were a chronic problem, so many operators experimented with electronic ordering in the hope that, by reducing the number of trips to the car, they could cut back on staff.[15] Up-and-coming chains like Red Barn and McDonald's simply dispensed with carhops, building self-serve outlets where customers had to park, order at a walk-up window, and return to their cars with food in hand. A few places, such as Royal Burger in Ottawa and the independent Frontier Drive-In in St. Catharines, used an early version of drive-thru service, although this seems to have been relatively rare until the late 1970s.[16]

With outlets designed to serve automobiles, it should come as no surprise that many observers saw fast food as a symptom of a faster society, where everybody was rushed, on the move, and less rooted in local communities.

McDonald's first Canadian outlet, opened June 1967, Richmond, British Columbia. At this point, the standard McDonald's outlet had no indoor seats. Customers typically ate in the car or took their food home. Six garbage cans are visible in the photo. McDonald's and other fast food outlets had to constantly battle blowing garbage.
City of Richmond Archives, 1987 61 3

"The phenomenal growth of fast food outlets in our fast-paced society is no surprise," a suburban reporter commented in 1971. "Ever-hungry teenagers want a fast snack. Families dashing off somewhere want to eat in a hurry."[17] Of course, every generation since the railway had lamented the acceleration of daily life,[18] but in the postwar period more and more families were dashing off somewhere in automobiles. Motor vehicle registrations in Canada more than doubled between 1945 and 1952, and they doubled again by 1964, far outpacing population growth in this period.[19] Car ownership continued to vary widely by region, type of municipality, and income, but it penetrated more deeply into the population across the country with each passing year. By the time McDonald's arrived in Canada, all but two provinces averaged one car per household.[20] Canadians did not simply integrate the car into their daily lives – they used it to transform them, adjusting family economies, rethinking housing possibilities, and reimagining the scope of mobility. These impulses reinforced, and were reinforced by, a whole constellation of government policies, pursued without much explicit coordination at every level of government, which smoothed the way for the automobile by widening roads, building bridges and superhighways, uprooting existing neighbourhoods, and even inventing new trade regimes.[21]

Yet cars had been transforming Canadian life since before the war, and road-side commerce had a longer history as well.

The Fast Food Gaze

"This is a country on the move," *Restaurants and Institutions* commented in 1956, "and because of this, road-side services have increased not only in number but, like the automobile, in sleekness and comfort. Motels, restaurants, service stations hedge our busy main roads, jostling for business and the favours of passers-by."[22] If carloads of hungry Canadians were on the move by 1956, this was because fast food chains had come to Canada at the end of a long evolution in roadside foodservice. Until about 1960 the restaurants "jostling for the favours of passers-by" remained ad hoc, local, and largely individual in organization. As car ownership increased in the early decades of the century (tripling between the end of the First World War and the beginning of the Depression), "auto gypsies" initially stopped at the roadside to eat, sleep, camp, and picnic.[23] Other travellers stopped at established restaurants with central locations in cities and towns since main highways still passed through downtown commercial sections. Any traveller approaching London, Ontario, on Highway 2 would have to slow down long enough to drive the length of the city's main street before proceeding on to Windsor or Toronto. Downtown restaurants, then, drew some passing tourists in addition to their core market, the "hundreds of businessmen and girls, bank clerks and others, whose time for eating is limited and who appreciate good food, served well in attractive surroundings."[24]

In between well-established communities, entrepreneurs soon responded to the growing network of drivers with ad hoc and haphazard efforts to capture the passers-by. Some gas station owners broadened their business into basic foodservice, either by offering simple meals in a cramped corner of their existing facility or by expanding the lot to accommodate a specialized eating area. "Auto courts" – a business offering camping space and occasionally cabin accommodation for automobile tourists – dotted the approaches to many cities and sometimes added restaurants to their offerings.[25] The most direct forerunners of fast food were individual entrepreneurs who set up roadside foodservice between the wars in hopes of grabbing the passing-by trade, often just on the edge of cities and towns. Buildings and menus were usually simple, and business was often seasonal since traffic dropped considerably in the winter.[26] In 1920 Nat Bailey set up a mobile food stand on South West Marine Drive outside of Vancouver, selling hot dogs and ice cream to passing motorists on Sundays. A decade later, he built a more permanent structure just outside the Vancouver city limits. At the other end of the country, Salter Innes opened a small drive-in outside Halifax in 1930, serving hot dogs and ice cream from a 100-square-foot shack beside a provincial highway. In London, Ontario, Earl Nichols couldn't afford a downtown location but soon discovered that his lot on Wharncliffe Road was perfectly located to capture a new market: tourists and local motorists who would drive a few extra blocks to take advantage of "curb service," where the car could be pulled up to the front of the restaurant, food could be ordered right from the driver's seat, and the meal could be delivered by a carhop in short order. The transient market soon formed the bulk of Nichols' business. By the late 1940s only 5 percent of Nichols' quarter-million annual customers arrived from the local neighbourhood.[27]

Over time, such fringe eateries became staples of the "approach strip," where numerous automobile-oriented businesses served drivers on the way in and out of town.[28] But despite complaints about the quality and reliability of these roadside eateries – concerns that would later be crystallized into the evocative term "food-easy" by industry observers[29] – the business of serving the car was the territory of local businesses rather than extensive chain restaurants until well into the postwar period. Efforts by chains to establish themselves at roadsides were few and largely unsuccessful. In 1929 a company called English Inns announced ambitious plans to build a chain of ten outlets along main tourist routes on both sides of the New York-Ontario border, combining motel accommodation, a fine dining room, and a quick-service lunch counter. The effort was unsuccessful, and the company was bankrupt by 1931.[30] Meanwhile, existing restaurant chains – outfits like Honey Dew, Muirhead's, and Murray's that had outlets in several cities across the country – stuck to their traditional eating-out market in downtown commercial and office areas, leaving the fringes to small entrepreneurs.[31]

The first phase of establishing chains at roadside saw a few entrepreneurs extend the drive-in philosophy of fringe locations and mobile customers after the war. Prewar drive-in operators often expanded their businesses but almost never tried to grow beyond their original, individual outlet. Nichols, for example, had diversified his menu and expanded the restaurant five times by 1947, increasing capacity from 24 to 103 seats to supplement his quick-lunch counter service, and he had paved a twenty-car parking lot at the side of the building. After his original outlet burned down in 1938, Innes added a dance hall, a dining room, and other attractions to his Sunnyside drive-in, which soon became a popular leisure spot for wartime youth. By 1950 business was good enough that the outlet's new owners began to open all year. But neither Nichols nor Innes grew beyond his original outlet.[32]

After the war, however, a few entrepreneurs built small chains that spanned local markets: Frank and Leo Fortin opened four Hi-Ho Drive-Ins (the first in 1938) around Windsor, Ontario, while Nat Bailey slowly expanded his White Spot drive-in empire in Greater Vancouver, jumping the water to set up in Victoria in 1961 and growing to eleven outlets by the late 1960s.

These local chains illustrated both a new phase and the relative backward-
ness of the Canadian drive-in industry. Although larger than single outlet
operations like Three Little Pigs, these chains paled beside the most progressive American companies like Howard Johnson's, Dairy Queen, and A&W,
which already had dozens of outlets throughout the United States by the
mid-1950s.[33]

While journalists were often impressed by the assembly-line production
of chains like McDonald's, what distinguished Canadian drive-ins from the
larger American chains was not just the efficiency of their operations but
also the scope of their imagination. In fact, drive-in entrepreneurs like the
Fortins took operations seriously, laying out efficient, streamlined procedures, attending restaurant conventions to learn about the latest innovations, and so on. White Spot restaurants under Nat Bailey sold so many
chickens that the company integrated back into chicken farming. In St.
Catharines, Ralph Markarian of the Linehaven Drive-In decided that the
best way to improve his operation was to learn from the most efficient assembly line in town, so he hired a General Motors engineer to streamline
his tiny hamburger stand.[34] But however much they modernized, integrated,
and improved their operations, hardly any of even the most sophisticated
Canadian operators spread beyond the confines of a single metropolitan
area before the late 1950s. As late as January 1959, then, the *Financial Post*
could reasonably observe that "the standard menu, standard service type of
roadside spot of the U.S. has no counterpart here."[35]

No one would have dared to make such a claim a half-decade later. "'Booming' aptly describes what the chain-operated drive-in business is doing in
Canada these days," *Restaurants and Institutions* reported in 1964, "and from
all reports there are no signs of this upsurge diminishing."[36] While a few
drive-in chains – A&W, Dairy Queen, and Tastee Freez, for example – had
been trickling into Canadian foodservice in the second half of the 1950s,
the pace of chain development increased considerably in 1959 (see Table
7.2). Surveying the drive-in scene in the mid-1950s, trade magazines profiled local operators like Barney Strassburger in Kitchener, Ralph Markarian
in St. Catharines, and Joe Young in Saskatoon. In the following decade,
even before McDonald's arrived, stories on such local innovators gave way
to coverage of early chains like Red Barn, A&W, Mister Donut, and Kentucky Fried Chicken – companies that reached out beyond a single city almost as soon as they began Canadian operations. From its Winnipeg
headquarters, A&W of Canada grew from its first outlet in 1956 to forty
outlets, stretching from Victoria to Montreal, four years later. By 1966 Red
Barn Hamburgers of Canada was only three years old but already had outlets across southern Ontario, with a branch operation in Alberta and plans
to expand to the Maritimes.[37]

Table 7.2

Fast food/drive-in chains established in Canada, 1955-65

Chain	Year	Product	First Canadian outlet
Dairy Queen	1955	Ice cream	Niagara Falls, ON
A&W	1956	Root beer/ fast food	Winnipeg, MB
Tastee Freez	1958	Ice cream	n/a
Kentucky Fried Chicken	1959	Fried chicken	Saskatoon, SK
Dog 'N Suds	1959	Root beer/ hot dogs	Saskatoon, SK
Chicken Delight	1959	Chicken	Winnipeg, MB
Johnny Johnson's	1959	Hamburgers	Scarborough, ON
Harvey's	1959	Hamburgers	Richmond Hill, ON
Royal Burger	1959	Hamburgers	Ottawa, ON
Burger Chef	1961	Hamburgers	Ontario
Henry's	1961	Hamburgers	Ontario
Frostop	1961	Root beer/ fast food	Manitoba
Dunkin' Donuts	1961	Donuts	Montreal, QC
Mister Donut	1962	Donuts	North York, ON
Tim Hortons Drive-In	1962	Hamburgers	Scarborough, ON
Tim Hortons Donuts	1963	Donuts	Scarborough, ON
Aunt Jemima Kitchens	1962	Pancakes	Scarborough, ON
Red Barn Systems	1963	Hamburgers	Scarborough, ON
Country Style Donuts	1963	Donuts	Toronto, ON
Dairy Belle	1964	Ice cream	n/a

Note: "Chain" refers to a business that grew to multiple outlets beyond a single metropolitan market. Canadian chains are in italics.
Sources: Canadian Hotel and Restaurant, Restaurants and Institutions, Financial Post.

Fast food arrived in Canada along the same paths as most other twentieth-century economic developments, migrating north of the border as branch plants or Canadian-owned versions of American mass-production outlets. Of the fourteen companies that controlled two-thirds of chain outlets in Canada by 1970, twelve came from the United States.[38] The most direct route, and probably the most numerous, saw a small Canadian entrepreneur buy an individual franchise from an existing American operation (or its Canadian subsidiary). A second approach was for Canadian entrepreneurs to purchase a territorial franchise from an established American company and then sell outlets to smaller operators in specific areas or simply operate the outlets themselves. Territories could vary in size from a specific city to the whole country. George Hansen of Kentville, Nova Scotia, already owned two independent roadside ice cream stands when he purchased the Maritimes franchise for Tastee Freez in 1957. He subsequently converted his existing outlets to the chain logo and had added four new locations by 1960. Harold Shneer had even bigger aspirations. Shneer spent a year researching US franchise opportunities before he purchased the Canadian rights to Red Barn Systems of Springfield, Ohio. In July 1963 he opened his first hamburger outlet in Scarborough, Ontario, and then sold other franchises to smaller operators like Frank Vetere, a former corporate executive who had yearned to go out on his own. For the Canadian rights to the hamburger chain, Shneer paid an up-front fee and promised to forward a percentage of his annual sales to Red Barn's American headquarters. When McDonald's finally came north in 1967, Ray Kroc created two Canadian master franchises, one outside of Ontario under George Tidball and one for Ontario under George Cohon. Eventually, Kroc bought the rights back from both entrepreneurs and created a single Canadian subsidiary under Cohon.[39]

These extensions of US firms were supplemented by a handful of Canadian operations. Yet many of these "home-grown" companies showed conspicuous American influence. Harvey's president George Sukornyk was a big player in the fast food game by Canadian standards. The hamburger chain started in 1959 and grew impressively (from twenty-five outlets in Ontario and Quebec in 1966 to forty-eight in 1968 and seventy-six by 1970). But Sukornyk was not an innovator, having taken over Harvey's after two years of "intensive research" of US hamburger chains.[40] In donuts, Tim Hortons began after company founder Jim Charade toured Mister Donut's Boston headquarters and decided that, based on his experience running a donut plant for Vachon Foods and his observations of the American operation, he could start his own chain instead. Returning to Toronto, Charade opened his first donut shop, called Your Donuts, on Lawrence Avenue East in Scarborough in 1963. The following year, he and partner Tim Horton opened their first franchised outlet on Ottawa Street in Hamilton.[41]

American chains made a few adjustments to the Canadian market, but only a few. McDonald's bowed to Canadian tastes by adding vinegar to french fry condiments. Other adjustments were not so simple. Red Barn's initial plans to simply import American procedures had to be rethought, particularly for choosing locations. Compared to the United States, Canada was a poorer country whose large centres of population were scattered thinly and separated by hundreds of miles, requiring more careful local-market studies. The company also discovered that Canadians were more "conservative" hamburger eaters, particularly concerning the distance they were willing to drive, so the estimated market area of an outlet was shrunk from four miles in the US to two miles in Canada.[42] These wrinkles should be weighed against claims about similarity and homogeneity. Some fast food capitalists suggested that regional boundaries *within* each country were harder to cross than the 49th parallel. "I can go into Alabama and feel more out of place than I do in Canada," noted Mister Donut's David Slater, whose chain was concentrated in the north-east United States and southern Ontario.[43] McDonald's discovered that local wrinkles often disappeared over time. "Every region seems to have its own preference for a particular condiment or flavor," commented McDonald's Alberta supervisor, Jared Kaufman, "but people everywhere soon come to prefer our way. It doesn't take long for the number of special grilling orders to level off and then decline."[44]

Kaufman may have been right, but in Canada "people everywhere" still did not have access to a McDonald's. Up to about 1975 the reach of McDonald's in Canada was somewhat limited, and McDonald's ultimate victory in the fast food war was hardly clear. In Canada the company got off to a late start and was actually losing money on its forty-three outlets when the chain consolidated Canadian operations under George Cohon in 1971. Only with increased capital from the American parent and a dramatic cut in prices (itself a risky attempt to attract Canadian consumers) did the seeds of McDonald's hegemony become clear: high per-outlet revenues, rapid growth (McDonald's of Canada gained quickly on existing leaders like A&W and Kentucky Fried Chicken), and increasingly sophisticated marketing (it was already using television to advertise to children, and its Canadian advertising budget would be $2 million by 1973).[45] South of the border, the chain was facing stiff challenges from companies like Burger Chef and Burger King, both backed by deep-pocketed food conglomerates. Indeed, corporate buyouts seemed the wave of the future as the capital requirements in fast food went up and existing food companies moved to establish a presence in the burgeoning fast food sector. Pilsbury took over Burger King, General Foods purchased Burger Chef, Servomation (a vending machine company) bought out Red Barn, and International Multifoods acquired Mister Donut. The list goes on, with echoes in Canada. General Foods bought White Spot, and Cara Foods entered the fast food market with Zumburger, its own creation. In the end, conglomeration was not the wave of the future – chains like Zumburger were largely unsuccessful, and the companies that stayed independent typically did the best – but this was not clear until later.[46]

In the early 1970s, moreover, the standardizing power of fast food remained partial since chains still grew on a regional basis, reflecting a combination of historical trajectories of companies and regional differences in disposable incomes and population patterns (see Table 7.3). American chains often found an initial base in the hometown of the Canadian entrepreneur who brought them north – Saskatoon, for example, for Dog 'N Suds and Toronto for Red Barn. And because they tended to cluster outlets, only a few companies reached out beyond their original regional base. In 1964 Red Barn opened outlets in Calgary through a partnership with a group of local entrepreneurs who claimed that they would "saturate the West with outlets," but the few western outlets that actually opened did not survive the

Table 7.3

Regional distribution of selected fast food chains in Canada, 1970

Chain	BC	Prairie provinces	ON	QC	Atlantic provinces	Total
Kentucky Fried Chicken	25	72	147	30	31	305
A&W	45	77	76	27	12	237
Dairy Queen (eastern Canada)[a]	–	–	132	77	22	231
Dairy Queen (western Canada)[a]	46	47	–	–	–	93
Harvey's Hamburgers	–	1	40	33	2	76
Red Barn Hamburgers	–	–	41	–	–	41
Dog 'N Suds[b]	12	17	1	–	5	35
McDonald's (two companies)[c]	12	7	10	–	–	29
Mister Donut	–	1	18	8	–	27
Country Style Donuts	–	–	21	–	–	21
Tim Hortons Donuts	–	–	16	–	–	16

Note: "Chain" refers to a company that opened outlets in more than one metropolitan area. Chains founded in Canada are in italics.
a   At this time, Dairy Queen outlets in Canada werê operated by two separate companies, one covering central and eastern Canada and one covering the Prairies and British Columbia.
b   Franchised units only. An additional eight units were company-owned.
c   In 1970 McDonald's was still split into two companies in Canada.
Source: Canadian Hotel and Restaurant, 15 March 1970, 43-44.

decade.[47] Dog 'N Suds spread as far as Atlantic Canada in its first decade but operated almost half of its outlets in its home province of Saskatchewan. Even companies with national coverage were often decentralized in some way. By 1970 Dairy Queen spanned the nation, but control was divided between a company in eastern Canada (231 outlets) and one in the West (93 outlets). When McDonald's arrived in Canada, then, only a few chains, like Kentucky Fried Chicken (135 outlets in all provinces by 1966) and A&W (158 outlets in 1966) had any real national presence.[48]

Yet the terms "national presence" and "regional basis" obscure as much as they reveal. To fast food companies, Canada was not so much a country as an archipelago of metropolitan and urban areas. Fast food companies normally entered an area by clustering outlets in major metropolitan markets before branching out.[49] When one trade magazine surveyed the largest fast food firms in 1968, most had located the bulk of their outlets in large cities (see Table 7.4). Of course, many companies also reported a number of outlets in smaller cities, but until at least the late 1970s a population of 30,000 seems to have been the key threshold (although it was never absolute). "Too many problems with small-town operations," commented Red Barn's Harold Shneer. "Many of them are marginal, and marginal is a nasty word to us."[50] In places below 30,000 people, the fast food market, when it was exploited at all, was left to limited-menu chains like Dairy Queen (which had very small requirements for population, but these outlets generally served only ice cream and closed in the winter) and to a lesser degree Kentucky Fried Chicken; the remainder of the market went to an assortment of independent operators. The idea of fast food could travel to communities without actual outlets – Canadians might visit a McDonald's or Red Barn while on vacation or hear about one through radio and television commercials – but these demographic targets had important consequences for understanding fast food's influence. While urban and metropolitan populations were gaining consistently in the postwar years, even by 1966, 44 percent of Canadians lived in communities too small to support a typical chain outlet. Leaving aside fast food's actual development, then, almost half of Canadians lived in communities where most fast food companies couldn't even *imagine* opening an outlet. In some areas of the country, particularly in the Maritimes, the figure was much higher, but even in Ontario fully one-third of the population lived well outside fast food's "gaze" (see Table 7.5).[51]

Within this urban archipelago, fast food's impact was further limited. Few outlets, whether chain or independent, located in urban downtowns until the mid-1970s, and on the fringes chains did not yet dominate the visual landscape, even along the busiest thoroughfares. Certainly, more and more chain outlets appeared on commercial strips, particularly in core metropolitan markets in southern Ontario and the Lower Mainland of British Columbia, pushing up real estate costs and leading to dire predictions of the end of independent operators.[52] This development was more often predicted than realized, however, as independents copied and borrowed concepts from larger chains or positioned themselves in niches not yet exploited

Table 7.4

Fast food outlets in Canadian cities with over 100,000 people, selected chains, 1968

Chain	Outlets in 100,000+ cities	Total outlets	%
A&W	63	184	34
Baron de Boeuf	22	22	100
Chicken Delight	23	33	70
Dairy Queen (eastern Canada)	77	217	35
Harvey's	44	48	92
Dog 'N Suds	16	32	50
Red Barn	18	20	90
Tastee Freez	6	11	55

Note: In 1966, 47 percent of Canadians lived in cities with over 100,000 people.
Source: Canadian Hotel and Restaurant, 15 May 1968, 47-51.

Table 7.5

The hamburger's gaze: Percentage of population living outside the potential reach of fast food, 1966

Place	%
Prince Edward Island	100
Yukon/Northwest Territories	100
Newfoundland	81
New Brunswick	72
Saskatchewan	71
Nova Scotia	61
Alberta	49
Manitoba	48
British Columbia	47
Quebec	38
Ontario	34
Canada	44

Note: Figures represent the percentage of the population living in communities considered to be too small to support a fast food outlet (30,000 people).
Source: 1966 Census of Canada, *Population—Urban and Rural Distribution* (Ottawa: Dominion Bureau of Statistics, 1968), Table 14.

by large companies. Indeed, on many suburban streets, the number of independent restaurants actually increased during the 1960s and 1970s. Driving along the typical drive-in strip until the 1980s was a lesson in what historians call "combined and uneven development," with many phases of drive-in commerce clustered together, competing for customers: older independents, longstanding local chains, extensive fast food companies, and newer independents all co-existed on the same strip (see Table 7.6).[53]

If fast food was homogenizing the Canadian roadside in the decade and a half after 1960, it was largely the result of many different companies and operators pursuing their own regional, local, and independent paths of development. Yet they all shared the basic vision of selling by the carload – the larger companies by defining precise rules about traffic volume and visibility, independents by the more commonsensical approach of opening on a busy strip. Whatever the precise strategy, however, a successful drive-in needed more than a big parking lot. As McDonald's stressed when it arrived in Richmond, the population around the outlet was as important as the number of cars going by. This reflected a broader truth in drive-in culture: businesses positioned themselves to catch transient consumers whose movements had been stretched out by the car, but everyone remained dependent on customers who were close to home. Based on a survey of marketing studies, the *Financial Post* claimed that "even along heavily traveled routes, sales to through-travelers make up a much smaller portion of a community's total business activity than was formerly supposed. Even gasoline

Table 7.6

Independent vs. chain restaurants

Location	Year	Independent	Chain	Total	% Chain
Kingsway, Vancouver[a]	1954	9	0	9	0
	1970	11	9	20	45
	1980	15	10	25	40
8th Ave. East, Saskatoon[b]	1950	1	0	1	0
	1960	6	3	9	33
	1974	12	3	15	20
	1989	23	11	34	32
Lundy's Lane, Niagara Falls[c]	1956	4	1	5	20
	1964	6	2	8	25
	1972	9	4	13	30
	1975	13	5	18	28
	1982	16	12	28	57

a From Willingdon Ave. in Burnaby to 10th Ave. in New Westminster.
b From Cairns Ave. to city limits.
c From Queen Elizabeth Way to Main Street.
Notes: Dates chosen partly reflect availability of city directories at the Toronto Reference Library. % chain = restaurants as percentage of total restaurants on strip.
Source: City directories, Toronto Reference Library.

stations, restaurants, and drive-in snack bars were found to be catering, to a large extent, to nearby residents."[54] As different operators fanned out across cities and regions in search of "solid, substantial family communities," they made the fate of fast food into a social question.

"Why Don't You Just Close Earlier?"

Fast food companies trickled north of the border at exactly the time that many Canadians were filling their hungry stomachs with restaurant meals. Precise figures were not collected comprehensively and consistently, but evidence suggests a trend toward more eating-out from the late 1950s through the 1970s, at least among urban middle classes in more affluent regions. The trend was dramatic enough that in the late 1970s Statistics Canada revised the Consumer Price Index to weight eating-out more heavily in its calculations. Industry observers responded with excitement, although Canadian eating-out never reached the lofty heights predicted by hopeful comparisons to the American market.[55] Like the rise in car ownership, this (uneven) trend of eating-out was nurtured by broader social developments. A key market for quick-service restaurants was the increasing number of families where the mother worked for wages. Increasingly, families were visiting restaurants or eating "take-out" meals, often in front of the television, as an alternative to mother's cooking. Long before feminists broke

into the mainstream with their critique of the double workday, restaura-
teurs had realized that mothers (whether "working" or not) wanted nights
off from cooking and appealed to their families with slogans like, in the
case of one Toronto drive-in, "Give Ma a Treat! Save Her Cooking a Meal
This Week-End."[56]

Of course, replacing maternal labour power with restaurant meals was easier
than ever for many Canadians since they had more money in their pockets
to spend. Real incomes almost doubled in the thirty years after the Second
World War. As usual, prosperity varied by class, gender, ethnicity, region,
and other factors, but the booming economy lifted thousands of Canadians
into the ranks of the mass consumer market, comprised of the section of the
populace, from skilled workers to white-collar professionals, that was "neither very rich nor poor," owned cars and houses, shopped at supermarkets
and plazas, and lived in nuclear families.[57] Fast food companies worked hard
to attract this middle market. "We look for churches and station wagons,"
declared McDonald's, a rule of thumb meant to symbolize the chain's commitment to solid, stable, middle-income communities. Other companies
described the same market in different ways. "In looking for lots," L.H.
Raymes, CEO of Dairy Queen Canada, commented, "we prefer a working or
middle class neighborhood. Even if we could get a permit I don't think we'd
set up a Dairy Queen in Forest Hill." For his part, Gordon Daly of P.K. Fish
and Chips added ethnicity and regional difference to this basic vision: "There
must be at least 12,000 people within [a] one-mile radius of the store; at least
50% of them must be of Anglo-Saxon background and so used to eating fish
and chips; the head of the average household must earn at least $7,500 a
year (this will be lowered for areas like the Maritimes); and the majority of
parents must be under 40 and so more likely to eat out with their young
families." Most often, however, differences of taste and background were
subordinated to income, housing choice, and family arrangement. Harold
Shneer revealed Red Barn's formula for success in similar detail, describing
an almost perfect demographic representation of the postwar middle class:
seek neighbourhoods of families with children aged six to eighteen living in
single-family homes valued at $15,000-$25,000 and with net household incomes of $4,000-$10,000 per year.[58] Of course, in the suburbs of the 1960s
few families earning $4,000 lived beside those earning $10,000, but with
market areas of two to four miles, built around highly mobile, auto-bound
customers, fast food companies sewed this broad middle market together.[59]

Yet middle-class families constantly complained about drive-ins. Aside
from noise, traffic, and garbage, residents worried that outlets would become magnets for youth. From the 1950s through the 1970s the complaints
remained the same, even if the language changed. Anger over "hoodlums,"
"gangs," and "hot-rodders" in the 1950s and early 1960s linked to adult
fears of juvenile delinquency.[60] "The scream of tires and drag racing make it

nearly impossible ... to sleep," one suburban couple wrote. "We have seen gangs with baseball bats and crowbars getting ready for a fight."[61] By the late 1960s these concerns intersected with more updated symbols of the generation gap, especially drugs and long hair. Although less known than the stereotypical image of hippie haunts along downtown streets in Yorkville and Kitsilano, the long-haired invasion of suburban shopping plazas and fast food joints seemed in full swing by 1968. Bad behaviour and long hair became virtually indistinguishable in the suburban imagination. "All the adults around here," complained one teen in Scarborough, Ontario, "if you don't have short hair, they think you're nothing but a plaza bum."[62] Three years later Edmonton's city solicitor complained of the "substantial percentage of hippy, yippy and yappy customers" who gathered on weekend evenings at a Jasper Avenue drive-in restaurant.[63]

Whatever the era, the parking lot was the common flashpoint. In trying to sell to the carload, fast food chains built enormous parking lots that became spaces in their own right, facilitating all kinds of alternative activities.[64] In 1966 residents neighbouring a Harvey's hamburger restaurant in Scarborough protested parking lot pastimes like "basketball games using tin cans for a ball and trashcans for a basket." Another suburban newspaper lamented that parking lots had become replacements for parks. "A group of eight boys were tossing a Frisbee around the parking lot of Tim Horton's donut shop until the cops came to break it up ... What Oakville needs is some kids space ... Just unstructured, open space to gather."[65] In other cases, complaints were more dramatic. Parking-lot fights between "gangs" of teenagers at three Winnipeg drive-ins led to the end of all-night service. In North York, Councillor Paul Godfrey's personal campaign against "booze and sex" at drive-in restaurants led to almost one hundred letters of support from local residents.[66]

Neighbourhood complaints raised troubling questions of marketing for fast food operators. In many ways, problems with youthful misbehaviour expressed the internal contradictions of selling by the carload, a lethal combination of large parking lots, cheap food, and baby boomer kids growing into self-directed and disrespectful youth. Large parking lots, while permitting fast food chains to sell by the roadside, also allowed young people to congregate; families with two or three kids were soon matched by gangs of rowdy youth. And middle-income communities meant that young people had enough disposable income that they couldn't just be ignored. Suburban hot-rodders and hippies were attracted to drive-ins for the same reason as their parents: the food was cheap, the service fast, the parking ample. It didn't hurt that automobiles provided semiprivate spaces for all kinds of illicit activities, although cars were never free of surveillance. When Vancouver police began to check drive-in patrons for alcohol bottles and flasks, youth reportedly hid liquor in their cars, pouring small amounts into two-ounce airline bottles to carry around the parking lot. As they turned to new inebriates later in the decade, the car served a similar purpose. "A check of a car in the parking lot of a drive-in restaurant on Lakeshore Road early this morning resulted in the arrest of a 22-year-old man on a charge of possession of narcotics," Oakville's *Daily Journal Record* reported in 1970.[67]

The constant claims of McDonald's and other companies that they ran clean, family establishments need to be understood in light of these problems. Yet to be effective, the business model of fast food had to include a range of subtle and explicit mechanisms of social control. At McDonald's, Ray Kroc banned jukeboxes, telephone booths, cigarette machines, and female employees, figuring that the combination would attract teenage boys and encourage hanging out. "We don't want music screaming out attracting kids just out for kicks," he commented during his first trip to the Richmond outlet.[68] Fast food owners also published detailed codes of conduct and occasionally hired off-duty police officers to enforce them. Others bragged about their own masculine prowess (one independent operator in Richmond claimed to be a former professional wrestler to scare rowdy youth, and a North York donut shop owner claimed to be a semiprofessional boxer), while some simply resorted to blanket bans. In 1969 several Halifax-area restaurants refused to serve long-haired patrons; a year later Tim Horton arrived at his Oakville, Ontario, outlet to announce a new policy: "no hippies." Suburban hippies responded to these kinds of actions by asserting their civil rights, using broader political ideas to claim access to consumer spaces. In the case of hippies, however, this rhetorical strategy faced real institutional limits: Nova Scotia's government, for example, claimed that it could do nothing about the bans since "appearance" was not listed in the Human Rights Act.[69] Whatever its legal status, rights-based language continued to be powerful: in Oakville, one youth writer reminded Horton that in "the early 1960s many restaurants in the southern states had similar policies dealing with black people."[70]

Solving the youth problem was rarely as simple as banning shaggy patrons. Young people, especially in the suburbs, were a lucrative market of their own, with abundant leisure time and (at least in the minds of marketers) considerable amounts of discretionary income, which they were more than willing to spend on fast food. Reflecting on the changing dynamics of eating-out in 1969, the president of the Canadian Restaurant Association pointed to a troubling fact for drive-in operators who were anxious to reach the family market: fourteen to twenty-two year olds had a taste for hot dogs and hamburgers and the money to buy them.[71] Since neighbourhood anger didn't always distinguish between violence, immorality, and more innocent horseplay, keeping neighbours happy might mean driving good customers away. Forgoing a share of the youth market was easier for a chain like McDonald's, which had high per-outlet revenues, but many smaller operations had no such luxury.[72]

If the combination of economic power and rowdy behaviour caused marketing problems for operators, youthful misbehaviour raised more troubling regulatory questions for neighbourhoods and municipalities. In 1970 Oakville experienced a minor moral panic near a Country Style donut shop, including dramatic claims of "sexual intercourse on lawns" and "urinating on sidewalks." Since the parking lot itself was private property, the town responded by passing an antiloitering bylaw that applied to nearby sidewalks and streets, hoping to empower local police to contain the immoral behaviour. The bylaw became the source of not inconsiderable ridicule and concern among civil libertarians, not the least because its wording – which banned occupying sidewalks and streets outside private businesses – appeared to outlaw picketing.[73]

The law may have been an overreaction, but the problem was real. By all appearances, drive-in parking lots were public spaces, but in law they were private property, over which operators had absolute control. If an owner was unwilling or unable to control youth on the lot, municipalities had little recourse. Some threatened to revoke licences, but no one seemed sure about whether they were empowered to do so. Scarborough police noted that regular patrols of area drive-ins helped to contain problems, but the costs were exorbitant and not really justified for a small number of private businesses. Moreover, a constant surveillance was unrealistic: officers might pass by to tell kids to quiet down or move along, but problems usually resurfaced once police drove on, if they arrived on time at all. "Last night, a bunch of hot-rodders were tearing around Tim Horton's donut shop for most of the evening," the *Daily Journal Record* complained in 1971. "Finally the police arrived. But all was quiet."[74]

Moreover, some of the simplest ways to control youthful misbehaviour – like closing early – caused other problems. As Edmonton's legal department noted, noise levels that might not be noticed during the day became "objectionable" at night,[75] so city officials across the country pressed outlets to close early. Conflict was almost automatic – operators wanted to stay open late, while neighbourhoods wanted them to close early – and municipal councils had to balance competing claims within the limits of their legal powers. In Richmond town officials issued the new McDonald's a licence only when the company agreed to close at 11:00 p.m., but many operators objected to similar procedures elsewhere, and even Richmond's reeve admitted that the town couldn't block the outlet.[76] In the longer term, municipalities could alter zoning regulations, but once permits were granted and the outlet was open, councils could only threaten and cajole. "We ... don't know the answer to this one," complained Vancouver's licence inspector in

1963. "I can not see any charges we can lay ... it is just a bunch of wild, exuberant kids making a racket."[77]

These institutional limits reflected a broader ideological problem. Michael Dawson points out that debates about closing times were as much about politics as consumption, playing on notions of democracy and freedom.[78] In a similar way, clashes over fast food outlets – both their use as consumer spaces and their hours of operation – expressed the longstanding tensions of liberal capitalism. Municipal councils struggled to balance claims about the community interest against the liberties accorded to private property and wondered how they might reconcile the "rights" of citizens to peace and quiet with those of businesses and consumers to legitimate market activity. Not surprisingly, then, the debate often turned on the question of legitimacy. While disgruntled neighbours and their sympathetic councillors pointed to any and all evidence of "promiscuity," fast food operators (and their sympathetic councillors) emphasized their family market, accused politicians of exploiting complaints for electoral advantage, and claimed to serve customers with genuine night-time needs. "Why don't you just close earlier?" one Scarborough councillor asked George Sukornyk of Harvey's before advocating a provincial law to make early closings mandatory. "I guess we want to make money," Sukornyk replied, noting that the late opening was for the benefit of shift workers, cabbies, and truckers, but "unfortunately we've attracted a lot of adult delinquents and children who should be in bed."[79]

A Drive-Thru Nation

Canadian fast food entered a new phase of development sometime around 1975. McDonald's climbed to the top of the Canadian fast food sector in late 1974, when it passed perennial leader A&W in annual revenues, signalling the final triumph of self-serve over carhops (even A&W began to close its older outlets and retreated to shopping-mall food courts).[80] About the same time, fast food menus began to expand. McDonald's introduced its breakfast menu in 1976, followed by a series of additions from McNuggets to salads, while other chains struggled to catch up.[81] Fast food chains also transcended their original boundaries after 1975, growing beyond their suburban locations to enter downtown neighbourhoods, smaller towns, hospitals, zoos, subway stations, and universities. If these innovations pulled fast food toward pedestrians, other changes plunged it deeper into car culture – particularly drive-thru windows (pioneered in Canada by Wendy's in 1975) and outlets in highway service centres – altering the balance between roadside location and the social dynamics of selling by the carload.[82]

If these developments produced the familiar fast food landscape that we know today, they also set it apart from the earlier phase of development, highlighting some important lessons for understanding the history of Canada's consumer society. Selling by the carload combined several key dynamics in postwar Canada: affluence, American economic and cultural influence, creeping homogenization, the mythic reach of the new middle class, the cultural hegemony of the nuclear family, the triumph of the automobile, and generational conflicts over legitimate forms of leisure. The early years of Canadian fast food, however, signalled both the limits and potential of postwar consumption. While many of these dynamics spread across the country, the early history of fast food was not really a "national" story, except insofar as fringe populations in metropolitan and urban centres shared some broad economic and social developments.

These limits and potentials, moreover, raise questions beyond those occasioned by the making and marketing of particular commodities. For the residents of Bennett Road, just as for George Tidball, there was no neat division between social, business, and political history: fast food operators spent as much time managing the social dynamics of suburban consumption as they did figuring out how to produce hamburgers; suburban residents responded ambivalently to the business developments that were transforming their communities; and municipal politicians struggled within real institutional limits to reconcile the conflicting impulses of liberal capitalism. Everyone had to confront the basic fact that suburban hot-rodders and hippies were attracted to drive-ins for the same reason as their parents: cheap food, informal surroundings, and lots of parking. Selling, and living, by the carload was a complicated proposition.

Notes

1 Tidball related this story retrospectively in *BC Business,* March 1993, 33. See also *Vancouver Province,* 3 October 1968, 20, and 4 December 1968, 25. For background on the early development of McDonald's in Canada, see John Love, *McDonald's: Behind the Arches* (New York: Bantam Books, 1995), 419-22; Ray Kroc, *Grinding It Out: The Making of McDonald's* (New York: Contemporary Books, 1977), 161.

2 Quotation from Richmond Planning Department, *The Brighouse Core Area,* March 1976, 9. On No. 3 Road and the Brighouse commercial area, see also City of Richmond Archives, Town Planning Series, file 3613, Richmond Planning Department, *Brighouse Commercial and Parking Study,* 1964; City of Richmond Archives, Richmond Planning Department, *Commercial Land Use Study,* November 1972; City of Richmond Archives, Richmond Collection, GP345, Richmond Planning Department, *Brighouse Commercial Core Area Parking Study,* October 1978.

3 *Richmond Review,* 28 June 1967, 10. Richmond's population more than doubled between 1956 and 1966 (25,000 to 52,000). Children aged one to fourteen and adults aged twenty-five to forty-four (broadly speaking, baby boomers and their parents) were overrepresented in the local population. Two-thirds of Richmond's population fell into these categories, compared to about 55 percent for both greater Vancouver and all of British Columbia. The area also had an above average number of single detached houses that were owned by their occupants. See Dominion Bureau of Statistics (DBS), *Census, Population Census Tracts,* Catalogue 92-615, App. B; DBS, *Census, Households and Families,* 1966, Catalogue 93-602, 93-610;

DBS, *Census, Population – Age Groups,* Catalogue 92-610, Table 22; DBS, *Census, 1966, House-holds and Families – Dwellings by Structural Type and Tenure,* Catalogue 93-602.

4   *Richmond Review,* 18 January 1967, 1. For more detail on town discussions of the outlet, see Town of Richmond, *Council Minutes,* 1966, 1542, 1562, 1557; ibid., 1967, 4, 25; and *Richmond Review,* 21 December 1966, 1.

5   *Canadian Business,* May 1978, 34.

6   *Mississauga News,* 22 May 1982, 7.

7   On McDonald's as an agent and symbol of globalization (and broader trends in popular culture), see George Ritzer, *The McDonaldization of Society,* rev. ed. (Westport, CT: Pine Forge Press, 2004); James Wilson, *Golden Arches East: McDonald's in East Asia,* 2nd ed. (Stanford: Stanford University Press, 2004); Joe Kincheloe, *The Sign of the Burger: McDonald's and the Culture of Power* (Philadelphia: Temple University Press, 2002); Tony Royle, *Working for McDonald's in Europe: The Unequal Struggle* (New York: Routledge, 2000); Maoz Azaryahu, "McIsrael? On the 'Americanization of Israel,'" *Israel Studies* 5, 2 (2000): 41-64; Mark Alfino, ed., *McDonaldization Revisited: Critical Essays on Consumer Culture* (Westport, CT: Praeger, 1998); Paul Ariès, *Les Fils de McDo: La McDonaldisation du monde* (Paris: Harmattan, 1997); and Benjamin Barber, *Jihad vs. McWorld* (New York: Times Books, 1995).

8   *Might's Toronto Directory* (Toronto: Might Directories Ltd., 1935); *Victoria Daily Colonist,* 2 October 1947, 12. According to fast food experts, fish worked best as an add-on product at a hamburger stand (the Filet o' Fish, introduced by McDonald's in 1962 to appeal to Catholic customers on meatless Fridays, being the most famous example) since only one person out of four might appreciate the variety. If fish was the only product on a restaurant's menu, the single fish eater was liable to be overruled by the rest of the group, who would instead choose a restaurant like McDonald's. On attempts to establish chains for fish and chips, see *Foodservice and Hospitality (FSH),* 12 September 1966, 5; *Globe and Mail (GM),* 6 September 1969, B1, and 23 May 1979, 7; *Canadian Hotel and Restaurant (CHR),* 15 March 1970, 27-31; and *Marketing,* 29 January 1973, 25. On the Filet o' Fish, see Love, *Behind the Arches,* 226-29.

9   *Vancouver Province,* 8 July 1964, 8; *Canadian Hotel Review and Restaurant (CHRR),* 15 January 1964, 33.

10   B.A. Ratcliffe, "A Survey of the Drive-In Restaurant Industry in Vancouver with Guidelines for Streamlining an Installation," (B.Comm. essay, University of British Columbia, 1968); James McLamore, *The Burger King: James McLamore and the Building of an Empire* (New York: McGraw Hill, 1997).

11   Ester Reiter, *Making Fast Food: Out of the Frying Pan and into the Fryer* (Montreal and Kingston: McGill-Queen's University Press, 1993). On fast food systems, see *CHRR,* 15 January 1968, 32-33, 15 May 1968, 44-51, 15 June 1969, 26, and 15 March 1971, 16-20; *Canadian Magazine,* 18 April 1970, 4; and *Financial Post (FP),* 12 October 1974, C1, C5.

12   *Richmond Review,* 18 January 1967, 1; *Scarborough Mirror,* 8 February 1967, 1. See also *Bramalea Guardian,* 27 January 1966, 1, and 3 February 1966, 2; *GM,* 25 July 1967, B5; and *FSH,* 29 August 1966, 5, and 21 November 1966, 4.

13   *Winnipeg Free Press,* 30 August 1966, 3.

14   On general issues of drive-in restaurants, see Chester Liebs, *Main Street to Miracle Mile: American Roadside Architecture* (Boston: Little, Brown and Company, 1985); Stan Luxemberg, *Roadside Empires: How the Chains Franchised America* (New York: Viking, 1985); Philip Langdon, *Orange Roofs, Golden Arches* (New York: Knopf, 1986); and John Jakle and Keith Sculle, *Fast Food: Roadside Restaurants in the Automobile Age* (Baltimore: Johns Hopkins University Press, 1999).

15   Customers would order through a microphone and speaker, and a carhop would bring the food to the car. This system had the added advantage of eliminating the use of horns and headlights to page the carhop, practices that annoyed neighbouring residents. The first use of electronic ordering in a carhop drive-in appears to have been at The Dog House in Winnipeg in 1956; see *FP,* 15 September 1956, 31. A&W used this system extensively into the 1970s.

16   In one 1973 Statistics Canada study, only 7.6 percent of franchised foodservice outlets reported offering a "car order pick up wicket," the category closest to what we would now

call a drive-thru window; see Statistics Canada, *Franchising in Canada's Food Service Industry* (Ottawa: Statistics Canada, 1973), Table 4. McDonald's did not open its first drive-thru window (located in Oklahoma City, Oklahoma) until 1975. The chain later adopted the window as a chain-wide strategy. By 1995, 90 percent of McDonald's freestanding units in the United States had drive-thru windows; see Love, *Behind the Arches*, 390-91. Among the large chains, Wendy's Hamburgers pioneered drive-thru lanes in 1970. The idea was a standard part of a Wendy's restaurant by the time the chain arrived in Canada in 1975; see D. Daryl Wyckoff and W. Earl Sasser, *The Chain Restaurant Industry* (Lexington, MA: Lexington Books, 1978), 100. The impact of drive-thrus in Canada is little studied, but see Borough of Etobicoke, *Restaurant Study, 1980*, Borough of Etobicoke Planning Department, 1 April 1980, 37-38 (Etobicoke is a suburb of Toronto).

17 *Oakville Daily Journal Record (DJR)*, 8 May 1971, 8.
18 See David Nye, *American Technological Sublime* (Cambridge, MA: MIT Press, 1994); Wolfgang Schivelbusch, *The Railway Journey: The Industrialization and Perception of Time and Space in the Nineteenth Century* (Leamington Spa, UK: Berg, 1986); and Stephen Kern, *The Culture of Space and Time* (Cambridge: Harvard University Press, 1983).
19 F.H. Leacy, *Historical Statistics of Canada*, 2nd ed. (Ottawa: Statistics Canada, 1983), series T147-194.
20 Newfoundland and Quebec were the exceptional provinces, at 0.72 and 0.98 cars per household respectively in 1966; see DBS, *The Motor Vehicle*, Catalogue 53-203, Table 3. On car ownership in this period, see also Sun Life Assurance Company of Canada, *The Canadian Automotive Industry* (Hull: Royal Commission on Canada's Economic Prospects, 1956), 21, 27; DBS, Prices Division, Consumer Expenditure Surveys Section, *City Family Expenditure, 1957* (Ottawa: Queen's Printer, 1961), 20.
21 On the development of car culture in Canada, and government involvement in it, see Dimitry Anastakis, "Multilateralism, Nationalism, and Bilateral Free Trade: Competing Visions of Canadian Economic and Trade Policy, 1945-70," in this volume; Richard Harris, *Creeping Conformity: How Canada Became Suburban* (Toronto: University of Toronto Press, 2004); G.T. Bloomfield, "No Parking Here to Corner: London Reshaped by the Automobile, 1911-1961," *Urban History Review* 17, 2 (October 1989): 139-58; and Stephen Davies, "Reckless Walking Must Be Discouraged: The Automobile Revolution and the Shaping of Modern Urban Canada," *Urban History Review* 17, 2 (October 1989): 123-38.
22 *Restaurants and Institutions (RI)*, September-October 1956, 23.
23 Leacy, *Historical Statistics of Canada*, 2nd ed.; *Toronto Globe*, 10 August 1920, 6; Warren Belasco, *Americans on the Road: From Auto Camp to Motel, 1910-1945* (Cambridge: MIT Press, 1979).
24 *CHRR*, 15 February 1937, 16-17.
25 *Fountains in Canada*, 15 May 1948, 20; Karen Dubinsky, *The Second Greatest Disappointment: Honeymooning and Tourism at Niagara Falls* (Toronto: Between the Lines, 1999). Motels did not come to Canada in great numbers until the 1940s; see *GM*, 22 September 1953, 7.
26 In some cities, drive-in restaurants continued to close in the winter well into the 1960s. In Saskatoon, for example, it was still common practice to close in the winter until 1965; see *FSH*, 20 December 1965, 3.
27 *Vancouver Sun*, 28 March 1978, 81; *Halifax Chronicle-Herald*, 26 June 1980, 22; *CHRR*, 15 August 1937, 16-17, and 15 November 1947, 26, 28, 72; Leacy, *Historical Statistics of Canada*, 2nd ed.; *Fountains in Canada*, 15 May 1948, 20.
28 Bloomfield, "No Parking Here to Corner"; Liebs, *Main Street*.
29 See, for example, *RI*, July 1959, 48. "Food-easy" was a play on the Prohibition-era term, "speakeasy," which referred to an underground drinking establishment.
30 *Toronto Globe*, 22 April 1929, 10.
31 Murray's Restaurants began as a small sandwich shop on Queen Street East in Toronto in 1924 and had expanded to seventeen outlets in Ontario and Quebec by 1938 and to eighteen outlets by 1955; see *CHRR*, 15 January 1938, 6-8, 16, and 15 February 1955, 7. Honey Dew was a chain of self-service cafeterias (founded in 1926) with thirty-seven outlets across central and western Canada in 1937: three in British Columbia, one in Manitoba, twenty-five in Ontario, and eight in Quebec. There were a few exceptions to this pattern of traditional

restaurants eschewing the drive-in market, but these tended to be local chains like Winnipeg's Salsbury House (founded in 1931), which started as a downtown eatery and branched out to drive-ins after the war. For a short time, Muirhead's owned a drive-in restaurant on the outskirts of Toronto, having purchased McKay's Drive-In in 1946. The outlet was sold in 1950. See *CHRR*, 15 March 1936, 7, 27, 15 December 1946, 58, and 15 March 1950, 64; and Canadian Chain Store Association, "Submission to the Royal Commission on Dominion-Provincial Relations," March 1938, 7.

32 *Halifax Chronicle-Herald*, 26 June 1980, 22; *CHRR*, 15 November 1947, 26, 28, 72.

33 In 1951 Howard Johnson's operated 255 restaurants spread across fifteen states, largely in the northeast of the United States. Dairy Queen grew from 17 locations in 1947 to 800 in 1950 and 2,100 in 1952. See Jakle and Sculle, *Fast Food*.

34 *Fountains in Canada*, 15 January 1959, 8, 10; Ralph Markarian, interviewed by author, St. Catharines, Ontario, 13 August 2001. Of course, many small operations were not so committed to efficiency, especially in practice. "I am inclined to believe," a University of British Columbia student wrote in 1968 after surveying local hamburger drive-ins, "that essentially a primitive process is being used"; see Ratcliffe, "Survey of the Drive-In," 16. It should be noted, however, that Ratcliffe's point of comparison for this conclusion was the "modern" automated hamburger machines (some quite bizarre in conception) that his thesis advocated.

35 *FP*, 31 January 1959, 22.

36 *RI*, September 1964, 11.

37 *Canadian Business*, May 1960, 132; *CHRR*, 15 August 1961, 36-40, 15 May 1964, 42-47, and 15 May 1966, 38-44; *CHR*, 15 May 1968, 44-51, 15 April 1969, 54, 15 March 1970, 43-49, and 15 March 1971, 20-23.

38 *GM*, 6 August 1970, B3.

39 *Canadian Business*, May 1960, 131; *CHRR*, 15 August 1963, 50, and 15 February 1964, 33; *FP*, 21 May 1966, 17, and 22 July 1974, F13; Love, *Behind the Arches*, 419-22.

40 On Harvey's, see *RI*, September 1964, 11; and *FSH*, 23 May 1966, 5, and 20 November 1967, 5.

41 Douglas Hunter, *Open Ice: The Tim Horton Story* (Toronto: Viking, 1994).

42 *GM*, 10 February 1971, B13; *CHRR*, 15 February 1964, 33-35, 50; *RI*, May 1965, 29.

43 *FP*, 8 April 1967, 5.

44 *CHR*, 15 May 1969, 24. In growing into international markets, McDonald's came to believe that playing too much to local tastes was distracting and unsuccessful; see Ian Brailsford, "US Image but NZ Venture: Americana and Fast-Food Advertising in New Zealand, 1971-1990," *Australasian Journal of American Studies* 22, 2 (December 2003): 10-24. The company has, however, introduced local wrinkles and different products in many countries. There is a succinct summary of this tension in Royle, *Working for McDonald's,* 27-30. See also James Watson, ed., *Golden Arches East: McDonald's in East Asia,* 2nd ed. (Stanford, CA: Stanford University Press, 2004).

45 Love, *Behind the Arches*, 419-22; *GM*, 10 February 1971, B13; *FP*, 12 October 1974, C5; *FSH*, October 1974, 17-20; *Marketing*, 16 April 1973, 42. On advertising to children, see Kathleen Toerpe, "Small Fry, Big Spender: McDonald's and the Rise of Children's Consumer Culture, 1955-1985" (PhD thesis, Loyola University of Chicago, 1994).

46 Jakle and Sculle, *Fast Food;* Love, *Behind the Arches;* Michael Bliss, *Northern Enterprise: Five Centuries of Canadian Business* (Toronto: McClelland and Stewart, 1987), 496-97; *Vancouver Province,* 7 September 1967, 20.

47 *CHRR*, 15 December 1964, 50, and 15 September 1964, 59.

48 *CHR*, 15 May 1966, 42.

49 Note that for its early outlets, McCan Franchises leapfrogged from Greater Vancouver to Calgary and Winnipeg; see *CHR*, 15 May 1969, 24. On Canada as an "urban archipelago," see Cole Harris, "Regionalism and the Canadian Archipelago," in L.D. McCann, ed., *Heartland and Hinterland: A Geography of Canada* (Scarborough: Prentice-Hall, 1987), 395-421.

50 *RI*, May 1965, 30.

51 The economic geography of fast food is further complicated by the fact that some of these small communities (those under 30,000 people) were located reasonably close to a larger centre with a fast food outlet.

52 *GM,* 6 August 1970, B3.
53 The classic study of combined and uneven development looked at industry in Britain in the nineteenth century; see Raphael Samuel, "Workshop of the World: Steam Power and Hand Technology in Mid-Victorian Britain," *History Workshop Journal* 3 (Spring 1977): 6-72.
54 *FP,* 24 March 1962, 65. See also Robert O'Dell, "An Analysis of Land Use at Highway 401 Interchanges between Toronto and London" (MA thesis, University of Guelph, 1974), 53-58; F.W. Boal and D.B. Johnson, "The Functions of Retail and Service Establishments on Commercial Ribbons," *Canadian Geographer* 9, 3 (1965): 154-69.
55 Changes in the pattern of eating out are frustratingly elusive, as survey strategies shifted over time (both in terms of who and what was asked), making direct comparisons difficult. Existing statistics do appear to indicate that industry observers were correct in identifying an increase through the 1960s and 1970s. In 1953, for urban families in the middle-income range, 8.7 percent of the weekly total food dollar was spent on eat-out fare (if other Canadians had been factored in, it is likely that the figure would have been lower); see DBS, *Urban Food Expenditure, 1953,* Catalogue 62-511, 11. In 1969, in a survey that included a broader geographic and income spectrum, the average Canadian spent about 17 percent of his or her food dollar away from home; see DBS, *Family Food Expenditure in Canada, 1969,* Catalogue 62-531, Table 2. By 1982 the average Canadian reported spending 25.3 percent of his or her food dollar at restaurants; see DBS, *Family Food Expenditure in Canada, 1986,* Catalogue 62-531, Table 1. Note that food eaten out, food eaten away from home, and food eaten at restaurants are not exactly the same thing, so these figures are offered as suggestive rather than conclusive. At all points, moreover, the figures varied by income, region versus province, urban versus rural, and other factors. On the change in the Consumer Price Index, see *FSH,* February 1979, 8. On Canadian-American comparisons, note that in the late 1970s Americans spent 35 percent of their food dollar eating out, while Canadians still hadn't reached this figure by as late as the early 1990s. Given the regional variations in Canada, however, a North American perspective that made regional comparisons but ignored the 49th parallel might indicate more similarities than differences. For suggestive comments on the more subdued nature of postwar consumption in Canada, see Joy Parr, *Domestic Goods: The Material, the Moral, and the Economic in the Postwar Years* (Toronto: University of Toronto Press, 1999), 64-83.
56 "Give Ma a Treat," Tasty Drive-In advertisement, *Weston Times and Guide,* 23 June 1960, 8. On take-out restaurants, see *CHRR,* 15 September 1955, 23-24; *RI,* July 1959, 28-29, 36; and *FSH,* 16 January 1967, 16.
57 Morgan Reid, quoted in *FP,* 21 February 1953, 32. On the postwar middle class, see Andrew Hurley, *Diners, Bowling Alleys and Trailer Parks: Chasing the American Dream in Postwar Consumer Culture* (New York: Basic Books, 2001); and Lizabeth Cohen, *A Consumers' Republic: The Politics of Mass Consumption in Postwar America* (New York: Vintage, 2003). On the connection between the mass market and family life, see Elaine Tyler May, *Homeward Bound: American Families in the Cold War Era* (New York: Basic Books, 1988), 162-82; and Harvey Levenstein, *Paradox of Plenty: A Social History of Eating in Modern America* (New York: Oxford University Press, 1993), 101-18. On the limits of affluence, see Robert Rutherdale, "Framing Fatherhood in Transition: Domesticity, Consumerism, and Resistance Narratives," paper presented to the annual meeting of the Canadian Historical Association, Quebec City, 2000; Alvin Finkel, *Our Lives: Canada after 1945* (Toronto: Lorimer, 1997), Chapter 1; and Bryan Palmer, *Working-Class Experience: Rethinking the History of Canadian Labour, 1800-1991* (Toronto: McClelland and Stewart, 1992), 305-7.
58 On McDonald's, see John Love, *Behind the Arches,* 164; Raymes quoted in *GM,* 10 April 1969, B5; on PK Fish and Chips, see *CHR,* 15 September 1970, 10; for Red Barn's market, see *CHRR,* 15 February 1964, 34. Note that Forest Hill is an affluent area in the heart of Toronto.
59 S.D. Clark, *The Suburban Society* (Toronto: University of Toronto Press, 1966); Harris, *Creeping Conformity.*
60 See, for example, *Bramalea Guardian,* 27 January 1966, 1, and 3 February 1966, 2; and *North York Mirror,* 10 August 1966, 13. On juvenile delinquency and concerns about teens, see Doug Owram, *Born at the Right Time: A History of the Baby-Boom Generation* (Toronto: University of Toronto Press, 1996), 136-58; Franca Iacovetta, "Parents, Daughters, and Family

Court Intrusions into Working-Class Life," in Franca Iacovetta and Wendy Mitchinson, eds., *On the Case: Explorations in Social History* (Toronto: University of Toronto Press, 1998); and Mary Louise Adams, *The Trouble with Normal* (Toronto: University of Toronto Press, 1997), 39-82.

61 *North York Mirror,* 20 July 1966, 3, quoting a letter to Councillor Paul Godfrey.

62 *Scarborough Mirror,* 28 August 1968, 6. On hippies more generally, see Owram, *Born at the Right Time,* 185-215.

63 *CHRR,* 15 August 1971, 35.

64 At shopping plazas, parking lots were so large that speeding became a problem, and provincial governments soon began to empower municipalities to enforce speed limits. See, for example, Province of Ontario, "An Act to Amend the Municipal Act," 22 June 1965, 27 (4), which empowered municipalities to set speed limits of fifteen miles per hour on privately owned parking lots upon receiving a written request from the owner. On the broader history of parking lots, see John Jakle and Keith Sculle, *Lots of Parking: Land Use in Car Culture* (Charlottesville: University of Virginia Press, 2005).

65 *DJR,* 15 May 1971, 4.

66 *FSH,* 21 November 1966, 4; *North York Mirror,* 20 July 1966, 3.

67 *Vancouver Province,* 25 May 1963, 2; *DJR,* 14 December 1970, 1. Far too little of the growing literature on drug use follows the story into suburban areas. This is unfortunate because smaller community newspapers often provide tantalizing – if sensationalist – clues about the grey economy of drug distribution in suburban schools, drop-in and community centres, and other places.

68 *Richmond Review,* 26 July 1967, 13; *Vancouver Province,* 20 July 1967, 12. During a labour shortage in the United States in 1968, Kroc relented and agreed to hire women; see Love, *Behind the Arches,* 291-93.

69 *Halifax Chronicle-Herald,* 9 July 1969, 9, and 10 July 1969, 20. On the broader import of rights-based language in this period, see Owram, *Born at the Right Time,* 166-67.

70 *Oakville Beaver,* 29 October 1970, A28. The analogy between hippies in the suburbs of Toronto and African Americans in the Jim Crow South is stretched to say the least, but it speaks to both the power of civil rights language in this period and to the link between rights and consumption. Mark Weiner explores the relationship between consumer symbols and civil rights campaigns in his "Consumer Culture and Participatory Democracy: The Story of Coca Cola during World War Two," in Carole Connihan, ed., *Food in the USA* (New York: Routledge Press, 2002), 123-42.

71 *GM,* 27 March 1969, B3. On youth as consumers more generally, see *FP,* 21 May 1966, 13; Serge Gouin, Bernard Portis, and Brian Campbell, *The Teenage Market in Canada: A Study of High School Students in London, Ontario, and Chicoutimi, Quebec* (London, ON: School of Business Administration, University of Western Ontario, 1967); and Ratcliffe, "Survey of the Drive-In."

72 In May 1971, McDonald's sought permission to open its Richmond outlet until midnight. Town Council agreed, but on a trial basis for that summer. Town of Richmond, *Council Minutes,* 1971, 810-11, 850. A year later, Council made the change permanent, noting that "the establishment has not been the source of annoyance as no complaints have been received." Town of Richmond, *Council Minutes,* 1972, 257-58. However, at other outlets, the declared willingness of McDonald's to forego the rowdy youth market never translated into the complete absence of rowdy youth; see, for example, *DJR,* 8 May 1971, 8.

73 *DJR,* 14 December 1970, 1; Town of Oakville, Bylaws of the Town of Oakville, 1970-98, "A By-Law to Prohibit Loitering and Nuisances on Public Highways," passed 7 July 1970; *Oakville Beaver,* 2 July 1970, 1, and 22 October 1970, A8. A *Toronto Star* editorial, 8 July 1970, 13, mocked the town for passing a "bonehead bylaw." The local Labour Council also protested the new bylaw, but with little effect.

74 *DJR,* 31 May 1971, 4.

75 *FSH,* 15 August 1971, 35.

76 See above, note 4.

77 *Vancouver Province,* 6 March 1963, 3.

78 Michael Dawson, "Leisure, Consumption, and the Public Sphere: Postwar Debates over Shopping Regulations in Vancouver and Victoria during the Cold War," in this volume.
79 *Scarborough Mirror*, 31 August 1966, 4. On accusations of exploiting complaints, see *North York Mirror*, 3 August 1966, 6, where one independent operator charged that "one of our ambitious politicians is using some of these complaints in addition to an imaginary one of his own as a vehicle to enhance his career."
80 *FSH*, September 1974, S2, and October 1974, 18-19; *Canadian Business*, May 1978, 32-36, and March 1982, 110-11; *GM*, 3 December 1977, B13.
81 *Marketing*, 21 June 1976, 2.
82 *FSH*, October 1974, 18-19; *CHR*, November 1975, 46. In 1980 one suburban planning study noted that drive-thru customers were generating 51 percent of the vehicle trips to the area's two Wendy's restaurants and 37 percent of such trips to McDonald's; see Borough of Etobicoke, *Restaurant Study, 1980*, Borough of Etobicoke Planning Department, 1 April 1980, 37-38.

Part 2
Diversity and Dissent

8
Leisure, Consumption, and the Public Sphere: Postwar Debates over Shopping Regulations in Vancouver and Victoria during the Cold War
Michael Dawson

Canadian historians have again set out in search of new, more reflexive ways to synthesize their many divergent areas of research.[1] As a result, it has become commonsense that we must leave room for contingencies and avoid proposing a narrow and exclusionary master narrative. In this endeavour, the history of the "public sphere," that rather amorphous social space in which rational public debate occurs, offers a promising field for exploration. One need not necessarily agree with Jürgen Habermas' pessimistic pronouncement on the decline of rational debate in Western society to recognize the value of exploring the history of public debate in Canada.[2] Given constant contemporary recriminations about the spiralling level of public debate during election campaigns, in newspapers, and in classrooms, one could argue that a history of how average, ordinary (as opposed to elite) Canadians have debated national, regional, and local problems is more crucial now than ever before. In this chapter I explore how Canadians in Vancouver and Victoria debated the controversial issue of store-hour regulation in order to demonstrate the utility of such an approach and to shed new light on the lived reality of the Cold War period.

Canadian historical inquiry into the postwar era has focused primarily on two related themes: the state and the family.[3] It is not surprising, then, that studies of the Cold War in Canada have focused on these two areas as well. Examinations of the role of the state, for example, have generally documented efforts to eliminate political dissent and ensure "national security."[4] Such studies confirm that the state intruded directly into Canadians' lives to limit political freedoms. Similarly well documented is the extent to which Cold War concerns informed family life in the postwar era, as expert opinion viewed both the "democratic" family and "normal" heterosexual gender roles as important bulwarks against the dangers of cultural decline and communism.[5] Such concerns contributed to a campaign for "domestic containment" in both Canada and the United States that, Franca Iacovetta reminds us, "involved the repression ... of individual rights and freedoms in the name of democratic rights and freedoms."[6]

However, the extent to which the Cold War affected Canadians' daily lives outside of the home and state institutions remains unclear. According to Doug Owram, the Cold War had a more muted cultural impact in Canada than in the United States but maintained "a brooding presence that reminded people that their current situation was tenuous."[7] This presence was ensured in part through the media. Paul Litt, for example, notes that celebrations of democracy and free enterprise, along with denunciations of communism, were standard fare in popular Canadian magazines, while Mary Louise Adams contends that an invasive US mass culture rendered "American cold-war hype" virtually unavoidable in Canada.[8] In addition, Peter McInnis has ably documented the determined public relations campaigns championing free enterprise and demonizing socialism that were waged by private enterprise during the reconstruction period.[9] But just how deeply these pronouncements permeated the consciousness of Canadians is unclear. Anecdotal evidence is certainly contradictory. On the one hand, it is hard to believe that a cultural climate that featured Watson Kirconnell and the Freedom Foundation determinedly campaigning to convince the public that water fluoridation was a Communist plot to brainwash Canadians could allow for anything but consistent angst and terror. On the other hand, that a 1952 Gallup poll reported that only 56 percent of Canadians had heard of the North Atlantic Treaty Organization (NATO) and that just 37 percent could explain what it was suggests that many Canadians, like many Americans, isolated themselves quite comfortably from Cold War tensions.[10] How, and to what extent, the "brooding presence" of the Cold War intersected with the reality of most Canadians' everyday lives outside of familial and government institutions remains an important but relatively unexplored question. Focusing on the local issue of shopping regulations in Vancouver and Victoria, this chapter offers preliminary answers to this question by examining the relationship between the Cold War and consumerism.

Only recently have historians begun to seek connections between the experience of the Cold War and the growing centrality of consumerism in Canadian life.[11] This chapter carries forward this research by documenting the complex way that Cold War rhetoric permeated debates regarding access to consumer goods and services.[12] Moreover, it does so by focusing on a previously neglected element of twentieth-century consumerism: small business.[13] After the Second World War merchants, employees, consumers, and local politicians in Vancouver and Victoria increasingly came to view the issue of store-hour regulation through the lens of the Cold War and expressed their views through rhetoric that drew on notions of free enterprise, political freedom, dictatorship, rights, and democracy. In doing so, these different groups employed the same Cold War language in ways that suited their own interests. In short, they employed Cold War idiom as a useful but malleable rhetorical weapon.

In examining the "larger field of utterance" in which Cold War rhetoric was employed, this chapter underscores two important points.[14] First, it demonstrates how individuals appropriated and recast cultural texts. Second, it highlights that postwar Canadian political culture was neither static nor uncontested.[15] Building on these two points, this chapter differs from earlier studies of Canada's Cold War culture by focusing not on "national" concerns such as the welfare state or immigration policy but on a very local issue. Most important, postwar debates over shopping regulations in Vancouver and Victoria offer a window onto the public sphere. In doing so, they provide an opportunity to explore the connections between the Cold War and consumerism and to evaluate more accurately the extent to which Cold War concerns permeated Canadians' everyday lives. The examples presented here suggest that while Cold War symbolism permeated Canadian society, it did so in unexpected and often contradictory ways.

Dogs, Garbage, and Store Hours: The Contentious Issue of Store-Hour Regulation, 1900-70

> "When I was very young in municipal government I was told that three things – dogs, garbage, and store hours – would occupy more time than anything."
> — Saanich reeve Hugh Curtis, 1966[16]

As the chapters by Becki Ross and Steve Penfold in this volume illustrate, regulation played an important role in the development of a mass consumer society in Canada during the postwar era. Both chapters implicitly highlight the role of municipal regulation. Municipal regulations determined which drinking and striptease establishments could obtain operating licences; they also determined where and when teenagers would be allowed to loiter outside of fast food franchises. Similar regulations or bylaws determined the hours of operation for retail merchants throughout the country. In British Columbia these regulations became the subject of a series of prolonged public debates.

These debates began in earnest in the first decade of the twentieth century when store clerks in Victoria petitioned their local government for a common half-day, mid-week holiday.[17] Embraced by many merchants in Victoria and Vancouver, the Wednesday half-holiday was enshrined in provincial legislation in 1916. Because retail clerks were otherwise unaffected by the province's Hours of Work legislation, they worked a five-and-a-half-day week. The Lord's Day Act ensured that they did not work on Sunday, and the province's Half-Holiday Act guaranteed an additional half-day off each week. In the absence of any specific hours of work legislation affecting retail clerks, store hours and hours of work became, for many employees, one and the same. Despite growing opposition in the 1920s and 1930s from merchants and other commercial interests (especially those in tourism-related businesses), the provincial government retained the Half-Holiday Act and amended it as needed to ensure its continued efficacy. The half-holiday in Vancouver and Victoria remained a controversial but workable compromise between consumers, merchants, employees, and larger commercial interests into the 1940s.

Ironically, an extension of the retail half-holiday to a full day of closing during the Second World War on the grounds of conservation and patriotism would prove the undoing of this compromise. Both cities adopted all-day closing on a voluntary basis during the war, and the elimination or retention of this temporary war measure became a key issue for civic voters once the war was over. In 1946 Victoria residents voted to return to half-day closing; in 1947 Vancouver residents voted to retain full-day closing. Seemingly decided once and for all, the issue of store-hour regulation was revisited in an angry and divisive manner almost annually until the early 1960s. From the mid-1940s to the late 1950s the debates focused primarily on the length of the shopping week. Retail clerks and many merchants fought to protect the five- or five-and-a-half-day week; they were opposed by outside commercial interests, tourism-related businesses, and other retail clerks and merchants that championed a six-day week as the most effective method of securing continued economic development. The six-day-week lobby eventually won out – but only after provincial legislation and union contracts were in place to ensure that store clerks themselves would enjoy a five-day work week. In 1957 Vancouver officially adopted a six-day shopping week, while in 1958 Victoria followed the lead of the neighbouring suburb of Saanich by rescinding its store-hour regulations, declaring city stores "wide open" and leaving merchants to set their own hours. Such decisions at the municipal level were now possible because the provincial government had finally opted to divest itself of responsibility for store hours in 1958 by revising its Municipal Act to transfer all regulatory power regarding store hours to local authorities. But the debate over store-hour regulations continued to rage. By the early 1960s the issue of evening shopping emerged as the key debating point before it was superseded by the issue of Sunday shopping in the 1970s and 1980s.

The postwar store-hour debates shared a number of characteristics with those that occurred before the war. In both eras, for example, the opponents and champions of store-hour restrictions failed to fit easily into tight categories. Clerks, merchants, and even chain-store representatives were frequently divided on the regulatory issue of the day. Moreover, during both

Store clerk at counter, c. 1940s.
City of Vancouver Archives, CVA 1184-1036, Jack Lindsay, Ltd., photo

eras the debates were structured by a tension between tradition and modernity.[18] Champions of store-hour regulations endeavoured to place limits on
the extent to which the emerging consumer culture dictated the rhythm of
their daily lives, while opponents of such regulations were loath to abandon the wealth-producing effects of any increase in trade. These store-hour
debates reflected the social tensions that emerged as leisure time was colonized by consumption and thus underscore that this development was resisted and contested in the public sphere throughout the twentieth century.
Finally, during both eras, while the debates in Victoria and Vancouver mirrored concerns over store hours elsewhere in Canada, the issue was understood by those involved as having a particular intensity in British Columbia.
Further comparative research is required to evaluate the validity of this observation, but it remained the dominant understanding during both eras.[19]
The key difference between the pre- and postwar debates was one of form
rather than content. Only in very rare instances did participants in these
debates before the Second World War employ overt references to political
ideologies and ideals.[20] After the war, however, the debates were imbued
with direct allusions to political ideology and Cold War rhetoric. It is this
development that I analyze here by focusing on three themes: differing
notions of personal and political freedom, the growing connection between
consumption and citizenship, and contrasting definitions of "democracy."

"A Half-Breed Monstrosity:" Free Enterprise, Freedom, and Dictatorship

Postwar store-hour debates were rife with references to personal and political freedom. Opponents of store-hour regulation consistently denounced government legislation and civic bylaws for infringing on the economic freedom inherent in a free-enterprise society. Logic dictated that supporters of store-hour restrictions were unable to make similar use of free-enterprise rhetoric. They drew instead on the language of personal and political freedom and, much more frequently, on notions of dictatorship. The result was a series of heated exchanges, infused with Cold War rhetoric, in which the growing power of consumerism was alternately celebrated and challenged.

Free Enterprise

The call to defend "free enterprise" was a common one among corporations, business lobby groups, and small businesses in the postwar era. However, just what proponents meant by the term varied considerably. In fact, such pronouncements drew on two competing understandings of the relationship between business and government – understandings that were weighted differently depending on the situation. One strain drew a stark distinction between entrepreneurship and government activity; this understanding virulently opposed government intervention on the grounds that such activity was destructive. Large corporations such as the Royal Bank of Canada and Hiram Walker gave voice to this strain in the 1940s when they embarked on advertising campaigns championing the free-enterprise system in an effort to rein in plans for an expansive role for government in the postwar economy.[21] Business lobby groups also drew on this understanding when they submitted briefs to the Massey Commission expressing concern over competition from the state-run Canadian Broadcasting Corporation and National Film Board.[22] Such pronouncements were an attempt to create a political consensus that would ensure that government interference with business pursuits was kept to a minimum. As Reg Whitaker and Gary Marcuse observe, such a "consensus cutting across classes" and "defending 'our way of life' – crucially including free enterprise – against the philosophy of Communism (and socialism) obviously appealed to businessmen contending with the demands of trade unions and fears of government intervention, nationalization, and regulation."[23] Expressed publicly, such pronouncements offered a vision of free enterprise that vilified intrusive government regulation and championed both entrepreneurial achievement and "consumer sovereignty," the liberal economic notion that consumers were readily equipped to make rational purchasing decisions.[24]

There was, however, a second understanding of free enterprise – one acknowledging that government played an important regulatory role in the economy. This understanding was perhaps best expressed by the British Columbia Chamber of Commerce. In a 1955 policy statement, the Chamber made the point implicitly. The "role of the government should be limited to the exercise of regulatory powers," it argued, because the "entrance of government into the field of production and distribution leads to socialism and dictatorship."[25] A decade later the Chamber had honed its phrasing to offer a bolder, more positive statement on the role of government. In its *General Policy Statements* for 1965, it explained that the "role of Governments is to create and maintain a favourable climate for enterprise." In doing so, the government would allow "competitive private enterprise" to "bring the greatest good to the greatest number of people of this province."[26] This strain of free-enterprise rhetoric was more easily reconciled with postwar demands by entrepreneurs and business lobby groups for government regulation. On this count, the selective approach to regulation adopted by BC tourism promoters in the aftermath of the Second World War is instructive. While protesting against what they considered unnecessary government regulations, such as mandatory BC automobile insurance for US visitors, civic tourism-promotion bodies endorsed a government act regulating tourist camps on the grounds that sanitary and enjoyable camping experiences would ensure repeat customers in the future. Camp operators themselves embraced these regulations in part because of the limitations that they placed on the number of facilities and thus on competition.[27] In a similar vein, as the wartime housing shortage was exacerbated by the arrival of returning soldiers, Vancouver Tourist Association officials co-operated with the National Housing Registry to frustrate the selfish designs of local accommodation operators endeavouring to charge exorbitant room rates.[28] Such actions and pronouncements illustrate the extent to which private enterprise embraced some forms of government regulation while eschewing others.

Free-enterprise ideology as expressed by private enterprise thus came in two variants. The first understood free enterprise as freedom from government regulation, while the second recognized that government regulations helped to create a positive entrepreneurial environment. The latter interpretation offered a more accurate understanding of the actual workings of Canada's free-enterprise system. It was, however, the former, more selective understanding of free enterprise that was expressed most consistently during the postwar store-hour debates. Merchants opposed to specific store-hour regulations worked from the assumption that any government regulation served to corrupt an otherwise perfect economic system. Faced with store-hour regulations that restricted their ability to sell goods, many merchants argued that government intervention was both unnecessary and a threat to Canada's free-enterprise system.

In 1954, for example, when Vancouver City Council considered appeasing local butchers by approving a ban on selling frozen meats and fish after 5:30 p.m., the frustration among small grocers was palpable. Earl W. Scott, proprietor of Scott's Grocery in the city's West End, vowed that he and other small grocers would find a way to continue selling meat and fish in the evening despite the new law. "It's getting so there's not much difference between the capitalist system and the communist system," he argued, before rationalizing that "this is supposed to be a free country, and if I want to operate 10 hours or 24 hours a day, that's my business."[29] Newspaper editorials and consumers expressed similar sentiments. Hence, in June 1957, the *Victoria Daily Colonist* voiced its frustration with the ongoing debate over store-hour regulation by drawing on free-enterprise rhetoric to point an accusatory finger at Victoria's City Council. "Confused and confusing discussion in city council over hours during which people may or may not do business in Victoria," an editorial argued, "serves to demonstrate the excessive regulation to which 'free' enterprise is subjected."[30] In advocating expanded night shopping in the Vancouver suburb of Burnaby, the *Vancouver Daily Province* echoed this line of argument and expressed its dismay at "the extent to which bureaucracy has been allowed to restrict what we are still pleased to call our free enterprise system."[31] Consumers, too, vented their frustration on this point. Retired Saanich resident Carl Fallas offered the following synopsis of his thoughts on the matter of store-hour regulations in 1958: "I am inclined to think, myself, that the bureaucrats are choking us to death. If a fellow wants to stay open, let him. If we are supposed to be living under capitalism, for God's sake let's have it and not a half-breed monstrosity such as we have now."[32]

While such concerns were widely felt among store-hour regulation opponents, they offered only a highly selective understanding of free enterprise – one that failed to acknowledge, unlike the BC Chamber of Commerce, that state regulations often served the interests of entrepreneurs. For as Tom Traves explains, "freedom of enterprise in Canada does not mean 'laissez-faire'" but reflects a system in which the "coercive power of the state" played an important role in regulating and stabilizing the business environment in the postwar years.[33] Focused, as these merchants were, on the specific issue of store-hour regulations, they conveniently overlooked this more complex understanding of the relationship between state regulation and entrepreneurial freedom.

In doing so, they echoed the pronouncements of businesses across the country that seized on the free-enterprise theme to challenge government intervention in the arts through briefs to the Massey Commission as well as to resist an expanded welfare state through advertising campaigns. For Canadians not attuned to debates over arts funding or the intricacies of postwar reconstruction, the debates surrounding shopping regulations ensured that they too were exposed to Cold War rhetoric championing free enterprise ideology and alerting Canadians to internal threats to their personal freedom. In this way, Cold War concerns informed not only debates about Canada's national destiny but more tangible local issues as well.

Freedom and Dictatorship

Closely related to warnings about threats to free enterprise were suggestions that store-hour regulations threatened both personal and political freedom and reeked of dictatorship – a spectre that could call forth threatening visions of both fascism and communism. As David Monod has demonstrated in his study of early-twentieth-century Canadian shopkeepers, retail merchants could be particularly enthusiastic champions of regulation when it came to erecting barriers to new competition or preventing underselling through resale price maintenance.[34] By requesting regulations that restricted the business activities of their competitors, supporters of store-hour legislation and bylaws could hardly make use of free-enterprise rhetoric. Nothing, however, prevented them from appropriating other aspects of Cold War ideology to serve their aims. Indeed, both opponents *and supporters* of store-hour regulations embraced rhetoric that championed personal and political freedom while raising the spectre of dictatorship.

Opponents of specific store-hour regulations frequently broadened their rhetoric to focus not simply on free enterprise but also on political freedom and its opposite, dictatorship. For example, a 1951 letter to the *Vancouver Sun* argued that co-ordinated attempts by store operators to have all stores in a given business class observe a common closing day were an assault on individual freedoms.[35] Seven years later the *Victoria Daily Times* echoed this sentiment by employing both the rhetoric of free enterprise and the theme of political freedom when it endorsed six-day shopping in Victoria: "Surely the whole debate comes down to ... the right of free citizens to carry on their businesses in a climate of freedom; to make money if they are efficient and hard-working, to lose it if they are inefficient or lazy."[36] The alternative to such a system, opponents of store-hour regulation charged, was totalitarianism or dictatorship – a point that they incorporated effectively into their arguments. Thus the Victoria Chamber of Commerce's Tourist Trade Group included in its 1946 resolution objecting to compulsory all-day Wednesday closing the charge that such compulsion "is definitely opposed to all British ideas of freedom of the individual and is akin to [a] totalitarianism form of government."[37] Not surprisingly, merchants were among the most likely to employ the spectre of totalitarian dictatorship.

As part of its 1957 campaign to overturn new provincial regulations that would restrict corner stores to selling a limited range of goods after 6:00 p.m., for example, Victoria's Independent Merchants' Co-operative Association called on the city's housewives to lend their considerable political clout to the association's efforts.[38] In a letter mailed directly to citizens' homes, association president William Palmer did not mince words in his appeal to citizens to support small shopkeepers in their continuing battle for survival against increasingly powerful chain stores that were coming to monopolize daytime sales. Evening operation, the association explained, was simply a matter of survival amid this increasing competition, and the provincial government was only making matters worse by restricting evening sales. In encouraging the city's housewives to attend a public meeting on the issue, Palmer challenged their political allegiance directly: "It is up to you to support this meeting, or are we going to wear the hammer and sickle?"[39] Employing the spectre of the Soviet Union as a potent symbol of overzealous government regulation was just one way that Palmer buttressed his campaign to oppose store-hour regulations. He also alluded to the broader, more amorphous threat of dictatorship. Palmer argued that in restricting evening sales, the provincial government was acting in the interests of the chain stores themselves. "Why should we be forced to follow the marketing pattern of the super-markets?" he asked. "Are we under the heel of a dictatorship?"[40] Unlike opponents of store-hour regulations who championed a selective understanding of "free enterprise," Palmer recognized that government regulation could aid private enterprise. What dismayed him was that provincial legislation seemed to be benefiting chain stores at the expense of small, independent grocers.

Store clerks at a Lux soap display at Spencer's department store in Vancouver, June 1944.
City of Vancouver Archives, CVA 1184-619, Jack Lindsay, Ltd., photo

Palmer was not alone in labelling restrictions on shopping hours "dictatorial." Indeed, the rhetoric of "dictatorship" emerged as early as December 1946 when Victoria merchant Doris Ashdown found her recently established "personal shopping service" threatened by the city's proposed bylaw on all-day Wednesday closing. With US visitors among her most important customers, Ashdown wrote to the *Daily Colonist* arguing that Wednesday closing would cost her dearly given her client base. In doing so, she cast the proposed regulations as threats to democracy, the British way of life, and even the beliefs of military veterans: "I wish to say that I am vitally opposed to compulsion as anything of the kind savors of dictatorship. I have lived during three wars in which the British Empire has given of her best and bravest to insure the democratic way of life. This is the way I believe in and that I desire to see continued, and I believe that is what the veterans – in the majority – who fought to insure it desires [sic] too."[41] Cold War rhetoric that equated provincial and civic regulations with dictatorial powers, and that blended antifascist and anticommunist sentiment, was clearly an appealing political tool for opponents of store-hour regulations.

However, neither the rhetoric of personal and political freedom nor the spectre of "dictatorship" were monopolized by those who sought to limit or eliminate restrictions on store hours. In 1953, for example, Oak Bay resident Alex MacLeod Baird, a salesperson with Standard Furniture, spoke out in favour of preserving the Wednesday half-day holiday by demanding to know "what authority the city council have to interfere with private business and their employees."[42] In a similar vein, when Victoria Chamber of Commerce member T.G. Denny voiced his concern that in its campaign to introduce six-day shopping the Chamber's Tourist Trade Group was ignoring a recent plebiscite in which the city's merchants had voted overwhelmingly to preserve the city's current store-hour regulations, he accused the group of "just being dictatorial."[43] Likewise, when Vancouver clothier A.J. Warner opposed the lifting of restrictions that prohibited Friday night shopping, he did so by suggesting that such an expansion of shopping hours was being "dictated by Safeway."[44]

The struggle against the tyranny of dictatorship also proved popular with D.A. Gilbert, national president of the Retail Merchants Association (RMA), who visited Victoria in April 1956 to survey merchants regarding the issue of store hours. Expressing the RMA's opposition to unrestricted store hours, he suggested that "the big operators have been calling the tune long enough." Gilbert explained that the RMA was "engaged in a nation-wide battle with the big chain stores which are trying to impose their will on the smaller stores" and promised that the RMA would oppose any attempt to alter the city's bylaws unless a majority of merchants approved of expanded shopping hours. "Everywhere in Canada today a few powerful organizations are seeking to eliminate all regulation of store hours ... Don't be dictated to by the big chain stores," he urged local store owners, "You can beat the power of wealth if you stand together."[45] By taking this line of argument, the RMA and its supporters were in surprising company. During the Massey Commission proceedings, business interests eager to voice their opposition to government involvement in cultural pursuits "equated state-sponsored culture with the threat of communist totalitarianism." In response, Paul Litt explains, the "cultural lobby countered that it was powerful business interests ... that presented the real threat to individual freedom and opportunity."[46] In closely resembling the latter position, grocery store owners' complaints that they were being victimized by a chain-store "dictatorship" reflect an important example of the extent to which cultural elites and commercial interests could share a common language – one that drew on Cold War rhetoric in an effort to silence opponents.

Reg Whitaker and Gary Marcuse have suggested that "the very essence of the Cold War mentality" was "to demand absolute and unthinking fidelity to the 'right' side in the apocalyptic struggle between good and evil."[47] The result of this mentality was a resort to a binary logic that imposed clear limits regarding "the boundaries of legitimate dissent" and that closed off "certain options and possibilities as illegitimate, disloyal, or even treasonous."[48] Tarring one's political opponent with the brush of communism, for example, proved a useful and potentially devastating ploy.[49] Participants in the store-hour debates rarely made explicit reference to communism. Instead, they drew on the notion of "dictatorship" and enthusiastically attached this label to the actions of those who either opposed their views or hindered their aims.

The charge of "dictatorship" was a popular one in Cold War Canada. Even progressive teachers used it in their campaigns against their conservative opponents.[50] By employing this loaded term, both supporters and opponents of store-hour restrictions seized on and appropriated a potent Cold War symbol. The binary logic of the Cold War had thus permeated even local debates about what time the corner store should close. It had done so, however, at the behest of both sides. Unlike other documented instances, then, the use of this binary Cold War logic did not close down debate by silencing one side. If anything, it raised the temperature of the dispute as each side appropriated the symbolism to suit its own purpose. Cold War rhetoric in this context was a politically useful but malleable weapon. Its use highlights the dynamic nature of postwar debates over consumerism. These debates reflected not a dormant public sphere in which consumerism's colonization of leisure time went unchallenged but one in which merchants, clerks, chain-store representatives, and the general public boldly offered their opinions and attempted to mobilize support for their views.

Consumption and Citizenship: The Right to Shop, the Right to Sell, and the Right to Leisure

Postwar debates about store-hour regulations were also infused with references to personal and political rights – a development that reflected the emergence of a culture of entitlement in Canada. In fact, the postwar era witnessed a blossoming of rights-based rhetoric. Throughout the 1930s and 1940s advocates of the welfare state downplayed an earlier emphasis on "charity" to embrace a line of argument that centred on "entitlement." Support for direct relief, family allowances, and pensions, for example, was infused with a language of citizenship that championed Canadians' right to government support.[51] Immersed in this growing culture of entitlement, both supporters and opponents of store-hour regulations incorporated rights-based rhetoric into their public campaigns and pronouncements. In doing so, they added another level of sophistication to these public exchanges in the public sphere.

Rights-based arguments in favour of decreasing or eliminating store-hour regulations took two complementary forms: the *right to shop* and the *right to sell*. Both were expressed most clearly during a 1946 debate over store hours in Victoria. In voicing its opposition to a proposal to legislate five-day shopping, for example, the *Daily Colonist* noted the possible deleterious effects that such a move might have on the city's tourism revenues before drawing its readers' attention to a more pressing issue: "The Canadian public is entitled to service upon an even basis" – something that would prove impossible if Victoria chose to restrict itself to a five-day shopping week and Vancouver did not.[52] The *Daily Times* agreed, arguing that the city's stores "have a definite responsibility toward the public."[53] If the right to shop provided one element of the rights-based rhetoric employed by those opposed to overzealous regulations, the right to sell provided the other. An example is merchant George MacDonald's blunt explanation of why he opposed Victoria's proposed five-day plan. "I'm not going to have any organization blackball me if I don't close my store on any particular day of the week," he argued, "this is not Germany, it is Canada."[54] The *Daily Colonist* brought both elements together when it argued "that many rights are involved. The public has a right to normal trading, having built its homes and businesses on that assumption ... Then there is the right of the proprietors who do not wish to close at midweek, but who value that trading day as much as any other trading day."[55] Such rhetoric championing both the right to shop and the right to sell reflected a growing connection between consumption and citizenship. Indeed, opponents of store-hour regulations in Vancouver and Victoria shared this notion of "economic citizenship" with Canadians who, during the 1940s, framed their protests against rising meat prices and restrictions placed on the availability of margarine in terms of citizenship rights.[56] This conflation of consumption and citizenship, as Lizabeth Cohen notes in the American context, underscores the growing power of consumer culture at mid-century.[57]

Yet consumerism's growing power did not go unchallenged. While merchants and the public employed free-enterprise rhetoric solely on the side of greater deregulation, the rhetoric regarding "rights," like that of freedom and dictatorship, was not nearly so one-sided. The champions of store-hour regulation developed their own rights-based arguments that focused on one's *right to leisure*. In 1953, for example, Victoria store clerk H.A. Napper voiced his opposition to a proposal that would see clerks' hours staggered over a six-day week and the elimination of their common mid-week holiday by calling the public's attention to "the right of retail clerks to take part, if they wish to, in group activities, such as cricket, football, baseball, or any other game they may fancy." "It took our fathers a long time to win this right," he explained, "and some of us don't want to lose it."[58] More dramatic was Harold Gray's letter to the *Daily Colonist*, which railed against "shop owners" who sought to "take away from some nearly 6,000 retail clerks, the right and privilege ... to enjoy together ... their weekly half-day holiday." "Go to all the clerks for permission to change their holiday," he warned, "but let it never pass that we the public should take away a privilege from others that is not rightfully ours to take."[59] Here, then, were two eloquent champions of workers' "right" to common leisure. Their arguments were echoed by Alex MacLeod Baird, who offered readers of the *Daily Times* a history lesson. "Following the history of our race if it were not for our laws – which preserve our rights – we would be wholly at the mercy of human greed," he argued. "Labor today represents a live potential section of the people – citizens who are taxpayers and represent a great proportion of the buying public, and are not a commodity as was thought years ago," Baird explained, tellingly equating workers' right to leisure with their role as consumers. It was this "right" that was now under threat and that required defending.[60]

Arguments in favour of retail clerks' right to leisure occurred in a context that was only just becoming familiar with such rhetoric. By the postwar era, Shirley Tillotson explains, leisure inhabited a secure place among the pantheon of "social rights" in Canada. The groundwork for this development had occurred in the 1930s when provincial governments across the country "put into law a new understanding of leisure as a universal citizen right" through legislation limiting hours of work and stipulating minimum annual holidays.[61] Government motivation during the Depression, however, was firmly focused on increasing employment. Hence, Tillotson explains, "the right to work, not the right to enjoy leisure, was the element of citizenship at issue."[62] Only in the 1940s and 1950s, she argues, was the right to leisure "explicitly asserted."[63] Such assertions coincided with a variety of

conflicting pronouncements from social scientists and cultural critics arguing about whether increased leisure time would improve or demoralize Canadians.[64] The debates over store-hour regulations add an important
dimension to these elite pronouncements: the voice of ordinary Canadians
championing leisure not only as a positive element of their lives but also as
an entitlement that they were determined to retain and protect. As they
had done with the rhetoric of freedom and dictatorship, both opponents
and supporters of store-hour regulations enlisted rights-based arguments to
champion their respective causes. The culture of entitlement that was firmly
in place by the postwar period allowed participants in these debates to employ these pronouncements confident that their statements would rever-
berate powerfully among their fellow citizens. In expressing themselves in
this manner, they were appropriating another element of Cold War rhetoric. Recognizing the presence of these voices in the public sphere highlights
an important but as yet overlooked fact: postwar debates about mass culture and democracy were not the sole preserve of cultural elites. Ordinary
Canadians were having their say as well.

Debating Democracy

Along with "freedom," "dictatorship," and "rights," "democracy" proved a
popular buzzword during the early decades of the Cold War. Psychologists
championed democratic approaches to childrearing, while cultural critics
worried aloud that a vibrant democratic political culture was being replaced
by a conformist mass culture.[65] Moreover, as Len Kuffert observes, there
existed in Canada's "Cold War environment" a tendency to equate "the
development of popular culture with political democracy and a kind of
'people's morality.'"[66] Many different interests thus claimed to be on the
side of democracy. Supporters and opponents of store-hour regulations were
no different. Democracy, along with rights-based arguments and the rhetoric focusing on freedom and dictatorship, was embraced by both sides of
the store-hour debates. The use of democratic rhetoric, however, was more
complex. While opponents of store-hour regulations deployed democracy
in general arguments that asserted shopkeepers' right to open or close their
stores, both sides in the debate invoked its spirit in detailed and intricate
arguments over the method by which decisions about a community's store
hours ought to be taken. These debates focused on who was an acceptable
participant in the decision-making process. Should the merchants determine store hours? Or should the public decide? The answer to these questions, not surprisingly, depended on the subject position from which one
viewed the debates.

In their general arguments, critics of store-hour regulations consistently
dismissed as undemocratic the civic bylaws and provincial statutes setting

out the restrictions.[67] Frequently, these critics pointed to what they understood to be flagrant inconsistencies in store-hour regulations and questioned
the democratic nature of the system itself. In February 1948, for example,
Mrs. M. Pratt, president of Pratt's Beauty Supply in Vancouver, questioned
the democratic nature of city regulations that obliged her store to close on
Wednesdays while drugstores exempted from the closing laws were competing directly with her business by selling virtually the same toiletry supplies.[68] Frustrated Victoria novelty-shop proprietor Kelly Porter shared Pratt's
concerns, asking rhetorically: "Is this a democratic country when the law
makes you close up whether you want to or not on a Wednesday afternoon?"[69] Such rhetoric continued into the mid-1950s. In 1954, voicing his
support for a six-day week in Vancouver, Vancouver Real Estate Board president Herbert R. Fullerton equated democracy with free enterprise: "Under
our democratic system of free enterprise, the individual is entitled to operate his business as he sees fit providing he does not injure the right of others
by doing so."[70]

By employing the rhetoric of democracy to suggest a direct connection
between democratic rights and their desire to be freed from unwelcome
government-imposed restrictions, opponents of store-hour regulations drew
on the binary mentality of the Cold War to cast themselves as defenders of
democracy and their opponents as threats to their democratic rights. Ideally,
such a manoeuvre would have succeeded in silencing the supporters of store-
hour regulations. However, when it came to determining the process by
which regulations should be approved, rejected, or rescinded, both opponents and supporters of store-hour regulations embraced the rhetoric of
democracy. Democracy, like so many other forms of Cold War rhetoric, was
appropriated by both sides of the debate.

By far the most prevalent argument employing democracy in the campaign to reduce or eliminate store-hour regulations centred around the demand that the public, rather than the merchants themselves, decide the
issue. This demand focused on two scenarios. One involved simply ensuring that civic officials solicited the public's opinion through referenda rather
than relying on the input of lobbying groups. A second scenario witnessed
opposition to the mechanism of specific bylaws, many of which stipulated
that classes of business could approve or repeal closing restrictions by ob-
taining the signatures of a certain number of business operators within a
given class.

The notion that civic government should be consulting the wider public
regarding store-hour regulations was motivated in part by the belief that
the public, as consumers, would inevitably embrace wider store hours. Frequently, referendum results proved this optimism wrong, but the rhetoric
itself remained consistent. Councillor H.M. Diggon led opposition in 1946
to Victoria's proposed bylaw on Wednesday closing by arguing that City

Council's decision was undemocratic because taxpayers had not had an opportunity to vote on the issue.[71] A meeting of Vancouver merchants in 1947 resulted in a similar call for a public referendum. While the majority of merchants at an RMA meeting favoured all-day Wednesday closing, dissenters calling for a referendum argued that it was "highly undemocratic for a small group of merchants to impose policy on the whole community."[72] R.H. Hiscocks, secretary of the local branch of the Native Sons of BC, went so far as to claim that Victoria's store-closing bylaws were in "direct violation" of democracy and majority rule. Retail stores, he argued, must be subject to the will of the people. Hiscocks thus rejected the bylaw's logic, which allowed for store hours to be set on the agreement of 75 percent of the businesses in a particular class. "The agreement of 75 per cent of the management in any given phase of business to petition the City Council to close the other 25 per cent to suit their convenience is a violation of the majority rule," he argued, "because the general public is the majority concerned."[73]

Former Victoria mayor and MLA Reginald Hayward went further in expressing his opposition to all-day Wednesday closing and his support for the city's decision to hold a referendum on the issue. Hayward equated consumption with citizens' decision-making power. In his understanding, merchants took on the role of politicians, while consumers voted with their pocketbooks. "Merchants have more than goods to sell: they have a service to perform," Hayward explained. "The public is the judge of the service it requires, not the merchants, and it is for the public to decide whether stores shall be compelled to close all day. The consumer, the customer, pays the bill." Consumers, he argued, "are the final judges of the service they require, or what they will buy or where."[74] Tellingly, Hayward thus incorporated a celebration of consumer sovereignty into his demand for a more democratic decision-making process.

For supporters of store-hour restrictions and of Wednesday closing in particular, the rhetoric of democracy was also crucial. However, the "majority" that was expected to approve or rescind such policies was not the general public but those whose lives were most directly affected by the regulations: the merchants and clerks. Such was Victoria councillor Edward Williams' understanding in 1946 when he urged his fellow council members to "do what the majority of the merchants in any specific class want... That is the most democratic way."[75] Reg Williams, president of the Victoria Meat Retailers' Association, pointed to the bylaws themselves as ensuring that the *real* majority had its say. Since in every case in which a bylaw regulating a particular class of business had been passed, at least 75 percent of the licensed dealers in that class must have requested the action, the bylaw had to be democratic, he explained.[76] In 1953 a group of Victoria clerks known as the Five Day Action Committee voiced its opposition to Victoria City

Council's plan to hold a referendum on the six-day week by directly questioning the public's right to decide its members' fate: "Why should the public be asked to vote on the working conditions of the retail clerks?" asked committee chairman Peter MacEwan. "When the banks and offices got their five-day week the public was not consulted. Nor was it, when the civil servants – who are actually paid by the taxpayers – went on to the Monday through Friday week. So why pick on the retail clerks, who are paid by private employers?"[77]

The argument that the public had no right to determine store-hour regulations was buttressed by a related claim that the public was not qualified to express its view on the issue. In a joint brief opposing a planned Victoria referendum on the six-day week, a coalition of organizations that championed the five-day alternative argued that "it is most illogical to expect the public to vote intelligently on a matter which merchants and their staffs find difficult to solve."[78] In Vancouver it was left to Councillor Syd Bowman to bluntly express this view: "The public has no place in telling me how to run my business. This is an issue that the businessman should decide, because the public isn't aware of the problems to be faced."[79] Support for Bowman's assertion came from the Retail Merchants Association. H.C. Boulton, secretary-manager of the association's national body, argued that "even in a democracy, there must be *some* rules as to who is eligible and who is not, to express an opinion." Retailing, he argued, was a specialized field, and only those who were part of this field should have a say in determining retail hours.[80] A number of merchants, employees, and other supporters of store-hour regulations thus appraised the public's ability to contribute meaningfully to resolving the store-hour controversy and found it wanting. They expressed this view through Cold War rhetoric that championed democracy but set clear and self-interested limits on which members of the public should have the opportunity to determine the outcome.

On one level, then, democracy was just one more symbolic weapon employed in the store-hour battle. It was a useful way to suggest that an opponent's views were beyond the pale of Canadian political culture. On another level, however, the exchanges regarding democracy serve to highlight a complex and rational debate in which participants evaluated the political decision-making processes that affected their daily lives as retailers, workers, and consumers. Participants in these exchanges argued not simply over the content of the regulations, but also about the process by which such regulations should be determined. This was a debate about how democracy actually ought to work and about the right of the majority to force its will on the minority. It was also a debate about who rightly comprised the majority. Depending on one's vantage point, the rightful majority ranged from all members of the voting public, to members of the public who purchased goods, to retailers and clerks employed in the retail trade.

Conclusions

"Public policy," Whitaker and Marcuse acknowledge, "is usually debated in terms that mix expressions of self-interest with assertions about the national or common interest." "The coming of the Cold War to Canada," they explain, "was most often discussed in lofty language and high rhetoric." Certainly, these postwar debates over store-hour regulation fitted this pattern. Opponents and supporters of regulation attempted to connect their own self-interests with national concerns about Canada's future.[81] As a result, the language of the Cold War permeated the experience of everyday life for merchants, clerks, consumers, and local politicians in very tangible and immediate ways. One lesson of this study, then, is that Cold War concerns were not restricted to broad debates about the nature of postwar reconstruction, family life, or government institutions. Indeed, in addition to these realms, Cold War rhetoric came to occupy a central place in very specific and local debates about one's access to consumer goods and services.

A second and related conclusion concerns the nature of public debate during the postwar era. Public debate was informed, but not solely shaped, by Cold War concerns. On one level, it is clear, as Whitaker and Marcuse have argued, that Cold War politics served to stifle real debate on a number of fronts.[82] However, as the store-hour debates make clear, Cold War rhetoric was appropriated to serve a number of different and often conflicting ends. Rather than closing down the debates over store hours, Cold War rhetoric served to fan the flames of conflict. Participants selectively employed notions of free enterprise, personal and political freedom, dictatorship, rights, and democracy to serve their own interests. Cold War rhetoric was thus a useful and malleable tool in the hands of opposing interests. Postwar Canadian political culture was hardly a pluralist paradise in which all groups had an equal say, but the examples cited here illustrate that Cold War symbolism was not monopolized by the state and its allies. Canadians also appropriated it for their own uses.

A third conclusion directly concerns the nature of the consumer society that existed between the end of the Second World War and the mid-1960s. These debates over store-hour regulations were clearly informed by both a rights-based rhetoric that mirrored the sense of entitlement expressed regarding welfare-state initiatives and a more atomistic understanding of human activity that denigrated government interference in the economy and instead championed the notion of consumer sovereignty. In her study of twentieth-century American consumer culture, Lizabeth Cohen identifies these two strands of consumer identity as comprising the "citizen consumer" and the "purchaser consumer." The former, she explains, rose to prominence during the 1930s as Americans demanded that their government protect their interests as consumers through regulation. This understanding of consumer identity, she argues, was trumped in the postwar era by the latter category, which expected consumers to contribute to the common good in a more limited and self-interested fashion. Simply by purchasing goods when and where they pleased, this line of argument suggested, Americans would be voting with their pocketbooks. Rather than directly influencing economic policy through government departments and regulations, the consumer now wielded influence indirectly while allowing business to remain as free as possible from undue regulation.[83] The debates over shopping regulations in Vancouver and Victoria suggest that both the "citizen consumer" and "purchaser consumer" ideals co-existed well into the postwar era in Canada. Demands for store-hour regulations mirrored the former understanding of consumer citizenship, while demands that stores be given the right to set their hours according to consumer demand reflected the latter. These competing conceptions of the consumer's role in society highlight not only the stresses and strains that emerged as consumerism colonized leisure time in twentieth-century North America, but also the extent to which citizenship came to be equated with consumption.

Finally, by focusing on the format and nature of these debates, and in particular on what the participants had to say about "democracy," this chapter points to an undeveloped but promising field of study for Canadian historians: the public sphere. Future research may well reveal that the debates examined here were, alternatively, part of a final fleeting wave of thoughtful debate, symptomatic of an already decayed public sphere colonized by a culture of consumption, or even that they formed part of a healthy public sphere that survived well into the twentieth century and perhaps beyond. Determining just where the arguments over store hours fit into the history of public debate will help us to gain an even deeper understanding of Canada's Cold War and postwar culture. More important, future research on the the way that Canadians have discussed and argued the issues of the day will also provide us with insights into the nature of democracy and critical debate in Canada. In doing so, such research will bring us closer to a history that draws on local, social, political, and other approaches to historical analysis as we attempt to answer overarching questions about what the nature of public debate in Canada is and has been and about how it has changed over time. As a step toward such a project, we should recognize that postwar debates over consumerism and leisure show the public sphere to have been more dynamic and vibrant than the existing literature on the Cold War period would suggest.

Acknowledgments
For their comments and suggestions, I would like to thank Catherine Gidney, Bob McDonald, the editors of this volume, and its anonymous reviewers. This essay forms part of a larger project examining the politics of postwar consumerism in Canada that was funded by a postdoctoral fellowship from the Social Sciences and Humanities Research Council of Canada.

Notes

1 Two recent examples are Ian McKay, "The Liberal Order Framework: A Prospectus for a Reconnaissance of Canadian History," *Canadian Historical Review* 81, 4 (December 2000): 617-45; and Gerald Friesen, *Citizens and Nation: An Essay on History, Communication, and Canada* (Toronto: University of Toronto Press, 2000).

2 Jürgen Habermas, *The Structural Transformation of the Public Sphere: An Inquiry into a Category of Bourgeois Society*, trans. T. Burger and F. Lawrence (Cambridge, MA: MIT Press, 1989). Such a synthesis, of course, would require Canadian historians to incorporate examinations of public opinion, public debate, and propaganda into their work. However, some useful departure points for such a synthesis might include Jeffery L. McNairn, *The Capacity to Judge: Public Opinion and Deliberative Democracy in Upper Canada, 1791-1854* (Toronto: University of Toronto Press, 2000); Paul Rutherford, *Endless Propaganda: The Advertising of Public Goods* (Toronto: University of Toronto Press, 2000); Russell Johnston, *Selling Themselves: The Emergence of Canadian Advertising* (Toronto: University of Toronto Press, 2001); Daniel J. Robinson, *The Measure of Democracy: Polling, Market Research, and Public Life, 1930-1945* (Toronto: University of Toronto Press, 1999); and Jarrett Rudy, *The Freedom to Smoke: Tobacco Consumption and Identity* (Montreal and Kingston: McGill-Queen's University Press, 2005).

3 On the creation and expansion of the postwar state, see Doug Owram, *The Government Generation: Canadian Intellectuals and the State, 1900-1945* (Toronto: University of Toronto Press, 1986); Nancy Christie, *Engendering the State: Family, Work, and Welfare in Canada* (Toronto: University of Toronto Press, 2000); Peter McInnis, *Harnessing Labour Confrontation: Shaping the Postwar Settlement in Canada, 1943-1950* (Toronto: University of Toronto Press, 2002); and Shirley Tillotson, *The Public at Play: Gender and the Politics of Recreation in Post-War Ontario* (Toronto: University of Toronto Press, 2000). On family history, for example, see Doug Owram, *Born at the Right Time: A History of the Baby-Boom Generation* (Toronto: University of Toronto Press, 1996); Mary Louise Adams, *The Trouble with Normal: Postwar Youth and the Making of Heterosexuality* (Toronto: University of Toronto Press, 1997); and Mona Gleason, *Normalizing the Ideal: Psychology, Schooling, and the Family in Postwar Canada* (Toronto: University of Toronto Press, 1999).

4 For example, state surveillance and the creation of a Canadian security state is the central theme in Reg Whitaker and Gary Marcuse, *Cold War Canada: The Making of a National Insecurity State, 1945-1957* (Toronto: University of Toronto Press, 1994); and Gary Kinsman, et al., eds., *Whose National Security? Canadian State Surveillance and the Creation of Enemies* (Toronto: Between the Lines, 2000). This theme also informs many of the essays in Richard Cavell, ed., *Love, Hate and Fear in Canada's Cold War* (Toronto: University of Toronto Press, 2004).

5 On these themes, see Gleason, *Normalizing the Ideal*; Adams, *Trouble with Normal*; Franca Iacovetta, "Making 'New Canadians': Social Workers, Women, and the Reshaping of Immigrant Families," in Franca Iacovetta and Mariana Valverde, eds., *Gender Conflicts: New Essays in Women's History* (Toronto: University of Toronto Press, 1992), 261-303; and Veronica Strong-Boag, "Home Dreams: Women and the Suburban Experiment in Canada, 1945-1960," *Canadian Historical Review* 72, 4 (December 1991): 471-504.

6 Franca Iacovetta, "Recipes for Democracy? Gender, Family, and Making Female Citizens in Cold War Canada," *Canadian Woman Studies Journal* 20, 2 (Summer 2000): 12-21 at 13. On domestic containment in the American context, see Elaine Tyler May, *Homeward Bound: American Families in the Cold War Era* (New York: Basic Books, 1988).

7 Owram, *Born at the Right Time*, 52-53. See also Doug Owram, "Canadian Domesticity in the Postwar Era," in Peter Neary and J.L. Granatstein, eds., *The Veterans Charter and Post-World War II Canada* (Montreal and Kingston: McGill-Queen's University Press, 1998), 205-23.

8 Paul Litt, *The Muses, the Masses, and the Massey Commission* (Toronto: University of Toronto Press, 1992), 58; Adams, *Trouble with Normal*, 22.

9 McInnis, *Harnessing Labour Confrontation*, 69-78.

10 Whitaker and Marcuse, *Cold War Canada*, 279, 281, 285.

11 See, for example, Julie Guard, "Women Worth Watching: Radical Housewives in Cold War Canada," in Kinsman, et al., eds., *Whose National Security?* 73-88; and Joy Parr, *Domestic*

Goods: The Material, the Moral, and the Economic in the Postwar Years (Toronto: University of Toronto Press, 1999), Chapter 4.

12 Following Jonathan Rose, I have understood rhetoric here to mean "a form of communication that has at its core an argument designed to elicit behavioral or attitudinal change in the audience." On the distinction between rhetoric and semiotics, see Jonathan Rose, *Making 'Pictures in Our Heads': Government Advertising in Canada* (Westport, CT: Praeger, 2000), 5-12, quotation at 7.

13 With the exception of David Monod's examination of early-twentieth-century shopkeepers, Canadian historians of retailing and consumption have focused exclusively on Eaton's in Toronto; see David Monod, *Store Wars: Shopkeepers and the Culture of Mass Marketing, 1890-1939* (Toronto: University of Toronto Press, 1996). On Eaton's, see Joy L. Santink, *Timothy Eaton and the Rise of His Department Store* (Toronto: University of Toronto Press, 1990); Cynthia Wright, "Feminine Trifles of Vast Importance: Writing Gender into the History of Consumption," in Iacovetta and Valverde, eds., *Gender Conflicts*, 229-60; and Donica Belisle, "Exploring Postwar Consumption: The Campaign to Unionize Eaton's in Toronto, 1948-1952," *Canadian Historical Review* 86, 4 (2005): 641-72.

14 The term comes from Gareth Stedman Jones, "The Determinist Fix: Some Obstacles to the Further Development of the Linguistic Approach to History in the 1990s," *History Workshop Journal* 42 (1996): 19-35 at 29.

15 This latter point is made explicitly in Nancy Christie and Michael Gauvreau, "Introduction: Recasting Canada's Post-war Decade," in Nancy Christie and Michael Gauvreau, eds., *Cultures of Citizenship in Post-War Canada, 1940-1955* (Montreal and Kingston: McGill-Queen's University Press, 2003), 17.

16 *Victoria Daily Colonist,* 2 August 1966, 17.

17 For a thoughtful survey of the retail clerks' campaigns for improved working conditions, see Andrew Neufeld, *Union Store: The History of the Retail Clerks Union in British Columbia, 1899-1999* (Burnaby, BC: United Food and Commercial Workers Union Local 1518, c. 1999). On the connection between these store-hour debates and Victoria's economic development, see Michael Dawson, "Victoria Debates Its Postindustrial Reality: Tourism, Deindustrialization, and Store-Hour Regulations, 1900-1958," *Urban History Review* 35, 2 (Spring 2007): 14-24.

18 Christie and Gauvreau, "Introduction: Recasting," 7, highlights the centrality of this tension in order to challenge the notion that a single political consensus existed in postwar Canada.

19 To date, Canadian studies addressing the regulation of commercial hours have focused almost solely on late-nineteenth-century Toronto; see Christopher Armstrong and H.V. Nelles, *The Revenge of the Methodist Bicycle Company: Sunday Streetcars and Municipal Reform in Toronto, 1888-1897* (Toronto: Peter Martin, 1977); and Santink, *Timothy Eaton.* Campaigns in support of store-hour restrictions are briefly addressed in Monod, *Store Wars,* 27, 42, 85, 92.

20 Of the 200 newspaper articles that I have found focusing on these debates between 1900 and 1945, only 2 make reference to political ideologies; see *Victoria Daily Times,* 28 August 1923, 4; and *Victoria Daily Colonist,* 17 June 1936, 4.

21 McInnis, *Harnessing Labour Confrontation,* 71-77.

22 Litt, *Muses,* 68, 105.

23 Whitaker and Marcuse, *Cold War Canada,* 13.

24 On the notion of "consumer sovereignty," see Parr, *Domestic Goods,* Chapter 4.

25 City of Vancouver Archives (CVA), BC Chamber of Commerce (BCCC) fonds, Add. MSS 370, vol. 1, file 13, BC Chamber of Commerce, *General Policy Statements and Resolutions* (1955), 2.

26 CVA, BCCC fonds, Add. MSS 370, vol. 3, file 1, BC Chamber of Commerce, "Submissions Received up to 29th March 1965 for Discussion at Fourteenth Annual Meeting," 1-A.

27 Michael Dawson, *Selling British Columbia: Tourism and Consumer Culture, 1890-1970* (Vancouver: UBC Press, 2004), 134-35; CVA, Add. MSS. 633, Greater Vancouver Visitors and Convention Bureau papers, ser. A, vol. 1, file 2, Board of Directors Minutes, Manager's Report, 11 March 1948.

28 CVA, Add. MSS. 633, Greater Vancouver Visitors and Convention Bureau papers, ser. A, vol. 1, file 1, Board of Directors Minutes, 9 August 1945.

29 *Vancouver Sun,* 15 January 1954, 16.

30 *Victoria Daily Colonist,* 26 June 1957, 4. Three months later the *Colonist,* 12 September 1957, 4, returned to this subject and argued that "in a supposedly free economy it should be a merchant's own business to decide when he will serve his customers."

31 *Vancouver Daily Province,* 1 August 1962, 4.

32 *Victoria Daily Colonist,* 22 May 1958, 13.

33 Tom Traves, *The State and Enterprise: Canadian Manufacturers and the Federal Government, 1917-1931* (Toronto: University of Toronto Press, 1979), 155-56. The central role of local and federal government agencies in US economic development is succinctly demonstrated in William Leach, *Land of Desire: Merchants, Power, and the Rise of a New American Culture* (New York: Vintage, 1993), 173-85, Chapter 12.

34 Monod, *Store Wars,* 27, 55, Chapter 6.

35 *Vancouver Sun,* 8 March 1951, 4.

36 *Victoria Daily Times,* 9 April 1958, 4.

37 Victoria City Archives, Victoria Chamber of Commerce fonds, 32-A-2, Board of Directors Minutes, 25 November 1946.

38 The central role of women in North American consumer activism at this time is well documented; see Guard, "Women Worth Watching"; Magda Fahrni, "Counting the Costs of Living: Gender, Citizenship, and a Politics of Prices in 1940s Montreal," *Canadian Historical Review* 83, 4 (December 2002): 483-504; and Lizabeth Cohen, *A Consumers' Republic: The Politics of Mass Consumption in Postwar America* (New York: Knopf, 2003).

39 *Victoria Daily Times,* 25 April 1957, 19.

40 A civic referendum in 1951, Palmer argued, had resulted in an overwhelming vote in favour of evening shopping at corner stores and had produced a civic bylaw allowing such. This bylaw was being rendered obsolete by the provincial government's revised Municipal Act; see *Victoria Daily Colonist,* 26 April 1957, 17.

41 *Victoria Daily Colonist,* 4 December 1946, 4.

42 *Victoria Daily Colonist,* 21 November 1953, 4.

43 *Victoria Daily Times,* 31 July 1951, 3.

44 *Vancouver Daily Province,* 20 May 1952, 15.

45 *Victoria Daily Times,* 27 April 1956, 6.

46 Litt, *Muses,* 105.

47 Whitaker and Marcuse, *Cold War Canada,* x.

48 Ibid., 268.

49 Canada's two most infamous witch hunts focused on NFB head John Grierson and diplomat Herbert Norman. Their stories are surveyed in Whitaker and Marcuse, *Cold War Canada,* Chapters 10 and 11. The federal government's campaign to tar the Housewives Consumers' Association with the brush of communism in order to hinder the association's postwar campaign for price controls is a particularly instructive example; see Guard, "Women Worth Watching."

50 Gleason, *Normalizing the Ideal,* 16.

51 On such rights-based rhetoric during the Depression, see Lara Campbell, "'A Barren Cupboard at Home': Ontario Families Confront the Premiers during the Great Depression," in E.-A. Montigny and L. Chambers, eds., *Ontario since Confederation: A Reader* (Toronto: University of Toronto Press, 2000), 284-306; and Lara Campbell, "'We who have wallowed in the mud of Flanders': First World War Veterans, Unemployment, and the Great Depression in Ontario, 1929-1939," *Journal of the Canadian Historical Association* n.s. 11 (2000): 125-49. On efforts to champion children's rights and women's rights respectively, see Dominique Marshall, "The Language of Children's Rights, the Formation of the Welfare State, and the Democratic Experience of Poor Families in Quebec, 1940-55," *Canadian Historical Review* 78, 3 (September 1997): 409-41 at 409; and Annalee Gölz, "Family Matters: The Canadian Family and the State in the Postwar Period," *Left History* 1, 2 (1993): 9-49 at 15. On the centrality of rights-based pronouncements to the creation of specific welfare-state policies, see Dominique Jean [Marshall], "Family Allowances and Family Autonomy: Quebec

Families Encounter the Welfare State, 1945-1955," in Bettina Bradbury, ed., *Canadian Family History: Selected Readings* (Toronto: Copp Clark Pitman, 1992), 401-37; and James Struthers, "Family Allowances, Old Age Security, and the Construction of Entitlement in the Canadian Welfare State, 1943-1951," in Neary and Granatstein, eds., *Veterans Charter*, 179-204.

52 *Victoria Daily Colonist*, 21 September 1946.

53 *Victoria Daily Times*, 10 October 1946, 4.

54 *Victoria Daily Colonist*, 26 October 1946, 3.

55 *Victoria Daily Colonist*, 9 October 1946, 4.

56 Fahrni, "Counting the Costs."

57 Cohen, *Consumers' Republic*.

58 *Victoria Daily Times*, 16 February 1953, 4.

59 *Victoria Daily Colonist*, 18 February 1953, 4.

60 *Victoria Daily Times*, 1 April 1953, 4.

61 Shirley Tillotson, "Time, Swimming Pools, and Citizenship: The Emergence of Leisure Rights in Mid-Twentieth-Century Canada," in Robert Adamoski et al., eds., *Contesting Canadian Citizenship: Historical Readings* (Peterborough: Broadview, 2002), 199.

62 Ibid., 204. On just one occasion was the "right to work" evoked in support of the six-day week; see *Victoria Daily Times*, 7 October 1958, 4.

63 Tillotson, "Time, Swimming Pools," 206.

64 Len Kuffert, *A Great Duty: Canadian Responses to Modern Life and Mass Culture, 1939-1967* (Montreal and Kingston: McGill-Queen's University Press, 2003), 96, 143-45, 157-58, 208; Litt, *Muses*, 87.

65 For pronouncements on democratic methods of childrearing, see Gleason, *Normalizing the Ideal*, 7, 16, 111; and Gölz, "Family Matters," 19, 27-28. For the concerns of cultural critics, see Litt, *Muses*, 106, 249.

66 Kuffert, *Great Duty*, 183.

67 *Victoria Daily Colonist*, 1 October 1946, 19; *Vancouver Daily Province*, 18 July 1957, 21.

68 CVA, City Council and Office of the City Clerk fonds – Clerk's Office, 28-D-7, File 1: Pratt's Beauty Supply Co. Ltd. 1948 re Wednesday Closing By-law, M. Pratt, Pratt's Beauty Supply Co. Ltd to License and Claims Committee, City Clerk's Office, 28 February 1948.

69 *Victoria Daily Times*, 12 January 1949, 7.

70 *Vancouver Sun*, 3 June 1954, 1.

71 *Victoria Daily Times*, 1 October 1946, 10.

72 *Vancouver Sun*, 7 January 1947, 8.

73 *Victoria Daily Colonist*, 11 October 1946, 2.

74 *Victoria Daily Colonist*, 6 December 1946, 4.

75 *Victoria Daily Times*, 7 October 1946, 3.

76 *Victoria Daily Colonist*, 27 October 1946, 3.

77 *Victoria Daily Colonist*, 14 November 1953, 17.

78 The joint brief was submitted by Standard Furniture Company, W. and J. Wilson, the Five-Day Action Committee, the Victoria Community Grocers Co-operative Association, Red and White Food Stores, and the Retail Meat Dealers' Association; see *Victoria Daily Times*, 24 November 1953, 10.

79 *Vancouver Sun*, 27 March 1954, 1-2.

80 *Vancouver Sun*, 4 July 1958, 4, original emphasis.

81 Their campaigns and pronouncements reflect the Italian Marxist Antonio Gramsci's recognition that successful attempts to obtain influence or hegemony in a society have a "national-popular" dimension. On this concept, see Roger Simon, *Gramsci's Political Thought: An Introduction* (London: Lawrence and Wishart, 1991), 43-46.

82 Whitaker and Marcuse, *Cold War Canada*, xi.

83 Cohen, *Consumers' Republic*, 18, 101, 147.

9

Men Behind the Marquee: Greasing the Wheels of Vansterdam's Professional Striptease Scene, 1950-75

Becki L. Ross

Fifteen to twenty police officers would come into the Penthouse on a raid and swoop down on you. But we had a system. Each club owner would phone: 'They just left my place. They're on the prowl.' We also had a lookout on top of the roof. If he saw a cavalcade of cars coming down Seymour St., he knew it was the police. So he would press the button and sound the alarm. That gave customers a chance to hide their bottles.[1]

Take a walk on the dark side of Chinatown where, like a sinister gargoyle, bird of carrion perched drooling on the corner of Pender and Main, once stood a perverse monument fully erected to deviant, diabolical depravity, the notorious Kublai Khan ... where lying in wait for you ... femme fatale sirens, luring in the men.[2]

Vancouver Heats Up after Dark

In the wake of the Second World War, Vancouver, British Columbia, basked in growing economic affluence, optimism, and new opportunities for leisure and recreation. After the penny-pinching Depression, the tragedies of war, and the upheavals of social and familial networks, Vancouverites looked ahead to a rosier future. Beginning in the 1950s, the erection of sleek modernist office towers, deluxe sports facilities, and diverse cultural venues announced the glitter and tinsel of a newly confident port city.[3] By the 1960s the entire city centre glowed from the electric energy of over 19,000 neon signs. Local citizens rejected the construction of an urban, elevated freeway that would have splintered the centre of town; this decision not only distinguished Vancouver from other major North American cities but also showcased the city's downtown as a compact, intimate locale.[4] Both the eight-lane Granville Bridge (built in 1954) and the rezoned, densely developed West End enabled easier access to the downtown district and to its flourishing after-dark scene of nightclubs, theatres, dance halls, movie houses, and restaurants.[5] After Canadian officials rescinded the racist Chinese Exclusion Act in 1947, Chinese immigration to Vancouver, or "Salt Water City," increased, and Chinatown – east of the city's downtown core – was marketed as the city's premiere "exotic destination."[6]

To Vancouver's workers who toiled long hours five days a week at dockyards, sawmills, factories, offices, shops, and department stores, night-time entertainment on weekends promised a much-welcome diversion. To suburban couples in New Westminster, Burnaby, Delta, Richmond, Coquitlam, North Shore, and Surrey, dressing up for a "night on the town" meant an exciting, temporary escape from the comfort and familiarity of detached homes, small children, and shopping malls. Indeed, many city residents had more discretionary income than ever before to spend on commercial leisure pursuits. To tourists on the lookout for adventure, the vibrant, pulsating beat of Vancouver's nightspots was as inviting as the city's dazzling natural beauty of mountains, forests, and Pacific Ocean. Live big band, swing, jazz, blues, soul, and rock music worked its influential magic on fun-seekers – young and old, urban and suburban, residents and visitors – who planned their evenings out in an era before television's monopoly on primetime viewing kept people at home.[7]

In the words of infamous night-beat reporter Jack Wasserman, "in the 1950s, Vancouver erupted as the vaudeville capital of Canada, rivalling and finally outstripping Montreal in the East and San Francisco in the south as one of the few places where the brightest stars of the nightclub era could be glimpsed from behind a post, through a smoke-filled room, over the heads of $20 tippers at ringside. Only in Las Vegas and Miami Beach, in season, were more superstars available in nightclubs."[8] *Vancouver Sun* journalist Patrick Nagle recalled a "show business railway" that moved performers up and down the Pacific Coast on a "west coast circuit," with stops in Los Angeles, San Francisco, Las Vegas, Portland, Seattle, and Vancouver.[9] The Canadian city's geographical proximity to the US-Canada border meant that American talent flowed steadily south to north much more than it flowed east to west over the physical and symbolic barrier of the perilous Rocky Mountains. In the context of a strong Canadian dollar, American nightclub acts were relatively affordable; moreover, many entertainers rehearsed brand new material in Vancouver to loyal fans, sometimes at discounted rates. Until the mid-1970s nightclub owners routinely booked cabaret-style revues that profiled combinations of singers, comedians, showgirls, chorus lines, acrobats, jugglers, and tap dancers, all of whom performed to live musical accompaniment.

In the 1950s and 1960s the art and industry of female striptease emerged in Vancouver (and elsewhere) as juicy, slightly naughty adult entertainment for locals and tourists alike. The growing profitability of exotic dancing was driven by the increasing postwar sexualization of popular culture peddled in risqué comic books, *Playboy* magazine (launched in 1953), pin-up calendars, and lurid pulp novels. "Bombshells" in Hollywood films such as Marilyn Monroe, Jayne Mansfield, and Kim Novak ramped up the erotica quotient, expanding the inventory of titillation for sale.[10] In the early twentieth century scantily clad can-can dancers, "hurdy gurdies," "walking dolls," and long-legged chorus girls earned their livelihood as vaudeville and burlesque performers.[11] By mid-century the regular appearance of internationally renowned, imported striptease queens in tasteful pasties and bejewelled g-strings at Vancouver nightclubs helped to cement the city's prevailing image as culturally and sexually permissive: a veritable Lotusland. And throughout the 1970s professional striptease redoubled its reach in the context of hippie culture, a "free love" ethos, decriminalized nudity (in British Columbia in 1972), and the recruitment of large numbers of Vancouver-based dancers onto the mushrooming stages of hotel "peeler pubs."

It seems hardly surprising that bawdy night-time entertainment in the booming port city stirred opposition in much the same way that it had decades earlier before the rough-edged, white-settler colony donned a mid-century veneer of sophistication.[12] In the early 1950s Vancouver's State Burlesque Theatre on East Hastings Street was raided and closed down, and in the 1960s and 1970s nightclubs suffered periodic social censure, police harassment, and charges for morality-related offences.[13] Dancers in particular were harshly judged for abandoning (and mocking) the venerated matrix of stay-at-home, full-time marriage, wifedom, and motherhood.[14] Indeed, expert opinion normalized the hetero-gendered roles of men and women in nuclear families as a bulwark against the looming peril of cultural decline and communism.[15] Yet antivice crusaders never successfully squelched the thirst for popular amusements. As Greg Marquis argues, Vancouver's vice industry met social needs and was *as vital* to the city's economic growth as were its railway facilities, sawmills, and grain elevators.[16]

In this chapter, rather than focus on the significant contribution of erotic dancers to the city's economic and artistic health, I examine the efforts of Vancouver's nightclub owners to create and stoke consumer appetite for "bump and grind."[17] The tricks these men employed, the risks they took, the profits they made, and the lines they both crossed and buttressed are revealed in archival and ethnographic data specific to the period 1950-75 – widely perceived as the "Golden Era" of striptease before the advent of "spreading," "split beavers," table-dancing, lap-dancing, champagne rooms, stage fees, and the Canadian government's Visa Program for "exotic dancers" from overseas.[18] Club owners openly exploited men's fascination with nearly naked female bodies, they operated quasi-legal establishments, and they were widely stereotyped as sleazy, low-life mobsters, bookies, pimps, and criminals. Their first-person memories of the contradictory facets of the "stripper business," supplemented by reflections of male musicians hired to accompany dancers on stage, open a window onto broader anxieties about gender, sexuality, race, and the Canadian nation in the third quarter of the twentieth century.

Fancy Nightclubs in the West End/Uptown

As the lights went out in Vancouver's vaudeville and burlesque theatres such as the Beacon and the State in the early 1950s, in their place emerged independent nightclubs clustered in both the West End/uptown and East End/downtown districts. Indeed, the east-west spatial divide – with Main Street as the principal bisector – was an already well-established fact in the metropolis. As summarized in the newly unveiled 1950s Gallery at the Vancouver Museum, "in the 1950s, your neighbourhood, especially the side of Main St. you lived on, was likely to reflect your income, ethnic origin, religion, and political affiliation."[19] Asymmetries of wealth, income, status, and education date back to the 1800s; moreover, racial and ethnic tensions have always been a central feature of life in the province's lower mainland.[20] In 1951 the city of 345,000 on the south-west coast of *British* Columbia comprised an Anglo-Canadian majority (93 percent) and small communities of non-Anglo Canadians who were overrepresented on the city's east side.[21] Like the colour line that divided Montreal's nightclub scene in the 1940s and 1950s, Vancouver's night-time entertainment reflected and reinforced the city's long-standing class-based and racialized separation of east from west.[22]

West End nightclubs – the Cave Supper Club (1937-81), Isy's Supper Club (1958-76), and the Penthouse Cabaret (1947-present) – were "la crème" of the city's night spots. Swanky and upmarket, these clubs enticed adventurous Vancouverites with their high-class acts, dancing to swing rhythms, and night-time razzle-dazzle. Much larger and more elegant than the East End/downtown cabarets (see below), they showcased "top drawer" entertainment, including the Everly Brothers, Mitzi Gaynor, Sophie Tucker, Liberace, the Platters, Sammy Davis, Jr., Wayne Newton, Lena Horne, the Supremes, and Sonny and Cher. Through connections to talent agents in Las Vegas, nightclub owners Isy Walters, Sandy De Santis, Joe Philliponi, Ken Stauffer, and Bob Mitten also began to book predominantly white American stripteasers with mainstream, cross-over appeal, including Sally Rand, the famous fan dancer; Evelyn West, the "Hubba Hubba Girl" with breasts insured by Lloyds of London for $50,000; Yvette Dare and her trained parrot; Lili St. Cyr and her infamous bathtub routine; the 6' 8" Glamazon, Ricki Covette; the multitalented, Seattle-born Gypsy Rose Lee; and the red-headed Tempest Storm.[23] Not until the mid- to late 1960s did local, Vancouver-based erotic dancers begin to appear on nightclub marquees, including Dee Dee Special, Miss Lovie, Daiquiri, Tequila Lopez, Princess

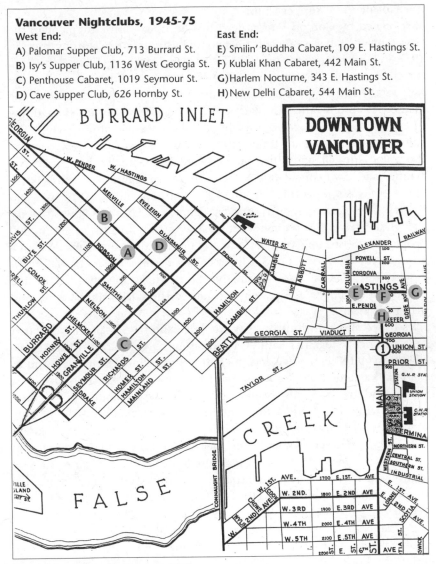

Vancouver Nightclubs, 1945-75

West End:
A) Palomar Supper Club, 713 Burrard St.
B) Isy's Supper Club, 1136 West Georgia St.
C) Penthouse Cabaret, 1019 Seymour St.
D) Cave Supper Club, 626 Hornby St.

East End:
E) Smilin' Buddha Cabaret, 109 E. Hastings St.
F) Kublai Khan Cabaret, 442 Main St.
G) Harlem Nocturne, 343 E. Hastings St.
H) New Delhi Cabaret, 544 Main St.

Map of downtown Vancouver, 1955.
Vancouver City Archives, Map Collection, no. 918, 1955, Vancouver, BC

Lillian, Bonnie Scott, Foxy Lady, Coco Fontaine, Tarren Rae, and April Paris, among others. By the early 1970s not only was there an increase in the availability and talent of Vancouver dancers, but club owners felt pressure to replace expensive, imported singers, comedians, and tap dancers with cheaper, exclusive line-ups of "exotics." As the demand sky-rocketed, there were more stages in local beer parlours than there were striptease dancers to fill them.

The Gothic Cave Supper Club

First owned by Gordon King, a Jewish, Winnipeg-born entrepreneur, the Cave Supper Club was officially opened for business at 626 Hornby Street in 1937 and quickly became one of the city's favourite nightclubs. Describing the club's interior for *Vancouver Life* magazine, Len Carlyle wrote that the King family had ingeniously dipped burlap in wet plaster and moulded the material around two-by-four outcroppings from the ceiling and floor; dimly lit and painted khaki green, they imparted a cave-like atmosphere.[24] The club changed hands many times: after King, it was owned by George Amato (from Portland, Oregon), then by Isy Walters, and finally in 1958 by Ken Stauffer and his nephew, Bob Mitten. To gossip columnist Denny Boyd, "the Cave was semi-gothic. They had a sculptured ceiling with plastic stalactites hanging from it, dusty artificial palm trees. For years, it was so busy they didn't have time for renovations. There were line-ups to get in, 800 people got dressed up – your best suit and tie, and the woman would wear a gown ... The crowd was not a stripper crowd, it was a Vegas entertainment crowd."[25] In 1954 the Cave – formerly a bottle club – was awarded the first dining-lounge liquor licence, which legalized the sale of liquor, wine, and beer with meals.[26] Walters no longer needed to rely on cover charges and sales of ice and soft drinks to pay the bills: the sale of alcohol (at often inflated prices), together with ever-increasing cover charges, made it possible to bankroll expensive acts, including professional striptease. And as Mariana Valverde notes, drinking moderate amounts of alcohol in public venues had, by the 1950s, assumed a degree of respectability as a method of enhancing social interaction, intimacy, and relaxation.[27] Despite the temperance-leaning provincial government of BC premier W.A.C. Bennett (1952-72), city-dwellers sought the pleasure of each other's company in social spaces where alcohol consumption and nightly entertainment were jointly sold. For many, Freudian-inspired "enlightened hedonism" supplanted the old-fashioned temperance ethos that had dominated the century's early decades.[28]

Isy Walters was one of Vancouver's most intriguing, enduring, and compelling movers and shakers in the world of entertainment and professional striptease. Born Isadore Waltuck in Odessa, Russia, in 1906, he arrived in Vancouver at age two with his working-class parents, Joseph and Marion – Jewish immigrants in search of a new life where it was rumoured "money was growing on the city's streets."[29] As a young boy, "bitten by the showbiz bug," he "sold candy and ice cream in every theatre in Vancouver."[30] Walters left home at fourteen to travel across the US and Canada with Browning Amusements and with the Conklin and Garrett carnivals. Once settled in Vancouver in the 1940s, after dabbling in the salvage business and then in the nightclub scene, he bought the upscale Cave Supper Club in 1952 and orchestrated Vancouver appearances of first-class "exotics": Lady Godiva (1952), Gypsy Rose Lee and her Royal American Beauties (1954), Lili St. Cyr (1955), Minsky's Follies (1954), and Ricki Covette (1956).[31] In addition to the striptease acts, Walters acknowledged that female dancers, regardless of their erotic explicitness, added dramatic action and sexy, Las-Vegas-style flare to any evening's program.[32] He was not ashamed to acknowledge that he always liked to "bring in the sex shows whenever things got quiet in the city." In 1975, a year before his death, Walters commented effusively, "It just seems that the girls always got me out of [financial] trouble. At first, they got me into trouble [with the morality squad], and then in later years, they kept getting me out of trouble."[33]

Richard (Richie) Walters, Isy Walters' son, followed in the footsteps of his impresario father and learned the ropes first-hand: "We had a lot of girls that were Australian or English. They were working in Vegas and then they'd be found by immigration and kicked out. So, they would come back to Canada and wait for their papers. They would come directly to us and work for us for awhile."[34] Richard Walters recalled that the showgirls were topless at the Cave, but they always wore g-strings and fancy headgear: "Mother would come down and watch them the first time to make sure everything was okay. We paid them $75 a week in the Fifties, which was not chicken feed – girls got $25 a week in a grocery store. Plus working a production line at the Cave was much more glamorous."[35] Most acts were booked for two-week stints, and the most bankable could expect repeat engagements.

Isy's Supper Club

After a six-year stint at the Cave, Isy Walters opened Isy's Supper Club in December 1958 and was granted a coveted dining-lounge liquor licence in 1959. Walters installed plush chairs, red-velvet curtains, big tables, seating for 260, and air conditioning, spending $100,000 to transform what was a former Chrysler garage. One wall was mirrored, and another wall in the entryway was full of eight-by-ten black and white photographs of all the acts: signed, framed, and screwed onto the wall. Here, Walters continued booking big American stars as well as lines of almost exclusively white erotic dancers, choreographed in-house by the talented Jack Card. In mid-1963 Walters' booking diary plots a shift to more explicitly sexual numbers, and the names of his acts reflect his ongoing love affair with the flash, sparkle, and erotic mystery of Las Vegas and Paris, among them: Burly Cue Revue (1963), Les Girls (1964), Vegas Girls (1964), Play Mates Review (1964), La Femme Revue (1965), Les Girls Revue (1965), Girls à la Carte (1966), Viva La Roma (1966), Card's Vegas Girls (1967), and SKIN Exotics (1969/1970). Both Sally Rand and Tempest Storm graced Isy's stage in 1970. None of these dancers performed nude, and with the exception of the SKIN show in 1969,

Jack Card, choreographer, Cave Supper Club and Isy's Supper Club, with dancers, ca. 1966.
Reprinted with permission of Jack Card, from his private collection; photographer unknown

they shared the nightly limelight with comics, accordion players, singers, illusionists, and magicians.

Jeannie Runnalls began her career as a go-go dancer in Calgary and, at nineteen, went to work at Isy's Supper Club, first as a cocktail waitress – "black lace top, hot pink skirt, black nylons" – and later as Isy's personal secretary. "Not only did Isy have a photographic memory," recalled Runnalls, "but he had the first liquor licence, the first Cadillac, the first penthouse."[36] Della Walters, Isy's stepdaughter, described her father's hectic pace until his death of a heart attack while working in his nightclub in 1976:

Program cover, Isy's Supper Club, "Viva la Roma," 1966. Reprinted with permission of Jack Card, from his private collection; illustrator unknown

Yvette Monjour, striptease start in Jack Card's production, "Viva La Roma," at Isy's Supper Club, 1966. Reprinted with permission of Jack Card, from his private collection; photographer unknown

He'd get up about 10:00 in the morning and spend an hour getting ready. He'd be gone by noon. And he was home at 6:00 on the nose. 6:15, he watched the news. Eat supper, watch the news, nap for a couple hours, then go and get changed and be gone again. He was a huge workaholic, didn't take vacations, except to California and Vegas – a mix of work and play. He was a big smoker, but he didn't drink. He was a master showman, huge charisma. He was larger than life. At his memorial, strippers came up to me after and told me how much he had meant to them.[37]

Isy Walters had high standards for "A-grade" dancers, and he admired professional stripteasers – not only from his standpoint as a risk-taking entrepreneur, but also as an aficionado of white beauty and glamour. Yet both he and his son were well aware of the need to ensure that what they viewed as tasteful did not slide into disgusting or offensive in the eyes of patrons, especially women. Richard Walters noted that women were quick to judge other women who doffed their clothing for a living: "You've got to remember that in the 1950s and 1960s, the average woman looked down on strippers ... maybe they really wanted to do it. How many women went home from these shows and stripped for their husbands? I bet some did. But they were hypocrites – they all thought strippers were prostitutes."[38] Isy was known to draw the line at what he considered respectable, proper female comportment. As Della Walters explained, "my father would never have let me become a dancer. Now there's a dichotomy for you ... When I was a cocktail waitress, I was approached by a man who wanted to take my picture for *Playboy* – $25,000. I was eighteen or nineteen. Isy said, 'No way my daughter's going to be on every goddamned musician's wall all over North America. No.' I think his main objection was that I was separate from all that at some level."[39] So on the one hand, Isy Walters refused to accept that stripping was cheap and tawdry, and on the other hand, he strove to protect his daughter from any involvement in the sex industry, thereby affirming the moral hierarchy that divided good "Marys" from evil "Eves."

In the early 1970s Isy Walters abandoned all pretence to a mixed, revue-style entertainment program: the "tease" in striptease was unceremoniously dead. In 1972, to coincide with a "Truck Loggers Convention," Walters launched "Strip City" – a weekly exclusive line-up of four or five "exotics" in response to the decriminalization of bottomless dancing, the new appeal of striptease in hotel beer parlours, and the soaring, prohibitive costs of big-name, Vegas-style production numbers.

The Penthouse Cabaret: "This Ain't Sunnybrook Farm!"
Like Isy Walters, Joe Philliponi became an extraordinarily visible and colourful club owner and impresario. In 1929, as a small boy, he arrived with

his Italian immigrant parents in Extension, British Columbia, from San Nicola, Italy. In 1933 the Philliponi family relocated to Vancouver, "the Manhattan of Canada." After what Joe's younger brother Ross Filippone[40] remembered as a happy childhood, three sons – Joe, Ross, and Mickey – served in the armed forces during the Second World War, and brother Jimmy and sister Florence stayed home to operate the family's messenger and delivery service, Eagle Time Delivery Company.[41] After the war, the family launched the Diamond Cab Company, which had the city's first limousines. In a building owned by the family at 1019 Seymour Street, Joe Philliponi began to entertain late-night guests in 1947 at a private club in his loft apartment, which he called the Eagle Time Athletic Club. According to Ross Filippone, "donations" to the club underwrote the family's sponsorship of amateur sports for youth, including lacrosse, basketball, bowling, football, hockey, and boxing. A very popular after-hours joint among celebrated invitees, Joe's loft was raided for liquor infractions in 1949 and subsequently reopened as the Penthouse Cabaret in December 1950.

In the Penthouse's heyday in the 1950s and 1960s, 600 patrons a night paid to enjoy the shows, which cost the Filippones nearly $300,000 a year. Throughout the 1950s the Penthouse had one of the few fine restaurants in town, the Steak Loft, and its brick-oven pizza and charcoal-broiled steaks – "grade 'A' Alberta beef" – were legendary. In the club's vast Gold Room, show business celebrities Tony Bennett, Sophie Tucker, Sammy Davis, Jr., Liberace, and Ella Fitzgerald entertained. Ross Filippone remembered: "We'd have the top people come to the club – lawyers, stockbrokers, doctors, professional athletes. Husbands came with the wives."[42] It was not the Orpheum. Nor was it the Cave or Isy's Supper Club, with their elaborate floorshows of skimpily clad dancing girls, elaborate choreography, and sumptuous stage sets. Yet it had heat. By the mid-1960s, in part to stay competitive with the Cave and Isy's, Joe Philliponi began to include showgirls in the nightly floorshows. In 1968 reporter Alex MacGillivray wrote that the Penthouse was "a watering spot for bookies and brokers, doctors and dentists, guys and dolls, ladies and gentlemen, and just about anybody who could smell a good time ... it was the city's oldest stationary funhouse."[43] It was Penthouse policy until the mid-1970s that all striptease dancers keep their g-strings firmly in place, although Joe (the booking agent) knew that dancers were performing nude in San Francisco in the mid-1960s. The Penthouse's owners were also beginning to feel the pinch of lost revenues to a revolutionary advance in media technology. As Ross Filippone astutely observed, "Television hurt the nightclubs. People sat in their living room and turned on the tube. They saw Ed Sullivan with all the name acts you could possibly mention, all in one hour! Four or five top-name acts in the business. And it didn't cost. So people stayed home – they didn't want to pay $1.75 for a drink."[44]

Until 1968 the Penthouse was a bottle club. While the Cave and Isy's were awarded liquor licences in the 1950s, the Penthouse was shut out, Ross Filippone mused, because of its alleged connections to organized crime – denied by Filippone to this day. He maintained that the hotels had a monopoly on liquor sales – they could legally sell draft beer, and "it was all political." He also claimed that the Penthouse was raided and harassed weekly in the 1950s and 1960s by fifteen to twenty Vancouver police officers at a time. Like other bottle clubs, the Penthouse sold patrons ice with mix and, sometimes, illegal bootlegged booze; they turned a blind eye to customers who arrived with liquor bottles in brown bags. Ross was frank about the hypocrisy: "You couldn't survive strictly as a bottle club when you're bringing in big-name acts. You had to have extra revenue. And the only way you could get revenue was by selling illegal booze, even though liquor could be bought at the 24-hour, government-run liquor stores." To prepare for imminent busts, Ross' brother Joe arranged a lookout on the nightclub's roof to watch for the detective crew. When he spotted the Dry Squad, he sounded an alarm and alerted the bar staff downstairs. Waiters then warned patrons to hide their jugs on built-in ledges, like utensil drawers, under the tables. Ross Filippone expressed indignation over the routine harassment: "It was a big farce. It was like the Keystone Cops coming in looking under tables for bottles with little flashlights. They'd never go to Hotel Vancouver. They'd never go to the Commodore. They would never go to the Cave. Because those places were high-class."[45] Effectively, the double standard reflected the city's class-stratified hierarchy: "high-status" clubs were entirely exempt from raids. The Penthouse was ascribed lower status in the West End/uptown, and it was targeted, although it occupied a higher rung than its East End/downtown rivals (see below).

The Penthouse quickly earned a reputation as the best place in the city to meet elite sex workers who frequented the club, bought food and drinks, and charmed a loyal clientele of locals and tourists. Despite the "live and let live" nonchalance of Penthouse staff and the lack of citizens' complaints, prostitution-related charges were laid against club personnel in December 1975 following a six-month undercover operation. Joe, Mickey, and Ross, cashiers Minerva Kelly and Rose Filippone (Mickey's daughter), and doorman Jan Sedlack were arraigned on charges of "living on the avails of prostitution" and "creating public mischief with intent to corrupt public morals."[46] According to the *Vancouver Sun's* former "Around Town" columnist Denny Boyd, "When people accused Joe of harbouring hookers and strippers, and living on the avails, he replied, 'I ain't Rebecca, and this ain't Sunnybrook Farm!'"[47] To Ross Filippone, the case meant negative consequences for his family: "My kids got ribbed. It was embarrassing. Didn't help my marriage either. I sat the kids down and told them, 'I want you to know one thing – we're not ashamed of anything. You can keep your heads up high, and you can know that your Dad did nothing wrong.' But inside they were hurt."[48]

In both the media and the courtroom, the Filippones were likened to pimps who profited from the tips and cover charges paid by prostitutes who solicited customers inside. Angrily, Ross Filippone pointed out a troubling double standard: "We argued in our defence that the Hudson's Bay [department store] sells working girls clothes, so why aren't they charged with living on the avails?"[49] In 1978, after sixty-one trial days over six months, forty-five witnesses, a padlocked closure of the Penthouse lasting almost three years, convictions, fines, appeals, $1.5 million in litigation fees, a Supreme Court appearance where nine judges dismissed the case, and $2 million in lost revenues, the accused were fully acquitted, and the Penthouse reopened for business, bruised but not broken.[50] Still open in 2007, it remains the longest-running striptease venue in Canada.[51]

The "Raunchy" East End Nightclubs: Smilin' Buddha, New Delhi, Harlem Nocturne, and Kublai Khan

Throughout the 1950s, 1960s, and 1970s, Vancouver's West End supper clubs – the Cave, Isy's, and the Penthouse – were owned by white men, regularly featured white striptease headliners, and catered to a white, well-heeled clientele (initially gender-mixed, then primarily male white-collar workers). In the East End, by contrast, a tightly knit circuit of nightclubs emerged and were deemed "minor league" and "B-list" in comparison to the West End's "A-list" nightclubs. Smaller, more run-down than West End supper clubs, and rented by men of colour, the East End cabarets – bottle clubs until the late 1960s – began to regularly feature "B-grade" and "novelty" striptease acts in the early to mid-1950s. Located in and around the working-class neighbourhood of Chinatown – a city in miniature – Lachman Das Jir's Smilin' Buddha (1953-89), Leo Bagry's New Delhi (1956-73), Jimmy Yuen's Kublai Khan (1970-80, formerly the Shanghai Junk), and Ernie King's Harlem Nocturne (1957-68) were more racially diverse than their West End competition in terms of staff, acts, and patrons. Part of the postwar transformation of Chinatown into a tourist site, these East End nightclubs catered to consumers' taste for the extraordinary and the unusual, as dictated by what the late Edward Said observed as the discursive tradition of orientalism.[52] Kay Anderson argues that hegemonic notions of a quintessential racial "other" produced and managed Chinatown as an enclave of adventure, intrigue, vice, and immorality – a destination for "entertainment, spice, colour and romance."[53] The area's nightclubs were well known for informal drug dealing, recreational pot use, an active sex trade, and a visible (white) police presence far removed from anything found in the tony, upper-crust, West-Side enclaves of Shaughnessy, Kerrisdale, and Point Grey. Club operators were also the first to introduce topless dancers minus pasties, although initially the City Licensing Department required that the women appear motionless.

In the immediate postwar decades, dancers of colour, especially black women, were more likely to work the Chinatown/Main Street clubs.[54] Italian Canadian jazz saxophonist Dave Davies (née Harold Loretto) recalled that "most of the girls at Isy's and the Penthouse that I played for were white, but down at the Hastings and Main Street strip, it was more a concentration of black girls."[55] For many people of colour in Vancouver, the cheaper, more accessible, and less formal Chinatown nightclubs were "the place to be." They became a popular destination for thrill-seeking white Vancouverites and tourists who crossed the city after seeing the "big stars" at the Cave Supper Club and Isy's Supper Club, much as white New Yorkers traversed neighbourhood borders to Harlem nightspots like the Hot Feet, the Clambake, and the Cotton Club and just as white San Franciscans sought out their city's Chinatown clubs.[56] To adapt the insight of Kevin Mumford, the interzone of Vancouver's interracial East End promised nonresidents entrée to somewhere exotic, foreign, and supposedly inferior.[57] For some white Vancouverites, voyaging to East End clubs was considered slumming it, in part because the East End lay adjacent to historic Skid Road – Vancouver's first so-called slum district, which overlapped with the city's original red-light district. Inhabited by waves of immigrants, unemployed poor, drifters, and mobile labourers for close to a century, the East End/Chinatown area was dotted with cheap, single-room-occupancy hotels and lodging houses. Geographer Jeff Sommers contends that the East End was a location where damaged masculinity, symbolized by the skid-row derelict, was linked to the deterioration of the central-city landscape.[58] At the same time, the predominance of male transients and resource workers meant a ready audience for relatively inexpensive floorshows.

Emcee and yo-yo specialist Harvey Lowe recalled that in the 1950s the Marco Polo nightclub featured a chorus line of "four pretty Chinese girls" in strapless bras, short skirts, and fishnet stockings – a spinoff from San Francisco's "Forbidden City" troupe – although the club never specialized in striptease performers.[59] Electric-bass player Sean Gunn, a Chinese Canadian and self-described "peoples' proletariat musician," cut his teeth at the Marco Polo club and formed the house band with "Lito, the Filipino keyboardist," and "Owen, the Hong Kong percussionist," at the Kublai Khan nightclub, where they accompanied strippers in the 1970s.[60] A club that attracted a mix of white and Chinese men and a regular complement of twenty to thirty prostitutes, the Kublai Khan was upstairs at 442 Main Street. Reminiscing about the notoriously "sleazy pleasure dome," Gunn not only takes wry pleasure in the Kublai Khan's free cover charge for Asian patrons, but tongue-in-cheek, also documents the commercial, physical, and emotional mystique of the "ubiquitous peelers" in the "deviant, diabolical, and depraved" Chinatown strip clubs.[61] An advertisement in the *Vancouver Sun* for the New Delhi Cabaret in February 1964 reads: "Battle of the Strippers, Jean Shaw, Harlem Cutie, Ebony Sexologist vs. Lovely Lolita, blonde bombshell from Montreal, MC Teddy Felton, and George Burney, featured on Ed Sullivan."[62] In July 1969 another advertisement for the New Delhi was published: "Stripperama, Vancouver's sin-sational, sex-sational girlie show, featuring direct from Hollywood, Susie Starr, Miss Ruthie, Frisky Miss Marcie, Stunning Miss Lena, 2 topless go-go girls, plus new chorus line."[63] By contrast, neither "stripper" nor "exotic" was used in promotional material for Isy's Supper Club or the Penthouse until the early to mid-1970s.

By the late 1960s bare-breasted "exotics" were *the* prized performers in the East End clubs; typically supplemented by an emcee and a singer, they practically owned the marquee at the Smilin' Buddha and the New Delhi. Jazz musician Mike Kalanj remembered the New Delhi: "It had a warm atmosphere – tables and chairs – the dancers had closets for dressing rooms. The dance floor was a hardwood floor in the middle of the room with a rope around it. They served East Indian and Canadian food. It was at Keefer and Main. You'd go up a long staircase and at the top was a ticket booth. Through the hole in the glass, you'd buy your ticket; they'd ring the buzzer and open the door."[64] The two-dollar admission charge covered the cost of one entrée – curried chicken, fried rice, veal cutlet, or pork chop.[65]

Isy's, the Penthouse, and the Cave advertised the city's best orchestras, which again reflected the compartmentalized geography of the local entertainment scene. Pianist Gerry Palken is a former band leader at Isy's: "I never played the East End. We all looked down our noses at those clubs – you didn't get paid very much. It was pretty low life down there – all the down-and-outers. There was a little café that drilled holes in the spoons so the junkies wouldn't steal them to cook up. I just didn't want to work down there."[66] Isy's Supper Club strove to distinguish itself by emphasizing tasteful, Vegas-style production numbers as opposed to second-tier exotics who strutted their stuff in "Stripperamas" to "B-grade" music for "the rough Chinatown crowd."[67] East End clubs openly promoted black dancers as "Harlem cuties, ebony sexologists, and Afro-Cuban specialists." And musician Gord Walkinshaw claimed that the New Delhi was the home of the first transvestites and "sex changes," some of whom worked as professional striptease dancers.[68] There is little doubt that the East End cabarets pushed hardest against the limits of postwar Anglo Vancouver's "community standards."[69] What remains uncertain is the extent to which East End and West End nightclubs actually competed in the 1950s, 1960s, and 1970s. Former Harlem Nocturne boss, Ernie King, recalled that there was seldom intersection between "the two different worlds."[70]

The "Jumpin'" Harlem Nocturne

Ernie King was born in Edmonton, Alberta, in 1919, the son of African Americans who left Oklahoma and the racism of the American South to make better lives in Canada.[71] His family moved to Vancouver in 1930 when King was a young boy; he later quit school to work at Hammonds Furniture Company for four years. After serving in the army during the Second World War and playing in the army band, King became a professional trombonist and started his own all-black band, the Harlem Kings. While touring in Edmonton, King met his future bride. Married in 1948 and settled in Vancouver, King joined the musicians' union, Local 145, and began working in East End cabarets. He recalled the barriers to better paying and more esteemed gigs in the West End supper clubs:

> I was qualified enough to play in the Cave, but they didn't want a guy like me. The owners wanted an all-white band, not a coloured band with me sitting in there. I would have never got a job as a houseman in the house band at the Cave – there were never any black musicians, unless it was a black band from the States. They knew our black musicians had as much talent or more than anybody else ... So I said I'd prefer to be with a couple of coloured guys, and maybe a couple of white guys, in the East End clubs.[72]

In 1958, frustrated with the owner of the New Delhi nightclub, who demanded that he take a cut in pay, King rented the main floor of 343 East Hastings Street, one and a half blocks from Main Street, and opened the Harlem Nocturne. It was the only black nightclub in Vancouver, not far from Vancouver's only black neighbourhood, Hogan's Alley.[73] American sailors in port for three to four days, regulars from Seattle, and local East Enders frequented the Harlem. Performers and tourists who travelled by train and bus to Vancouver found both stations within several blocks of the Main Street nightclubs. Black entertainers enlivened the scene nurtured by King and his wife, Choo Choo Williams, who jointly operated the club with King and performed striptease there. King spoke with pride: "We had Choo Choo and other black dancers – Miss Lovie, Lottie the Body, and Tequila. We had the Mills Brothers, Ike Turner, Montgomery Brothers, Pearl Brown, Thelma Gibson, Ruth Brown – a jazz singer – Billy Daniels, Ernestine Anderson. T-Bone Walker did a solo act. He'd work the Delhi and then come over to the Harlem."[74]

Denied liquor licences until 1969, East End nightclub owners like Ernie King, Leo Bagry, and Jimmy Yuen milked the "forbidden" aura of their unlicensed bottle clubs and suffered much more intense police scrutiny than did their West End rivals. Ernie King was not alone in devising strategies to subvert police action and the threat of arrest. Laughing, he recalled a creative tactic: "I trained my customers. I had them put their booze in an empty coke bottle, or 7-up bottle, and they'd pour rum in there, or vodka or gin. And the cops never bothered them! It took the cops a year to wise up!" Other Chinatown clubs put liquor in tea pots. And while the Penthouse nightclub endured years of police intimidation and forced closure – occupying a liminal third space somewhere in the middle of Vancouver's East-West divide – the Harlem Nocturne was subject to unique pressures. Ernie King harboured bitter memories: "No one was harassed more than me. No one. It got to the point they would harass me two or three times a night. Because I was the only man that owned a black nightclub! I couldn't get a liquor licence. I could only sell food and soft drinks. After eight years of owning that place and fighting with the cops and letting them get away with all kinds of stuff, I finally said, 'To hell with it, I'm closing up.' I sold the place, and I got on out of there. I went into the trucking business, and I didn't have to be harassed by the police."[75]

Ernie King's recollection of these regulatory times is confirmed by gossip columnist Denny Boyd: "Vancouver Vice Squad was insane in those days! It was probably the perception of a couple of high-ranking cops that 'We must stamp out evil. We must shape the morals of our citizens. We can't let them condemn themselves to hell.'"[76] In 1966, fifteen years after the State Burlesque Theatre was raided for the second time, the city's chief licence inspector, Mitch Harrell, cautioned the Harlem Nocturne and another club: "Two cabarets were warned: the attire on their girls was too skimpy. One involved dancers with transparent, black chiffon blouses. The by-law forbids any person to produce in any building or place in the city any immoral or lewd theatrical performance of any kind."[77] To quell fears of unchecked permissiveness, and to rationalize their own regulatory practices (and budgets), law enforcers and social reformers sought to administer striptease as a social problem through normalized interventions, particularly in the East End clubs.[78] By necessity, club owners, staff, and entertainers balanced what was at times a lucrative (yet fickle) business with tense relations with police and moral reformers. Even after full nudity was decriminalized in 1972, strip joints remained easy prey for moral conservatives and their "clean-up" campaigns.

How much policing of the Harlem Nocturne and other East End nightclubs was fired by vestiges of early-twentieth-century temperance ideology and other elements of a moral reform agenda? What role did institutionalized police and societal racism play, including the congealed, intractable myth of exotic Chinatown as a vice town? How great a factor was the century-old conflation of the city's East End with female prostitution and "sex deviance" more broadly (a conflation reaffirmed by the raid on the Penthouse and subsequent pressure on sex workers to move eastward)? Surely, multiple forces were at play; calculating the strength of each at any given time is a vexing task largely because they continually reinforced one another. What is clear is that East End nightclubs and their staff were relentlessly made scapegoats in the 1950s, 1960s, and early 1970s by moral reformers, city politicians, Vancouver police, and mainstream journalists. And this intensity of focus had significant implications for the conditions under which "B-list" professional striptease was produced and consumed.

Concluding Thoughts

From the 1950s to the mid-1970s commercial striptease made its mark in Vancouver: it enhanced the city's reputation as "home to the hottest night-clubs north of San Francisco" during a time of more continuity than change in the business.[79] Headlining erotic dancers promised adventurous patrons in both East End and West End venues something new, something special, and something daring before the advent of cable television, VCRs, and the grave economic downturn of the 1970s. Yet teetering on the edge of legality, nightclub owners who routinely booked "strippers" could never take for granted the respect extended to so-called legitimate small-business operators, even within their own ethnic communities, whether Italian, Jewish, Chinese, South Asian, or African Canadian. Until the expansion of erotic entertainment into downtown and suburban hotels in the mid-1970s, Vancouver's nightclub owners had "made it" – they were gainfully employed, paid taxes, set down roots in the city, married and raised children, staffed their clubs with workers, and supported community activities such as sports teams, boxing, and the Variety Club.[80] By certain conventional measures, these business owners were model Canadian citizens. Yet in the eyes of critics, the combination of *who* they were (first- and second-generation non-Anglo immigrants), *what* they did (promote striptease), *where* they did it (in nightclubs, some of which were in the disreputable East End), and *when* they conducted business (at night, not from 9:00 a.m. to 5:00 p.m.) disqualified them from the roster of "businessmen of distinction."

Although never hobbled – as dancers were – by the unflinching whore stigma, nightclub owners habitually faced pressure from antivice factions to clean up the acts. From 1950 to 1975 raids, fines, arrests, and closures engineered to stamp out immorality, revitalize law and order discourse, and justify a bigger policing budget were commonplace; although not unique to Vancouver, they took a toll on all business insiders, particularly East Enders. The city's hotspots were never shut down en masse à la New York City in the 1940s.[81] However, clubs such as the State Theatre, Penthouse Cabaret, Harlem Nocturne, New Delhi, Smilin' Buddha, Kublai Khan, and Café Kobenhavn were forever at risk of incursion. Vancouver police exercised significant discretionary power to lay charges of "lewd and obscene exhibition," illegal liquor sales and consumption, gambling, minors on the premises, and myriad prostitution and drug-related offences.[82] Ironically, in the decades following the Second World War, although Vancouver's economy needed erotic spectacle, moral reformers screeched that it ruined communities, family values, the nation, and national security.

Nightclub owners who invested in striptease made a comfortable living as hard-working entrepreneurs, yet they never escaped insidious moral opprobrium. On the one hand, they were grudgingly admired not only for surviving but also for thriving as agents of free enterprise and defenders of personal and political freedom. On the other hand, commonplace lore alleged that they aided and abetted men's sexual perversions, degraded and victimized women, and took part in a range of illicit goings-on. Certainly, female dancers experienced intensely complex relationships with their bosses, the men behind the marquee – sexist and racist paternalism, sexual harassment, unsavoury recruitment strategies, resistance to improved working conditions, and anti-union tactics.[83] At the same time, no amount of Vegas-style glamour or humanitarian goodwill erased the caricature of all male club owners as shady, seamy hustlers who stimulated and capitalized on other men's desire for "exotics." Disentitled practically and symbolically to membership in the city's wealthy, Anglo business and professional class, nightclub owners were perpetual outsiders. Indeed, their outsider status underscores the need for more research into the tangled, differently racialized and class-bound contradictions and convolutions of postwar masculinities.[84]

Acknowledgments

I would like to thank Magda Fahrni and Robert Rutherdale for co-ordinating this anthology, the anonymous reviewers, and my research assistants, Michelle Swann, Kim Greenwell, Erin Bentley, Christine Harris, and Genevieve Lapointe. I am sincerely grateful to all the business insiders I have had the privilege of interviewing. The Social Sciences and Humanities Research Council of Canada and the University of British Columbia's Hampton Fund supplied much-welcome financial support. In Douglas Coupland's *City of Glass: Vancouver* (Toronto and Vancouver: Douglas and McIntyre, 2000), 138, he notes that the *New York Times* referred to Vancouver as "Vansterdam," in recognition of the city's permissive sensibility regarding sex and marijuana.

Notes

1 Interview with Ross Filippone, Vancouver, 15 June 2000.
2 I am grateful for this excerpt from Sean Gunn's unpublished poem, "Kublai Khan Ten," p. 1, Vancouver, 2001.
3 To date, Vancouver's postwar striptease scene has been conspicuously absent from historical writing. For instance, Douglas Cole erases "bump and grind" from the city's cultural traditions: opera, the symphony, radio, visual and literary artists, poetry, theatre, architecture, modern dance, and professional and recreational sports. See his "Leisure, Taste and Tradition in British Columbia," in Hugh Johnston, ed., *The Pacific Province: A History of British Columbia* (Vancouver and Toronto: Douglas and McIntyre, 1996), 344-81.
4 On postwar Vancouver's lively and profitable downtown, see Robert North and Walter Hardwick, "Vancouver since the Second World War: An Economic Geography," in Graeme Wynn and Timothy Oke, eds., *Vancouver and Its Region* (Vancouver: UBC Press, 2001), 207. On American downtowns, see Michael Johns, *Moment of Grace: The American City in the*

1950s (Berkeley and Los Angeles: University of California Press, 2003), 42; and Jane Jacobs, *The Death and Life of Great American Cities* (1961; reprint, New York: Modern Library, 2003).

5　On West End development, see Sherry Mckay, "'Urban Housekeeping' and Keeping the Modern House," *BC Studies* 140 (Winter 2003-04): 11-38. On the emergence of fast food restaurants, see Steve Penfold, "Selling by the Carload: The Early Years of Fast Food in Canada," in this volume.

6　See Kay Anderson, *Vancouver's Chinatown: Racial Discourse in Canada, 1875-1980* (Montreal and Kingston: McGill-Queen's University Press, 1991), 144-77; and Graeme Wynn, "The Rise of Vancouver," in Wynn and Oke, eds., *Vancouver and its Region*, 141-42.

7　See Brandon Yip, "Rockin' Back the Clock," *Vancouver Courier*, 7 July 2004, 1-5.

8　Jack Wasserman, "Saloon Crawler's Notebook," *Vancouver Sun*, 19 October 1971, A5.

9　Interview with Patrick Nagle, Victoria, 28 July 2000.

10　For selected work on the sexualization of postwar commercial culture, see Angus McLaren, *Twentieth-Century Sexuality: A History* (Oxford: Blackwell, 1999), 143-92; Mary Louise Adams, *The Trouble with Normal: Postwar Youth and the Making of Heterosexuality* (Toronto: University of Toronto Press, 1997); Andrea Friedman, "Sadists and Sissies: Anti-Pornography Campaigns in Cold War America," *Gender and History* 15, 2 (August 2003): 201-27. On the genealogy of "bombshells," see Kristina Zarlengo, "Civilian Threat, the Suburban Citadel, and Atomic Age American Women," *Signs: Journal of Women in Culture and Society* 24, 4 (1999): 925-58.

11　For selected histories of early-twentieth-century showgirls, see Charlene Kish, "A Knee Bone Is a Joint and Not an Entertainment: The Moral Regulation of Burlesque in Early-Twentieth-Century Toronto" (MA thesis, York University, 1997); Andrea Stuart, *Showgirls* (London: Jonathan Cape, 1999); Linda Misejewski, *Ziegfeld Girl: Image and Icon in Culture and Cinema* (Durham and London: Duke University Press, 1999); Allison Latham, *Posing a Threat: Flappers, Chorus Girls and Other Brazen Performers of the American 1920s* (Hanover and London: University Press of New England, 2000); Lael Morgan, *Good Time Girls of the Alaska-Yukon Gold Rush* (Vancouver: Whitecap Books, 1998); Rosemary Neering, *Wild West Women: Travellers, Adventurers, and Rebels* (Vancouver: Whitecap Books, 2000), 87-90; and Rachel Shteir, *Striptease: The Untold History of the Girlie Show* (New York: Oxford University Press, 2004).

12　See Beatrix Zumsteg, "Promoting Censorship in the Name of Youth: The Council of Women's Activism against Vaudeville in the 1920s and 1930s in Vancouver" (unpublished paper, University of British Columbia, 1998), 2.

13　"5 Convicted of Indecent Stage Show," *Vancouver Sun*, 18 January 1952, 25; "Burlesque Show closed; appeal next," *Vancouver Sun*, 19 January 1952, 6. The theme of state/police surveillance during the Cold War decades, particularly in relation to "sex deviants," is treated by Gary Kinsman, "The Canadian Cold War against Queers: Sexual Regulation and Resistance," in Richard Cavell, ed., *Love, Hate, and Fear in Canada's Cold War* (Toronto: University of Toronto Press, 2004), 108-32.

14　After the Second World War the marriage rate in Canada jumped, while the nuclear family was extolled by social scientists as the most stable, mature arrangement of domestic relations. By 1956 the age of marriage had plummeted: on average, women married at 21.6 and men at 24.5. "Especially for women," argues Doug Owram, "the completion of [high] school, engagement, marriage, and the birth of the first child were more or less consecutive events"; see his *Born at the Right Time: A History of the Baby-Boom Generation* (Toronto: University of Toronto Press, 1996), 18. See also Veronica Strong-Boag, "Home Dreams: Women and the Suburban Experiment in Canada, 1945-1960," *Canadian Historical Review* 72, 4 (December 1991): 471-504.

15　For a valuable discussion of how Cold War symbolism permeated Canadian society, specifically the regulation of store hours, see Michael Dawson, "Leisure, Consumption, and the Public Sphere: Postwar Debates over Shopping Regulations in Vancouver and Victoria during the Cold War," in this volume. On "normal" postwar families, see Mona Gleason, *Normalizing the Ideal: Psychology, Schooling and the Family in Postwar Canada* (Toronto: University of Toronto Press, 1999).

16　Greg Marquis, "Vancouver Vice: The Police and the Negotiation of Morality, 1904-1935," in *Essays in the History of Canadian Law*, Vol. 6, *British Columbia and the Yukon*, ed. John

McLaren and Hamar Foster (Toronto: University of Toronto Press for Osgoode Society, 1995), 243-44.

17 This essay is drawn from my larger book project on commercial striptease in Vancouver's postwar decades. On the experiences of retired dancers, see Becki Ross, "Striptease on the Line: Investigating Trends in Female Erotic Entertainment," in Deborah Brock, ed., *Making Normal: Social Regulation in Canada* (Toronto: Thomson Nelson, 2003), 146-78.

18 On the "Golden Era" of striptease, see Linda Lee Tracey, *Growing Up Naked: My Years in Bump and Grind* (Toronto: Douglas and McIntyre, 1997). On the contemporary striptease scene, see Chris Bruckert, *Taking It Off, Putting It On: Women in the Skin Trade* (Toronto: Women's Press, 2002); and Lily Burana, *Strip City: A Stripper's Farewell Journey across America* (New York: Hyperion, 2001). On migrant, transnational sex workers, see Deborah Brock, Kara Gillies, Chantelle Oliver, and Mook Sutdhibhasilp, "Migrant Sex Work: A Roundtable Analysis," *Canadian Woman Studies Journal,* 20, 2 (Summer 2000): 84-91. On the demise of the Visa Program, see Robert Fife, "Feds Stop Giving Visas to Strippers," *Vancouver Sun,* 2 December 2004, A5; and Marina Jiménez and Campbell Clark, "Volpe Ends Exotic-Dancer Program," *Globe and Mail,* 2 December 2004, A4.

19 Mounted text, 1950s Gallery, Vancouver Museum, 1100 Chestnut St., Vancouver.

20 For selected histories of class and racial/ethnic clashes in Vancouver, see Robert McDonald, *Making Vancouver: 1863-1913* (Vancouver: UBC Press, 1996), 3-32, 149-74; Cole Harris, *Making Native Space: Colonialism, Resistance, and Reserves* (Vancouver: UBC Press, 2002); Patricia Roy, *The Oriental Question: Consolidating a White Man's Province, 1914-1941* (Vancouver: UBC Press, 2003); and Adele Perry, *On the Edge of Empire: Race, Gender and the Making of British Columbia, 1849-1871* (Toronto: University of Toronto Press, 2001).

21 The total population of British, French, and other Europeans in British Columbia was 93.2% in 1951, 93.4% in 1961, and 92.4% in 1971, while the Asian population for these years was 2.4%, 2.5%, and 3.5% respectively, the Aboriginal population was 2.2%, 2.4%, and again 2.4%, and all others comprised 2.2%, 1.7%, and again 1.7%; cited in Veronica Strong-Boag, "Society in the Twentieth Century," in Johnston, ed., *Pacific Province,* 276.

22 See the documentary film *Show Girls: Celebrating Montréal's Legendary Black Jazz Scene,* directed by Meilan Lam, National Film Board of Canada, 1998.

23 Mizejewski, *Ziegfeld Girl,* 8-9, argues that musical director Florenz Ziegfeld's "Glorified American girls [1920s-1940s] were not supposed to be recent immigrants from southern and eastern Europe, hence not ethnic, dark-skinned, or Jewish," and that Ziegfeld rewarded his white girls for not getting summer suntans. For a pictorial history of Vancouver's Cave Supper Club (1937-81), see Claire Hurley, *Remember the Cave* (Vancouver: Goalgetter, 1982).

24 Len Carlyle, "The Show Business Phenomenon Called the Cave: Why Stars like Berle, Berman, Damone and Carter Go out of Their Way to Play Vancouver," *Vancouver Life,* July 1966, 46.

25 Interview with Denny Boyd, West Vancouver, 2 August 2001.

26 "City Cafes Get Wine Licenses," *Vancouver Sun,* 22 April 1954, 1. On the history of liquor regulations in Vancouver, see Robert Campbell, *Sit Down and Drink Your Beer: Regulating Vancouver's Beer Parlours, 1925-1954* (Toronto: University of Toronto Press, 2001).

27 Mariana Valverde, *Diseases of the Will: Alcohol and the Dilemmas of Freedom* (Cambridge: Cambridge University Press, 1998), 97.

28 Ibid. Importantly, argues Robert Campbell, not all Vancouverites had equal access to the purchase and consumption of alcohol: "Prices, comportment, and outright discrimination often kept First Nations men and women out of [nightclubs]" in the 1950s, and the government refused to allow Aboriginal people to purchase liquor off reserves except in licensed places until 1962. See his "A 'Fantastic Rigamarole': Deregulating Aboriginal Drinking in British Columbia, 1945-62," *BC Studies* 141 (Spring 2004): 81-104 at 91, 96.

29 Isy Walters, interviewed by Meyer Freedman, Isy's Supper Club, Vancouver, 1975, tape recording in possession of Della Walters. My thanks for access to this material.

30 Ibid.

31 Jewish Canadian fashion icon Harry Rosen was raised by a father who arrived in Canada (northern Ontario) from Poland in 1925 "hardly employable." Harry's father got a pushcart and collected scrap to provide a livelihood for his family. According to Harry, some Jewish men (like his father and Isy Walters) found that the salvage business "permitted them to

take Friday afternoon and Saturday off to observe the Sabbath." Personal correspondence
with Harry Rosen, 18 May 2005.
32 The history of postwar striptease dancers and shows in famous Las Vegas clubs near and on
"The Strip" – Tropicana, Dunes, Stardust, Caesars Palace, Desert Inn, and the Sands –
remains unwritten. Clues can be found in Robert McCracken, *Las Vegas: The Great American Playground* (Reno: University of Nevada Press, 1996), 69-86.
33 Isy Walters, interviewed by Meyer Freedman, Isy's Supper Club, Vancouver, 1975, tape
recording in possession of Della Walters.
34 Interview with Richard Walters, Vancouver, 8 July 2000.
35 Ibid.
36 Interview with Jeannie Runnalls, Port Coquitlam, 21 June 2000.
37 Interview with Della Walters, Vancouver, 20 September 2001.
38 Interview with Richard Walters, Vancouver, 8 July 2000.
39 Interview with Della Walters, Vancouver, 20 September 2001.
40 "Filippone" is the anglicized version of the original, "Philliponi," invented by a racist immigration officer when Joe (the eldest) and his parents arrived in British Columbia from
San Nicola, Italy, in 1929.
41 Interview with Ross Filippone, Vancouver, 15 June 2000.
42 Ibid.
43 Alex MacGillivray, untitled column, *Vancouver Sun*, 29 December 1968, 14.
44 Interview with Ross Filippone, Vancouver, 15 June 2000.
45 Ibid.
46 See Les Wiseman, "Not Your Average Joe," *Vancouver Magazine*, April 1982, 60-64, 68, 84.
47 Interview with Denny Boyd, West Vancouver, 2 August 2001.
48 Interview with Ross Filippone, Vancouver, 15 June 2000.
49 Ibid.
50 See John Faustmann, "Joe Philipponi's [sic] World," *Vancouver Courier*, 12 August 1979, 15.
51 John Lowman, a criminologist at Simon Fraser University, claims that the closure of the
Penthouse Cabaret in 1975, combined with the closure of other venues in Vancouver,
played a decisive role in the shift to street prostitution and a ghettoization of the sex trade
in the city's East End. Outdoor sex workers became increasingly vulnerable to violence and
murder – a trend that we still see today, most graphically in what is now commonly termed
the Downtown Eastside, where more than seventy sex workers have been murdered. See
John Lowman, "Street Prostitution in Vancouver: Some Notes on the Genesis of a Social
Problem," *Canadian Journal of Criminology* 28 (1986): 1-16.
52 Edward Said, *Orientalism* (New York: Vintage Books, 1979), 71.
53 Kay Anderson, *Vancouver's Chinatown: Racial Discourse in Canada, 1875-1980* (Montreal
and Kingston: McGill-Queen's University Press, 1991), 206.
54 June Sochen, *From Mae to Madonna* (Lexington, KY: University of Kentucky Press, 1999),
8-9, argues that not only did black female vaudevillians in the US in the early twentieth
century face the whorish image associated with show business, but the additional barrier
of the colour line meant that dark-skinned women were rarely booked into shows. On the
racialization of the Vancouver striptease scene, see Becki Ross and Kim Greenwell, "Spectacular Striptease: Performing the Sexual and Racial Other in Postwar Vancouver, 1945-1975," *Journal of Women's History* 17, 1 (April 2005): 137-64.
55 Interview with Dave Davies, Vancouver, 27 June 2000.
56 On racialized entertainment in postwar Montreal, see Meilan Lam's documentary film
Show Girls: Celebrating Montréal's Legendary Black Jazz Scene, National Film Board of Canada,
1998. On slumming, see George Chauncey, *Gay New York: Gender, Urban Culture and the
Making of the Gay Male World, 1890-1940* (New York: Basic Books, 1994), 246-47; Kevin
Mumford, *Interzones: Black/White Sex Districts in Chicago and New York in the Early Twentieth
Century* (New York: Columbia University Press, 1997), 135-56; and Benson Tong, *The Chinese Americans* (Westport, CT: Greenwood Press, 2000).
57 Tong, *The Chinese Americans;* Mumford, *Interzones,* 135.
58 See Jeff Sommers, "Men at the Margin: Masculinity and Space in Downtown Vancouver,
1950-1986," *Urban Geography* 19, 4 (1998): 287-310 at 287.

59 Alex Louie and Harvey Lowe, interviewed by Bernice Chan, Vancouver, 15 December 2003. Radio Archive, Canadian Broadcasting Corporation, Vancouver.

60 Interview with Sean Gunn, Vancouver, 18 March 2004.

61 I am grateful for this excerpt from Sean Gunn's unpublished poem, "Kublai Khan Ten," p. 1, Vancouver, 2001.

62 Advertisement, *Vancouver Sun*, 21 February 1964, 23.

63 Advertisement, *Vancouver Sun*, 26 July 1969, 25.

64 Interview with Mike Kalanj, Vancouver, 5 July 2000.

65 See Maxwell Smith, "The Downtown Scene," *Vancouver Life*, January 1968, 24.

66 Interview with Gerry Palken, Vancouver, 18 February 2002.

67 Interview with Ross Filippone, Vancouver, 15 June 2000.

68 Interview with Gord Walkinshaw, Vancouver, 27 June 2000. For more on male-to-female transsexual and crossing-dressing strippers, see Don Paulson, with Roger Simpson, *An Evening at the Garden of Allah: Seattle's Gay Cabaret* (New York: New York University Press, 1996).

69 In the late 1960s Café Kobenhavn was a bottle club allegedly owned by "bikers" on Main Street in the East End. In February 1971 undercover police officers charged the club's four managers and four dancers with staging an "obscene performance." In September 1972 provincial court judge David Moffet acquitted the club and its employees of all charges, inciting four other clubs to "take it all off." See Les Wiseman, "Young, Sexy, and Well Heeled," *Vancouver Magazine*, March 1982, 29-35, 45.

70 Interview with Ernie King, Vancouver, 4 February 2002.

71 Ernie King died on 10 June 2004 at the age of eighty-five in Vancouver. This essay is dedicated to his memory. Also see Bruce Shepard, *Deemed Unsuitable: Blacks from Oklahoma Move to the Canadian Prairies in Search of Equality in the Early Twentieth Century Only to Find Racism in Their New Home* (Toronto: Umbrella Press, 1997).

72 Interview with Ernie King, Vancouver, 4 February 2002.

73 See the documentary film *Hogan's Alley*, directed by Andrea Fatona and Cornelia Wyngaarden, Video Out, 1994; the first-person stories in Daphne Marlatt and Carole Itter, eds., *Opening Doors: Vancouver's East End* (Victoria: Aural History Program, 1979); and Wayde Compton, *Bluesprint: Black British Columbian Literature and Orature* (Vancouver: Arsenal Pulp, 2001).

74 Interview with Ernie King, Vancouver, 4 February 2002.

75 Ibid.

76 Interview with Denny Boyd, West Vancouver, 2 August 2001.

77 George Peloquin, "Go Go Cabarets Can't Go Topless," *Vancouver Sun*, 19 September 1966.

78 Michel Foucault, *The History of Sexuality*, vol. 1 (New York: Vintage Books, 1980), 68.

79 Jack Wasserman, "Saloon Crawler's Notebook," *Vancouver Sun*, 19 October 1971, A5.

80 The exception to the image of the "family man" was Joe Philliponi – a life-long bachelor and "playboy" with a legendary "fondness for the ladies."

81 On twentieth-century raids and closures of burlesque and striptease venues, see Andrea Friedman, *Prurient Interests: Gender, Democracy, and Obscenity in New York City, 1909-1935* (New York: Columbia University Press, 2000); and Ross, "Striptease on the Line." On the policing of striptease in North America during the 1980s and 1990s, see Judith Lynne Hanna, "Undressing the First Amendment and Corseting the Striptease Dancer," *Drama Review* 42 (1998): 38-69.

82 On mid-century prostitution in Vancouver, see Michaela Freund, "The Politics of Naming: Constructing Prostitutes and Regulating Women in Vancouver, 1939-1945," in John McLaren, Robert Menzies, and Dorothy Chunn, eds., *Regulating Lives: Historical Essays on the State, Society, the Individual and the Law* (Vancouver: UBC Press, 2002), 231-58.

83 On efforts by Vancouver-based dancers to unionize in the past, see Becki Ross, "'Trouble-makers' in Tassels and G-Strings: Striptease Dancers and the Union Question in Vancouver, 1960-1980," *Canadian Review of Sociology and Anthropology* 43, 3 (August 2006): 307-22.

84 For work that historicizes masculinities in Canada, see Christopher Dummitt, "Finding a Place for Father: Selling the Barbecue in Post-War Canada," *Journal of the Canadian Historical Association* 8 (1998): 209-23; Robert Rutherdale, "Fatherhood and the Social Construction

of Memory: Breadwinning and Male Parenting on a Job Frontier, 1945-1966," in Joy Parr and Mark Rosenfeld, eds., *Gender and History in Canada* (Mississauga, ON: Copp Clark, 1996), 357-75; Steven Maynard, "Queer Musings on Masculinity and History," *Labour/Le Travail* 42 (Fall 1998), 183-97, and Gary Kinsman, *The Regulation of Desire: Homo and Hetero Sexualities in Canada*, 2nd ed. (Montreal: Black Rose Books, 1996).

10

New "Faces" for Fathers: Memory, Life-Writing, and Fathers as Providers in the Postwar Consumer Era

Robert Rutherdale

"He was the meanest customer. He's had Fred out on a limb for months. He'd say he'd be right up to the office and Fred would wait for him and he wouldn't come." Fred Cress was an insurance salesman working in Barrie, Ontario, in the early 1950s. In this excerpt and those that follow, his wife, Ruby, was writing to her sister, working into her letter complaints about daily problems that her husband faced trying to sell insurance: "Fred waited all Sat. morning for him to come in and he didn't show up. Fred phoned him and he said he'd phone him back sometime between then and bed time and let him know ... Really he was the most inconsiderate person and Fred had to stay around and have it hanging over his head." Ruby at home supported Fred's work to earn the family income. Their "companionship" marital partnership, as parents and providers, took shape in a more prosperous era than that of their parents.[1] On the one hand, middle-class fathers pursued more opportunities than their fathers could to secure employment, but on the other hand, they were also expected to spend more time at home in the new era of family togetherness. Saturdays at work could be as stressful as missing the sales bonus. This particular client, it seems, finally did sign off on a policy but not in time for Fred to include it in his year-end report. As it turned out, he could not get "credit for it on his year to get the bonus," Ruby lamented: "Poor Fred, he gets awful breaks at times. This has been a terrible strain."[2]

The strain of supporting a family can be reflected in the different relationships that all family members have to fathers as providers, whether growing up as children, as marriage partners, or as young adults on the threshold of leaving home. Baby boomer Carol Ann Cole remembered her father – a mechanic and gas station owner in Nova Scotia's Annapolis Valley – at times drunk, at times physically abusive, and at times in deep financial trouble. "While Mom, was raising her girls," recalled Cole about her situation, shared with two siblings, "Dad spent most of his time at the service station in Middleton and hanging out with his buddies at the air force base." Shortly after graduating from high school at eighteen, she managed to get out of town. A hidden escape fund put aside by her mother, an aunt in faraway North Bay, Ontario, and an entry-level job there soon put her on the road to an executive-level career with Bell Canada. Her father's failure in business at this juncture appeared also to put her at a crossroads with him, with Carol on her way up, her father down. Despite all, she also recalled a perpetual longing for his approval, especially before she left home. She just could not express it above her anger: "I knew Dad's business was not doing well, and Mom had hinted that he wasn't even paying his phone bill. Before I left I confronted him about the phone being disconnected. 'So I understand we aren't even going to have a telephone,' I said in a very flippant tone ... By this time, I felt that if I could give as good as I would get with my father in terms of confronting him, at some point he would see me as an equal."[3]

The letters of Ruby Cress as a postwar housewife and Carol Cole's memories as an angry teenager point toward the complex bonds to family men that all family members have. A husband and father's relative success or failure as a provider does not determine the full range of sentiments that he inspires, but it establishes basic parameters, from the sympathy of a spouse to the disgust of a dependant. This chapter considers the evidence of fathers as providers from the postwar era to the early 1970s as inscribed in life-writing or recalled in oral history. My samples show signs of fathers' rising expectations either for themselves or for their children, shaped by the obvious signs of expansion in manufacturing, urban infrastructure, suburban sprawl, and family-based consumerism.[4] Emphasis is placed here on broadening our understanding of breadwinning to consider how fathers during Canada's baby boom, and other family members too, experienced in social and cultural terms what was seen as a particular economic family strategy based on the patriarchal primacy of male breadwinning. The problem for historians of fatherhood has been to place the "absent presence" of breadwinning within the active role of being both a provider and a father, situated in the overlapping spheres dividing public from private life.

According to John Demos, studies of fatherhood across many historical contexts present researchers with a conundrum and an opportunity. Fathers are, in part, private-sphere subjects whose gender power as breadwinners ordinarily originates outside the home. Since the gendered lives of fathers, as spouses, parents, workers, or community members, cross the thresholds of private family life, they take shape through an array of what Demos calls "faces." As fathers navigate back and forth, from home to interacting in public communities, most often at work, these multiple faces reflect the private-public duality of their daily lives. Each of the faces that Demos discusses, from father as *anachronism* (the outdated father as seen by his maturing children), to father as *shield, intruder, incompetent, chum,* and so on, are posited as potential conceptual approaches to fathers as diverse and, until recently, overlooked subjects in history.[5]

By the beginning of the twentieth century, the provider's role stood as the most encompassing image for family men whose earnings were, through prescribed models of the *ideal* father, to be devoted to providing for family as a matter of duty, if not pride. Meanwhile, Canada's fathers struggled throughout their working lives to earn a "family wage," a sacrosanct benchmark of family breadwinning entitlement in the context of class struggle.[6] How could a family man get by without being able to provide food, clothing, and shelter to his dependants? Of course, many had to get by, many did, and many other hands in poorer families, mothers and children, worked for sustenance.[7] But a father's greatest disappointment could be when his reach as a provider far exceeded his grasp, when his inability to secure an adequate family wage marred his self-concept as providing father. As a Cape Breton coal miner, destined to stand up against the British Empire Steel Corporation, put it in 1902:

> I grew up and got married, and we had a sweet little baby girl. The house we lived in had a brick floor. One did not need to mud-patch it ... My wife used to wash it every day ... All the wives in that miners' row did this. We were very happy, my wife and baby and I. But at night when we would sit by the fire, just the three of us, my happy feeling would go smash looking at the damned floor of yellow bricks ... Why could I not get something better for those I loved?[8]

This yearning, expressed by J.B. McLachlan not long before he took up a radicalized torch for Canadian labour, strikes at the core of histories of frustrated providers. The end of four years of global war that had hastened the end of a decade of economic collapse hardly ended great challenges faced by Canada's working-class providers. Nonetheless, as the baby boom approached, new perceptions of male breadwinning can be discerned, partly based on a faith that better times lay ahead, as reflected in the consumer advertisement images of domestic goods. A new generation of fathers pursued higher expectations: of gaining employment, of being able to provide material goods and services for their families, and of combining citizenship with consumption, all positive signs of manful achievement.

Significantly, the 1948 passage of the Industrial Relations Disputes Investigation Act granted new powers to organized workers in industrial unions that then comprised some 30 percent of the nonagricultural workforce. Labour politics entered a period in many industries in which traditional class politics were challenged by a new consumer-citizen ethic.[9] It was in this context that breadwinning fathers across Canada's economy forged their individual life paths as parents and as marital partners. Their intimate relations with all family members determined how fathers were seen by their dependants at home, their work determined how they saw themselves as men, and the threshold between the two converged in the faces of the providing father that reflected his job, his income, and the unique circumstances of his private life.

Some important caveats should be addressed. Notions of fathers as successful breadwinners, rising prosperity and expectations, and the good life remained a middle-class illusion, even long after 1945. Work by Alvin Finkel, in particular, underscores this. Finkel estimates that "forty-one percent of Canadians were living outside the stereotypes of prosperity commonly applied to the post-war period."[10] Given the rising proportion of married women in the paid workforce from the mid-1950s onward, and given the complexity of changing family income strategies throughout the postwar years, an analysis of gender power in family regimes, vis-à-vis fathers' incomes, would require other methods.[11] Here, I wish to consider autobiographical texts illustrating how family men in the postwar era were either construed or constructed themselves as providers.[12]

Why consider fathers as providers rather than fathers simply as breadwinners? In a study of gender and breadwinning in two southern Ontario towns, Joy Parr emphasizes that supporting a family, whether carried out by women or men, intersects with a diverse range of relationships. Seldom, however, are the connections and complexities between providing economic sustenance, kinship ties, and fashioning family roles throughout the life cycle fully contemplated: "There is clearly something more," Joy Parr notes, "to the family man than the imagery of economic man can comprehend, something more complicated governing his relations with others in his household, both female and male, than his relations to the market alone can explain."[13]

This "something more" requires historians to think beyond the structural indices of breadwinning and family fortunes in a changing economy.[14] Thus this chapter addresses five themes: (1) fathers *getting settled* as part of a new generation of family men; (2) fathers *building or improving homes* as part of their provider function; (3) *absent fathers*, whose work kept them from home; (4) intimate portraits of *involved* fathers; and finally (5) *failed providers*, whose children grew up to recall fathers who could not live up to the expectations of the period.[15]

Getting Settled

In the family stories treated here, marriage and fatherhood were ordinarily considered something that should be financially anchored on the primacy of male breadwinning. The return to normalcy that characterized the postwar period reinforced the profoundly gendered aspects of public policy, pay-scale discrimination, job availability, and job promotion. From state and corporate employment practices to taxation legislation and consumer marketing strategies, the significance of this basic fact underscores how difficult sole providing was for women breadwinners. These structures also indicate the deeply embedded gendered regime of primary versus secondary breadwinning faced by women and men.[16] A man's capacity to provide economic support for a wife and prospective family underpinned his prospects as a family man, expectations that became possible for higher proportions of Canada's marriageable men by the late 1940s.

A southern Ontario hardware merchant, Ted Finley, recalled how he "won" permission from his father-in-law to marry his daughter. Their marriage lasted more than a half-century. Finley fondly noted, at one point during an interview, having celebrated his golden wedding anniversary in a marriage that produced nine children with many grandchildren. Born in 1926 and raised in Beaverton, Ontario, Finley remembered vividly the situation that he faced coming out of the military in 1945 with marriage on the horizon: "I think I had, at that time, $1,200 dollars in the bank, which was considered at lot of money at that particular time. Well, of course, as I say, I didn't drink, and so on and so forth. So that, ah – the money collected! And anybody that had $1,200 dollars in the bank at that stage, was y'see, almost a millionaire [chuckles]." At this point, Finley remembered an important meeting, structured by the rules of a patriarchal courtship system, with his future father-in-law. He asked him for "permission," as he put it, to marry his daughter. He sought her hand in matrimony as a good provider, someone sober and sensible. And as a serviceman with a good record, he was likely a good prospect: "I think that was one of the things that my father-in-law considered when he, when he gave me permission to marry his daughter – was the fact that his three sons drank heavily, and I didn't drink. And I was a Vet. And these two things seem to sit well with him. So I think that was one of the things that made him not have any doubts about his daughter being in good hands."[17]

Finley, who would later become a provincial government administrator, recalled a sense that better times were coming. The masculine work ethic of the family man seemed in tandem with job opportunities. This certainly became true first and foremost for the middle class, whose gains from the good life that began in the early 1950s set a pattern, but it was not a pattern that all working-class families could follow. Many wage earners found that their expectations exceeded their paycheques. Maria Coletta McLean illustrates this through an intimate memoir of her father, Mezzabotte Coletta.[18] He had emigrated from Supino, midway between Rome and Naples, to Toronto some twenty years before. Then just nineteen, with little money, formal education, or fluency in English, Coletta depended on his aunt's and uncle's support as a landed immigrant.

Coletta belonged to a generation of the city's Italian community whose lives were shaped by class and ethnic boundaries. His parenting in the postwar years was marked by sustained struggle as a wage labourer, something that Franca Iacovetta has adeptly examined for "such hardworking people" of Italian origin in the period. In his role as a father and provider, his daughter cast him as striving to get ahead in difficult times yet forever optimistic. She recalled his basic faith: life will be better for his children. "My father," she writes, drove "a truck for Toronto Macaroni, delivering boxes of pasta to Italian supermarkets all over Ontario." His absence while on the job was punctuated by her strong sense, as a child in the early 1950s, of his vital presence at home:

> Before my mother turned 30, she had my brother Don, my sister, and me. He was gone before we got up for school and often not back for dinner. I remember the sound of his black metal lunch box as he sat it on the kitchen counter, the slight scrape of the chair as he pulled it up to the mother-of-pearl Arborite table, the way he slipped some vegetables off my sister's plate onto his own because she hated to eat them. Sometimes he'd tell us about his trip to Sudbury, Thunder Bay, Sault Ste. Marie. The boss always gave him money for meals and a motel on those long trips, but he took his lunches, skipped the comfort of a motel whenever he could and drove straight through. That's how he managed to make it home the next day.[19]

Improved opportunities for newcomers gradually opened up after the war, but job markets were far from open. Marketable skills, formal education, and what sociologist John Porter calls the "vertical mosaic" of Canadian society, with its "charter group" of dominant anglophone males in senior management positions and the professions, remained formidable barriers.[20]

Morris and Janet Gibson arrived in Canada in 1955 with their school-aged daughter, Catriona, from the bomb-scarred city of Hull in Yorkshire. Their middle-class power might be defined, in part, by their ability to make choices, to leave their professional practices in England – both were family physicians – for a Canadian adventure, come what may. They settled first in Okatoks, Alberta. They left the United Kingdom because of their hopes for the future – both sought better careers in Canada – and because they felt that they had been pushed away by a poorly supported public health system. Before the year was up on the Prairies, however, Gibson reached a point of decision: "Those nine months had been like a wonderful holiday in many ways – a total change from the daily grind of general practice in Hull. People weren't well off, but they were independent to a degree, and if they did not have ready cash or some small service, we would find a dozen or two eggs or a chicken brought to the door. Some people brought us little presents, butter and eggs, beef, just to introduce themselves and say they'd come to see us if we were needed." He adds: "There was friendliness all around that was refreshing and enticing – but – we weren't making a living!" While "living expenses were low" in the West, "even by British standards," the $2,000 that he and his wife had earned so far in Canada "would not keep the wolf from the door for long!" At the moment when they were considering separate offers from a Regina clinic, "quite unexpectedly, we received word that $10,000 could be transferred from England to our bank in Canada. It was the beginning of a gradual change in our fortunes. Suddenly we felt wealthy, and we decided that we would build our house at once." Again, a sense of an unfolding adventure appears in his memoir: "but it must be built on land where we had a view of the mountains."[21] Things moved even more quickly after that.

Part of their struggle lay in negotiating their own gender regime as a family. Morris, for instance, recounts the double haul that Janet, who had no intention of giving up practice, expressed: "She was that rare creature, a woman doctor and, as she said, a woman doctor in what was largely a man's world. 'You see,' she said, as we talked things over, 'I have to wear about three hats. I have to be your wife, but it's also very important that I should be Catriona's mother. So I go to school and attend parent-teachers' meetings, and take an interest in school affairs, and in the little one's new friends.' When she did this she was 'Janet,' or 'mom.' But 'when I work in the office' she added, she was the 'doctor.'"[22] Morris' public face, on the other hand, as a providing father was inextricably bound to his identity as "doctor." He does not note any corresponding angst about his primary role as a father in his everyday movements in and out of private life.

Few men could speak of this with Gibson's flair for recall. Many I interviewed remembered this period of their lives as simply a sudden surge forward: having emerged from their gruelling, young bachelor days during the early war period, they experienced an unexpected acceleration of life-course transitions beginning with the end of the war and continuing throughout the 1950s as they became young dads. As Toronto journalist Scott Young recalls, the arrival of his second-born, a child destined for fame as a singer-songwriter for a generation of baby boomers, caught him in the midst of a frantically paced career. A neighbour "whom we hardly knew" asked him how he and his wife, Rassy, were getting ready for the moment, adding: "How is your wife going to get to the hospital?" Young admitted: "I hadn't thought of that. Probably by cab." For Young, this period shortly after 1945, during which he became a father for a second time, seemed to interweave his roles as provider and parent into a sweeping set of life-course passages: "I found Rassy pale, and wan, and happy, and baby Neil with a lot of black hair. We both wept a little. All this happened within two months of my navy discharge. New home, new baby, new job. Things were working out."[23]

The assumption that things were indeed working out for young couples was often rooted in the division of domestic labour and paid labour sanctioned by the state, a fundamental split between a mother's prime responsibility at home and the father's outside of it. The corresponding integration between the gendered household economy and the gendered wage economy was based on the primacy given to male breadwinning, something that Nancy Christie has concluded underpinned the "'personal responsibility' of the male head of household, whose exclusive duty it was to defend the polity against the threat of social dependency by securing his own family's economic self-sufficiency."[24]

Getting settled, for middle-class fathers especially, often meant getting a job that supported a financially dependent wife at home so that she could fulfil her primary care responsibilities for the children. Providing and dependency were often recast as role-divided partnerships within companionship marriages throughout the 1950s. The patriarchal system that structured this model became a prime target of second-wave feminists in the following decade. While the consumption demands of the postwar era increasingly prompted married women to reenter the paid workforce as supplemental earners, the face of fathers as providers in an ideal sense renewed traditional notions of separate spheres.

Upgrading and Building Homes

Fathers in the postwar years parented in an era that celebrated home-centred living. If moms had jobs to do in homemaking, so did dads in house making. By the 1950s the face of providing fathers as home builders, renovators, and home fix-it men had been restored. Those I interviewed often emphasized their material accomplishment as family men, especially how they built, repaired, or expanded their family dwellings. When, for instance, Earl Baxter of Burlington, Ontario, recalled his first house as "just a two bedroom bunglow, actually," he spoke for many when he described what came next: "It needed a lot of work ... I did some of the things I learned as an electrician. The first thing I did was put an electric hot water heater in."[25] Men like Baxter often recalled, distinctly, the first houses that they owned and the end of their days living in rented accommodations.

Applying capital and labour to family housing created considerable opportunities for fathers to expand or build new homes, especially those men with new or growing families who had a clear sense of purpose in renovating. According to Richard Harris, about one-third of new homes built between 1945 and 1955 fell into this category in Canada.[26] Owner-built housing became an additional element in the new face of fathers as providers in the postwar period, as did upgrading and home improvements. Prior to the rise of the corporate suburb, Canada's housing shortage in the late 1940s and early 1950s gave rise to a special opportunity for men as fathers to build, improve, or expand their stake in their existing stock. This was also, to a certain extent, part of a longer, often overlooked tradition in Canada, especially in working-class families: "It was 'men of family' who took charge of building," as Harris puts it. "Single men lived at home, boarded, or rented. Building was something done by those with families, who thereby lost their leisure time on evenings and weekends."[27] A father's role as provider meant that work in both paid labour and in housing provision, which included some degree of sweat equity, was commonplace, except among upper-class professionals.

On occasion, a question about memories of the first-born would lead to stories that quickly segued into home-improvement narratives. Charles Gilroy, a retired car salesman, storeowner, and construction worker from Burlington, Ontario, recalled how his son was born while he was at work, both on the job and at the construction site of his own property:

> I remember, they were doing, ah, commercial building on Brant Street, when there was no Burlington, no Burlington hospital in those days. And I had to take Kay to Hamilton, for – take her in, drop her off, and back to work, eh? – in those days. Oh sure. Yeah. I think she was in for a full day, until about five o'clock the following morning – before Bruce was born, y'see. Well, that particular day we were working on the floor. On the second floor of this two story building. And hammer and nails in the wooden floor all day, no machines, no nailers, y'know, all by hand. Oh, every couple of hours, I think, I'd maybe call in, see how things – "Nothing happening, nothing happening." And the doctor, 'course, had the number where I was working. And just nothing happened all day long! Went home that night, and ... I can't remember whether – I don't even think I, I had an opportunity to go to Hamilton that night! Before he was born the next morning. Yeah, just wait for the phone call. "He's born, everything's all right." Simple as that. As I say, we were living on Nelson Avenue by that time. I built that property. I worked for father all day, and worked on this building all night. So, to put, y'know, to get it going. I remember Hallowe'en night, they – y'know how the pranksters would do things? So I sat over there that night, because we had just set the window frames up. And had them propped. I didn't want anybody to come along and knock them down. Sure, so I just sat there all evening, and made sure nobody knocked those down on us.[28]

A tendency to conflate birth with building can also be found in life-writing from the father's perspective. In his autobiography, *Fate and Destiny*, Frank Roosen, a Dutch-born horticulturalist from Deep Cove, British Columbia, not only lists, in painstaking detail, the items and costs of his home-improvement project, but also inserts the birth of his first child, a daughter, into his ongoing house renovation project. As he puts it: "Insulating a house, walls 1 cent per square foot / Insulating a house, ceilings 1 1/2 cents per square foot / Install duroid roofing, 3 cents per square foot. At those rates it took a helluva lot of hours to make headway paying those bills to the oil company, but slowly and surely we are gaining and most of all, they started to trust us and we got finally some 'credit' with them!" Then, immediately following this passage, he adds: "I must have laid awake 'one night too many.' 'Joka' is again getting these familiar, morning sicknesses. Somehow we must have missed the 'Rhythm Method' by a few hours! And there she is. A beautiful baby girl. Wow, just what Daddy wanted and somehow she was named after my mother, with a little change though. She's to be called 'Deborah Joan,' in short Debbie, and she was a 'beauty.' It was May 7th, 1960."[29]

Both stories foreground masculine ways of describing the material act of building or renovating, and both do so while referring to the birth experiences of their wives as a basic fact of life for which they had to prepare as fathers. But this part of their stories stays in the background as they cast themselves as self-reliant, if not self-made, men, tidily summarizing the birth events with phrases like "He's born, everything's all right," "Simple as that," or "And there she is. A beautiful baby girl," noting a *father as progenitor's* pride in naming a daughter partly after one's own mother. While women certainly played active roles in home improvement, for fathers this aspect often stood out as an important part of how they saw themselves *as providers*.[30]

Absent Fathers

Most fathers I interviewed admitted, often in no uncertain terms, that the single biggest regret in their lives was the time spent away from home, at work. Wives, too, expressed regret at absent fathers, with a sense of loss shaped by their particular family-earning/homemaking strategy. From Sydney, Cape Breton, Helen Mleczko, an English war bride, recalls her husband's work bringing with it unwelcome absences. In her autobiography, Mleczko describes in considerable detail how her husband, army veteran Henry Mleczko, worked in the pit, as it was still called, with the Dominion Coal Company of Glace Bay, nearly a half-century after J.B. McLachlan. His basic concern as a provider in the pit was comparable to McLachlan's, although now he could afford to, and did, build his own house.[31]

Helen Mleczko's memories of becoming a wife and mother by the early 1950s are suggestive on several levels. She recalls their optimism as a newly married couple very much in love and very much hoping to make a fresh start after the war. The "one thing that I wanted was to bear Henry a son," to which she adds "it was a real disappointment to think that the first child we had conceived in love was a male and we had lost him." She suffered a stillbirth. Their struggle included raising a daughter whose difficult birth had left one arm disabled. Helen's labour proved a medical crisis. Henry's job meant that he could not be there on the night she was born. She never forgot it: "Henry was working, we had to phone, so poor Ma had to struggle through deep snow down the Avenue to phone the doctor." Helen's memories of birth and early childcare seem to displace Henry almost altogether, with only a few references to his presence in the kitchen, the nursing bedroom, or at the father-and-toddler stage.[32]

For many men, job security did not come before marriage or even before the arrival of children. Provincial northern locales, for instance, displayed a highly uneven boom-and-bust record of stable employment during the postwar period.[33] From northern Saskatchewan, Tom Briden's road to self-sufficiency as a farmer, fisherman, logger, and a Government of Saskatchwan smokejumper (air-dropped firefighter) was marked by a long, hard search for security. He raised seven children but rarely felt settled in various roles as a provider. Briden recalled this as something that shaped much of his fatherhood through to the early 1970s. He stated several times that his Métis heritage came to determine much of his sense of identity as a father and, later, as a grandfather; but this also contributed to racist exclusion, something that he claimed hit him hard. A lack of job promotions, of wage equality, and even of worksite living quarters as a smokejumper, which would have kept his family together, were each cited as he told his story.[34]

He began his account of becoming self-sufficient after his wartime service ended with demobilization in 1945. The next few years were difficult, particularly in getting established as a family breadwinner supporting "the country girl," as he put it, he had married, a woman of Cree heritage: "I was always thinking about the future – put it that way. Like ah, I worked on the railroad. And, in between times – commercial fishing. And I was always doing something. But it wasn't anything that was, y'know I could foresee that I'm going to be a few years from now ... sitting idle and be grateful that I had a successful life, type of thing. There wasn't anything like that in what I was doing."[35]

A change of government in Saskatchewan, a change in direction in forest management, and as he clearly remembered, a change in attitude in hiring policies for a select few government forestry jobs in the early 1950s made a new outlook on the future possible: "When I got the letter that I'd get a permanent job with government, I thought 'O Jesus, here's security!' This is what I was dreaming for. So, I figured, well, I didn't know what a smokejumper was, but I figured, well, it will be a start." Briden held the position, without promotion, for the next sixteen years, although it forced prolonged absences that kept him from his wife and children. His seasonal yet small income was something that he could not give up. Commuting from La Ronge to Prince Albert, Briden remembered, was more than difficult. He recalled, bitterly, how he tried to keep in touch with a family that began to disintegrate. During the long fire season, he simply could not be at home as much as he needed to be. That, he claimed, became clear only when it was too late.[36]

Story after story that I collected included recollections of the prolonged absences from the family circle that paid work entailed. Most interesting was Roy Best's description of how his surveying business, run for many years from his downstairs office at home in Abbotsford, British Columbia, imposed a stark barrier between work and family under one roof: "I had my own business, and I ran it out of the basement of the house. You know, if I had any spare time I usually went back into the office and worked. Even at night. I spent a lot of time working at night ... so anything that had to be done upstairs my wife did it."[37] Best recalled long hours, even a feeling, to which he admitted, of actually looking forward to work: "When I look back now, I can't remember what the hell I – how I spent my average days, you know, my average years. I was so involved with my work. I like working. I worked hard. I worked long hours. And I couldn't wait for Monday morning to come around."[38] Life on the job could be stressful, but it involved a routine that men preferred, freeing them from the uncertainties of domestic chores involving infant children.

For some men, like Cyril Barnard, a former Oakville plant foreman, breadwinning required absences, but these were seen simply as justification for a clear division of labour in the home. "You gotta remember," as Barnard put it, "she was a housewife and I was a breadwinner, and a housewife's job in those days, you [housewives] do the necessary chores – take care of the kids, washing, ironing, the whole bit, laundry, cooking, the whole bit."[39] His reference to "those days" as "something you gotta remember" for their division of labour was anchored in a *natural* assumption maintained by many men of his era.

Barnard's life story, like many others, also presents one of the most important elements of fatherhood: a spectrum, from intense involvement to aloofness or near complete absence, on which an individual fathering personality might be placed, with this placement indicating the degree to which a father takes an active or passive role in childrearing and the domestic chores of parenting. Sociologists, led by the pioneering work of Meg Luxton, have frequently concluded from empirical studies that fathers seldom extended their efforts beyond a "helping" capacity.[40]

One avenue by which fathers could embrace both married life and parenting was through the new, middle-class familial ideal of "togetherness," a popular ideal of family closeness in the postwar years. Togetherness embraced the notion of family life as a profoundly *shared* experience. "Togetherness" in the 1950s, Jessica Weiss concludes, "encapsulated both the comforts and conflicts of baby boom family life. As an ideology, it provided a solution to the dilemma couples with large families faced by combining family time and couple time. But togetherness turned out to be a leaky vessel on which to navigate through the family life cycle."[41] Like suburbia, it attracted its critics.

Chatelaine weighed in with several articles. "Is togetherness vital?" Joan Morris asked in the April 1960 issue. Citing a Montreal-based study by Nathan Epstein, she noted that "communication" between family members was more important than mere "togetherness" in the same space at the same time. Contact itself could be too much. So could guilt for being away. "The desirability of being together is played up so much in our culture these days," Epstein remarked, "that a person feels guilty if he wants to be alone." Epstein also made a pointed reference to the face of fathers as successful providers as one that was still primary – indeed, essential: "What did appear to influence the family's well being," he concluded, "was that the children witnessed their father's growing success in business, and their own consequent improvement in economic and social status."[42] Powerful fathers, he suggested with an interpretation more than tinged with patriarchy, make compelling examples. "Togetherness is Awful," wrote June Callwood to head up an article in "10 Reasons Why Marriages Fail," citing a Montreal social worker who declared, "vehemently," that marriages were now so "full of clatter" that there was "no time for man and wife to be apart from the family."[43] Despite such warnings, which seemed to come on the heels of a new face of marriage and childrearing as a *shared* enterprise, fathers as *involved* parents had nonetheless found their champions in the new postwar family. Breadwinning took time, often too much, as many of my interviews indicated. Few fathers could live up to the ideal of togetherness or even wanted to. If anything, this new face for fatherhood stood as a counterpoint to the realities of fathers' prolonged absences from home while engaged, simply as breadwinners, in providing as a purely economic function.

Involved Breadwinners and Intimate Portraits
Precisely how the nurturing father and providing father came together, however, was not always a neat melding of identies. This is not to say that as the birth rate increased up to the early 1960s, fatherhood reinforced a neglectful absence by the working family man; involved fatherhood, in the form of engaged, active participation in family life at home and in the local community, often went hand-in-hand with personal motivations that could fit in with postwar paid-work demands.

As recreation opportunities become more institutionalized, both fathers and mothers were expected to participate in childrearing within these structures and according to their gendered roles as parents. In hockey arenas, on baseball diamonds, and in a growing array of local community recreational settings, the faces of involved providers proliferated from city to suburb, from small-town Canada to the metropolitan YMCAs. In Brantford, Ontario, as Shirley Tillotson argues, this transition took place against a backdrop in 1953 of paid professionals displacing "citizen" volunteers; nonetheless, parents maintained a key role in supporting their children's participation.[44] On the one hand, to cite a notable instance, Walter Gretzky, then a Brantford-based Bell Telephone lineman, who admits that he may have been rather complacent about the birth of his five children, beginning with Wayne in 1961 ("a little too blasé, I think, in [his wife] Phyllis's opinion"), missed one birth altogether while at a hockey tournament with his destined-to-be-famous son.[45] On the other hand, he recalls that there soon "was so much to fit in" to his busy life as a father of four sons and a daughter. From then on, as he remembers his parenting, a

> snapshot of the Gretzky family during the '60s and '70s, if you could get us to stand still long enough to pose, would show you a growing young family that loved sports and always had some kind of activity on the go, be it hockey, baseball, lacrosse or track and field. Sometimes, the kids' hockey games would go one after another down at the arena, in order from Peewee to Bantam, so we'd be able to watch Glen, then Keith and then Wayne in one place. Other times we would travel around to different places to watch them play. Phyllis and I would often divide that up. I think we decided pretty early on that our kids would get equal time with us as much as possible. She'd take them to early-morning practices, since I was such a night owl and didn't like to get up, and had to go to work anyway. And I'd go to their games.[46]

The image of the father juggling work and family time – as unbalanced as the actual sharing of childcare between spouses tended to be – was repeatedly championed in the popular discourse of the era. The May 1961 issue of *Chatelaine*, for instance, profiled the married life of Bob Eadie in a "Chatelaine Personal Experience Story" related by his wife, Betty. Bob was ten years older than Betty and had been paralyzed by polio from the waist down since he was an infant. He required a wheelchair but had built a successful career in printing management and was employed as an assistant manager of the print division of Cornwall's city newspaper, the *Standard-Freeholder*. He was also the father of two adopted sons, aged eight and ten when their story appeared. Betty Edie described an active family man, on the job, in the community, and at home: "With so many interests forever demanding Bob's time, you might think he has little left over for our boys. You would be quite wrong. Bob is, I think, an ideal father, who believes that 'parents should spend time with their children, not just palm them off on teachers and counselors.' He lives by his beliefs, too." She went on to describe the outdoor pursuits that they enjoyed together and spoke fondly of his frivolities

The face of father as provider in the spring of 1967: This father-and-child photograph was taken at Expo 67, in April of Canada's Centennial year. With his child aloft on his shoulders, possibly to witness an Expo spectacle, the father holds a transistor radio in one hand as he steadies his child with the other, with a map of Expo, it appears, stuffed into his jacket pocket.
Library and Archives Canada, Canadian Corporation for the 1967 World Exhibition fonds, R869-0-8-E/e001096650

with their kids at home. "A favorite game involves the boys trying to pin their father's exceptionally strong arms and shoulders to the floor. They haven't succeeded yet."[47]

Ideal portraits tended to reify concepts of a gendered spectrum of masculine domesticity. At one end stood the good fathers, the involved fathers – those who actually did participate in aspects of familial togetherness. At the other stood fathers who were too busy to be home from work and were, at worst, too busy to care. For many men I interviewed, family vacations with children served as significant settings to recall involvement in recreational moments, particularly when viewed as part of what a provider's role for fathers *should* entail. "Ruth and I always had a vacation," Bob Wright recalled. Wright was managing an agricultural wholesale supplier in Abbotsford, having grown up on a farm before joining the Royal Canadian Air Force (RCAF) in 1941. He married in Canada during the war and later raised two girls and two boys from the war's end to the mid-1960s. "We always used to take the children to Birch Bay, for a week," he related: "They always had a week in Birch Bay. We went there for, ah, I'd say fifteen years, fifteen or sixteen years. Yeah, then we bought a trailer there in '71. Course the kids were grown up then." His youngest turned twenty that year, suggesting that the resort had been a key spot for all of them throughout the period. "I know that it was $100.00." That "was the price that we paid," he noted succinctly. "And it was $30.00 for the cabin and $70.00 to, I think the kids got ten bucks each, or something, y'see. But a hundred dollars would do a week at Birch Bay." "We had our cabin there, and the two kids [his older two, looking at a family photograph] went roller skating every day, and that was their big thing. And those two [his younger two] they always seemed to have, they'd find a couple of chums, y'know. And, of course, they played and went in the water. And Ruth and I, of course, we never were, and still aren't, water people. We went down there for the ... well, we had a good rest, y'know."[48]

But how much time did fathers actually give to intimate interaction with their children, even when providing a vacation? In many cases, including this one, it is difficult to say, although the ideal, of course, was for fathers to care and to be there with the family. Father *as clown* and father *as buddy* were not necessarily the preferred faces, but father *as provider* was. In fact, based on a comprehensive reading of popular representations of fatherhood throughout the 1950s, Ralph LaRossa concludes that patriarchal images became more predominant toward the end of the decade than they had been at the beginning.[49]

Arguably, the best measure of where fathers stood on individual spectrums can be found in memories of children, especially when they recall leisure times that increasingly meant spending some portion of the family's disposable income. In his Ontario-based memoir, *Last Resort: Coming of Age in Cottage Country*, Linwood Barclay remembers his close relationship with his father, who succumbed to lung cancer when his son was still in high school. His father worked both as a commercial artist in a Toronto suburb and as a resort operator in the summer months in northeastern Ontario. The story of Everett Barclay, as told by his son, is also the story of how fathers and sons interact at home and on a jobsite that was shared, one of the many histories of fathers rearing sons to the worlds of work. Here, the informal model of father as co-worker is suggested. Increasingly, in the summer months at their trailer-park resort near Fenelon Falls, Ontario, as Barclay recalled:

Dad sought my help. Many of the chores needed a second pair of hands, and I was getting old enough to be useful. I helped him clean out the rental boats ... We hauled the boats up on shore, and while one of us tipped it on its side, the other sprayed it with the hose. We took turns ... Dad didn't do this just for our boats. He did it for everyone's. The guests must have viewed this as, if not nuts, at least overly cautious. But there is something comforting about coming down to the lake early in the morning, as the mist was lifting, and seeing all the fishing boats linked together from dock to dock, like a line of nursery-school kids being taken out for a walk.[50]

Barclay's depiction of an engaged father casts him as a family man at the positive end of the involvement spectrum, juggling work and family life.

Walter Gretzky's memories and Betty Edie's account of her husband likewise construct this kind of father. These narratives, along with Bob Wright's
recollection of his passive presence near, but not actually *in*, the water, illustrate how familial togetherness, rooted in sharing the fruits of labour after
work or on vacation, ordinarily ranged from fathers wrestling with children
on the floor to the stand-offish dad on the beach well aware of what everything was costing. Some fathers claimed, or were constructed to claim, that
they were simply too tired to do much else.

Popular depictions of the haggard breadwinner and failed provider generated steady streams of prescriptive reporting on what became a salient trope
of postwar domesticity: the insensitive wife and mother versus the over-
worked husband and father. *Chatelaine*'s case studies of the late 1950s and
early 1960s offered several prominently featured illustrations: "June looked
at Bill in utter disbelief," one male psychologist reported in a November
1960 article entitled "Is Your Husband Happy in His Job?" "He had just fin-
ished telling her of his resignation from a perfectly secure post in which he
had risen consistently. Moreover, there seemed nothing else in sight for
him." The problem was his family. Its demands proved too much. He could
not even talk about it before it was too late. "Even worse he seemed to blame
[June] in some way, and the depth of his bitterness shocked her. Everything
for which they had worked seemed to be lying in ruins around her."[51]

The face of fathers as providers within the spectrum from family as burden
to the rejuvenating family weekend was open to a critique seldom discussed
in the pages of *Chatelaine*. Family men could simply avoid, as breadwinners,
the realities of family togetherness. And little was said of this as long as the
money flowed in. As part of a gendered system of expectations, father's
roles were heavily scripted to afford men a dividend, a right to emotional
time off from the family circle, restricting his fatherly involvement to the
margins. The closer he might choose to move toward the centre, toward
meaningful contact with children and spouse, the better. But this was not
always easy, or so it was claimed. This is partly because their very maleness
was essentialized, even medicalized, in simplistic case-study prescriptions
featuring psychological assessments of Canadian dads that failed to consider, critically, how these men continued to exercise the privileges of family patriarch.

Children seldom see, nor do adults often remember, their fathers in these
terms. Often the intimate portraits that they draw converge in a face of
working fathers that interweaves breadwinning with a simplistic but powerful
sense of the social identity of male parents. Such patterns of perception and
memory tend to construct individual fathers as each belonging to a special
breed of men, somehow empowered or marked through their work. This is
usually the case when children are fascinated by the personae of their fathers

as gainfully employed workers or when they see some aspect of their fathers' jobs as intrinsic to them as public men.

Wayne Johnston's intimate portrait of his father as the focal point of his family's Newfoundland heritage is a case in point. His father, Art, completed his formal training as an agricultural technician in 1948, graduating from the agricultural college in Truro, Nova Scotia, just before the province entered Confederation. Art Johnston claimed to have left the Avalon Peninsula to study agriculture in order to help save modern Newfoundlanders from their traditional reliance on the sea. He then worked at an experimental farm near St. Johns, set up under Premier Joey Smallwood, which ultimately closed. From there, he moved on to a fisheries research station in the city's downtown core. His job in a modern, lab-coat environment working on projects to improve the marketing and exploitation of cod and other species seemed to negate his anachronistic sense of island pride. "He lived in denial of these contradictions," his son maintained: "By my time, he was well used to it. He had become what my mother called a 'fishionary,' part missionary, part visionary when it came to fish. Though he still regarded the sea with a mixture of awe, dread and revulsion, he preached the gospel of the fishery, predicted the imminent invention, by scientists and technologists like him, of new and more efficient ways of catching and preserving fish. Where the farm had failed, 'the Station' would succeed."[52]

His father also taught him all that he thought he should know about fish, from the Latin nomenclatures of cod, herring, turbot, and mackerel to his clowning imitations of a flatfish's prey-roving eyes, which "always sent me into hysterics."[53] In his son's eyes, Art Johnston's provider's face, like much about this misplaced man, could never be separated from a romantic sense of island nationalism that, fundamentally, defined his father for him.

David Zieroth grew up on a family farm in Manitoba in the 1950s. His close contact with a providing father, which his agricultural upbringing necessitated, was in this case fondly remembered. Perhaps to emphasize this fact, Zieroth chose a present-tense narration: "I love my father, and he loves me," began one passage describing a father who

> shows me how to handle a machine, or we bend our heads over a tool, and, and he talks to me, and sometimes we laugh about something I don't understand. He tells me what to do, and I do it. I'm eager to help because I believe it will gain entry to my father ... I can tell my father is looking at me from the distance of the forty-five years he's already put under his belt when I'm born, the last of his four kids ... After lunch, before he goes back to his work, he lies on the couch in the living room to snooze for fifteen minutes, not really sleeping, eyes closed, doing some private calculation that restores him.[54]

Zieroth recalled trying to get as deeply as possible into the mindset of his father, especially when he worked. Most telling was Zieroth's yearning to know everything that his father appeared to know about the world around them: "I would like to follow him into his dreams, to see him the way he sees himself. Since I can't, I stay close to him, go where he goes."[55] Zieroth suggested how his father became a young boy's guide to the world of work partly because they lived on a farm but fundamentally because his role as a manful provider melded with masculine role modelling that held a special appeal for young Zieroth.

"Providing could be seen and felt," as Demos suggests, "as an enlargement of paternal nurturance." A father's work could seem "mysterious and wonderful, and his ability to negotiate the treacherous routes through 'the world' might be positively heroic."[56] For children especially, the experiences of seeing, hearing, even smelling fathers as providers could be visceral. They could leave deep, sensory impressions, in memory, that combined the breadwinning father with a sense of the father's presence altogether. Like the episodic recall of sight and sound of Maria Coletta Mclean's description of her father's black metal lunchbox scraping against the kitchen counter and of his chair as he pulled it up to their mother-of-pearl Arborite table, sensation, emotion, and presence became intertwined. Her father's return, perhaps from a long-haul drive as he struggled to help make ends meet, was experienced first from a child's perspective through the concrete record of the senses.

When I asked Janet Gilroy-Jones of Burlington, Charles Gilroy's daughter, what she remembered best about her working father, she did not hesitate: cigars – their smell, even their taste when "Dad used to let me bite off the tips of them." As she put it: "my grandfather had a construction company in St. Petersburg, Florida. So, Dad would go down and build homes, on off times. So, grandmother still had the house down there. So we would drive down to Florida. And, I [chuckles] used to get *terribly* car sick. And we'd sit in the back of the car, and my dad would have the window down *a crack* [chuckles]. And he would be smoking a cigar. O God." Gilroy-Jones also recalled the sound of Stompin' Tom Connors blaring in a Bronco cab rigged for local snow removal contracts, another mid-winter part-time job for her father: "He was an incredibly hard worker. In the wintertime he plowed snow. I remember going in a little, ah, it must have been, like, a '69 Bronco ... And I would go out and plow snow with him. And we'd have an 8-track tape of Stompin' Tom Connors playing. And he would plow snow – he would take us to Guelph line, where Jumbo's plaza is, where the ice-cream place is." When asked if she grew up with a good sense of what her father did, she said simply "yes, it was feast or famine."[57]

Fathers as providers became in some children's mental diaries masculine beings whose work, in myriad ways, connected them to the often alluring, exotic world of adults in the public realm. The private-public duality of fathers as providers could lend them a powerful presence in their children's eyes. What distinguished fathers in this generation from previous ones were their higher expectations of securing employment, of working in jobs at all levels that valorized family manhood through material acquisitions. Home spaces, domestic goods, and leisure consumption, from houses to cars to family vacations, often served as masculine markers of success that became specific to this generation's hopes and disappointment through to the early 1970s, perhaps especially for the many fathers across Canada who never really saw much of the good life.

Faces of Failure

I interviewed Roy Phillips in Sault Ste. Marie in 2004. He had served overseas in the infantry in France, rising to the rank of lieutenant. He had also lost his first job back in Canada, when the Department of Veterans Affairs reorganized its local benefits administration. In fact, with little formal education, he found himself stuck for work in 1946 despite his record. He had married the day that war broke out in 1939. His children, two girls and a boy, were born from the early war to just past the peak of the baby boom in 1958. But he really felt the pressure when he was laid off. He had no real alternatives besides a labourer's job, working shifts, at a pulp mill in Espanola, two hours by car down the road from where he had to leave his wife and children in the Sault. They stayed with his parents. A few months later, he was able to move them into a company-owned house, near the mill. Then his father paid a visit. He never forgot that day:

> You see, what sticks in my mind is a comment my father made one time, when he came to visit us. He said: "Son, have you *any* idea how fortunate you are?" "What'd ya mean?" He said: "Look at your house. There's a place for everything – and everything in its place. It's *spotless!*" He said: "Look at the kitchen, look at your cupboard. It's ordered. There's – I wouldn't say it's plentiful." But he said: "Your wife has done what she can do with whatever income there is – and made it work!" We went upstairs into the bedroom. He pulled open the closet door. He said: "I'm not invading your house – but look what you got here! Clean shirts, hanging on coat hangers." And he pulled out the drawer. He said: "Look!" Dad was impressed with it because, in his words, he'd "seen all sorts of people who, y'know, they had last Tuesday's shirt on. What the hell. As long as it wasn't wet – wear it!" Hah – that's the extreme. But he had seen all that. He was pointing out how fortunate I was to have married a girl who could *do* that. Of course, she learned it from her mother who had *absa-bloody-lootly-nothing!*[58]

Phillips' father, who knew first-hand the hard times of providing in the 1930s, held higher hopes and expectations for his son than Phillips could, at least at that moment. His end would pick up. He should be sincerely grateful that his wife was holding up so well. Phillips endured his setback, gained training along the way, and eventually was able to make his way back to the Sault to work the balance of his career in a quality-control laboratory.

Some fathers, of course, really did fail. Although the postwar years, as an era, can hardly be cast as years of failure for most family men, dependants felt the *fear* of jobs and families lost to alcohol, marital infidelity, crime, and other tragedies even if they were momentarily spared. As an imagined horror, images of fathers as failed providers became a staple on the pages of magazines like *Chatelaine* through a steady stream of short stories, case studies, and prescriptive discourse. Bankruptcies, layoffs, and other economic failures, to be sure, took their toll. But providers were, somehow, expected within the postwar social order to bounce back like never before. If not, notions of young, healthy fathers as victims in the Canadian job system, on an ideal level, made no sense. Failed providers were, simply put, failed fathers. Reading the signs of behavioural disfunction leading to a crisis for fathers as providers became, as it were, a modern science. Patterns of abuse or poor moral character could seldom be hidden for long. Except when revealed by accidents or sudden illnesses, the faces of failed providers were not apparent; they emerged.

Ian Ferguson remembers his father, Hank, differently. In 1959, the year he was born, his parents drove a rickety Ford Zephyr from Edmonton over 500 miles north to Fort Vermillion. His father was a con man: "My father hailed from Radville, Saskatchewan," Ferguson explained. He "got out of there as quickly as he could. At the time he met my mother, he was calling himself a salesman, but he had aspirations to be a minor-league grafter. He had previous experience as an actor, a card shark, a pool hustler and a musician."[59]

Now he had to leave Edmonton in a hurry. This time he was selling insurance policies quite unlike those of Fred Cress. When an outraged customer came to call, Ferguson fled. Heading north, with no real plan, he picked up word along the way that the Peace River Separate School District was desperately short of teachers. "The superintendent hired him on the spot." From there, he was sent north, over 500 miles from Edmonton to Fort Vermillion, a tiny settlement of Natives, Métis, and other local families with a residential school about to close.

Unusually, it seems at first glance, Hank settled down. Over the next few years the Fergusons even expanded their family in the North. Hank's Achilles' heel, however, proved to be his school's principal: "We had to move," his son remembered, then ten years old: "because my father got fired. Gene Rogers, tired of my father's insubordination, and of losing softball, had looked at his original application and uncovered my father's lack of a teaching certificate. The jig was up." He "gleefully passed the information on to the school board, and my father was dismissed on the spot ... My parents had spent ten years in Fort Vermillion. Three of their four sons were born there. They owned property, and they had recently fixed up their house. But they had very little money left. Putting in the plumbing had used up almost all their savings. My father needed to find some other way to support his family. He spent a few miserable weeks working on a road crew south of High Level, but he wasn't any good at it. He cashed in his pay check and that was that."[60]

They then moved on to Regina, where Hank enrolled in teacher's college, his last effort to become legitimate. Then things got ugly: "One time my father simply didn't come home. He was gone all day Saturday and all day Sunday. We were in bed asleep when the front door slammed on Monday night."[61] That marked the end of the Ferguson nuclear family. "My father was pretending to be quiet, but we could hear him as he came stumbling up the stairs. He went room to room to give us all a kiss goodnight. I pretended to be asleep, but I could smell the alcohol on him. He went to join my mother, and they had a long, hissing argument that lasted well into the morning. My father had started drinking again. He never stopped after that. He eventually died from it. Cirrhosis."[62]

As a good provider, Hank wore a mask. His son remembers his mother telling him later: "Your father got tired of the long con. Those first ten years we had together were the best ten years of my life, but he was only pretending to be that person, to be a good husband and a good father and a good teacher, and after a while he couldn't pretend any more. When we moved to Regina, he decided to pretend to be someone else."[63]

Conclusion

These stories, each unique yet linked to broader histories of fatherhood as providers, indicate the degree to which successful breadwinning, particularly in male-dominated labour markets, resurrected a traditional model of fatherhood. Moreover, the fathers themselves often used gendered language to tell their family stories accordingly – to meld together, if not confuse, providing with becoming new fathers, with parenting children, with their identities as men, and with a discernable desire for material gains and status secured through family-based consumption. The varieties of fathers' activities as postwar providers – from getting settled, to building and improving houses, to prolonged absences at work – took place at a time when more was expected by fathers and by families than could have been the case in prior eras.

Approximately one-half of the age cohort that I have considered here, comprising over two million men in Canada, served in the Second World War. About half, like Ferguson's father, did not. It is important to emphasize, too, that the war did not end simply with the peace of 1945. There remained, often for younger families, a discomforting, sometimes appalling, period of adjustment, from a very real housing shortage across the country up to the mid-1950s to the personal horrors of war that some men brought back home. With respect to living standards, many fathers had to wait for pay raises that did not outpace mild inflation throughout the period.

But expectations grew. Bruce McCall's father, who had served in the RCAF, simply dreamed of getting something new, fun, and exciting, sometimes outrageous: "One Sunday it would be the little Grumman Seabee amphibian plane he was going to buy; the next, a mighty new DeSoto with Fluid Drive; a week later, a phonograph with an automatic record changer was practically due for delivery at 101 Union Street. We'd get a movie camera and projector, showing color film. All the bounty of postwar technology was heading our way." But as McCall puts it, striking a note of realism, the "truth was, of course, that T.C.'s six-thousand-dollar annual salary as a medium-level Ontario civil servant barely covered the basic costs of food and shelter and clothing for his brood and he couldn't afford a week's vacation or a used car, much less an airplane or a movie camera. McCall family life was not about to be revolutionized anytime soon. Save for the postwar scientific breakthrough of plastic bubbles you could blow up and keep, like balloons, life would go on much as before. He knew it and so did I, but I forgave him and his fantasies. It was, after all, 1947."[64] As Magda Fahrni has argued in a local study of Montreal war veterans, these men returned not only to a variety of stresses and expectations, but also to family lives of constrained prospects and frustrated realities.[65]

This was something that the men I interviewed widely perceived as distinctive to their place in history as a generation of fathers supporting dependants at younger ages than their fathers had and in proportionally more conjugal families between the late 1940s and the end of the baby boom in the early 1960s. In a parallel study, I have considered how fathers' constructions of family memories, from the perspectives of the men themselves, emphasized pride in home ownership, material gains, and securing a "settled" household through male breadwinning. Their life stories of becoming fathers, and both productive and consuming citizens, bore many signs that embraced the consumerist ethic of the baby boom period that began with the arrival of the children themselves in the late 1940s.[66]

Central to an economy that became increasingly oriented to provisioning demands fuelled by the rising rate of family formation was the conjugal nuclear family itself, a kinship model that reemerged following the war years as powerful as it had been during the development of middle-class norms that had governed bourgeois family formation patterns since the early nineteenth century. The return to normalcy, so eagerly sought by younger couples raising children during Canada's baby boom, revived and reconfigured the father's central role as provider within families that strove for security through income, consumption, and demonstrated social status. Only in the latter 1960s did many of the gendered and patriarchal assumptions upheld by this generation of fathers begin to break down in any significant way. The provider's role for fathers endured nonetheless, having recently survived even greater challenges just a generation before: "The Depression attacked, and sometimes shattered, fathers in their central role as providers," as Demos observes. Nevertheless, "the role itself survived until the return of better times, and flourished thereafter. The wars separated millions of fathers from their families for months or years at a stretch, but the ensuing peacetimes brought a renewal (even a reinforcement) of traditional domestic arrangements."[67] My own oral history fieldwork and life-writing drawn from the multiple positions of all family members express the unique and particular ways that individual life stories and the period combine. On different terms, however, all address a role – both traditional and modern – for fathers as gendered subjects and identify fatherhood as a category of experience that historically crosses thresholds separating private from public spheres, a category that we are only now beginning to examine.

Notes

1   The concept of "companionate marriage," as debated in the late 1920s, should not be confused with the *companionship* (also "companionate") marriage models of the 1950s. The former referred to trial heterosexual cohabitation and conjugal intimacy prior to a legal marriage with faith-tradition sanction. It had appeared in monograph form with the controversial publication of Ben B. Lindsey and Wainwright Evans, *The Companionate Marriage* (1927; reprint, New York: Arno Press, 1972). On the use of the term at this time in America, see Steven Mintz and Susan Kellogg, *Domestic Revolutions: A Social History of American Family Life* (New York: Free Press, 1988), 114-15. During the 1950s, notes Jessica Weiss, *To Have and To Hold: Marriage, the Baby Boom and Social Change* (Chicago: University of Chicago Press, 2000), 116, a new discourse of "togetherness" was popularized in the print media and in the relevant postwar prescriptive literature on partnership relations in married life: "The ideology of 'togetherness,'" Weiss explains, "sprang out of a century-long dichotomy in prescriptions for American middle-class marriage. Historians identify two conflicting patterns that emerged during the nineteenth century – 'separate spheres' and companionate marriage." Weiss concludes that married life during the postwar, baby boom period did not necessarily bring about a shift toward the companionate ideal, although many elements of that model were championed in the new, optimistic discourse advocating "togetherness" in married life.

2   Ruby Cress, *Haven't Any News: Ruby's Letters from the 50's,* ed. Edna Staebler (Waterloo, ON: Wilfrid Laurier University Press, 1995), 5.

3   Carol Ann Cole, with Anjila Kapoor, *Comfort Heart: A Personal Memoir* (Toronto: ECW Press, 2001), 18.

4   For a useful overview of postwar domesticity at mid-century, see Doug Owram, "Home and Family at Mid-Century," in *Born at the Right Time: A History of the Baby-Boom Generation*

(Toronto: University of Toronto Press, 1996), 3-30. On the penetration rates of domestic goods and a comparison of American and Canadian patterns, see Joy Parr, *Domestic Goods: The Material, the Moral, and the Economic in the Postwar Years* (Toronto: University of Toronto Press, 1999).

5 Writing in the mid-1980s, Demos could refer in American contexts to a noticeable gap in the historiography that has since been addressed in several major studies, including Robert L. Griswold, *Fatherhood in America: A History* (New York: Basic Books, 1993); Scott Coltrane, *Family Man: Fatherhood, Housework, and Gender Equity* (Oxford and New York: Oxford University Press, 1996); Ralph LaRossa, *The Modernization of Fatherhood: A Social and Political History* (Chicago and London: University of Chicago Press, 1997); Stephen M. Frank, *Parenthood and Masculinity in the Nineteenth-Century American North* (Baltimore and London: Johns Hopkins University Press, 1998); and Shawn Johansen, *Family Men: Middle-Class Fatherhood in Early Industrializing America* (New York and London: Routledge, 2001). Comparable monographs, drawn from Canadian settings, have yet to be published. See John Demos, "The Changing Faces of Fatherhood," in *Past, Present, and Personal: The Family and Life Course in American History* (New York and Oxford: Oxford University Press, 1986), 41-67.

6 An insightful summary of this issue appears in Cynthia R. Comacchio, *The Infinite Bonds of Family: Domesticity in Canada, 1850-1940* (Toronto: University of Toronto Press, 1999), esp. Part 1, "Making the New Nation: Domestic Adjustments, 1850-1914," 15-62.

7 By far the single best study of family strategies among the poor in industrializing Canada is Bettina Bradbury, *Working Families: Age, Gender, and Daily Survival in Industrializing Montreal* (1993; reprint, Toronto: Oxford University Press, 1996).

8 Quoted in David Frank, "Cape Breton Red: J.B. McLachlan and Canadian Labour Radicalism," Second Annual Robert S. Kenny Prize Lecture, 28 April 2000, University of Toronto Library, Thomas Fisher Rare Book Library, Robert S. Kenny Prize, http://www.library.utoronto.ca/fisher/kenny-prize/david-frank.html.

9 As Peter S. McInnis argues in *Harnessing Labour Confrontation: Shaping the Postwar Settlement in Canada* (Toronto: University of Toronto Press, 2002), the postwar settlement between the state and industrial workers brought consumer-directed citizenship under the umbrella of business unionism. Higher productivity, higher wages, and higher levels of consumption lent a new legitimacy to industrial capitalism that undercut traditional class-based politics. Union membership supported bureaucratic measures based on a postwar ideal: economic redistribution took place through negotiated settlements that meant higher wages and higher levels of consumption of industrial outputs.

10 Alvin Finkel, *Our Lives: Canada after 1945* (Toronto: Lorimer, 1997), 9-10.

11 Both Veronica Strong-Boag and Doug Owram cite figures for the increase in the participation rates of all women and, as its own category, of married women in the paid workforce in the postwar period. As early as 1951 the proportion for all women in the paid workforce stood at 25%, compared to an interwar average of 20% (Owram). Married women's participation moved from 11.2% in 1951 to 22% by 1961. See Owram, *Born at the Right Time*, 29; and Veronica Strong-Boag, "Home Dreams: Women and the Suburban Experiment in Canada, 1945-1960," *Canadian Historical Review* 72, 4 (December 1991): 471-504 at 479-80.

12 The postwar baby boom period considered here – from the beginning of a significant increase in the birthrate in 1949 to its relative collapse in the early 1960s – should not be oversimplified as one of dramatic, uncomplicated rupture from the years of depression and war that preceded it. The drive for security, launched by expectations and Cold War fears, had resonance on both sides of the border. On the Canadian context, see Reg Whitaker and Gary Marcuse, *Cold War Canada: The Making of a National Insecurity State, 1945-1957* (Toronto: University of Toronto Press, 1994); and Richard Cavell, ed., *Love, Hate and Fear in the Cold War* (Toronto: University of Toronto Press, 2004). On family life and the Cold War in America, see Elaine Tyler May, *Homeward Bound: American Families in the Cold War Era* (New York: Basic Books, 1988). Periodizations that mark the end of the Second World War as a dramatic, largely progressive, new beginning belie a 1950s-based presentism. Considerable shifts in state governance and social change occurred up to 1955. See Nancy Christie and Michael Gauvreau, "Introduction: Recasting Canada's Postwar Decade," in Nancy Christie and Michael Gauvreau, eds., *Cultures of Citizenship in Post-War Canada* (Montreal and

Kingston: McGill-Queen's University Press, 2003), 3-26. On the housing shortage for a specific locale, Prince George, British Columbia, see Robert Rutherdale, "Approaches to Community Formation and the Family in the Provincial North: Prince George and British Columbia's Central Interior," *BC Studies* 104 (Winter 1994-95): 103-26 at 124.

13 Joy Parr, *The Gender of Breadwinners: Women, Men, and Change in Two Industrial Communities, 1880-1950* (Toronto: University of Toronto Press, 1990), 244.

14 On the historical processes that contributed to gendered (patriarchal) state/society assumptions, legislation, and public policies in Canada from the First World War to the early baby boom years, see Nancy Christie, *Engendering the State: Family, Work, and Welfare in Canada* (Toronto: University of Toronto Press, 2000). On Quebec's school system and gendered family allowances from the war period to the mid-1950s, see Dominique Marshall, *Aux origines sociales de l'État-providence: Familles québécoises, obligation scolaire et allocations familiales, 1940-1955* (Montreal: Presses de l'Université de Montréal, 1998).

15 Samples in this study (eight oral-history interviews and twelve life-writing texts) have been selected from different class and ethnic identities and regional settings not to pursue rigorously a structural hypothesis for any of these dimensions but to consider how a gendered sense of identity as breadwinning family men often crossed social and spatial boundaries as the Canadian economy grew after the war.

16 On the ambivalence of this model as experienced in Canada's postwar suburbs, see Strong-Boag, "Home Dreams." On the discriminatory barriers and hardships that single mothers in Ontario faced, see Margaret Jane Hillyard Little, *No Car, No Radio, No Liquor Permit: The Moral Regulation of Single Mothers in Ontario, 1920-1997* (Toronto: Oxford University Press, 1998).

17 Ted Finley interview, Sault Ste. Marie, Ontario, 2 June 2004. Pseudonyms are used for the names of all interviewees.

18 Maria Coletta McLean, *My Father Came from Italy* (Vancouver: Raincoast Books, 2000).

19 Ibid., 17-18. On Toronto Italian family, work, and community life in this period, see Franca Iacovetta, *Such Hardworking People: Italian Immigrants in Postwar Toronto* (Montreal and Kingston: McGill-Queen's University Press, 1992).

20 John Porter, *The Vertical Mosaic: An Analysis of Social Class and Power in Canada* (Toronto: University of Toronto Press, 1965).

21 Morris Gibson, *A Doctor in the West* (Toronto: HarperCollins, 1983), 141, 144.

22 Ibid., 142.

23 Scott Young, *A Writer's Life* (Toronto: Doubleday, 1994), 145-46.

24 Christie, *Engendering the State*, 311.

25 Earl Baxter interview, Burlington, Ontario, 17 July 2001.

26 Richard Harris, *Creeping Conformity: How Canada Became Suburban, 1900-1960* (Toronto: University of Toronto Press, 2004), 148.

27 Richard Harris, *Unplanned Suburbs: Toronto's American Tragedy, 1900-1950* (Baltimore: Johns Hopkins University Press, 1996), 206-7.

28 Charles Gilroy interview, Burlington, Ontario, 19 July 2001.

29 Frank Roosen, *Fate and Destiny* (Deep Cove, BC: Roosendal Farms, n.d.), 68-69.

30 For the role of women in owner-built housing in this period, see Harris, *Creeping Conformity*, 150.

31 Helen Mleczko, *My Book of Memories: Picking Up the Pieces* (Glace Bay, NS: Robertson Print Craft, n.d.), copy of text provided by the author, August 2002.

32 Ibid., 56-58.

33 On resource exploitation and job instability, see Kenneth Coates and William R. Morrison, *The Forgotten North: A History of Canada's Provincial North* (Toronto: Lorimer, 1992).

34 Tom Briden interview, Saskatoon, Saskatchewan, 5 July 2004.

35 Ibid.

36 Ibid.

37 Roy Best interview, Abbotsford, British Columbia, 5 March 1997.

38 Ibid.

39 Cyril Barnard interview, Burlington, Ontario, 25 July 2001.

40 As Luxton remarked of a Flin Flon, Manitoba, case study: "Most significantly, it was still assumed that women were primarily responsible for domestic labour and that men were 'helping out.'" See Meg Luxton, "Two Hands for the Clock: Changing Patterns in the Gendered Division of Labour in the Home," in Meg Luxton, Harriet Rosenberg, and Sedef Arat-Koç, eds., *Through the Kitchen Window: The Politics of Home and Family,* 2nd ed. (Toronto: Garamond Press, 1990), 47.

41 Weiss, *To Have and To Hold,* 116.

42 Joan Morris, "Was the Victorian Father So Bad after All?" *Chatelaine,* April 1960, 44-52.

43 June Callwood, "10 Reasons Why Marriages Fail," *Chatelaine,* January 1961, 63.

44 See Shirley Tillotson, "The Meanings of Citizenship Participation: Brantford, 1945-1957," in *The Public at Play: Gender and the Politics of Recreation in Postwar Ontario* (Toronto: University of Toronto Press, 2000), 104-27.

45 Walter Gretzky, *On Family, Hockey, and Healing* (Toronto: Random House Canada, 2001), 38.

46 Ibid., 40.

47 Betty Eadie, as told to Sheila Kieran, "The Wonderful Man I Married," *Chatelaine,* May 1961, 68.

48 Bob Wright interview, Abbotsford, British Columbia, 13 March 1997.

49 Ralph LaRossa, "The Culture of Fatherhood in the Fifties: A Closer Look," *Journal of Family History* 29 (2004): 47-70.

50 Linwood Barclay, *Last Resort: Coming of Age in Cottage Country* (Toronto: McClelland and Stewart), 62.

51 Douglas M. Jones, "Is Your Husband Happy in His Job?" *Chatelaine,* November 1960, 45.

52 Wayne Johnston, *Baltimore's Mansion: A Memoir* (Toronto: Vintage, 2000), 124.

53 Ibid., 128.

54 David Zieroth, *The Education of Mr. Whippoorwill: A Country Boyhood* (Toronto: Macfarlane, Walter and Ross, 2002), 7-8.

55 Ibid., 8.

56 Demos, "Changing Faces," 52.

57 Janet Gilroy-Jones interview, Burlington, Ontario, 31 July 2001.

58 Roy Phillips interview, Sault Ste. Marie, Ontario, 4 May 2004.

59 Ian Ferguson, *Village of the Small Houses: A Memoir of Sorts* (Vancouver and Toronto: Douglas and McIntyre), 31.

60 Ibid., 107-8.

61 Ibid., 120.

62 Ibid.

63 Ibid., 121.

64 Bruce McCall, *Thin Ice: Coming of Age in Canada* (Toronto: Random House of Canada, 1997), 89.

65 Magda Fahrni, "The Romance of Reunion: Montreal War Veterans Return to Family Life, 1944-1949," *Journal of the Canadian Historical Association/Revue de la Société historique du Canada* n.s. 8 (1998): 187-208. See also Fahrni, *Household Politics: Montreal Families and Postwar Reconstruction* (Toronto: University of Toronto Press, 2005) for a comprehensive study of how families adapted to postwar conditions in Montreal. On barbecuing practices as an aspect of consumerism and family leisure, see Chris Dummitt, "Finding a Place for Father: Selling the Barbecue in Postwar Canada," in *Journal of the Canadian Historical Association/Revue de la Société historique du Canada* n.s. 8 (1998): 209-25. See also Dummitt, *The Manly Modern: Masculinity in Postwar Canada* (Vancouver: UBC Press, 2007) for a thematic examination of masculine responses to postwar modernity, drawn largely from Vancouver examples.

66 See Robert Rutherdale, "Fatherhood and Masculine Domesticity during the Baby Boom: Consumption and Leisure in Advertising and Life Stories," in Lori Chambers and Edgar-Andre Montigny, eds., *Family Matters: Papers in Post-Confederation Family History* (Toronto: Canadian Scholars' Press, 1998), 309-29.

67 Demos, "Changing Faces," 63.

11

"We Adopted a Negro": Interracial Adoption and the Hybrid Baby in 1960s Canada

Karen Dubinsky

In September 1961 *Star Weekly* magazine published a heart-tugging story about adoption. "The Children Nobody Wants" paints a sorry portrait of daily life for parentless multiracial children in Canada. "Some are infants, others have waited (in foster care or institutions) twelve years. It is the same story across Canada, nobody wants them. Red skinned, brown or yellow, they have committed the unforgivable sin of having one parent who wasn't white. Because of this they'll never know security, never be part of a family." Abruptly, the story moves from the child to the nation: "For years we've been told Canada is the bridge between Old world and New. Couldn't we build another bridge? In a fast changing world, new Afro Asian nations are being born. The white Anglo Saxon has lost supremacy. Couldn't our future citizens of mixed race brought up in white homes, knowing the best of both backgrounds instead of the worst, be Canada's ambassadors for peace? In a country that's gone on record against apartheid, it's worth considering." The story ends on an upbeat note, introducing the Open Door Society, a group of white Montreal parents who have made a project of adopting nonwhite children, or in the words of this journalist, "Canadian parents putting Christianity quietly to work and delivering their own smashing blow against prejudice."[1]

A version of this tale, featuring identical dramatis personae and leaping from the fate of individual babies to the tribulations of nations, appeared in just about every mass circulation newspaper and magazine in North America through the late 1950s and 1960s. The practice of interracial adoption and the activism of parent groups such as the Open Door Society helped to create a public persona for the transracial adopted child, a figure I call the "hybrid baby." "Hybridity" has a long and complex cultural meaning and has travelled some distance from its origins in what Robert Young termed "the vocabulary of the Victorian extreme right."[2] More likely now to describe cultural rather than physiological or biologized moments of cross-racial connection, recent commentators nevertheless stress the political dimensions of the term. "Hybridity is constituted and contested through complex hierarchies of power," write two British postcolonial theorists.[3] I am drawn to the term – which in this context can signify the multiracial origins of adopted children as well as the origins of children of one race (black, Native, or Asian) who are raised by parents of another race (almost always white) – because it can accommodate relations of hierarchy and power as well as cultural exchange *and* because, quoting Young again, "wherever it emerges it suggests the impossibility of essentialism."[4] Of course, this is hardly the first time in history that racial lines were crossed in the raising of girls and boys – white children have been cared for by brown and black women around the globe for generations. But the adopted hybrid baby acquired a specific configuration and social meaning in 1960s North America and came to signify a spectrum of interracial understandings, politics, and conflicts, as this little snippet of journalism suggests. My current project, of which this chapter forms a part, is about the process by which babies become symbols or icons, especially when they cross boundaries of race and/ or nation. The social category "child" is at once real and metaphorical – powerful as a cultural construct but equally as forceful in flesh and blood. Like women, children have often been bearers, but rarely *makers,* of social meaning.[5] In the highly publicized and frequently debated case of interracial adoption in the 1960s, an iconic child was fashioned from the experiences of actual children. By exploring the histories of children alongside the cultural and political narratives that were formed around them, I want to illuminate how social anxieties operate through the bodies of children. Why and how have children been used as markers of racial and national boundaries? When children cross these boundaries, either through interracial or international adoption or as refugees in times of crisis, war, or revolution, how do national or racial groups construct their claims to custody or parenthood? How, and by whom, is racial or national identity conferred?

For Margaret Edgar and the handful of other parents who organized themselves into the Open Door Society in Montreal in the late 1950s, racial boundary crossing occurred in the most intimate setting imaginable: their own families. While black children had been cared for in white foster homes in Montreal since the 1920s, the Edgars became, in 1958, among the first white parents to legally adopt nonwhite children in North America (some versions of the story say that they were the first). They, along with the two other sets of adoptive parents, organized the Open Door Society (ODS), which was initially intended as a small support group but very quickly became involved in advocating for interracial adoption, mixed-race families, and the integration model of civil rights. They attracted enormous media attention, and they helped to spark similar organizations across the United States and Canada.[6] Over the next twenty years, Montreal's ODS maintained an extensive international communications network, lobbied governments

"Mixed Racial Adoption: A Community Project":
front cover of a Montreal Open Door Society
pamphlet, ca. 1963.
Author's personal collection

to change antiquated adoption laws, worked with Montreal's black community to promote civil rights and teach black history and culture to adopted children, and organized international conferences and prompted the first stirrings of academic research on race and adoption, all the while searching for a politics of transracial adoption that was unifying, not colonizing.

If Margaret Edgar is Canada's founding mother of interracial adoption, Muriel McCrea is the midwife. McCrea was the executive director of the Children's Service Centre (CSC), one of Montreal's oldest welfare organizations (an incarnation of the Protestant Infants Home, established in the early nineteenth century). McCrea, seemingly single-handedly, and alone in North America, overturned decades of adoption practice by facilitating – in fact, encouraging – cross-racial placements in the late 1950s. This defied the common custom of scrupulously matching parents with children of the same race, "the paradigmatic feature of modern adoption" according to historians, which of course made adoption and its ugly stepsisters, illegitimacy and infertility, easier to hide.[7] For the first half of the twentieth century, needy children were divided into two categories: adoptable and nonadoptable. While never exact, "nonadoptability" fused the racial, the social, and the moral to render certain kinds, and colours, of children permanently nonadoptable. One rare study of nonadoptable Canadian children in the 1940s defined them as being of "unknown paternity," or as having mothers who were of "low mentality" or promiscuous, or as possessing undesirable features such as "asthma, TB, epilepsy or Negroid blood."[8] Of course, "blood" itself was hardly a stable category. In Alberta, for example, it was Ukrainian and Métis children who were defined out of the domestic adoption system; instead, they were allegedly "trafficked" to unsuspecting adoptive parents in the US and Central America (a remarkable turnabout on the baby-selling scandals that haunt contemporary Central America).[9]

In 1955 Muriel McCrea announced to the Annual General Meeting of the CSC: "the wonderful fact is that when we began looking we found that there were many people who could take some chances, so that this year we were able to place Brian with a club foot, Joyce with a cleft palate, Nadia with Central European ancestry, and even Paul who had some coloured blood." With this statement, she was both challenging and confirming the social hierarchies that informed adoption practice in the twentieth century.[10] In fact, according to the CSC, 75 percent of the "Negro or partly Negro" children in orphanages or foster care in 1950s Montreal – over one hundred children in total – were legally adoptable. McCrea's willingness to break adoption's colour bar brought black children into the adoption system. A publicity campaign was undertaken, which targeted first black and then white parents for these newly categorized "adoptable" children. Enter Margaret Edgar and the ODS, which was formed in November, 1959.

Despite what I argue here about the cultural importance of the hybrid baby and the influence of the Open Door Society, the numbers of such children in English Montreal were in fact very small. Montreal, like the rest of Quebec, was of course a city whose majority of citizens were French-speaking, although it was also home to the vast majority of the province's anglophones and immigrants. Child-welfare services were, on the whole, divided along religious and linguistic lines, particularly so for adoption agencies since religion-matching laws were in force at this time.[11] The statistical landscape for interracial adoption in the past is complicated and, like racial classification schemes everywhere, capricious and unreliable. However, my best estimate is that about three hundred and fifty children who were labelled nonwhite were placed for adoption by the CSC in Montreal between 1955 and 1969 (the last year for which I have found statistics), three hundred of whom were adopted by whites. This represents about twenty-five to thirty adoptions per year, when the total number that this agency dealt with ranged from approximately four to six hundred annually. Black children made up the vast majority of these children, followed by a small number of Asian and Native children.[12] So the hybrid baby was definitely more powerful than the numbers alone would suggest, for it carried huge cultural weight. As popular culture heralded its birth – even television's *The Brady Bunch* featured an episode on the topic – many looked *through,* not at, these children and saw in the hybrid baby the promise of racial reconciliation. The processes of adoption, of course, denaturalize the family in basic and fundamental ways. Adoption exposes that family relationships are no more real or pregiven than any other sort of human relationship. Such ties are socially negotiated, not biologically ordained. All adoptive parents in this era were in the curious position of reconciling essentialist notions of blood, heredity, and familial sameness and security – mainstays of North American culture in the mid-twentieth century – with the practice of introducing complete genetic strangers into their lives forever. What happened when adoption began to breach the apparently secure biological borders of race as well? My answer to this question is based in large part on my reading of hundreds of adoption case files from the CSC, remarkable vignettes of the encounter between birthmothers, babies, and adoptive parents as well as the social workers who mediated their relationships.[13] Through these stories, we can observe an extended conversation about the social meaning of race in the 1960s, which took place mostly among white people, a group not accustomed to such exchanges. Whether they invested race and racial difference with enormous social meaning or downplayed its significance entirely, whether they feared it, ignored it, attempted to "cure" it, or embraced it, all of these discussions began from the premise that the racial identity of *children* was something quite distinct.

According to two academic studies at the time, white parents who adopted across racial lines in Montreal were not, demographically speaking, hugely different from other adoptive parents. They were a little older, a little richer, and a lot more educated – 70 percent of cross-racially adopting men had postsecondary education, for example, compared to 48 percent of same-race adopting men and 9 percent of the Canadian labour force.[14] But this generation of adoptive parents *felt* themselves to be different. They described themselves as "liberal thinkers," "freethinkers," "internationalists," "rebels at heart." As one social worker delicately described a potential adoptive mother, "she gains a certain amount of security from being different from the run of the mill." Another was described, somewhat less delicately, as "inclined to get on a soapbox."[15] Adoptive parents and social workers alike constantly denied explicitly political motives while speaking publicly. "We're not tilting at windmills," one adoptive mother told *Maclean's*. "Don't make us out to be do-gooders," another told *Good Housekeeping*. Even *Ebony*, the US magazine catering to a black readership, assured its readers in 1961 that "mother love provides the only motivating force" for many white adopters of black children.[16] Yet privately, social workers looked for signs – generally expressed in what we might now call the language of therapy or personal growth – that potential parents understood interracial adoptions to be different. "I went into their attitudes towards Negroes quite fully with them and found they did not have the strength," wrote one social worker in 1960, "they feel quite guilty about this."[17] "They have the necessary streak of independence and unorthodoxy," wrote a social worker of another couple enthusiastically, and "they are not concerned about what other people think."[18] Qualities such as "strength," "independence," and the ability to "handle risk" were endorsed approvingly by social workers examining potential parents. Many decades later, former CSC social worker Grace Gallay recalled that part of her effort to recruit white parents for interracial adoption involved "seeing how far I could stretch them."[19] Thus the explicitly political discourse of interracial co-operation and civil rights was muted, but not erased, in the language of the helping professions, and race remained, like epilepsy or blindness, one more "risk" that not everyone could "handle." "She will be the kind of mother who will help her children fight their own battles," wrote one social worker of a new applicant, a suburban housewife, a keen endorsement of her parenting potential *and* an acknowledgement that all the "mother love" in the world would not inoculate black children against future conflicts.[20]

Why would self-described "freethinkers" and "rebels" – most drawn from the cozy confines of Montreal's West Island suburbs or stately downtown Westmount – choose interracial adoption to express their independence? The majority were convinced by the international publicity, much of it generated by the CSC and the ODS, about the grave problems facing "hard to place" nonwhite children. As one Westmount adoptive father explained – one of many featured in flattering stories in the media in and beyond Montreal – "interracial understanding and communication was one of the greatest needs in today's world, and since we wanted another child anyway, we felt that this was a way in which we could do our part."[21] The use of media both by the adoption agency and later by the parents' group was extremely effective; the CSC estimated that forty adoptions of nonwhite children occurred in the first two years of the ODS' existence directly because of publicity.[22] While these stories were almost always accompanied by photos of adorable babies, the ODS was not naive about what US historian Laura Briggs has termed "the visual iconography of rescue."[23] They complained, for example, about the "Wednesday's Child" column in the *Montreal Star,* which profiled individual children needing adoptive homes, objecting to its "syrupy" and "pitying" tone and noting the strong objections of Montreal's black community to such advertising. They also decided against inviting journalist Doris Giller, who had just published a long and flattering feature on interracial adoption, to cover the annual ODS/Negro Community Centre picnic, worrying that this would look like a "publicity stunt" and antagonize their friends in the black community. Yet they were also adamant that interracial families needed to show the public that they were functioning in what they termed "a very ordinary manner" and thus needed to "offer themselves as subjects for questioning and photographing." Such stories, they insisted, "produce more adoption applications, which is the sole reason we do them."[24] This was beyond dispute, for the "we adopted a Negro" narrative became a quintessential feel-good story, and most people who came to the CSC willing to adopt mixed-race children said that they were prompted to do this by interviews with multiracial adopting parents. If one was drawn to adoption by the argument that it was "selfish" to reproduce when the world had so many needy children – and many applicants voiced concerns about the so-called "population explosion," itself a highly racialized notion – it followed that the more needy the children were, the more good parents were doing by adopting them. Like burning one's draft card, coming out of the closet, or tallying who did the dishes, adopting a "hard to place" child made the personal political, and vice versa.[25]

So by the time Prime Minister Lester Pearson posed with a multiracial adoptive family to proclaim Brotherhood Week in 1966, the mixed- or multirace adopted child had clearly become symbolic of hope, optimism, and good. While groups like the Open Door Society soon emerged in many cities across North America, Montrealers were never permitted to forget that theirs had been the first, that Montreal was, as one parent put it, "the mecca for multi and interracial adoption." In addition to receiving hundreds of requests for information from researchers and child-welfare agencies throughout North America, ODS parents also found themselves in the unusual position of advising nervous Americans about which US hotels and restaurants might welcome mixed-race families and even about which US cities had integrated neighbourhoods. As the US magazine *Coronet* put it in 1964, "only in Montreal are mixed race adoptions an honor, not a stigma." Montreal's position in the vanguard of interracial adoption reinforced several longstanding Canadianisms: that this was a land of much greater racial tolerance and liberalism – always positioned against the US – and that Montreal edged out Toronto as Canada's most sophisticated city. Many, including *Chatelaine,* concurred that interracial adoption reflected the worldliness of Montreal's citizens. "Montreal has been quietly demonstrating the message of Man and His World for eight years through the activities of our Open Door Society," proclaimed another parent during Expo 67. When a similar project was launched in Toronto in 1962, the Committee for the Adoption of Negro Children found Montreal's example "encouraging" but constantly worried that Toronto lagged far behind.[26] The hegemonic goodness of Montreal's mixed-race adopting parents was also evident in the comments of those who considered but declined the attempts made by the CSC to find homes for nonwhite children, most of whom refused because, as one typical couple told the agency, they "admired people who could do this but were simply not big enough people."[27]

Yet a willingness to cross one racial boundary in no way suggested that white adoptive parents had divested themselves of *all* of their culture's tropes of race. As this first generation of white parents contemplated raising black, Native, and Asian children, they faced myriad uncertainties and anxieties about the cultural meaning of race within their families and communities. A clear pattern of racial preference emerged, in which "full Negro" children were at the bottom, and mixed-race Asian or Native children (always imaged in white-nonwhite groupings) were at the top, although details of this hierarchy varied by region. It was commonly believed among social workers, for example, that Native children were difficult to place for adoption in the prairie provinces, that black children were especially "hard to place" in Halifax and throughout most of the United States, and that Asian (especially Eurasian) children were always relatively easy placements.[28] One woman, the wife of a clergyman, told her social worker in 1959 that "she was ashamed to admit it but she had difficulties with Negroes, though she thought Orientals were fine."[29] Another set of parents worried that their small town was "too sticky" for black children, but part-Native children would be welcome. A white foster mother declared that she would welcome a "coloured" child in her home and neighbourhood, but she feared that her country club would not; "Orientals," however, would be no problem.[30]

Many adopting parents imagined race as a kind of disability that could be overcome, perhaps even be made to disappear, with the love and care of good parents. This way of thinking located race in the body, but it opened the possibility of transcendence. Some parents attempted to depoliticize and "forgive" their black children's bodies, suggesting, for example, that one son's black skin was the same as another biological son's birthmark or comparing a black daughter's "kinky" hair to a white son's "big ears."[31] Another suggested that their black daughter got teased just as much as a neighbour's red-haired, freckled daughter. More than one likened their child's complexion to a tan, which most people "have to sit in the sun and suffer for."[32] This disability-transcendence model of racial identity appealed to the media, for it seemed especially appropriate for children. Interracial adoption became symbolic of racial harmony and integration in large part by

imagining children as the ultimate race liberals. "Children have no prejudice," announced one headline, a theme repeated in countless stories.[33] From
this perspective, it was not difficult to separate race from bodies altogether
and reimagine adopted children as virtually raceless. "What does color matter
when a child strokes your cheek and tells you she loves you?" declared one
anonymous adoptive mother to the *Toronto Star* in 1964. Another parent
told *Parents* magazine how their newly adopted child had finally won the
hearts of her disapproving grandparents: "it's hard to hold a grudge against
a baby."[34] As children grew up, some parents continued to work to contain
racial difference. An ODS membership canvass in the early 1970s, for example, revealed a wide array of ideas, including the perspective of one white
father who declared that he "believed black people should take on Canadian culture and is bringing up his girl to be a Canadian first."[35]

Of course the flipside of the transcendence model was the tendency to
exoticize, another common feature of press commentary. References to "dark
skinned Tahitian princesses" and "tiny Oriental pixies" filled pages of testi-
monials from new parents. And as historian Veronica Strong-Boag has explored, adoption advertising of the era relied on finding a positive new spin
for old racialized tropes – describing, for example, boys who possessed "the
typical Indian child's gentle disposition." Adoptive parents continually complained about what they called the "overbearing attention" that their
nonwhite children received from strangers, and ODS activist Irene Henderson
recalled advising prospective parents who "couldn't stop talking about how
cute Negro children were."[36]

Black children provided the greatest scope for parents to ponder the minutiae, and meaning, of racial difference. Following the logic of providing
help for the "hard to place" child, some parents preferred to adopt "full-
Negro" children – even though they also believed that racial ambiguity would
make their families' lives even more complicated. Indeed, many ODS parents felt that it would be easier to cope with "obvious" children, who could
"not escape the reality of difference."[37] Rarely were the undertones of mis-
cegenation acknowledged publicly. A typically forthright Margaret Edgar
once told a reporter about the "sensation" caused when she and another
adoptive mother strolled through a small resort town with their eight children, including two "part Negro babies." "The natives are still wondering
what we'd been up to," she declared.[38]

Edgar laughed this off, but others pondered the appearance of black children quite gravely. In contrast to those parents who sought out "full-Negro"
children for adoption as a means of confronting difficulties head-on, many
parents believed that raising light-skinned black children would be "easier"
to manage – in predominantly white neighbourhoods, for example, or when
introducing adopted mixed-race children to recalcitrant grandparents. Even

those who believed the adage "the lighter the easier" had questions about the possibility of "Negro blood" emerging in grandchildren; indeed, US social workers told *Newsweek* in 1969 that many adoptive parents considering mixed-race children were scared off when asked to ponder the possibility of "even blacker grandchildren."[39] One Montreal father wondered whether his newly adopted mixed-race son might "assert his Negro race aggressively" in the future.[40] Social workers almost always accepted preferences for lighter-skinned children – although one interracial couple was finally rejected after they declined three successive black children because they were deemed too dark and lacking "good hair." Generally, however, the CSC facilitated these hierarchies, taking scrupulous physical descriptions of the birthmother and father (if possible) and examining newborns closely to see whether they "showed their colour." "Watch for colour in this baby," read a typical file notation in 1960, "there is coloured blood in the putative father's family."[41] Rae Rambally, one of the few black social workers employed in Montreal in this era, remembers the regular adoption-placement meetings that she attended at the CSC, during which the skin colour and hair texture of black children was detailed with precision.[42] When paternity had not been divulged by a white birthmother, occasionally doctors were called into the hospital at birth to pronounce the race of the child. Ambiguous or absent racial signifiers – understood generally as complexion and hair type – were generally seen to work in the baby's favour, making him or her more "adoptable" (particularly since in such cases even this groundbreaking agency occasionally declined to disclose the whole truth about a child's racial origins to adoptive parents).[43]

All of this helps to explain the paradoxical treatment of white and black birthmothers and their offspring in this era. Robert Young notes that hybridity "always carries an implicit politics of heterosexuality." One of the longstanding, and highly romantic, beliefs about the hybrid baby in this era was that most of the "black" adopted children in Montreal were of mixed race, the offspring of liaisons between whites and blacks.[44] This narrative of cross-racial adoption depends on and helps to sustain a host of other fictions, including the perception that most such liaisons involved unmarried white women and black men and that these relationships, and especially the children that they produced, were doomed because of still-rampant social intolerance. When unmarried black mothers do enter this story, they and their offspring quickly disappear into the great void known as "black culture" – a monolithic classless and genderless block that, in this instance, holds that unwed black women reject adoption in favour of extended family networks. A corollary of this is that black families were uninterested in or unmotivated to adopt through the child-welfare system – why should they, when they were perfectly able to "take care of their own."

This narrative of doomed interracial romance certainly fuelled media interest in and public representations of needy black children, especially as interracial dating was emerging as an issue of civil rights. To the press, mixed-race children were "unwanted victims of racial discrimination" or "strange, contemptible victims in no man's land." Yet this was also their potential; through interracial adoption they became, as one Christian periodical put it, "innocent bearers of racial reconciliation."[45] For generations, hybrid babies, the offspring of various interracial encounters, challenged one of the central fictions of colonial hierarchy: that the boundaries separating the colonizer from the colonized were self-evident and thus easily drawn and maintained. Mixed-race children (perhaps the ultimate child-standard bearers) symbolized the contagion of indigenous (black, brown) women and the susceptibility of white men and threatened almost all of the classification schemas on which racism rests.[46] As racial identities and relationships were recharted in 1960s North America, perceptions of interracial romance and adoption ran parallel. Interracial love became, as historian Renee Romano terms it, "a metaphor for the possibilities of racial equality."[47] When the public face of interracial adoption was the mixed-race child, white adoptive parents of these children found another claim on which to base their parenthood. Some might think it was "wrong to take the child out of his milieu," Margaret Edgar told a reporter in 1962, "but what is the child's milieu? If he's half coloured and half white, does he belong in the coloured milieu or the white milieu? The fact is he doesn't belong in either."[48]

This origin story is true to a point. In my sample of 100 nonwhite children whose births attracted the attention of the CSC, almost one-third were the offspring of white women and nonwhite (mostly black) men. The vast majority of mixed-race couples, almost 90 percent, relinquished their children. The mixed-race origins of these children joined a long list of factors shaping unmarried white mothers' choices. The almost complete lack of social, familial, psychological, and economic support for single motherhood was not *caused* by having a mixed-race baby, although such progeny might make unmarried white women feel their ostracism and isolation more acutely. Even as adopting a black child was becoming an act of goodwill, giving birth to one as a white woman signified immorality.[49] Thus putting such a child up for adoption provided, as it did for almost all white unmarried mothers in this era, what US historian Barbara Melosh has termed "the best solution," so long as they played by the rules. Shame and remorse, as well as seclusion during pregnancy (preferably in either a home for unwed mother's or while doing domestic labour for middle-class women), followed by instant relinquishment of the baby and a willingness to convince at least their social workers of their unshaken belief in the moral rightness of their culture (as the CSC social workers put it, to "profit by experience" or "mature through mistakes"), offered redemption for countless white women, both in Montreal and throughout North America. The adoption records, and everyone's lips, were sealed – at least until this punitive model of single motherhood and adoption began to crumble, allowing birthmothers to assert themselves in their own histories.[50]

Yet there is another origin story for Montreal's black adopted children, one that relies less on stories of thwarted interracial love and more on black women's limited labour and migration options. This story starts with the Domestic Immigration Program of 1955, which partially relaxed Canada's immigration colour bar and recruited almost three thousand English-speaking black West Indian women to work as domestic servants in middle-class homes. Their story is often told – at the time and by subsequent historians – as a tale of loneliness and rejection, for they were scorned as housemaids by both whites and established Canadian blacks and rendered almost freakishly lonesome by the absence of black male company in Canada – the only sexual interest publicly imagined for these women. Watching a West Indian community dance one evening in Montreal in 1961, a reporter noted the "sad excess" of women, mostly domestics, who outnumbered the men five to one. "Women like mangoes in this place," claimed a black West Indian student, "abundant and at low price." (This same reporter also learned that students at an unnamed Montreal university forbade domestics from attending West Indian social events.)[51] Given the extent of such musings about the sexual and moral perils posed by – as well as to – single black women in Canada's cities, it would likely have come as no surprise to anyone at the time that West Indian immigrant women soon began to turn up at the doorstep of the CSC as unmarried mothers. And then, like all unwed mothers in this era, these immigrant black birthmothers promptly disappeared from public view. Of course, the very existence of a global black underclass in Canada complicates our beloved national narrative of anticonquest. No wonder, then, that their tale has been eclipsed by feel-good stories about the rescue of their children.

There were twice as many black women as white in my sample of the birthmothers of nonwhite children. Of these women, 80 percent were pregnant by black men, and almost half of them decided against adoption and chose to keep their "illegitimate" children. That, overall, approximately 30 percent of women seen by the CSC decided against relinquishing their babies throughout the 1960s (peaking at 43 percent by 1969) definitely seems to confirm the commonsense view, expressed in the social-welfare literature and anecdotally for decades, that "black women keep their children" – at least more so than white women.[52] The lengths to which unmarried black mothers went to hold on to children were remarkable. Typically, they took advantage of the agency's provision for four months of postnatal foster care – paid for by the mothers themselves – in order to cobble something together. Between working long shifts, usually in Montreal's garment or service industry, they cajoled extended family members in the West Indies to move to Canada to help with childcare, made private arrangements with foster mothers for extended care, and even found friends who were willing to become roommates and help raise their children. Occasionally, they returned home with the child, intending to leave it with a relative and return to work in Canada; even more occasionally, they convinced the birth father to support them. Not surprisingly, sometimes such plans, conceived in desperation with meagre resources, failed, and children were returned to agency care, causing social workers to grumble about women who "produce coloured children, leaving the upbringing for society."[53]

Despite what CSC staff once described as a "strong cultural need" for West Indian women to keep their children – ironically, in this instance, when the unmarried mother in question arrived at the agency having survived a botched abortion – half of them didn't. Furthermore, black birthmothers were generally encouraged by social workers to plan to keep their children, advice rarely dispensed to white women in this era. Usually, this took the form of repeatedly warning them that their child – particularly "full-Negro" children – would fare poorly in the adoption system and may stay in the foster system indefinitely. Pregnant black women considering adoption were told, for example, "the hard reality that to give up her child for adoption could not be considered until she had given birth, then the full force of her emotional feelings will have a different meaning to her."[54] Having reviewed hundreds of case files, I simply cannot imagine a white woman hearing this. Black women – such as one twenty-two-year-old Barbadian immigrant who arrived in Canada pregnant and wanted neither single parenthood nor even marriage because, as she said, "people in the West Indies get married too early" – often had to fight their way into the adoption system.[55] In their way stood agency staff who treated them alternately like children ("a good deal of firmness is required with this one") or, as the decade progressed, with a great deal of fear.[56]

Encounters between blacks and white social workers speak volumes about changing racial politics in 1960s Canada. In the early years, a social worker congratulated himself for using the washroom in a black client's home, imagining this as an act of tolerance that helped to win the trust of the potential foster parents he was investigating.[57] Slowly, social workers began to note a new restiveness on the part of their black clientele; as one wrote of an unmarried mother in 1965, "I suspect she's not quite so servile as she appears on the surface."[58] By the end of the decade social workers were perplexed: black women, even the young, pregnant, and vulnerable ones, had changed. They were "stubborn," "aggressive," "challenging," full of "pride." They felt that "society owed them something," and worse still, they had become "color conscious" and had begun to complain about "discrimination."[59] This powerful combination, then, of fearful, often hostile responses to black female clientele and a lingering rebuff of "full-Negro" children due to their "hard to place" status helped to create a different experience for unmarried black birthmothers, one in which the boundaries between distinctive black culture and racism are difficult to untangle. Writing of this era in the US, Melosh terms adoption "a strategy of upward mobility that, in practice, benefited whites almost exclusively."[60] I've come to believe that rather than assuming blacks' disinterest in adoption, both as adoptive parents and as birth parents, it might be more accurate to say that blacks mistrust the adoption *system* – mostly because historically it has treated them poorly.[61] Adoption case files tell a complicated story, one that includes the shamed white birthmother who redeemed herself through adoption but also includes a variety of racial and ethnic combinations, a group of people for whom the redemption narrative was far less available.

Of course, the racial understandings of people who flatly refused to consider moving beyond their own racial and national group in adoption provide equally interesting perspectives on children and racial identity in this era. Many lumped race, nation, and ethnicity together with confident if confused eugenic understandings of history, appearance, temperament, and even language. They could not adopt a German baby, to take one example, because they'd lived in London during the Blitz. Or they had grown up on the Prairies near a Ukrainian settlement and "feel very sure that this group has different facial characteristics and they don't want a child with Slavic features."[62] Or, very commonly, they did not want a "swarthy" child with a "difficult" temperament and therefore preferred to avoid the "Latin races." (Several were of the opinion that Italians were "lazy," and predictably, a few refused Québécois babies because they found francophones "trying.")[63] National prejudices were difficult to untangle from appearance preferences. Even though the tide was turning toward honesty in adoption – indeed, this agency worked very hard to convince adoptive parents to tell the truth to their children – many parents clearly wanted to adopt children whom they perceived as matching themselves and their biological children. "We don't want a child who would stand out like the ugly duckling," explained one father.[64] Perhaps this explains the large number of adoptive parents who said that they could accept any national mixture but insisted that they did not want a child with red hair.

Yet interracial adoption produced another discourse of racial difference that neither exaggerated nor denied its existence: the integrationist civil rights philosophy espoused by the ODS.[65] There were certainly a range of people attracted to this group. A few were liberals or leftists who had given issues of racism and civil rights some thought before deciding to adopt. But most ODS activists were politicized *because* they parented black children, not beforehand. In other words, it was the experience of raising black children in 1960s Montreal that turned these parents toward the civil rights movement. As one black social worker explained to me recently, "those parents had never encountered racism, and they simply walked around in shock for a few years."[66] There's nothing like having your black child – possibly the only one in his or her class – offered the role of black dog in the school play to make white adoptive parents realize, as Margaret Edgar explained, "love is not enough."[67]

Of course, also unfolding in Canada's, and Montreal's, black community over the course of the 1960s were big demographic and political changes, detailed in Dorothy Williams' history of black Montreal, *The Road to Now*.[68] Just what kind of "black" child was waiting at the adoption agency? West Indian? Canadian? Was "black" a racial, social, or political designation? The combination of watching their children move from cute "raceless" babies to youngsters exposed to adult-sized racism, as well as the changing demographics and politics of the black community, had huge reverberations for ODS parents.

The response of North American blacks to interracial adoption is a large and complicated topic, and on this score there are similarities with the cultural trajectory of interracial marriage. Blacks moved from an initial approval of both phenomena – symbolic of the meaninglessness of racial difference and consistent with the view that these were acts of cross-racial solidarity – to a more skeptical assessment that interracial marriage and adoption were "engines for assimilation." From the perspective of blacks in the US, as segregation gave way to expanded individual opportunities for some, integration via marriage appeared as just one more route to success, a means to evade racial solidarities.[69]

There is much more to learn about the history of civil rights and black nationalism in Canada in this era. There are suggestions, however, that the politics of transracial adoption played differently in the black community in this country. In 1972 the Association of Black Social Workers in the US famously condemned the hybrid baby, claiming that interracial adoption distorted and undermined African American racial identity because white parents could never teach black children how to survive in a racist world. They also charged that the child-welfare system discriminated against black adoptive families.[70] White adoptive parents groups on both sides of the border believed that such polarization around adoption was much more profound in the US. Certainly, the ODS had enjoyed a long history of cordial and I think meaningful relations with local and national black community leaders and organizations – including Martin Luther King, Jr., himself – throughout the 1960s. The politicization of Montreal's white adoptive parents – at least the open-minded among them – at once reshaped their notions of race, citizenship, and parenthood. As Irene Henderson, a white adoptive mother of three black children recalled, the weekend that she spent as one of the only white delegates at the National Black Coalition's founding conference was a personal turning point, for "it helped me see what my kids live every day."[71] But as the decade progressed, perhaps Christmas parties and children's picnics at the Negro Community Centre were not sufficient to address the changes in North American race politics. Like interracial marriage, adoptions across the colour line began to look less like a gesture of solidarity and more like cultural annihilation. I have found no Canadian equivalent to the apocalyptic statement of the US black social workers. And it's certainly possible that disinterest was the fall-back position among blacks in this country. One long-time black community worker in Montreal told me that "we hardly noticed" the activities of the ODS.[72] But there were certainly moments in this country when Canadian blacks viewed interracial adoption through nationalist tropes of family. The Afro-centric Montreal newspaper *UHURU*, for example, labelled interracially adopted children "misfits" in 1970 and called for a black CSC.[73] In this story, headlined "Do Black Parents Care?" the hybrid baby was both a social embarrassment (blacks were not doing their part for needy children) and a symptom of the racism of the child-welfare system (blacks were shut out of the foster and adoption system). *URUHU* described as "black liberals" those black activists who co-operated with the ODS and chided them for their too-cozy relationship with whites. There was also a now-legendary meeting between black students of Sir George Williams University and ODS parents, which exists vividly in the memories of everyone who was there, for at one point one of the black students stood up and demanded that the white parents "give us back our children" (the line that everyone remembers).[74]

Yet, as others have found, Canadian black history in the 1960s does not follow a linear narrative from quiescence to integration to revolutionary nationalism.[75] The hybrid baby left its infancy behind in the turbulent late 1960s, but in some quarters it remained symbolic of optimism, a site of cross-racial solidarity. ODS parents co-operated with black community leaders in the early 1970s to create a Black Studies Centre, staffed and run by black (volunteer) teachers, which provided, among other things, instruction in black history and culture to interracially adopted children and their white siblings. This was accompanied by the creation of a 900-title lending library of books on black history and culture, including children's titles, maintained by the ODS. Thus, for several years during the 1970s, every Saturday morning white parents brought their children, white and black, downtown for classes, music, and other activities.

This certainly opened a new set of possible meanings around racial identity for children of this generation, anticipating as it does postmodern debates about the relationship between bodies, unstable identities, and "authentic" selves by several decades. Several ODS parents told me, with amusement, that white neighbourhood children were jealous of black-studies classes and Negro Community Centre picnics; they wanted to go too. Within the amusement lies many of the most intriguing questions about identity of our day: what happens when essentialist conceptions of race are unhinged from biology and family?

Conclusion

> Montreal was gripped by notions of grandeur in the 1960s that
> only a generation later look like a preposterous flight of fancy.
>
> *– New York Times,* 3 October 2004, 21

Written in a story about the closing of Montreal's Mirabel Airport, these words could, perhaps, describe many social movements of the era, including the campaign to promote interracial adoption. The hybrid baby reached adulthood in a climate vastly different from today's. Yet this epitaph for a generation is excessively smug and totalizing. Babies make great metaphors. A hopeful sign of cross-racial tolerance, an unfortunate in need of rescue by tender white care, a measure of either the superior culture of Montreal or the superior social values of Canadians, a marker of the political weakness of the black community – the hybrid baby could be read as all of these and more. The fanfare around its appearance suggests something about how the frontiers of race and nation were recharted in 1960s Canada.

Acknowledgments
I received insightful comments from several friends and colleagues on a draft of this chapter; thanks to Susan Belyea, Roberta Hamilton, Susan Lord, Daniel McNeil, Sean Mills, Veronica Strong-Boag, and Barrington Walker. Thanks also to the editors of this anthology.

Notes
1 "The Children Nobody Wants," *Star Weekly,* September 1961.
2 Robert Young, *Colonial Desire: Hybridity in Theory, Culture and Race* (London: Routledge, 1995), 10.
3 Annie E. Coombes and Avtar Brah, "Introduction: The Conundrum of 'Mixing,'" in Avtar Brah and Annie E. Coombes, eds., *Hybridity and Its Discontents: Politics, Science and Culture* (London: Routledge, 2000), 7.
4 Young, *Colonial Desire,* 27.
5 The distinction between "bearers" and "makers" of social meaning is well explained in Judith Walkowitz, *City of Dreadful Delight: Narratives of Sexual Danger in Late-Victorian London* (Chicago: University of Chicago Press, 1991). On symbolic and social anxieties about youth in the Canadian context in this era, see Mary Louise Adams, *The Trouble with Normal: Postwar Youth and the Making of Heterosexuality* (Toronto: University of Toronto Press, 1997).
6 Grace Gallay, "Community and Family," in *First International Conference on Mixed Race Adoptions, May 1969* (Montreal: Open Door Society, 1970), 41. It seems that Montreal was also ahead of the rest of the country in placing black children in white foster homes. As of the

late 1950s the Toronto Children's Aid Society placed children of "Negroid appearance" in institutions rather than white foster homes. See A. Lenore Schwalbe, "Negro and Partly-Negro Wards of the Children's Aid Society of Metropolitan Toronto" (MSW thesis, University of Toronto, 1958), 24. That Open Door Society parents were the "first" in North America to adopt transracially comes from Rita J. Simon and Howard Altstein, *Adoption across Borders* (Lanham: Rowman and Littlefield, 2000), 1.

7 Ellen Herman, "Families Made by Science: Arnold Gessell and the Technologies of Modern Child Adoption," *Isis* 92, 4 (December 2001): 684-715 at 691.

8 Rosemary Landsdowne, "The Concept of Non-Adoptibility," (MSW thesis, University of British Columbia, 1949), 46. See also Herman, "Families Made by Science."

9 Karen Balcom, "The Traffic in Babies: Cross-Border Adoption, Baby-Selling and the Development of Child Welfare Systems in the U.S. and Canada, 1930-1960" (PhD thesis, Rutgers University, 2002).

10 Children's Service Centre, *Annual Report, 1955* (Montreal). These, and all other children's names in this chapter, are pseudonyms.

11 Some years after the founding of the ODS, an analogous organization, Spadete (Société pour l'adoption d'enfants de toutes ethnies) was founded by a Montreal college teacher – and adoptive parent – explicitly to serve the francophone Catholic population. Spadete worked with the Société d'adoption et de protection de l'enfance in Montreal. See "La société d'adoption Spadete, il n'est jamais question de races," *Le Petit Journal*, 29 June 1969. On the history of adoption laws in Quebec, see Dominique Goubau and Claire O'Neill, "L'adoption, l'Eglise et l'Etat: Les origines tumultueuses d'une institution légale," in Renée Joyal, ed., *L'évolution de la protection de l'enfance au Québec* (Sainte-Foy: Presses de l'Université du Québec, 2000), 97-130; and Ann M. Paquet, "Study of Current Adoption Law and Practice in the Province of Quebec" (MSW thesis, McGill University, 1959).

12 Open Door Society, *Mixed Race Adoption: A Community Project* (Montreal, 1967).

13 I read 800 case files from the years 1956 through 1969, about a 20 percent sample of the total. Of this sample, approximately one hundred involved nonwhite children and/or interracial placements.

14 Ethel Roskies, "An Exploratory Study of the Characteristics of Adoptive Parents of Mixed-Race Children in the Montreal Area," (MA thesis, University of Montreal, 1963), 40. See also Grace Gallay, "A Study in the Motivation Expressed by White Couples Who Adopt Non-White Children" (MSW research report, McGill University, 1963).

15 Children's Service Centre case files (hereafter CSC case files). To ensure confidentiality, all identifying information, including file numbers, have been removed from these sources.

16 "We Adopted a Negro," *Maclean's*, 19 November 1960; "When Noel Came Home," *Good Housekeeping*, November, 1965; "Many Interracial Adoptions Are Triggered by Chance," *Ebony*, August 1961.

17 CSC case file.

18 CSC case file.

19 Interview with Grace Gallay, Montreal, 27 June 2003.

20 CSC case file.

21 "Sure There Were Problems, but Not of Color, Say Parents of Mixed-Race Adopted Child," *Westmount Examiner*, June 1968.

22 Open Door Society correspondence, October 1961.

23 Laura Briggs, "Mother, Child, Race, Nation: The Visual Iconographpy of Rescue and the Politics of Transnational and Transracial Adoption," *Gender and History* 15, 2 (August 2003): 179-200.

24 ODS Executive Minutes, January 1969 and September 1970; ODS correspondence, September 1970. On advertising children for adoption in Canada, see Veronica Strong-Boag "Today's Child: Creating the Just Society One Family at a Time in 1960s Canada," *Canadian Historical Review* (forthcoming).

25 On the racialization of the "population bomb" in the 1960s, see Laura Briggs, *Reproducing Empire: Race, Sex, Science and U.S. Imperialism in Puerto Rico* (Berkeley: University of California Press, 2002).

26 Letter to the editor, *Montreal Star*, 7 September 1967, 19; "New Hope for Canada's Homeless Children," *Chatelaine*, December 1963; "Color Keeps them Apart," *Toronto Star*, 1 June 1963; "Should White Parents Adopt Colored Babies?" *Coronet Magazine*, December, 1964.
27 CSC case file.
28 See, for example, Gallay, "Community and Family," 42; Interview with Grace Gallay, Montreal, 27 June 2003; "The Scandal of our Orphanages," *Christian Outlook*, October 1961. In 1967 the Child Welfare League of America established the Adoption Resource Exchange Program of North America (ARENA), a network of adoption agencies in the US and Canada, in order to surmount what they termed "regional prejudices that prevent homeless children form being adopted"; see ODS correspondence, 1967.
29 CSC case file.
30 CSC case file.
31 CSC case file.
32 "Too Often They Are Through at Age of Five: That Is Fate of Multi-racial Children Here," *Montreal Star*, 18 February 1967.
33 "Children Have No Prejudice," *Montreal Monitor*, 18 February 1960.
34 "A Child Is a Child," *Toronto Star*, 23 November 1964; "Interracial Adoptions: How Are They Working?" *Parents Magazine*, February 1971.
35 ODS correspondence, Telephone Survey, 1971. See also Lawrence Scyner, "Towards Adolescence and Young Adulthood," paper presented at the Second International Conference on Transracial Adoption, Boston, November 1970.
36 See, for example, "Popularity Is Her Only Problem," *Vancouver Sun*, 10 September 1969; "Multi-Racial Children – Their Need is Great!" *North Shore News*, 5 June 1969; Strong-Boag, "Today's Child"; Interview with Irene Henderson, Winnipeg, 23 July 2003.
37 CSC case file.
38 "The Children Nobody Wants," *Star Weekly*, 23 September 1961.
39 "Adopting Black Babies," *Newsweek*, 3 November 1969.
40 CSC case file.
41 CSC case file.
42 Rae Tucker Rambally, *Practice Imperfect: Reflections on a Career in Social Work* (Montreal: Shoreline, 2002); Interview with Rae Rambally, Montreal, June 2003.
43 CSC case file.
44 Young, *Colonial Desire*, 11.
45 "How We Adopted an Interracial Family," *Chatelaine*, December 1966; "Color Bar Hits Helpless Youngsters," *Montreal Gazette*, 26 October 1965; "The Scandal of Our Orphanages," *Christian Outlook*, October 1961.
46 Ann Stoller, *Carnal Knowledge and Imperial Power: Race and the Intimate in Colonial Rule* (Berkeley: University of California Press, 2002). See also Adele Perry, *On the Edge of Empire: Race, Gender and the Making of British Columbia, 1849-1871* (Toronto: University of Toronto Press, 2001).
47 Renee C. Romano, *Race Mixing: Black-White Marriage in Post-War America* (Cambridge: Harvard University Press, 2003), 37.
48 "Mixed Race Adoption – Something of a Crusade," *Montreal Gazette*, 28 April 1962.
49 Romano, *Race Mixing*, 75.
50 Adoption histories in the US include Barbara Melosh, *Strangers and Kin: The American Way of Adoption* (Cambridge: Harvard University Press, 2002); Julie Berebitsky, *Like Our Very Own: Adoption and the Changing Culture of Motherhood, 1851-1950* (Lawrence: University of Kansas, 2000); E. Wayne Carp, *Family Matters: Secrecy and Disclosure in the History of Adoption* (Cambridge: Harvard University Press, 1998); Rickie Solinger, *Wake Up Little Suzy: Single Pregnancy and Race before Roe v. Wade* (New York: Routledge, 1992); and Rickie Solinger, *Beggars and Choosers: How the Politics of Choice Shapes Adoption, Abortion and Welfare in the United States* (New York: Hill and Wang, 2001). This history is yet to be fully explored in Canada, although much work is underway. A preliminary study is Patti Phillips, "Blood Not Thicker Than Water: Adoption and Nation Building in the Post-War Baby Boom" (MA thesis, Queen's University, 1995).

51 "The West Indians: Our Loneliest Immigrants," *Maclean's*, 4 November 1961. See also Violet King, "Calypso in Canada," *Canadian Welfare* 34 (November 1958): 178-83; Ian R. Mackenzie, "Early Movements of Domestics from the Caribbean and Canadian Immigration Policy: A Research Note," *Alternate Routes* 8 (1988): 124-43; and Dorothy Williams, *The Road to Now: A History of Blacks in Montreal* (Montreal: Vehicule Press, 1997).
52 Children's Service Centre, *Annual Reports, 1960s* (Montreal).
53 CSC case file.
54 Ibid.
55 Ibid.
56 Ibid.
57 Ibid.
58 Ibid.
59 Ibid.
60 Melosh, *Strangers and Kin*, 153.
61 Lost in the volumes of social work literature on black disinterest in the adoption or foster-care system is a US study revealing that, when class and financial status are taken into account, black families are *more* likely to adopt through the child-welfare system than white families; see Elizabeth Herzog and Rose Bernstein, "Why So Few Negro Adoptions? A Reappraisal of Evidence," *Children* 12, 1 (January-February 1965): 14-18.
62 CSC case file.
63 Ibid.
64 Ibid.
65 The story of Canada's civil rights movement has yet to be fully told, so it is difficult to contextualize groups such as the Open Door Society. Important information about early civil rights campaigns is contained in Constance Backhouse, *Colour-Coded: A Legal History of Racism in Canada, 1900-1950* (Toronto: University of Toronto Press, 1999); Ross Lambertson, *Repression and Resistance: Canadian Human Rights Activists, 1930-1960* (Toronto: University of Toronto Press, 2005); and James St. George Walker, *"Race," Rights and the Law in the Supreme Court of Canada: Historical Case Studies* (Waterloo: Wilfrid Laurier University Press, 1997).
66 Interview with Carole Kristianson, Vancouver, September 2003.
67 Margaret Edgar, "Black Children – White Family: A Problem of Identity," unpublished paper (c. 1970); interview with Margaret Edgar, Galiano, September 2003.
68 Williams, *Road to Now*.
69 Romano, *Race Mixing*, 218.
70 There is an extensive literature, mostly in the US, about this debate. See, for example, Amuzie Chimezie, "Transracial Adoption of Black Children," *Social Work* 20, 4 (July 1975): 296-301; Alicia Howard, David D. Royse, and John A. Skerl, "Transracial Adoption: The Black Community Perspective," *Social Work* 22, 3 (May 1977): 184-89; Bernice Q. Madison and Michael Schapiro, "Black Adoption – Issues and Policies: Review of the Literature," *Social Services Review* 47, 4 (December 1973): 531-60; Maye H. Grant, "Perspectives on Adoption: Black into White," *Black World* (November 1972): 66-75; Joyce Ladner, *Mixed Race Families: Adopting across Racial Boundaries* (Garden City: Anchor Press, 1977); Elizabeth Bartholet, "Where Do Black Children Belong," *University of Pennsylvania Law Review* 139, 5 (May 1991): 1163-1256; Elizabeth Bartholet, "Race Separatism in the Family: More on the Transracial Adoption Debate," *Duke Journal of Gender, Law and Policy* 2, 1 (Spring 1995): 99-105; Peter Hayes, "The Ideological Attack on Transracial Adoption in the USA and Britain," *International Journal of Law and the Family* 9, 1 (1995): 1-22; Randall Kennedy, *Interracial Intimacies: Sex, Marriage, Identity and Adoption* (New York: Pantheon, 2003); and Sandra Patton, *Birth Marks: Transracial Adoption in Contemporary America* (New York: New York University Press, 2000).
71 Interview with Irene Henderson, Winnipeg, July 2003.
72 Interview with Jasmine Smith (pseudonym), Kingston, August 2004.
73 "Do Black Parents Care?" *UHURU*, 13 July 1970, 4. See also "Black and White Liberals Discuss Black Problems," *UHURU*, 1 June 1970.

74 Interviews with Irene Henderson and Jody Boyer, Kingston, June 2002; interview with Frances Bayne, Montreal, July 2003.
75 See, for example, Daniel McNeil, "Afro(Americo)centricity in Black (American) Nova Scotia," *Canadian Journal of American Studies* (forthcoming).

12
"Chastity Outmoded!" *The Ubyssey,* Sex, and the Single Girl, 1960-70
Christabelle Sethna

The Association of Women Students (AWS) kicked off the 1960s at the University of British Columbia (UBC) with a pitched debate on the topic "Resolved that Chastity Is Out-Moded." Speaking for the affirmative, one Miss Grossman contended that given an increase in the age of marriage, in educational expectations, and in "sexual awareness" among the youth of her day, chastity for university students was virtually impossible to maintain. On the opposing team, a cheeky Mr. Calamitsis challenged Miss Grossman to uphold her beliefs by naming "the time and the place." Although she deftly declined his sexual invitation by invoking the strict moral code that her parents had taught her to follow, Miss Grossman allowed that emancipated women now had the same right as men to practise "sexual promiscuity." The majority of the 1,000 audience members voted in agreement. *The Ubyssey,* the main student newspaper on the most populous campus in western Canada, trumpeted the decision on its front page the following day: "Chastity 'outmoded!'"[1]

Long judged one of the most valuable Christian virtues, chastity was often equated with purity, celibacy, and morality. In women it has traditionally been associated with premarital virginity. A rigorous double standard held that women, not men, who lost their virginity before marriage were unchaste.[2] During the 1960s an influx of female students into universities, the debut of the birth control pill, and the advent of a "New Morality" brought a so-called sexual revolution to campus doorsteps across Canada. This revolution condoned in attitude, if not always in behaviour, heterosexual sexual intercourse for young, single, white, middle-class women.[3] While debate continues to rage about whether the shift in the sexual mores of the decade can be justifiably identified as revolutionary,[4] little is documented about how Canadian university students experienced this shift, even in histories of universities, in accounts of the 1960s, in chronicles of second-wave feminist organizing, or in studies of New Left student activism.[5]

In an attempt to understand some male and female students' experiences of this shift on campus, this chapter focuses on *The Ubyssey*'s coverage of the sexual revolution between 1960 and 1970. Originally titled *The Ubicee, The Ubyssey* was established in 1918 and became a member of the Canadian University Press. The student newspaper evolved into an award-winning publication that provided a reputable training ground for future journalists like Pierre Berton, Joe Schlesinger, Ian Brown, and Katherine Monk. Still, its elevated status did not prevent some critics from damning it "the vilest rag" and "the best argument for censorship that could be produced."[6] Like many other student newspapers, *The Ubyssey* was primarily occupied with showcasing student clubs, social events, sports, hijinks, and complaints. The publication also covered topics of local, national, and international interest. Over the years, items dealing with racism against the Japanese in Canada, antimilitarism, communism, and anti-Semitism punctuated its pages. In the 1960s, under the helm of a male-dominated editorial board "determined to create a professional, powerful, influential newspaper," the publication adopted an overt, New Left political slant. It turned its attention to pressing global social-justice concerns such as the civil rights movement, the Vietnam War, nuclear disarmament, and student power.[7]

During this decade the UBC student society, the Alma Mater Society (AMS), published the newspaper three times a week between September and March, the span of two university semesters. Publication virtually ceased in April and December; in the remaining months it was sporadic. For this chapter, *Ubyssey* back issues dating from 1960 to 1970 that are on deposit at Library and Archives Canada were combed for headlines, articles, editorials, letters to the editor, cartoons, captions, advertisements, drawings, reviews, and photographs dealing with themes often associated with the sexual revolution: sex, sexuality, sex education, marriage, pregnancy, contraception, abortion, and women's liberation. At first, this relevant material was photocopied from microfilm. It was downloaded from the Internet once the UBC Archives digitized the newspaper in 2004. All material collected was catalogued by theme and date of publication.[8]

Although historians have used student newspapers to study the history of universities, educational trends, or campus life in general, newspapers are problematical historical sources of information.[9] They can be read, variously, as a record of events, as a force for social change, as an expression of editor bias, or as a reflection of popular sentiment.[10] But recent accounts suggest an alternative point of view. Printed media can be viewed as a particular "construction of reality" produced interactively by editors, reporters, advertisers, and readers. Moreover, this construction serves as a vehicle for "codes of meaning" that privilege assumptions, values, and norms. These codes are embedded in "dominant discourses" that need to be uncovered, examined, and critiqued.[11] Applying such an approach to *The Ubyssey*'s dominant discourse of the sexual revolution reveals that both men and women students simultaneously feared, celebrated, and questioned single women's sexual freedom, objectified single women's bodies through an androcentric lens, and interpreted single women's sexuality in ways that reinforced many sexist, heterosexist, and racialized stereotypes. In fact, *The Ubyssey*'s cocky coverage often belied the progressive New Left student radicalism considered so typical of the decade.

UBC and the Baby Boom

After the Second World War, Canada experienced an increase in births that has been identified demographically as a baby boom. Despite quarrels over the precise timing of this boom, scholars agree that a surge in live births occurring roughly between 1946 and 1966 entailed a "major departure from the long-term trend" of declining fertility.[12] During this period, the age of women giving birth for the first time decreased, resulting in three to five births per female of childbearing age.[13] The baby boom was much more than a demographic phenomenon. Due to sheer volume, it forced momentous adjustments on society, resulting in what Doug Owram has referred to as a "shock wave."[14] Much of this shock wave was evident at universities in the 1960s. Full-time enrolment at the university level skyrocketed by 213 percent between 1960-61 and 1970-71. The enrolment of female students contributed significantly to the overall increase. The total university enrolment rates for the male population aged 18-24 years rose from 10 to 17%. For females in the same age group, the numbers climbed from 3 to 10%.[15] By the end of the decade, males accounted for 64% of the university student population, down from 75% at the beginning.[16] It was difficult to find statistics that would reliably indicate the racial composition of students. Data on foreign students show that they constituted a very small minority at universities. There were more Canadians studying abroad than there were foreign students in Canada.[17]

The University of British Columbia, which was founded in 1915, benefited greatly from this period of expansion. It was situated in a province where university enrolment in the 18-24 age group jumped overall from 9.6% in 1960-61 to 14.4% in 1970-71. UBC absorbed the largest number of students. By the end of the decade, it had the highest student enrolment (20,156) of all the universities in the western provinces. It was closest in size to McGill University in Quebec (15,178) but still lagged behind the largest university in the country, the University of Toronto (26,568).[18] Based on the model of Oxford and Cambridge, UBC's statutes technically allowed for the co-education of women. Yet the university's history on this score was chequered. Support for the equal education of women increased parallel to the putative eugenic threat posed by the immigration of nonwhites to British Columbia. Educated white women were touted as key to the regeneration of the Anglo-Saxon race because of the positive genetic contribution that they could make to their offspring. Over the years, allowances were made for the inclusion of women in certain UBC faculties and disciplines, but the goal of higher education was often subsumed by the expectation that women's ultimate destiny was marriage and motherhood.[19]

The New Morality

Nevertheless, white, middle-class women entering university in the 1960s were nothing if not ambitious. The role of postwar suburban wife, in which many of their mothers languished, was not going to be their fate. This young, educated cohort would flourish: "*We* were students," notes Myrna Kostash of her baby boomer peers, "we would be clever and we would travel and have adventures. And then we would marry, and *we* would be in love. We would build an interesting home and raise bright children."[20] Anne Petrie, a nineteen-year-old UBC student in the 1960s presumed, as did Kostash, that "we should follow any dream we had."[21]

Such ambition was understandable given the New Morality sweeping campuses across the country. The term was used to describe the hip sexual and political counterculture of youths. The New Morality encapsulated contemporary Quaker and Protestant nonjudgmental theological reflections that rejected traditional approaches to sexuality. In youth counterculture, the past symbolized respectable bourgeois Christian sexual morality. For men, it signalled marriage, fatherhood, and economic responsibility; for women, it meant premarital virginity, marriage, and motherhood. Many youths argued that contemporary sexual relations outside the bounds of marriage were not necessarily immoral per se. Rather, dishonesty among sexual partners was.[22] The New Morality also encompassed the hodgepodge of ideas that constituted the New Left. The student, not the working class, was in the vanguard of society. Discontent stemmed from the family, not class relations. Direct action, not theory, was the key to the democratization of society. Here, the university could be a pivotal force, training students to resist the status quo by examining the relations of power, exploitation, and exclusion, by condemning American imperialism, and by condoning participatory democracy on and off campus.[23]

The New Morality made the separation of the political from the sexual impossible.[24] Barbara Ehrenreich has determined that a white, male, middle-class revolt against the "breadwinner ethic" was already evident in the 1950s. Many men began to refuse the role of husband, father, and wage earner in favour of the persona of the swinging heterosexual bachelor epitomized in soft-porn magazines like *Playboy*.[25] The former represented the dull trap of commitment to one woman, while the latter promised erotic escape with as many women as possible. In the 1960s this revolt gathered steam, celebrating men's unfettered sexual access to women outside the bounds of marriage – so much so that sex, according to Beth Bailey, became a political "weapon" of choice against moribund mores. More often than not, this weapon was wielded in misogynist fashion, promoting – in both language and imagery – shock, vulgarity, and explicitness in the name of sexual and political liberation.[26]

The Birth Control Pill and the Illegality of Birth Control

An unwanted pregnancy was an obvious wrench in the works. For young women pregnant out of wedlock, there were few options apart from a shot-gun marriage to legitimate the pregnancy or a retreat to a home for unwed mothers.[27] The Criminal Code had outlawed abortion as well as the sale, dissemination, and advertisement of contraception since the late 1800s. The early birth control movement had eugenic underpinnings, advocating the passage of sterilization legislation in Alberta (1928) and in British Columbia (1933). The courts ruled in 1936 that contraception was legal if shown to be "in the public good." After 1945, Western population-control experts' belief that overpopulated countries in Asia, Latin America, and Africa would destabilize the world order to such an extent that thermonuclear war would result helped to make birth control a respectable goal. These experts held that the hallmark of a modern nation was a manageable birth rate. Therefore, they considered many Third World countries backward because their population numbers were deemed too high. In contrast, Canada's population numbers were quite low. Still, Canada could not be designated a modern nation because its birth control laws were outdated. To Western population-control experts, a reduction of the birth rate in countries such as India, Haiti, and Puerto Rico was proof of modernity. In Canada, reform of outdated birth control laws would constitute the same.[28]

Due to loopholes in the Criminal Code, the pill was introduced into Canada in the late 1950s, first as a menstrual regulator and then, in 1961, as a prescription contraceptive. The pill was intended primarily as a family-planning aid for married, not single, women in the First World and as a population-control tool in the Third. The possibility that the pill would release single women from the risk of an unwanted pregnancy and, there-fore, promote sexual promiscuity was recognized early on. However, hetero-sexual dating patterns had already changed long before the pill became generally accessible to single women in the late 1960s.

During the postwar search for stability on the home front, the popularity of group dating waned in favour of exclusive steady relationships between heterosexual couples. Petting was considered acceptable preparation for marital relations, but young women going steady were expected to main-tain their virginity until marriage.[29] Although many young women who became pregnant within a steady relationship wedded their partner, rates of illegitimate pregnancy began to increase. In the 1960s sexual intercourse for young women with steady *or* casual male partners outside the promise of marriage became more acceptable. This change, which sociologists have identified as a sexual revolution, occurred within a larger landscape of social transformation that contributed to the growth of secularism and consumerism.[30]

The Ubyssey Tackles the Sexual Revolution

Reminiscing about working on *The Ubyssey* with a staff characterized by a bent for beer and a fondness for "debunking, irreverent fun," *Globe and Mail* columnist Michael Valpy recalls: "We had no friends outside *The Ubyssey*, few if any interests outside *The Ubyssey*. We even explored the sexual revolution within *The Ubyssey*."[31] The sexual revolution was not as straightforward a matter as Valpy's pleasantry may suggest.

Rather, as the fallout from the AWS-sponsored debate on chastity demonstrates, the sexual revolution was uneven and contested from the start of the decade, especially in regard to single women. The debate unleashed a flood of contradictory responses that *The Ubyssey* splashed across its pages. Students Brian Dawson, David Fraser, Mac Etter, and Barry Mawhinney wrote individually to the newspaper's editor to protest the lewdness of the topic, the female debators' crudeness, and the rudeness of the newspaper in publicizing the debate.[32] One *Ubyssey* reporter responded by conducting a mock sex survey of the UBC community only to discover that many students did not know how to define chastity, the crux of the debate.[33] Mrs. Buda Brown, a member of the province's Social Credit government, got in on the exchange by charging that the debate revealed a "lack of virtuousness" among UBC students.[34] In reaction, *The Ubyssey* reprinted a *Victoria Times Daily* editorial that denounced Brown and called for "more Socreds [Social Credit members] with a college education."[35]

Ultimately, AWS president Fran Charkow and *Ubyssey* editor-in-chief Fred Fletcher jumped into the fray. Charkow insisted that because women students were part of a "modern society," the university was a respectable public forum for a debate on chastity.[36] Fletcher was far wilier. In an editorial, he praised the AWS for sponsoring the debate but assured readers that the newspaper was "in favour of chastity."[37] Fletcher's claim could not have been more disingenuous. Tellingly, the original front-page article on the chastity debate shared space with a technically unrelated but eye-catching photo of a pretty brunette student surrounded by donations of textbooks destined for universities in Japan and Pakistan. A sly caption referred concurrently to the brunette's books and breasts: "Brother are these ever stacked – the books we mean."[38]

The sexual revolution now provided the newspaper with the opportunity to up the ante on the sexualization of single female students. On the one hand, *The Ubyssey* derided physically unattractive women for their sexual undesirability to men. In one issue that devoted front-page coverage to the election of UBC's first woman chancellor, an editorial asked: "What's wrong with Canadian women?" Came the answer: "Nothing. If you like them bow-legged, flat-chested or knock-kneed."[39] On the other hand, the newspaper objectified women considered physically attractive. *The Ubyssey* did have a longstanding penchant for roguish photos showcasing comely co-eds.[40] However, over the decade, the image of cheesecake pin-up increasingly gave way to the likeness of a soft-porn centrefold. In the most blatant ongoing example, the newspaper's art director established a tradition of printing a photo puzzle poster of a different nude female in every final autumn issue. Whether she was a UBC student or a professional model is unknown. The instructions encouraged male readers to clip out and glue together "Mary Christmas." The masturbatory implications of this holiday gift were obvious: "Included as a special festive treat is Mary Christmas, who goes to pieces each year until fumbling fingers rectify her."[41]

The Pros and Cons of Premarital Sex

A scant two years before the chastity debate, UBC suspended a student nurse from classes for two weeks for kissing her boyfriend in a parked car just outside Vancouver General Hospital.[42] As the 1960s wore on, it became impossible for universities to regulate student premarital sexual activity under longstanding *in loco parentis* regulations. Studies confirmed that a notable proportion of male and female students would have sexual intercourse for the first time while at university because of a direct relationship between age and coital experience.[43]

Initially, *The Ubyssey*'s coverage of premarital sex was careful, displaying journalistic even-handedness with the opinions of pundits on its pros and cons. In one of the earliest articles on the topic, British professor George Carstairs waxed that youths had transformed society, making sexual experiences "a sensible preliminary to marriage." Ignoring the very real possibility that sexual experiences among unmarried students would not necessarily lead to wedlock, Carstairs couched his commentary safely within the context of future marital bliss. For Carstairs, premarital sex only increased the "probability that marriage would be a mutually satisfying partnership."[44]

Just one month after Carstairs was featured, another article on a Lutheran pastor's speech to 300 UBC students took the opposite tack. Reporter Ann Burge quoted him as saying that the furtive, "back-seat calisthenics" practised by singles were not just wrong but, in fact, "destructive, against historic morality, and against God's way of a full life for man [sic]." The pastor's suggestion that university students should say a firm no to sex before marriage was apparently met with noticeable groans from the back of the room. That Burge found it unnecessary to elaborate on the significance of these utterances presumably indicates that they were best understood as dismay over the speaker's advice.[45]

The Pill, the Church, and Male Self-Interest

When discussions about the morality of premarital sex inevitably touched on contraceptives, particularly the pill, the newspaper leaned toward pro-contraceptive pronouncements. Frequently, these were predicated on male self-interest. For example, *Ubyssey* columnist Jack Ornstein hailed the pill as a magic bullet that would, by reducing the risk of an unwanted pregnancy, stoke single women's sexual desires, make single men and women happier, and eliminate the need for an illegal abortion. But he also lavished praise on oral contraception for alleviating the "hell" that a single man experienced while waiting for his girlfriend's menstrual period to arrive on schedule. The hell reference spoke to a single man's fear of the negative consequences of impregnating his sexual partner. One consequence would have been a shotgun marriage to legitimate the pregnancy, thereby locking him into the breadwinner ethic. Given the benefits of the pill to both single men and women, Ornstein concluded that doctors and lawyers should make oral contraception accessible by prescription to all women, regardless of their marital status. Still, he acknowledged that the medical and legal professions "would need a shove or two – from you and I."[46]

Ornstein's support for the pill implied that all students were in common cause with the sexual revolution. Yet not every UBC student was a sexual revolutionary. In response to news of the firing of University of Illinois biologist Dr. Leo Koch for suggesting that contraceptives be made available to students on campus, *The Ubyssey* conducted an informal poll. Reporters found that respondents generally disagreed with Koch. One student was quoted as saying that contraceptives should not be used "just to allow people to indulge their physical desires." Another thought that the more society condoned sex, "the more it will get out of hand." Still another commented that while it was "natural" for couples going steady to engage in sexual intercourse, "it's bad to allow wholesale sexual indulgence." Faculty members appeared to agree. Dr. E.I. Signori, head of the Department of Psychology, warned that "if the society or the university officially permits more indulgence, then morals will get looser and looser."[47]

Father W. Ring was even more orthodox in his views. His comments to Student Christian Movement members at the University of Western Ontario, which were picked up by *The Ubyssey,* had him avowing that contraception was "evil." This Catholic priest confirmed that sex was for the purposes of procreation within marriage; therefore, the use of contraceptives by all couples, married or single, was immoral.[48] Wulfing von Schleinitz, a popular *Ubyssey* columnist, refuted much of Ring's message in a piece on the history of marriage. He wrote that marriage sanctified by the church was fast becoming an outdated institution. The church's emphasis on chastity meant that couples wed with little knowledge of sex. For von Schleinitz, sex was clearly about sexual intercourse. The lack of sex education, he posited sardonically, must have led to "interesting situations" on a couple's wedding night as no one "knew what was going on or where to put it."[49]

Similar anti-Catholic sentiments were divulged at the decade's halfway mark in yet another UBC student debate on the still-hot topic of chastity. This time, when the team from the Faculty of Nursing spoke out in favour of chastity, arguing that it was a sought-after ideal, Les Harowitz from the Faculty of Law countered that the church had "used chastity to control the people." The effect of such control was that many individuals had abandoned the church to indulge in sexual relations. In a crowd-pleasing final flourish, Steve Tick, Harowitz's debating partner, won the audience over by revealing a chastity belt worn under his lawyer's robe.[50]

The Vatican figured prominently in much of the publication. Pope Pius XII had agreed that Catholic women could use the pill only as a treatment for reproductive problems. Although it was considered unacceptable for contraceptive purposes, the popularity of the pill had forced Pope Paul VI to reconsider the relationship of the church to birth control.[51] Not surprisingly, when the Archbishop of Vancouver spoke to 150 UBC students on campus, the newspaper's account focused on his comments about birth control. Feeling positive about the commission that the Vatican had struck to reflect on the matter, Archbishop Johnson asserted that the church "appreciates that the world is demanding a definite yes or no answer on recent developments in birth control methods."[52] Unmoved, and cynical about the church's promised pronouncement on birth control, von Schleinitz contended that scripture should no longer hold sway on such matters. The church's stance against birth control had forced couples to play a risky "Russian Roulette" with an unwanted pregnancy.[53]

The topic of unwanted pregnancy figured prominently in the film *Bitter Ash*. So too did the flight from the breadwinner ethic on the part of the lead male character. Written and directed by UBC student Larry Kent and featuring student actors from the Theatre Arts Department, the film focused on a young, unmarried, sexually active white heterosexual couple. The young woman has missed a menstrual period. The young man turns down a shotgun marriage. The on-screen portrayal of a young man bucking the role of husband, father, and wage earner as dictated by respectable bourgeois Christian sexual morality proved to be wildly popular with UBC students. Regardless, the AMS banned the film because its sexual content and nudity drew the wrath of parents and Vancouver film critics alike. Conversely, *Ubyssey* reviewers praised the film for its "raw reality."[54]

For von Schleinitz, the raw reality of premarital sex required that the pill be made available to single women. Unlike married women, who had an easier time accessing the pill on prescription, single women had to resort to what von Schleinitz called "other cruder methods" of birth control. This comment was not related to women's need for more effective contraceptive security. Rather, it was linked to men's sexual pleasure in the condom-free sexual intercourse that the pill made possible. Posing a question that disparaged condoms as an example of those other cruder methods, a coy von Schleinitz asked his readers: "Would you wash your feet with your sox on?"[55]

The Population Explosion as a Rationale for Birth Control
Whereas birth control for single students engendered much debate, birth control in regard to the putative population crisis rarely did. In an article entitled "Universities check population growth," *The Ubyssey* reported that due to large numbers of undergraduates seeking admission, a number of universities were raising their entrance standards.[56] The title was an obvious nod to increased enrolments at Canadian campuses. It also reflected Canadians' growing preoccupation with overpopulation, especially in the Third World. One speaker to the campus, Dr. Norman Alcock, identified as the head of the Canadian Peace Research Institute, informed a UBC symposium of several contemporary anxieties. In addition to the prospect of nuclear war and the growth of the gap between rich and poor nations, he cited the population explosion as one of the areas in which universities needed to bring about "changes in attitudes."[57]

UBC president John Macdonald fleshed out these changes in his inaugural address. He began by sounding the alarm over the population crisis, noting that the world's population was increasing by the amount of the population of Canada every four months. To solve the problem, countries needed to commit "capital, trained men and education" to the situation. It was a mistake, he noted, not to deal with overpopulation in underdeveloped nations for moral, religious, or cultural reasons. There were only two ways to cope with the situation: "the first is to kill; the second is to limit reproduction."[58] Macdonald's seemingly pragmatic approach to controlling the fertility of brown, black, and yellow peoples was tellingly devoid of any analysis of race. Critiques of the racism of population-control experts surfaced toward the end of the decade in response to the publication of *The Population Bomb* (1968) by American professor Paul Ehrlich. A supporter of sex education, contraception, and abortion, Ehrlich advised that developed countries like Canada should work together to restrict food aid to nations that they identified as underdeveloped and overpopulated.[59]

Massimo Verdicchio, a *Ubyssey* reporter, proposed another, attention-seeking solution to overpopulation: sex with older women. The assumption was that they would be infertile.[60] A student countered in a letter to the editor that the solution to overpopulation was the propagation of fewer men who were "as corrupt, immoral and filthy" as Verdicchio.[61] Ornstein added his voice to the overpopulation scrap, musing that those single women who became pregnant while at university graduated with a BA in "Bastard Augmentation." While he demanded that unmarried women must have access to the pill, his language use indicated that his target audience was male, not female: "Can a student (YOU) be happy without being sexually satisfied? Can you concentrate on your studies when sex rears her beautiful head? Must you sublimate your sex via sports, religion and/or booze?"[62] Ornstein's rant earned him the wrath of one first-year male student who blamed him for being as emotionally immature as a child and asked why the newspaper functioned as "a medium for such trash."[63]

The threat of overpopulation in the Third World provided many Canadians with an almost foolproof rationalization for challenging Canada's outdated birth control laws. In early 1965 a newly formed UBC student group, the Demographic Society, announced its intention to distribute birth control information to students. Perhaps to show its support for the society and for oral contraception, *The Ubyssey* bracketed its front-page masthead with the phrase: "A pill a day keeps the doctor away." One of the society's first acts was to ask MLA Gordon Dowding, a Vancouver lawyer, to speak at UBC about the legal aspects of birth control.[64] The society soon became embroiled in a dispute with the AMS over the legality of its constitution because it had included a clause on the dissemination of birth control literature. The clause was removed under pressure from the University Clubs Committee. Its removal did not prevent the society's founder, Sieglinde Streda, from maintaining that birth control information would continue to be distributed. To this end, the society presented a film called *The Story of Human Fertility*, restricted to those eighteen years of age and older.[65]

Student Health Services at UBC

The society's attempt to bring birth control information to students was a response to the dearth of birth control services on campus. University health services everywhere typically provided students with frontline medical care. But given the illegality of birth control, the moral strictures on premarital sex, and the fear that an institution of higher education dispensing contraceptives would be exposed to negative public scrutiny, most university health services were cautious to a fault. When the American College Health Association (ACHA) surveyed its member institutions across Canada and the United States, only 4 percent of respondents reported that their health services provided contraceptives for the unmarried who had attained the age of majority and only 3.74 percent reported doing so for those who had not yet attained majority.[66] Married students and students engaged to be married fared better with pill prescriptions. So too did female students who were prescribed the pill for menstrual disorders.[67]

A small number of respondents to the ACHA survey, 9.65 percent, reported pressure from institutionally related groups to loosen their policies on contraceptive prescriptions.[68] Some of this pressure came from students themselves.[69] In late September 1965 *Ubyssey* reporter Ann Ratel deigned to test the stated reluctance of UBC's Student Health Services (SHS) at Wesbrook Hospital to prescribe the pill to single female students in an undercover sting operation. Following the SHS' public declaration that it provided oral contraception *only* to married students, Ratel borrowed a wedding ring, assumed a false last name, and presented herself to the SHS as a newlywed. After first speaking to a nurse, Ratel consulted an SHS physician who enquired about her relationship with her fictitious husband and then provided her with a two-year prescription for Ortho-Novum. Under the pun-filled front-page headline, "Un-Ortho-Dox: Our bachelor girl perforates leaky Wesbrook pill policy," *The Ubyssey* printed Ratel's prescription with the physician's signature blacked out.[70]

Ratel's stunt ignited a firestorm. One student wrote to *The Ubyssey* to blame the SHS for forcing single students to gamble on an unwanted pregnancy. Others reproached Ratel, reasoning that the SHS would now require women to produce marriage certificates if they wanted the pill. Still others accused the newspaper of sensationalism. The bluntest letter writer allowed that all Ratel did was to confirm that the SHS would provide oral contraception only to married students.[71] Perhaps in response to Ratel's actions, AMS president Byron Hender declared his support for a proposal by the Canadian Union of Students (CUS) to defy the birth control laws, stating: "The ban on contraceptives is a foolish part of the criminal code and it should be amended." According to the ambitious CUS proposal, fifty preselected single women would ask co-operating pharmacists in Vancouver and Victoria for contraceptives to force a test case of the law.[72] Shortly thereafter, in yet another UBC debate on the topic of chastity, students declared openly: "sex is for the single girl."[73]

Single female students' difficulty accessing oral contraception on campus had important repercussions for the Vancouver Family Planning Clinic. Canadian family-planning clinics were traditionally meant to service poor married women seeking birth control, often in keeping with eugenical imperatives.[74] When it first opened in 1965, most of the Vancouver clinic's clientele was married. But between 1968 and 1969, 71 percent of the patients were unmarried women, 45 percent of whom were university students. It was speculated that the change in the numbers was related to the fact that university health services were reluctant to prescribe contraceptives to single women. Surveys revealed that while single female university students attending the Vancouver clinic displayed "fear of disapproval," they were well adjusted and goal-oriented. Furthermore, they "appeared to have come to terms with any anxieties about premarital sexuality as shown in a realistic, pragmatic approach to the use of contraception and the frankness with which they acknowledged the probable disapproval of others."[75]

Women's Rights

Betty Friedan's runaway hit *The Feminine Mystique* (1963) had already made its way to the UBC campus,[76] but feminist content in *The Ubyssey* during the first half of the decade was rare. In one such exception, an editorial by an anonymous "Ubyssey Staff Writer" identified the sexual double standard as "one of the most conspicuous hypocricies [sic] of modern society." Women, the author noted, were expected to be chaste, but men were not. The double standard was based on the false belief that women had no sexual urges. The author compared women who laboured under this belief to "Negroes" who were told that they were inferior to whites.[77] Such a comparison obfuscated the very real power differentials between white women and black men and black women, while ignoring the fact that some women were also black. Yet given the era's focus on civil rights, American race relations between blacks and whites were regularly invoked as analogous to the dominant and subservient status of certain groups.[78] At times the analogy was dismissed outright. When one *Ubyssey* editorial compared university students to African American slaves because Canadian universities were similarly beholden to their American overlords, some letter writers bridled, calling the commentary "smug" and "ignorant."[79]

Occasionally, reportage dealing with abortion betrayed a feminist sensibility. Espousing his candid views on abortion to a group at UBC's International House, New Democratic Party MLA Dave Barrett stated that a society that did not provide abortion services to unmarried women was "crazy."[80] Not to be outdone, von Schleinitz argued that he could condone abortion from the standpoint of overpopulation but also supported it as every woman's right. Ever-quotable, he insisted, "I consider it a woman's right to decide for herself whether or not to put another child into the world (not just canon-fodder for some political or religious creed)."[81]

After 1965 some readers of *The Ubyssey* – if not the newspaper itself – displayed greater sensibility toward women's rights. When a misogynist polemic by John Kelsey appeared, angry readers inundated the publication with letters. An editor for the Friday page, Kelsey professed that the American-led warfare sweeping the world had its origins in "momism's ugly breast."[82] Momism, a term coined by Philip Wylie in his book *Generation of Vipers* (1942),[83] referred to the supposedly pathological child rearing techniques employed by American mothers who smothered their children and, especially, their sons. Daughters of such mothers grew up to be dominating women, while sons developed into submissive, possibly homosexual, men.[84]

Kelsey did not explain why momism was responsible for global conflict. But his polemic reflected widespread disgust with the American invasion of Vietnam. This disgust was communicated in a powerful graphic published in the late 1960s in *The Ubyssey*. It consisted of a naked bearded man labelled "USA" lying on top of a naked long-haired woman named "Vietnam."[85] The words "Reluctant to pull out" appear underneath her body. The play on both male pleasure in coitus and the American military presence in Vietnam worked as a powerful symbol of oppression precisely because of the sex, sexual orientation, and sexual position of the couple involved. Even though it theoretically cast heterosexual relations for women in a negative light, the graphic underlined the subjugated status of women, non-whites, and Third World nations. For some students it was not obscene but all too appropriate given the current state of affairs. Al-Mujahid, a student with roots in Southeast Asia, dismissed potential criticism of the graphic, denouncing imperialism as "a monster which rapes a nation." Vietnam was merely the most recent victim.[86]

Kelsey did extrapolate on Wylie's work to avow that Western civilization had collapsed because of the power women had secured at the expense of men via universal suffrage and the institution of marriage. Kelsey stated that suffrage had "let women out of the kitchen" only to plunge into men's "shoes (and pants and wallets and cars)." Similarly, in marriage every wife became a "shrew" who wanted to "castrate" her husband. Kelsey's solution to this unhappy state of affairs, where women now ruled over men, was for men to decline the breadwinner ethic. The best alternative was for couples to live together. "Only then," remarked Kelsey, "can a shrew be tossed onto the nearest sidewalk, lingerie showering around her."[87]

In response to the obvious misogyny of the piece, one letter writer lamented that women were being used as a "scapegoat" for all the ills of Western society.[88] Another intoned melodramatically that Kelsey was a Communist who had "bastardized the morality of Canada" and "slandered the holy name of woman."[89] The ubiquitous von Schleinitz disagreed strongly with Kelsey over universal suffrage but admitted that nothing good could be said about the institution of marriage. He praised Kelsey for recommending cohabitation to couples but suggested that such a living arrangement required at least some equality between the sexes. Implying that only full-time married housewives, not live-in girlfriends employed outside the home, could be expected to keep house without a man's assistance, von Schleinitz cautioned: "Take note Mr. Kelsey, you would have to do the dishes and clean the house once in a while since your partner in this affair will undoubtedly have a regular job."[90]

The Women's Liberation Movement

In 1967, stirred by the demands of Laura Sabia, president of the Canadian Federation for University Women, the federal government struck a Royal Commission on the Status of Women (RCSW). The commission catalyzed the growth of a women's liberation movement across the country and the beginning of a period now commonly known as second-wave feminism. In quick succession, women's liberation groups like the Toronto Women's Liberation (TWL), the Feminist Action League (FAL), and the Vancouver Women's Caucus (VWC) were established. Women's liberation operated, as some historians have noted, in keeping with the counterculture views of the decade, including "a preference for openness and self-expression, and a rejection of customary standards of dress, behaviour, and sexuality."[91]

From 1968 onward, the influence of women's liberation on campus resulted in an uneasy partnership between *The Ubyssey* and feminism. The newspaper maintained its bawdy emphasis on sex even when it rankled many a reader. Tim Hicks, a third-year science student, told the editor: "I'll just say that I'm sick and tired of all the fucking and the fuck-you's and the free lovers. Please clean up your crude articles."[92] When another male student grumbled that the content of a reprint about "balling" to music was immature, the editor's rejoinder was defensive: "Obviously, since you think balling to music is perverted, you have never tried it ... It is because people like you exist that we run such stories – to attempt to better students' lives by opening their eyes to things joyful and pleasant."[93]

The newspaper did discontinue Mary Christmas in November 1968, replacing her with a naked male figure called "Hippie New Year."[94] Yet even though *The Ubyssey* sometimes reported cases of sexual assault against female students on university grounds,[95] its pages continued to be adorned with photos and captions that reinforced the idea that single women were toys for men and decorations for the campus. By way of example, a voluptuous, bikini-clad belle sprawled invitingly on a blanket was identified as one of many "luscious" co-eds "eagerly awaiting the lascivious looks" of male students.[96] Simultaneously, the publication began to give voice to some of the distinctive projects of second-wave feminism, such as the remaking of gender roles. Ruth Dworkin suggested that gender roles were culturally, not biologically, determined. She explained that women were raised to be submissive to men and were expected to rear their children. She asserted that women's inability to control their own fertility had pushed them to the margins of society. She praised the pill not because it provided a woman with sexual freedom but because it allowed her to choose whether or not to become a mother.[97]

A year after Dworkin's piece appeared, *The Ubyssey* carried a front-page spread on the women's liberation movement positioned below a photo of Vancouver university and high school students demonstrating against the

Vietnam War. The juxtaposition of the spread and photo seemed to legitimate women's liberation as one of the major protest movements of the decade. Indebted to some of the arguments made by Friedan, authors Victoria Smith and Judy Fitzgerald concentrated on the ways that women's bodies were objectified in advertising. The advertising industry created bodily insecurities in young women. As a result, they became lifelong consumers of clothing, make-up, and hair products intended to enhance their appearance. Although most advertising was directed at white, middle-class women, it had the power to seduce women of all races and classes. Therefore, all women became "captives" of an industry whose corporations sought only to "expand markets and increase profits."[98]

The spread included an advertisement for Exquisite Form brassieres as an illustration of the objectification of women in advertising. Ironically, a sidebar to the left of the spread that contained an advertisement for Tampax tampons highlighted even more trenchantly the main points that Smith and Fitzgerald had made. Appropriating an image associated with youthful protest, the advertisement displayed a photo of a trouser-clad young woman carrying a placard emblazoned with the words: "GIRL POWER." Ironically, the advertising copy reflected the same feminine stereotypes that second-wave feminists set out to critique. Tampax, noted the advertisement, was a part of "all those little tricks every woman knows. Like tilting your head at exactly the right angle when you ask a special favor. Or knowing just when to wear that particular dress."[99]

At least three letter writers roundly condemned the spread for portraying women as gullible fashion victims. Karen Atrens of the Psychology Department blamed the hypocrisy of "groovy 'liberated' men" who pursued "chicks" influenced by fashion magazines, as opposed to real women. She concluded that gender roles were as stultifying for men as they were for women but added, in a stereotypical tone, that the only men disputing masculine stereotypes were homosexual.[100] Terry Atkinson, a commerce student, refused to believe that women could be manipulated to the extent that the authors had indicated. He retorted that "if the average Canadian woman had as low mentality as is credited to her by the women's liberation movement ... she has nothing to gain by being 'liberated.'"[101] A law student identified only as D. McCrimmon was more succinct, labelling the spread "poppycock." McCrimmon accused women of creating problems in their "simple minds." Furthermore, he blasted *The Ubyssey* for turning itself into "a crying towel" for women.[102]

This last accusation rang hollow because the mainly male editorial board of the newspaper was preoccupied with its own struggle over feminism. On the editorial page of *The Ubyssey,* male staff often came in for ribbings over their supposed talents, quirks, and/or religious affiliation. For example, news editor Paul Knox was known as "a master of the fine arts of journalism and eye-rape;" managing editor Bruce Curtis was "rumoured to be more-than-a-casual smoker of LSD"; and city editor Nate Smith was nicknamed "Super Jew." Yet when the editorial board introduced readers to its crop of female staffers – some of whom reported on the women's liberation movement – it did so with glib wink-wink, nudge-nudge one-liners that sexualized their appearance, ethnicity, and politics. Sandy Kass was complimented for being "one of our dazzling girl staffers," who wanted "the new position (horizontal?) of society editor." Christine Krawczyk was labelled a "lovely Polish lass." Robin Burgess was identified as the "staff midget" who was "known for her position (vertical) on the women's liberation issue." In a direct reference to the spread on the objectification of women's bodies in advertising, Burgess was teased about "shoplifting every available can of 'special girlie deodorant' in an act of protest."[103]

The newspaper framed its greeting to the female staffers in much the same way as it appraised all women as inviting – in fact, desiring – male sexual appreciation. In the same issue, a sketch of a young, shapely, large-breasted, naked woman gazing intently at the reader accompanied a review of a local cinema's skin-flick. The film came highly recommended for its displays of female genitalia, or as the reviewer phrased it in the vernacular, "unobscured beaver ... with good close-ups too."[104] And like *Playboy*'s tendency to mix soft porn and serious journalism, this issue was packed with articles on the oppressive conditions under which different populations suffered: the famine ravaged in Biafra, the striking grape workers in California, and the exploited Native beet harvesters in Alberta. Even women teachers, professors, and office workers were accorded some sympathy regarding salary inequity.[105]

Birth Control for and by Students

In 1969 the long-awaited reforms to the Criminal Code occurred. The Trudeau government legalized contraception and liberalized the abortion law. These reforms to birth control subjected sexuality, contraception, and reproduction to even further regulation by the medical profession. Many contraceptives could now be purchased "over the counter," but a few, like the pill and the intra-uterine device (IUD), could be acquired only with a doctor's prescription. Procuring a legal abortion became a convoluted process marked by lengthy delays and arbitrary decision-making. Under the new law, women had to submit their application for an abortion only to a Therapeutic Abortion Committee (TAC) at an accredited hospital. TACs were composed of doctors invested with the power to grant or to deny requests for a therapeutic abortion based on their evaluation of the negative impact of the pregnancy on the woman's life or health.[106]

The *Ubyssey* devoted several column inches to publicizing a McGill University student manual on birth control called the *Birth Control Handbook*. First published in September 1968, while the legal ban on birth control was still in effect, the *Handbook* was the brainchild of the Students' Council of the McGill Students' Society. Concerned with the problem of illegal abortion, the council mandated the publication of a student-friendly manual on birth control. The *Handbook* was filled with information about reproductive anatomy, contraceptives, sterilization, and abortion. It also contained editorial commentary that took Western population-control experts to task for their racism and that supported women's reproductive rights as a function of women's liberation.[107]

The *Ubyssey* praised the *Handbook* for its factual accuracy, lauded its availability at the SHS and at the AMS, and agreed that it be disseminated to everyone. However, upon reviewing the *Handbook,* one anonymous *Ubyssey* staffer marginalized women's concerns. The author stated that the "most questionable aspect" of the *Handbook* was the editorial commentary that began with a discourse on the population explosion and ended up "as a testimony for liberated women." The staffer's facetious solution to the population explosion was not intended to interrogate the racism of Western population-control experts but to "knock off" the enrolment lists those single female students who had been knocked up. He or she implied that women's liberation was a point of contention because it marginalized men; UBC male students who read the *Handbook* might feel ignored by the *Handbook's* focus on women's reproductive rights.[108] AMS secretary Isobel Semple similarly depoliticized the *Handbook's* feminist message in her statement to *The Ubyssey*. She told the newspaper that the AMS' distribution of the *Handbook* was not undertaken "in order to keep Frosh chicks from getting pregnant." Rather, it provided "things to be learned by students of all ages and sexes."[109]

The *Handbook* became a smash hit on campuses across North America. The UBC campus quickly ran out of copies. While waiting for the delivery of another batch, Maurice Bridge, a *Ubyssey* advice columnist, told his readers that many Vancouver doctors would provide the pill or other contraceptives to "chicks" without overt "hassling" about their age or marital status. Bridge expressed the hope that given the recent reforms to the Criminal Code, the local campus shop, the Thunderbird, would soon stock birth control supplies.[110] In a move that won *Ubyssey* approval, the AMS next agreed that male students could buy condoms from dispensers installed in men's washrooms as part of the "progressive services" that the AMS had put in place.[111]

The SHS did come under fire from some students. When a women's liberation group distributed a questionnaire via *The Ubyssey* about students' experiences of birth control, the vast majority of the 460 respondents (340 females and 120 males) reported that they wanted a birth control clinic at

UBC. Of the 53 females who said that they had requested contraceptives at the SHS, 38 said that they had been refused. Dr. A.M. Johnson, the SHS' director, bristled at the results. He allowed that the SHS always provided married students with contraception, while it sometimes turned down single students. However, Johnson defended the SHS. He insisted that single students who were refused contraceptives were referred instead to birth control clinics in the city. These referrals help to explain why so many single female university students flocked to the Vancouver Family Planning Clinic in the late 1960s. Johnson also declared that although birth control was still a topic of medical controversy, he supported the judgment of every SHS doctor making decisions about contraception on a case-by-case basis. Finally, Johnson concluded that the ultimate responsibility for contraception lay with the individual student, not with the SHS.[112]

Due to the doctor's remarks, *The Ubyssey* published a step-by-step outline of what a student seeking contraceptive care could expect at the SHS. A student could expect to consult a doctor in private. If the doctor agreed to prescribe oral contraception, she would receive a renewable one-year supply based on a physical exam, a pelvic exam, and a pap smear. The doctor would also inform her of the principal side effects of the contraceptive. The outline confirmed that those single students whose requests for a contraceptive prescription were denied were sent to downtown Vancouver birth control clinics. However, it also revealed that an SHS doctor's refusal of such requests was based on his or her determination of the emotional maturity of the student. Such practices reinforced the power of physicians to micromanage single females' sexuality.[113]

Our Bodies, Our Lives

As frustration grew over a new abortion law that did little to alleviate the dangers of illegal abortion, *The Ubyssey* ran a number of articles on women's reproductive health and contraceptive care on and off campus. The newspaper even publicized abortion teach-ins sponsored by campus organizations such as the AMS.[114] But even in this instance the tone was salacious. One information session on contraception and abortion that approximately 1,000 students attended was described as "recreation without procreation" and as a "group grope."[115]

However, when the VWC became involved in providing abortion counselling, *The Ubyssey* announced the location of the group's downtown service.[116] The newspaper also began to run a regular column called "Speak Easy." Named after the campus drop-in centre established by student social workers, the column invited students to write in, call, or visit with their concerns. The column carried warnings against backstreet abortionists, gave information about the new abortion law, and discussed three options for dealing with an unwanted pregnancy: raising the child on one's own, adoption, or abortion. The option of a shotgun marriage was conspicuously absent. If a pregnant student sought an abortion, she was advised to contact the VWC or to arrange for an abortion in England or Japan.[117] *The Ubyssey* advertised inexpensive flights to the cities of London and Osaka under the aegis of the AMS. Once clinics in the United States began to provide abortions for Canadian women, the newspaper also carried advertisements from American abortion-referral services that had sprung up to meet the demand.[118]

The RCSW delivered its report in 1970. Among its many recommendations, it suggested abolishing TACs, thereby making the process of acquiring an abortion easier.[119] The VWC went one step further. With other women's groups across the country, it sponsored a campaign demanding repeal of the new abortion law. *The Ubyssey* tracked the campaign, which culminated in the journey of an Abortion Caravan from Vancouver to Ottawa. The Caravan, which was based on the "On to Ottawa" protest during the Great Depression, showcased a casket filled with coat hangers, the symbol of illegal abortion. In promoting the campaign in the student newspaper, Vicki Goodman conveyed her resentment over the fact that while some women were able to access out-of-province abortions, the young and the poor did not have the funds to do so. This class analysis was representative of the socialist-feminist politics of the VWC. Yet Goodman's other charge – that women seeking abortions either had to "degrade" themselves in front of the primarily male doctors on TACs or risk becoming "'brood' animals" birthing children that they did not want – spoke to the burgeoning popularity of radical feminist sentiments.[120]

Radical feminists opined that men's control over women's bodies was the prime reason for female subjugation. Thus, the repeal of the new abortion law would strike a blow against this control. As the 1970s dawned, men's control over women's bodies factored into a number of *Ubyssey* opinion pieces that cast doubt on the validity of the sexual revolution for women. Ellen Woodsworth of the VWC took the organizers of UBC engineering students' annual Lady Godiva event to task. She blasted the tradition, which highlighted the parade of a topless woman astride a horse, as an example of the sexual objectification of women. Posing a politically – and grammatically – convoluted question, she asked men to evaluate their relationship to women in feminist terms: "Can you only relate to yourself as an animal who has erections with no feelings for the individual or are you so afraid of this woman that you must objectify her to deal with her at all?"[121]

By the end of the decade, radical feminist politics tied the objectification of women to the exercise of female sexuality. In a reprint of an article that appeared in *Ramparts,* a widely read, left-wing American magazine, Susan Lydon praised William H. Masters and Virginia E. Johnson, authors of *Human Sexual Response* (1966).[122] Drawing on their findings that women's orgasms were centred in the clitoris, not in the vagina, Lydon argued that putative vaginal orgasms functioned as status symbols for male, not female, sexuality. She complained that "sexual liberation for women is wrongly understood to mean that women will adopt all forms of masculine sexuality." Lydon's complaint spoke to radical feminists' growing disillusionment with the sexual revolution. Furthermore, it hinted at the possibility of lesbianism as a political reaction to this disillusionment, but the author did not pursue this point further.[123] In the 1970s radical feminists and radical lesbian feminists began emphasizing that heterosexual relationships mirrored women's subservient position in patriarchal society. They called for a revisioning of female sexuality grounded in the pleasure of clitoral orgasm.[124]

Conclusion

Throughout the 1960s UBC's award-winning student newspaper, *The Ubyssey*, depicted the sexual revolution as a much-needed hedge against respectable bourgeois Christian sexual morality. Although not everyone agreed with the newspaper's ribald approach to relations between the sexes, there is no doubt that the publication's dominant discourse on the sexual revolution almost exclusively identified sex as heterosexual, sexual activity as penile penetration, and single women as ornamental trinkets designed for male sexual pleasure. Although this discourse was usually couched in male adolescent-style humour, something far more serious was at work. The coverage of the sexual revolution targeted women for male derision and desire. It celebrated young men's unbridled access to recreational sex free from the demands of the breadwinner ethic as an example of progressive lefty politics. Finally, it constructed women's sexuality in ways that betrayed a fundamental unease with the presence of single female students on campus. It is ironic that the newspaper's juvenile misogyny, often stylized as politically and sexually cool, coexisted with newsworthy reports on the distress of oppressed peoples around the world.

The impact of the women's liberation movement on some of the publication's coverage was evident toward the end of the 1960s. Pieces inspired by second-wave radical feminism, in addition to material on contraception and birth control, contested the benefit of the sexual revolution to women. This new slant on the sexual revolution, which was predicated upon radical feminists' demands for women's control over their bodies, mounted a major challenge to the traditional masculinist bias of *The Ubyssey*. In this respect, *The Ubyssey*'s dominant discourse of the sexual revolution may be viewed as a period piece that lends credence to second-wave feminists' disenchantment with the sexual politics of the time. Or it may be upheld by third-wave feminists as an ongoing lesson in the contradictory gains and limitations of the use of sexual relations as a vehicle for political liberation. In an era when right-wing political agendas threaten sex education as well as women's reproductive rights and gay rights, when HIV/AIDS decimates populations already marginalized by poverty and racism, and when the war on terrorism has become an excuse to abrogate citizens' civil rights, third-wave feminists should take no revolution – sexual, political, or otherwise – for granted.

Acknowledgments
I am grateful to the Social Sciences and Humanities Research Council of Canada for its support and to my research assistants, Amélie Chrétien, Corrie Level, Marion Doull, and Stacey Loyer. I appreciate the insightful comments of the two anonymous reviewers. I also thank the Dillon family for the time spent at their cottage writing this chapter. A version of this chapter was presented at the Canadian History of Education Association/L'Association canadienne d'histoire de l'éducation and the American History of Education Society, University of Ottawa, 26-29 October 2006, and at the European Social Science History Conference, Royal Netherlands Academy of Arts and Sciences, Amsterdam, The Netherlands, 22-25 March 2006.

Notes
1 Bob Canon, "Chastity 'outmoded!'" *Ubyssey,* 27 January 1961, 1.
2 Kathleen Coyne Kelly, *Performing Chastity and Testing Virginity in the Middle Ages* (New York and London: Routledge, 2000).
3 Brooke E. Wells and Jean M. Twenge, "Changes in Young People's Sexual Behavior and Attitudes, 1943-1999: A Cross-Temporal Meta Analysis," *Review of General Psychology* 9, 3 (2005): 249-61.
4 Charles W. Hobart, "Sexual Permissiveness in Young English and French Canadians," *Journal of Marriage and the Family* 34, 2 (May 1972): 292-303; Sheila Jeffreys, *Anticlimax: A Feminist Perspective on the Sexual Revolution* (New York: New York University Press, 1990); David Allyn, *Make Love, Not War: The Sexual Revolution: An Unfettered History* (New York: Routledge, 2001); Beth Bailey, "Prescribing the Pill: Politics, Culture, and the Sexual Revolution in America's Heartland," *Journal of Social History* 30, 4 (Summer 1997): 827-56; Hera Cook, *The Long Sexual Revolution: English Women, Sex, and Contraception, 1800-1975* (Oxford: Oxford University Press, 2004).
5 Martin L. Friedland, *The University of Toronto: A History* (Toronto: University of Toronto Press, 2002); Myrna Kostash, *Long Way from Home: The Story of the Sixties Generation in Canada* (Toronto: James Lorimer and Company, 1980); Doug Owram, *Born at the Right Time: A History of the Baby-Boom Generation* (Toronto: University of Toronto Press, 1996); Nancy Adamson, Linda Briskin, and Margaret McPhail, *Feminist Organizing for Change: The Contemporary Women's Movement in Canada* (Toronto: Oxford University Press, 1988); Dimitrios Roussopoulos, *The New Left in Canada: Our Generation* (Montreal: Black Rose Books, 1970); Norman Sheffe, ed., *Issues for the Seventies: Student Unrest* (Toronto: McGraw-Hill, 1970).
6 "Vile Rag," a 1956 *Ubyssey* editorial excerpted in J.E. Clark, ed., *Back Issues: 80 Years of the Ubyssey Student Newspaper* (Vancouver: Ubyssey Publications Society, 1998), 44.
7 Michael Valpy, "Foreword," in Clark, ed., *Back Issues,* 49. For additional information, see Harry T. Logan, *Tuum Est: A History of the University of British Columbia* (Vancouver: UBC Press, 1958), 238.
8 The *Ubyssey* Index is available at http://www.library.ubc.ca/archives/ubyssey_index_revised.html.
9 A.B. McKillop, *Matters of the Mind: The University in Ontario, 1791-1951* (Toronto: University of Toronto Press, 1994).
10 For more information, see Michelle Muir, "Producing Educated Women: Eveline LeBlanc and the University of Ottawa" (MA thesis, University of Ottawa, 2003).

11 Frances Henry and Carol Tator, *Discourses of Domination: Racial Bias in the Canadian English-Language Press* (Toronto: University of Toronto Press, 2002), 5-6. See also Valerie J. Korinek, *Roughing It in the Suburbs: Reading* Chatelaine *Magazine in the Fifties and Sixties* (Toronto: University of Toronto Press, 2000), 70-101.
12 Roderic Beaujot, *Population Change in Canada: The Challenges of Policy Adaptation* (Toronto: McClelland and Stewart, 1991), 72.
13 Ibid., 75.
14 Owram, *Born at the Right Time*, xiii.
15 Statistics Canada, *Education in Canada: A Statistical Review for the Period 1960-61 to 1970-71* (Ottawa: Statistics Canada, 1973) 30, 47, 48-49, 52, 57, 58.
16 Statistics Canada, *University Education Growth, 1960-61 to 1971-72* (Ottawa: Information Canada, 1974), 13.
17 This trend reversed in the 1970s. See Statistics Canada, *From the Sixties to the Eighties: A Statistical Portrait of Canadian Higher Education* (Ottawa: Statistics Canada, 1979), 69. Statistics based on the racial or ethnic background of Canadian-born students during this time period have been difficult to find.
18 Statistics Canada, *Education in Canada*, 48-49.
19 Lee Stewart, *"It's up to You": Women at UBC in the Early Years* (Vancouver: UBC Press for the UBC Academic Women's Association, 1990). See also Logan, *Tuum Est*, 8, 24, 35.
20 Kostash, *Long Way from Home*, 167. For two accounts of women in suburbia, see Betty Friedan, *The Feminine Mystique* (1963; reprint, New York: Dell, 1983); and Veronica Strong-Boag, "Home Dreams: Women and the Suburban Experiment in Canada, 1945-1960," *Canadian Historical Review* 72, 4 (1991): 471-504.
21 Anne Petrie, *Gone to an Aunt's: Remembering Canada's Homes for Unwed Mothers* (Toronto: McClelland and Stewart, 1998), 14.
22 Allyn, *Make Love, Not War*, 112-13.
23 Owram, *Born at the Right Time*, 216-47.
24 Julyan Reid, "Some Canadian Issues," in Tim Reid and Julyan Reid, eds., *Student Power and the Canadian Campus* (Toronto: Peter Martin and Associates, 1969), 15; Allyn, *Make Love, Not War*, 112-13.
25 Barbara Ehrenreich, *The Hearts of Men: American Dreams and the Flight from Commitment* (New York: Anchor Books, 1984), 42-51.
26 Beth Bailey, *Sex in the Heartland* (Cambridge, MA, and London, UK: Harvard University Press, 1999), 54-174.
27 Petrie, *Gone to an Aunt's*, 2.
28 Angus McLaren and Arlene Tigar McLaren, *The Bedroom and the State: The Changing Practices and Politics of Contraception and Abortion in Canada, 1880-1997*, 2nd ed. (Toronto: Oxford University Press, 1997), 133-55.
29 See Beth L. Bailey, *From Front Porch to Back Seat: Courtship in Twentieth-Century America* (1988; reprint, Baltimore and London: Johns Hopkins University Press, 1989).
30 See Allyn, *Make Love, Not War*, 8.
31 Valpy, "Foreword," in Clark, ed., *Back Issues*, 49.
32 See "Letters to the Editor," *Ubyssey*, 2 February 1961, 2.
33 "Sex Investigated: A.G. conducts personal survey," *Ubyssey* insert: *Without Prejudice*, 16 February 1961, one, four.
34 Fred Fletcher, "'Shocking, immoral' – Brown," *Ubyssey*, 24 February 1961, 12.
35 "The big smear," guest editorial, *Ubyssey*, 2 March 1961, 2.
36 Fran Charkow, "AWS Answers" letter to the editor, *Ubyssey*, 2 February 1961, 2.
37 "Pen Pals??" editorial, ibid.
38 See photo in *Ubyssey*, 27 January 1961, 1.
39 "Canadian Women," editorial, *Ubyssey*, 29 November 1961, 2.
40 See also Clark, ed., *Back Issues*, 43.
41 "Your Christmas Present," *Ubyssey*, 1 December 1967, 1.
42 Kathryn McPherson, "'The Case of the Kissing Nurse': Femininity, Sexuality, and Canadian Nursing, 1900-1970," in Kathryn McPherson, Cecilia Morgan, and Nancy M. Forestell,

eds., *Gendered Pasts: Historical Essays in Femininity and Masculinity in Canada* (Toronto: Oxford University Press, 1999), 179-98.

43 F. Michael Barrett, "Sexual Experience, Birth Control Usage, and Sex Education of Unmarried Canadian University Students: Changes between 1968 and 1978," *Archives of Sexual Behavior* 9, 5 (1980): 367-90 at 385.

44 George Carstairs, quoted in "Chastity may be outmoded, British psychologist says," *Ubyssey*, 8 January 1963, 9.

45 Ann Burge, "Pre-marital sex hampers full life," *Ubyssey*, 12 February 1963, 3.

46 Jack Ornstein, "Don't legalize abortions," *Ubyssey*, 29 September 1961, 2.

47 Richard Simeon, "Beware of warping your mentality," *Ubyssey*, 19 October 1962, 5.

48 "Minister says: Sex still a mess despite publicity," *Ubyssey*, 14 February 1963, 8.

49 Wulfing von Schleinitz, "That old custom way back when," *Ubyssey*, 8 October 1964, 3.

50 Jack Khoury, "Chastity stripped in Brock," *Ubyssey*, 18 March 1965, 3.

51 Bernard Asbell, *The Pill: A Biography of the Drug that Changed the World* (New York: Random House, 1995), 244-65.

52 Steve Brown, "'Vatican sees God in others,'" *Ubyssey*, 25 February 1965, 2.

53 Wulfing von Schleinitz, "If you must be discreet about it ..." *Ubyssey*, 8 October 1965, 9.

54 *Bitter Ash* debuted at UBC on 7 October 1963; see Clark, ed., *Back Issues*, 59.

55 Wulfing von Schleinitz, "If you must be discreet about it ..." *Ubyssey*, 8 October 1965, 9.

56 "Universities check population growth," *Ubyssey*, 6 March 1962, 4.

57 Mike Grenby, "Alcock says: World problems our challenge," *Ubyssey*, 13 February 1962, 5.

58 "Dr. Macdonald enumerates ... grave responsibilities: Man faces war, poverty, population explosion," *Ubyssey*, 2 November 1962, 2.

59 Paul R. Ehrlich, *The Population Bomb* (New York: Balantine Books, 1968).

60 Massimo Verdicchio, "Motherly Love: Why use the pill? Try older women," *Ubyssey*, 8 October 1965.

61 "Dissent: Sex laid low," letter to the editor, *Ubyssey*, 15 October 1965, 13.

62 Jack Ornstein, "Let's take the hex off sex," *Ubyssey*, 17 January 1964, 4.

63 Stan Dosman, "Immature emotion," *Ubyssey*, 24 January 1964, 4.

64 Ian Cameron, "New group bucks birth control ban," *Ubyssey*, 8 January 1965, 1.

65 Don Hull, "Control clause deleted," *Ubyssey*, 19 January 1965, 3.

66 Lewis Barbato, "Study of the Prescription and Dispensing of Contraceptive Medications at Institutions of Higher Education," *Journal of the American College Health Association* 19, 5 (June 1971): 303-6.

67 Elsie R. Carrington, "Menstrual Problems in College Women," *Journal of the American College Health Association* 15 (May 1967): 35-41 at 35, 41.

68 Barbato, "Study of the Prescription," 303-6.

69 See also Christabelle Sethna, "The University of Toronto Health Service, Oral Contraception and Student Demand for Birth Control, 1960-1970," *Historical Studies in Education/ Revue d'histoire de l'éducation* 17, 2 (2005): 265-92.

70 Ann Ratel, "Un-Ortho-Dox: Our bachelor girl perforates leaky Wesbrook pill policy," *Ubyssey*, 30 September 1965, 1.

71 George Reamsbottom, "That 'Ol Control: Some pills please," *Ubyssey*, 5 October 1965, 4; "Comment: Readers speak out on Ubyssey's Wesbrook birth control story," *Ubyssey*, 8 October 1965, 13.

72 "Hender backs plans for a birth-test ban," *Ubyssey*, 26 November 1965, 2.

73 Sue Granby, "Yes, SEX is for the single girl," *Ubyssey*, 3 December 1956, 2.

74 T.M. Bailey, *For the Public Good: A History of the Birth Control Clinic and the Planned Parenthood Society of Hamilton, Ontario, Canada* (Hamilton: Planned Parenthood Society, 1974).

75 Kathleen Belanger and Eleanor J. Bradley, "Two Groups of University Student Women: Sexual Activity and the Use of Contraception," *Journal of the American College Health Association* 19, 5 (June 1971): 307-12 at 311. A similar pattern was observed at the Scarborough Family Planning Clinic; see Marion G. Powell, "Changing Profile of a Family Planning Clinic," in Ben Schlesinger, ed., *Family Planning in Canada: A Source Book* (Toronto: University of Toronto Press, 1974), 196-98.

76 "Public Forum," *Ubyssey*, 20 March 1964, 10.

77 Staff writer, "The double standard must be exposed," *Ubyssey,* 7 February 1963, 2.
78 For example, see Paula Giddings, *When and Where I Enter: The Impact of Black Women on Race and Sex in America* (1984; reprint, New York: Bantam Books, 1988), 308. See also Jerry Farber, *The Student As Nigger* (New York: Contact Books, 1969).
79 See "Canadaghetto" and "Fools," letters to the editor, *Ubyssey,* 19 September 1968, 4.
80 "'Abortions should be legalized,'" *Ubyssey,* 8 October 1964, 2.
81 Wulfing von Schleinitz, "Abortions: The woman's prerogative," *Ubyssey,* 15 October 1965, 3.
82 John Kelsey, "Women, I hate [wedding] 'em," *Ubyssey,* 7 January 1966, 11.
83 Philip Wylie, *Generation of Vipers* (New York: Rinehart and Co., Inc., 1946).
84 Jennifer Terry, *An American Obsession: Science, Medicine, and Homosexuality in Modern Society* (Chicago and London: University of Chicago Press, 1999), 316.
85 Clark, ed., *Back Issues,* 56-57.
86 Al-Mujahid, "Nation-rape," letter to the editor, *Ubyssey,* 21 November 1969, 4.
87 Kelsey, "Women," 11.
88 "Scapegoat," letter to the editor, *Ubyssey,* 20 January 1966, 3.
89 "Communist," letter to the editor, *Ubyssey,* 11 January 1966, 5.
90 Wulfing von Schleinitz, "Sex," letter to the editor, *Ubyssey,* 11 January 1966, 5.
91 Alison Prentice et al., *Canadian Women: A History* (Toronto: Harcourt Brace Jovanovich, 1988), 343-49, 353.
92 "Garbage," *Ubyssey,* letter to the editor, 19 September 1968, 4.
93 Daniel E. Meakes, "Gross out," letter to the editor, *Ubyssey,* 30 September 1969, 4.
94 See editor's note on the death of Mary Christmas and the birth of Hippie New Year, *Ubyssey,* 29 November 1968, 4.
95 "Fort girls want better protection," *Ubyssey,* 20 September 1963, 1.
96 See photo and caption, *Ubyssey,* 9 September 1969, 1.
97 Ruth Dworkin, "Women: Why are they inferior?" *Ubyssey,* 19 September 1968, 4.
98 Victoria Smith and Judy Fitzgerald, "The Woman Market," *Ubyssey,* 18 November 1969, 5-7.
99 "Girl Power," advertisement, *Ubyssey,* 18 November 1969, 6.
100 Karen Atrens, "Shackles," letter to the editor, *Ubyssey,* 28 November 1969, 4.
101 Terry Atkinson, "Women," letter to the editor, *Ubyssey,* 21 November 1969, 4.
102 D. McCrimmon, "More Women," letter to the editor, *Ubyssey,* 21 November 1969, 4-5.
103 See editor's note, *Ubyssey,* 28 November 1969, 4.
104 Roon, "Films and where to avoid them," *Ubyssey,* 28 November 1969, PF5.
105 See the following articles that appeared in the *Ubyssey,* 28 November 1969: "Students hit war in Biafra," 8; John Lingley, "Demonstration to be held in support of grape strike," 3; John Ferguson and Barry Lipton, "Racism in Alberta: One lump or two?" 10-11; and Krista Emmott, "Women persecuted by lower job positions," 27.
106 Janine Brodie, Shelley A.M. Gavigan, and Jane Jenson, *The Politics of Abortion* (Toronto: Oxford University Press, 1992), 20-21.
107 Christabelle Sethna, "The Evolution of the *Birth Control Handbook:* From Student Peer Education Manual to Feminist Self-Empowerment Text, 1968-1975," *Canadian Bulletin of Medical History/Bulletin canadien d'histoire de la médecine* 23, 1 (2006): 89-118.
108 Staff writer, "Anti Preg Mag," *Ubyssey,* 12 September 1969, 7.
109 Murray Kennedy, "Overcrowding? Why not try birth control information?" *Ubyssey,* 12 September 1969, 13.
110 Maurice Bridge, "Flower in a concrete plant," *Ubyssey,* 19 September 1969, 2.
111 "Praise, at last," editorial, *Ubyssey,* 30 September 1969, 4; "SUB washrooms modernized: prophylactic popularity rises," *Ubyssey,* 7 October 1969, 6.
112 Sibylle Klein, "Questionnaire shows clinic wanted," *Ubyssey,* 6 February 1970, 5.
113 Jan Davies, "Contraception controversy," *Ubyssey,* 6 February 1970, 5.
114 "Two days of abortion clinics," *Ubyssey,* 27 October 1970, 5; "Abortion teach-in," *Ubyssey,* 13 November 1970, 1; "Teach-in tells the facts of abortion," *Ubyssey,* 17 November 1970, 2.
115 Sandy Kass, "Popping the Pill is the answer," *Ubyssey,* 20 November 1970, 16.
116 Sandy Kass, "Abortion advice available through newly created clinic," *Ubyssey,* 9 January 1970, 7.

117 "Speak Easy," column, *Ubyssey,* 6 February 1970, 2, 23 October 1970, 21, and 30 October 1970, 8.
118 "AMS Charter Flights," advertisement, *Ubyssey,* 10 October 1969, 20. See also the advertisements "Your Questions on Abortion" and "Abortion Counsel, Referral and Assistance," *Ubyssey,* 24 November 1970, 8, 9.
119 Prentice et al., *Canadian Women,* 354.
120 Vicki Goodman, "A Valentine's Day protest for control of our bodies," *Ubyssey,* 13 February 1970, 2.
121 Ellen Woodsworth, "Why such overt contempt for women?" *Ubyssey,* 6 February 1970, 3.
122 William H. Masters and Virginia E. Johnson, *Human Sexual Response* (Boston: Little, Brown, 1966).
123 Susan Lydon, "Orgasm: Dispelling some repressive myths," *Ubyssey,* 20 March 1970, 7.
124 Annette Koedt, "The Myth of the Vaginal Orgasm," in *Notes from the Second Year: Women's Liberation – Major Writings of the Radical Feminists* (New York: Radical Feminism, 1970), 37-41.

13
Law versus Medicine: The Debate over Drug Use in the 1960s
Marcel Martel

In the 1960s Canadians had conflicting views about recreational marijuana use. For some, it was a harmless drug and its legalization was imperative. Marijuana was "no more a physical or mental danger to its user than orange juice is to the women who just can't let a morning escape without the habitual early morning glass of juice."[1] For others, marijuana was a threat to user health and social values. Consequently, repression should be maintained and perhaps strengthened. "Mothers and fathers can see their children growing long hair and dressing in unorthodox fashions. [The] knowledge that marijuana and other drugs are in common use amongst hippies causes alarm ... They are against hippies, against drugs and want the police to do something about both."[2]

The issue of drug use, like those of alcohol consumption, prostitution, exotic dancing, sexual behaviour, and gambling, constitutes an excellent example of what Meier calls "morality policies and politics."[3] To summarize Meier's thesis, some social actors construct these social realities as dangerous behaviours and activities. They do so because they are anxious to impose their moral judgment and to control individual behaviour. These actors wish that their moral judgment, which often condemns these activities, would lead to their ban or, at the very least, to a coercive regulation. To quote Hunt, they are eager to influence "the conduct of human agents" so that individual behaviours suit their values and convictions.[4] In certain circumstances, these social actors do not hesitate to put pressure on the state so that it legislates in a way favourable to their moral judgment.[5] In her study of the reformist movement at the beginning of the twentieth century, Valverde approaches the domain of morality policies. She looks at the role of interest groups and their efforts to fight vice and impose virtue. By analyzing issues such as alcohol use, prostitution, immigration, and urbanization, she demonstrates that "the state has no monopoly on moral regulation, and private organizations – notably, the medical and legal professions and the philanthropic groups – have exercised crucial leadership in the regulatory field."[6]

In the context of recreational drug use and the counterculture movement of the 1960s, individuals and social groups, such as police forces, parents' associations, certain religious organizations, and physicians, wanted to modify the behaviour of recreational marijuana users. This behaviour was not constructed as a vice per se but as a bad habit to be discouraged in order to prevent a breakdown of social order. However, the religious tone that had been part of the moral reform movement at the beginning of the century was absent. By condemning illegal drug use, opponents did not try to achieve "the regeneration of the individual through personal purity," as did moral reformers at the beginning of the twentieth century.[7] They justified their opposition by the fact that they defined marijuana use as a harmful and wrongful activity. Recreational marijuana use was a condemnable means to escape stress and other difficulties associated with daily life in a postwar society. Opponents pressed the federal government to refrain from softening its marijuana legislation, as was being suggested at the time, because they feared that this would trigger change to the overall antidrug strategy, which was based on repression.

Meier argues that morality policies are very popular because they appeal to a large segment of public opinion. However, they are inefficient since they fail to change the individual behaviour that they target. Furthermore, the state apparatus has difficulties with enforcement. For example, the attempt to drastically reduce alcohol consumption through prohibition in the early 1900s revealed the limitations of state intervention and proved that prohibition was an inefficient regulatory policy.[8]

The drug issue constitutes another example of morality politics that led to the implementation of morality policies. The legal framework that regulates drug use in Canada was put in place at the beginning of the twentieth century. The federal government criminalized certain drugs, such as opium in 1908 and marijuana in 1923. The possession, cultivation, and trafficking of these two substances were designated criminal offences.[9] During the 1960s drug classification became a topic of discussion in the public domain. Drug use reemerged as an issue partially because it was a manifestation of the counterculture, a highly visible socio-cultural movement that challenged mainstream values. At the same time, interest groups intervened in the debate over recreational marijuana use because they wanted to impose their notion of what constituted illegitimate drug use and proper social behaviour, and they expected that their views would prevail.

The drug issue is an excellent case with which to study the competing and conflicting agendas of social actors and their strategies to shape the public debate. In the context of the drug debate in the 1960s, I argue that two interest groups, law enforcement agencies and the medical community, came to dominate the debate over how the state should handle the drug issue. Had the law proven itself the best means by which to reduce drug supply and deter individuals from recreational drug use? Or should health and educational programs and strategies be introduced to reduce drug demand by treating those who had developed an addiction and by educating others about their drug use? The challenge for these two groups was to convince the federal government of the merits of their respective approaches. However, physicians undermined their own lobby effort. They were divided over which position to adopt and thus over which message to convey both to the population at large and to politicians in particular; there was no consensus on the best course of action to pursue. Capitalizing on these divisions, law enforcement officers won the battle over the orientation and goals of public drug policy.

The Medical Community: Offering a Health Approach in the Handling of the Recreational Drug Issue

Members of the medical community intervened in the drug debate in the 1960s. Many of them expressed their views through their professional organization, the Canadian Medical Association (CMA), a federation of provincial medical associations created in 1867. By working within their provincial and national organizations, physicians gave more weight to their intervention, but also they were aware that the CMA had relatively easy access to provincial and federal politicians and bureaucrats, something that was often denied to individual physicians.

During the 1960s several issues compelled the CMA to act while offering it the opportunity to measure its influence in shaping public policy. For instance, the federal government launched a new series of social-welfare policies during the decade, including Medicare. This triggered a conflict with physicians. The debate focused on access to health services, regardless of the individual's capacity to pay, and on physicians' reluctance to see their practice restricted by state intervention.[10]

Access to abortion was another debate that mobilized individuals and physicians. This debate was framed in terms of the rights of women to a free abortion and the legal protection required by physicians who performed them. In her account of the women's movement, Alison Prentice mentions that the 1960s offered women an opportunity to gain control over their own bodies. In this context, gaining control meant greater autonomy at the expense of religious and other interest groups that had successfully convinced the state to enforce their moral views over the termination of pregnancies. In the battle over free access to abortion, women's groups had quarrelled with the medical profession. The abortion issue led physicians to promote change that would transfer the power of regulation from the state to the medical profession since its members defined the termination of a pregnancy as a medical act and therefore under the control of the medical profession.[11]

At the same time, the CMA and health professionals in general came under suspicion for how they assessed health risks associated with drug use. At the beginning of the 1960s, news reports alerted the public about the dangers of thalidomide. The birth of infants with missing limbs "worked powerfully on the popular imagination,"[12] sparked a debate, and made the public aware that this drug was not as safe as indicated by physicians and other health officials. Another example was lysergic acid diethylamide (LSD), used for recreational purposes. News reports linked its use to suicide and other tragic experiences and triggered a public fear. As stated by Dyck, "the recreational use of psychedelic drugs and the crisis created by the thalidomide tragedy seemed to suggest that the medical community did not have sufficient knowledge of, or control over, its drugs."[13]

It was in this context that the CMA intervened on the drug issue. The CMA asked its Council on Community Health Care to formulate its position based on an assessment of medical, social, and legal implications of the illegal drug issue. In 1969 the council asked the Subcommittee on the Misuse of Drugs to prepare a report. Dr. Lionel Solursh, a psychiatrist at Toronto Western Hospital and a psychiatry professor at the University of Toronto, chaired the subcommittee. Due to his research on LSD, Solursh was a recognized authority on drug use and abuse. He believed that changes were required for the classification of drugs and particularly for marijuana. Due to the unique context of the counterculture movement and youth rebellion, Solursh adopted a very liberal approach. He expressed his views in a personal brief to the Commission of Inquiry on the Non-Medical Use of Drugs, known as the Le Dain Commission.

The Le Dain Commission was appointed by the federal government in May 1969 and chaired by Gerald Le Dain. The commissioners were Heinz E. Lehmann, Ian Lachlan Campbell, J. Peter Stein, and Marie-Andrée Bertrand, the French-speaking representative. With the commission, the federal government enlarged the debate, which became a public forum for any concerned citizen or interest group to express a view on the issue. However, the commission was a device to delay any legislative action on the issue of the legalization or decriminalization of marijuana, as evidenced by the federal government's statement that it had to wait until the submission of the commission's final report before deciding on a course of action.

In his submission to the Le Dain Commission, Solursh argued that marijuana use was not as dangerous as many believed. He asserted that it was a matter of frequency, dosage, environment, and the users' mental and physical health. He called on the federal government to make a courageous political gesture by legalizing the possession of marijuana for anyone over twenty-one. However, his solution was proposed as an experiment, with a two-year

Members of the Le Dain Commission at the University of Toronto for a
public hearing, 20 October 1969.
York University, Clara Thomas Archives and Special Collections, Toronto Telegram fonds, image no. 724

period, and Solursh invited the Le Dain Commission to make a recommendation on the idea. Solursh's audacious proposal was also justified by the
consequences of the criminalization of marijuana. Up until 1969 penalties
for possession of marijuana included a jail term of up to seven years, as
stipulated by the Narcotic Control Act. Furthermore, Solursh pleaded for
legalization as a reaction to law enforcement methods. Youth were targeted
and often ended up with a permanent criminal record that could handicap
their future. Because of the law and the way it was enforced, Solursh judged
that the time had come to dramatically change the legal status of marijuana.[14]

The Le Dain Commission and the Ministry of National Health and Welfare did not adopt Solursh's recommendation. However, the Toronto psychiatrist used his position as chair of the subcommittee to launch a
conceptual revolution over the drug issue that he hoped would lead to a
successful liberalization of public drug policy.

The subcommittee had an agenda: to propose a health approach as an
alternative to the prohibition and criminalization of drug use. The new
approach was based on two key concepts: prevention and education. These
concepts were linked to a new definition of what constituted drug abuse.
The term "abuse" would be replaced by "misuse." "The term 'abuse,'" wrote
Dr. Unwin, a member of the subcommittee, "implies value judgments which
at the present time are contentious, especially if 'abuse' is held to mean any
drug use without medical supervision."[15] The proposed definition of "misuse" was "the use of a substance beyond the generally accepted limits of

medical therapy or the limitations imposed by current laws."[16] With adoption of the term "misuse," it became necessary to promote the idea that all drugs, regardless of their legal classification, had the potential to be misused, sometimes even when they were prescribed by the medical profession. But when the officials of the CMA debated the subcommittee's report, they rejected it. Instead, they settled for a restrictive definition of "drug abuse," applying the term to the use of any substance without proper medical supervision. Regarding possible abuse of prescription drugs, the CMA stated that health professionals could best police themselves.[17]

Besides its attempt to redefine the notion of drug abuse, the subcommittee of the Council on Community Health Care dealt with the divisive issue of recreational marijuana use. Its members were aware that this substance was more than a simple drug. Within the counterculture movement, marijuana had acquired political and symbolic meanings. Many people used marijuana in order to promote new cultural values, lifestyles, and philosophies. For others, smoking marijuana was a rebellious gesture against a society that was seen as hypocritical in how it managed drug use. Users questioned the legal classification of drugs by pointing out that certain drugs, such as alcohol, were legal. To them, alcohol was a good example of how hypocritical or inconsistent society was in its handling of drugs in general. Despite its health risks for users, alcohol was defined as a socially accepted drug – in contrast to marijuana, which was seen as dangerous for individuals and society because it affected personality and led to criminal behaviour. Here was proof that moral judgment shaped public policy on marijuana and that the time had come to put an end to it.

The report submitted to the CMA tried to balance scientific knowledge with the political and legal consequences of the criminalization of marijuana. The authors of the document acknowledged that there were still many unknowns about the health consequences of marijuana use, although the dose, frequency, and characteristics (gender, age, physical and mental health) of users had to be taken into consideration. However, it was impossible to formulate a definitive opinion since studies that had been done at the time were incomplete or biased and since most of them had not involved human beings.[18] By acknowledging these unknowns, the authors of the report tried to distinguish between the limits of current knowledge and giving credibility to possible change, conscious that marijuana had triggered a debate that had produced numerous emotional and sensational statements. The report's authors argued that marijuana was not as dangerous as some studies claimed. This was a controversial statement, and members of the subcommittee backed up their report by referring to studies such as the 1968 report of the British Advisory Committee on Drug Dependence. Its authors stated that marijuana, if used moderately, did not have dangerous health consequences.[19]

The report rejected legalization but advocated a softening of the penalties associated with marijuana. The time had come to make the punishment fit the crime, especially in cases of possession for personal use. If this was not enough to persuade CMA members and officials, the report stated that marijuana was not a narcotic and that it should be transferred from the Narcotic Control Act to the Food and Drugs Act – a possible move discussed by National Health and Welfare bureaucrats at the time. Under this scenario, penalties for marijuana offences would be lowered.

CMA officials adopted the recommendation to transfer marijuana to the Food and Drugs Act.[20] However, this gave rise to further disagreement within the CMA. Many feared that the CMA was about to justify greater use of marijuana despite its knowledge that marijuana was not a harmless drug. When CMA members debated the issue during annual meetings, their divisions became public.

At the 1971 General Council, members approved a proposal arguing that "simple possession of any psychoactive drug should not be punishable by [a] jail sentence."[21] Capitalizing on this resolution, the Subcommittee on the Non-Medical Use of Drugs of the Council on Community Health Care submitted its resolution on recreational marijuana use at the 1972 General Council. It recommended the liberalization of the repressive approach. CMA members, however, decided otherwise.

The members preferred the resolution presented by psychiatrist Conrad J. Schwarz, chairman of the British Columbia Medical Association's Committee on [the] Non-Medical Use of Drugs and board member of the Narcotic Addiction Foundation of British Columbia. The resolution asked members of the medical profession to discourage marijuana use because of its dangers.[22]

At the 1974 General Council, members once again debated the marijuana issue. They agreed that marijuana should continue to "be regarded as an unlawful act but that it not be classified as a criminal offence in the normal usage of that term."[23]

In addition to debates within the CMA, divisions among physicians and other health professionals became public during the hearings of the Le Dain Commission. In their Interim Report, released in 1970, commissioners reproduced a series of letters from individuals that illustrated the divisions in society over the marijuana issue. Two of the letters came from health professionals, and both advocated some change to the legal status of the drug.

A psychiatric nurse who had extensive experience with drug addicts argued that marijuana was not dangerous except "in the hands of irresponsible and immature adolescents and adults for whom the abuse of this substance is an escape from the responsibilities and realities of life to the degree that it interferes with their ability to function and produce effectively." Consequently, changes were required to the Narcotic Control Act since jail terms would not discourage drug use. In fact, sending a young person to jail constituted a greater crime than the crime itself. "To expose such a youngster to hard-core addicts, thieves, prostitutes and the lot is a damaging and very disillusioning traumatic experience from which it would take a great deal of personal strength to recover intact."[24]

In another letter, a student nurse shared similar concern about the criminalization of marijuana. In an attempt to justify a softening of the federal drug legislation, the student indicated a list of positive outcomes for anyone who smoked marijuana. "I found it made contemplation, constructive introspection, the fulfilling of creative potential ... and appreciation of subtleties in music and art much easier due to heightened perceptions and increased sensitivity." The student even suggested that the insights gained by using marijuana helped one "to appreciate more freely the wonder of the universe and the sacredness of life."[25]

However, not everyone shared this positive assessment. Other health professionals and organizations expressed opposite views, warning the Le Dain Commission that it should take into consideration studies that pointed to the mental, psychological, and other health dangers of marijuana. Among the opponents to legalization and decriminalization was Conrad Schwarz, who made his views known in order to undermine the pro-marijuana lobby within the CMA and in the public domain. He participated in conferences such as the 1968 Loyola Conference on Student Use and Abuse of Drugs and appeared before the Le Dain Commission. In the case of the commission, he submitted his comments on various commission reports. His opposition was based on the assertion that marijuana was a dangerous drug with unknown health effects. Therefore, physicians had the obligation to discourage its use and the state should maintain its repression.[26]

Schwarz worked within the British Columbia Medical Association in order to give more weight to his antimarijuana campaign. In June 1974 the association supported the views of its Drug Habituation Committee, chaired by Schwarz, and criticized the content of the final report of the Le Dain Commission. It deplored that the commission did not "update its comments on marijuana in the light of recent research that proves the dangers of this drug."[27]

The debate over recreational drug use proved that reaching a consensus on marijuana, since this drug dominated public debate, was a difficult process. The divisions within the CMA became public, and some physicians worked outside of the CMA to make their point of view known and to influence decision makers. These divisions encouraged the pro-marijuana groups since they contributed to undermining the image of medical science. They also prompted law enforcement agencies to intervene.

Law Enforcement Agencies: Preserving the Status Quo
In the 1960s the Narcotic Control Act and the Food and Drugs Act were the legislation that constituted the core of Canadian public policy on drugs.

Since 1923 marijuana has been an illegal substance in Canada. From 1961 it was classified under the Narcotic Control Act, which, among other things, increased legal penalties for possession, trafficking, exportation, importation, and cultivation while removing the minimum penalties for most offences. Henceforth, anyone charged with possession of marijuana could face a maximum penalty of seven years in jail. Law enforcement was the responsibility of the Royal Canadian Mounted Police (RCMP), except in major urban centres such as Toronto and Vancouver, where municipal forces worked with the federal agency.

The RCMP's influence was substantial because of its expertise in drug-related law enforcement. It was the RCMP, rather than the Food and Drug Directorate of the Ministry of National Health and Welfare, that was responsible for controlling the illicit traffic of narcotics and other illegal drugs. Moreover, the RCMP was a member of the International Criminal Police Organization (Interpol).

Law enforcement agencies' understanding of the drug issue was based on data collected by the RCMP on offences committed under the Narcotic Control Act and the Food and Drugs Act. In 1962-63, 20 Canadians were charged under the Narcotic Control Act for marijuana offences such as possession, possession for trafficking, trafficking, cultivation, and importation/exportation. Only in 1965-66 did the number of people charged under the Narcotic Control Act for marijuana offences begin to increase significantly. That year 162 persons were charged, 398 the following year, and 1,678 in 1967-68. In its annual reports, the RCMP provided a regional breakdown. Most of the individuals charged were in the southwest Ontario division, which included Toronto. In 1965-66, 46 percent of those charged were from this division, and this region continued to occupy first place in the following years. Behind southwest Ontario, British Columbia and Quebec came second and third respectively. Besides individuals charged, the RCMP compiled data on narcotic drug seizures. Until 1966 heroin was the major concern and the main focus of law enforcement officers. In 1967-68 the RCMP seized 53.5 kilograms of marijuana.[28] It concluded that recreational marijuana use had become a major problem, if not an epidemic, in the country.

Since the state chose repression in order to affect drug demand and supply, the RCMP used these data to justify its law enforcement work and pleaded for more financial and human resources to fulfil its mandate. This plea encountered strong criticism from the public, especially from young people. Although the RCMP never publicized any data about the number of people charged and convicted based on age and gender, young people argued that they were being targeted by law enforcement officers. Comments made by RCMP officers and other police officers from municipal forces were used by young people to prove their case. For instance, an officer with the Vancouver Police Force said that although he had no problem with young people

Police officers posing before several bags containing drugs, 22 November 1968.
York University, Clara Thomas Archives and Special Collections, Toronto Telegram fonds, image no. 718

and hippies, they disturbed him when "they sprawl all over public lawns, wrecking the grass and making suggestive remarks to old ladies." Because these behaviours were judged unacceptable, hippies should not complain about being harassed by police officers. On the contrary, they constituted a public nuisance and should face the consequences of their behaviour.[29]

Law enforcement officers and the RCMP in particular felt uneasy about the counterculture and the flower-power revolution. Although some police officers stressed that they were dealing with a minority, others equated the counterculture with "an increase in lawlessness," "acts of senseless vandalism," "runaway youngsters," and the use of drugs.[30] The RCMP began to feel that it was under siege. Since illegal drug use was a victimless crime – most drug users did not represent a threat to anyone other than the individual in possession of the substance – the federal law enforcement agency was forced to collect information through the use of informers and undercover officers. These law enforcement practices, known as the "methodical suspicion" approach, soon came under fire. Through methodical suspicion, or the profiling of suspects, police targeted particular types of individuals in the enforcement of drug legislation.[31] Undercover activities in school and university premises and in areas where youth gathered, such as Gastown in Vancouver, Carré Saint-Louis in Montreal, and Yorkville in Toronto, became a matter of public concern. For instance, in November 1969 the *Winnipeg Tribune* reported that an undercover RCMP officer used "pot" and sold illegal drugs during his activities. The RCMP was quick to deny this by pointing out that it was an Edmonton City Police officer, not a member of its force.[32]

Given possible changes to public drug policies, the RCMP developed a strategy aimed at preserving the status quo. Its objectives were to maintain law enforcement and to prevent the decriminalization or legalization of marijuana. It was crucial that the RCMP build up the credibility of its position. Thus current practices were defended and were determined to be an appropriate means to reduce the overall supply of drugs. To back up this approach, the RCMP paid attention to interest groups, including the Commission of Inquiry on the Non-Medical Use of Drugs (the Le Dain Commission), which was in a position to shape public opinion and influence the choice that federal politicians would make once they received the commission's final report. As stated by the RCMP, its role was "to convince" the commission of its "point of view, but also to present to that Committee all the known facts relating to drug abuse and to offer them every assistance within our control."[33]

To make the preservation of the status quo a valid public policy, the RCMP publicized the dangers of marijuana and developed support outside law enforcement agencies, especially among the medical community. Since the medical community was divided, the RCMP was able to refer to studies that emphasized the health dangers of marijuana. It relied on provincial health organizations, such as the Narcotic Addiction Foundation of British Columbia, and on professionals who conducted research on marijuana use. For instance, the RCMP referred to Dr. Luis Souzo, who had concluded that marijuana use damaged chromosomes. It mentioned Dr. Constandinos J. Miras of the University of Athens, who had conducted research on regular marijuana use by long-time smokers and had concluded that there was "a clear connection between marijuana-induced brain damage and deranged behaviour." His research was also conducted on rats exposed to marijuana for a twelve-month period. "The injections were halted for three months and the rats were given sleeping pills. They slept longer periods than rats given similar pills [that] had not been exposed to marijuana." His conclusion was that "something had happened to their brains."[34] However, the RCMP played down that Canadian and international medical communities were divided on the health dangers of marijuana.

In its strategy to counteract those who pressed the federal government to amend its drug legislation, the RCMP emphasized the social dangers that accompanied marijuana use. Although its evidence was thin, it argued that marijuana was a stepping-stone drug that led inevitably to the use of hard drugs like heroin. The RCMP depicted drug culture as a grave danger to society and the pro-marijuana lobby as a moral and social threat. To substantiate the latter, the RCMP relied on its manpower. Law enforcement officers, undercover officers, and informers helped the RCMP to construct a specific profile of drug users.

The RCMP's construction of marijuana users targeted young people. This age group was singled out because it was imperative to discourage young people from consuming marijuana. The RCMP argued that if youth started using marijuana, they would inevitably become drug addicts and cause serious social problems. The RCMP targeted hippies since many young people embraced this new cultural phenomenon. For the RCMP, this iconic group of the counterculture movement constituted a threat, and it was crucial to undermine their image of innocence.

Since hippies were the target group, RCMP undercover officers were sent to observe and report on them. When public accounts were published, officers refrained from making any direct negative comments on hippies' values and lifestyle. However, in descriptions of their "physical" transformation in order to infiltrate the hippie community, RCMP officers expressed different views. In a case in Vancouver in October 1967, constable Brown "quickly sprouted whiskers which became a healthy beard in jig time." For his part, constable Cardinal's face "remained as smooth and hairless as a billiard ball, but his hair had grown to near shoulder length." Besides their physical transformation, they had to assimilate drug street jargon such as "speed," "narcs" (for drug-squad men), "fix," "score," and "hit."[35] Before entering Yorkville in 1968, Constables Frank Hummell and Jean-Yves Côté insisted on disguising themselves as the people who called themselves "disciples of love." Of course, long hair and a beard were prerequisites, but so too was clothing that the officers described as "the worst," taking for granted that hippies had no taste.[36] Both stories concluded that the undercover operations had been successful.

In their private reports, RCMP undercover officers displayed a strong personal animosity toward hippies. To some undercover officers in Calgary, hippies in general – their behaviour, clothing, and other attributes – were quite repulsive. They were described as "mainly filthy with no pride in their appearance," and their hair was "generally very long, dirty and untidy." In terms of living habits, the focus was on lack of cleanliness. Hippies "live in houses and apartments resembling 'pig pens' with an accumulation of garbage and rubble throughout. In one particular house there was a toilet which had overflowed and it appeared there had been no effort to rectify the situation." In terms of work habits and ethics, the officers said that "they think nothing of shop lifting, writing bad cheques and then turn around and beg money from the respectable citizens on the street." In terms of engagement with society, the officers found nothing positive to say: "These people have no desire to put forth any effort to better their education; however, some attend university to promote the use of drugs and nothing else. They do this to obtain government funds in the form of student loans." In the area of attitudes toward family and sex, the officers found that they believed "in free love and stress this as much as possible." In their conclusions, they

A celebration of love, life, and freedom in Toronto,
30 June 1968.
York University, Clara Thomas Archives and Special Collections, Toronto Telegram
fonds, image no. 734

emphasized that drugs defined hippies' way of life and limited their aspirations, contrary to accepted social values: "During the time we acted in an undercover capacity we knew no persons with an apparent scholastic potential who had discontinued their education after being initiated to the drug milieu."[37]

In the face of attempts by the Ministry of National Health and Welfare to win Cabinet ministers' support for its own proposal, the RCMP argued that legislative change had in fact already taken place. Indeed, the federal government had already done what many were asking it to do, which was the reduction of penalties for possession of marijuana. Starting in August 1969, the possibility of a fine rather than a jail term was introduced into the Narcotic Control Act. In 1969 and prior to the August amendment, about 74 percent of the 349 individuals convicted for possession of marijuana in Montreal, Toronto, and Vancouver had received a suspended sentence – evidence that the law was already lenient. As far as the RCMP was concerned, nothing more was required. Otherwise, the Narcotic Control Act would lose its deterrent effect.[38]

In the debate, the RCMP acted as an interest group and a social-control agent. Its views were supported outside law enforcement agencies and medical circles. Within the federal bureaucracy, the Ministry of Justice was considered an ally since it judged that law enforcement, as a method of control of drug supply, was at stake and should remain part of the public drug policy. Outside the state apparatus, some interest groups used RCMP data to support their opposition to the legalization of marijuana – for instance, the National Council of Women of Canada. In a brief prepared for the chair of the Senate committee that studied a bill softening marijuana-related penalties in 1974-75, the council opposed the legalization of marijuana because of "new scientific evidence," without being more specific, about the dangers of marijuana use. These dangers included the drug's tendency to cause "chromosome damage, disrupt cellular metabolism, cause impotence and other hormone disorders, damage the lungs and, most serious, cause potentially irreversible brain damage." The council used the RCMP's views in its plea for retaining a possession offence as a deterrent, concluding that "marijuana impairment is as hazardous as alcohol impairment when it comes to driving."[39]

Municipal councils adopted several of the arguments put forward by the RCMP. For instance, in 1970 several Ontario municipal councils warned the Le Dain Commission that they were opposed to the legalization of marijuana. The municipalities of Brockville, Preston, Sarnia, and Woodstock justified their stance by arguing that marijuana had no use in the treatment of illnesses and that its absorption could trigger serious mental, psychological, and physical health problems, such as "over-confidence, poor judgment, intoxication, hallucinations, and torpor (numbness and apathy) and without subsequent toxicity or 'hang-over' or positive detection, as is possible with alcohol intoxication." They concluded their opposition by embracing the view that marijuana was a stepping-stone drug since its users were tempted to try morphine and heroin.[40]

In 1972 several Ontario municipalities, responding favourably to an initiative by the County of Renfrew, pressed the federal government not to legalize "soft drugs" and suggested that a referendum be organized on the issue. Furthermore, the resolution invited the federal government to increase penalties for those found guilty of selling drugs and to make certain drugs, such as speed, illegal. It pressed governments to allocate more resources to addiction treatment and to better training of police forces. In June 1972 Toronto City Council lent its support to the resolution, except the parts concerning the call for a national referendum and more resources for treatment and training.[41]

Solving the Debate over Recreational Marijuana Use

The federal government took more than seven years to publicize its views through a piece of legislation introduced in the Senate in 1974. In 1968 the minister of national health and welfare, John Munro, hinted at the views of his department on the justification for change in the case of the offence of marijuana possession, especially when the criminal was a young individual. At the annual meeting of the Canadian Pharmaceutical Association, Munro argued that "the teenager, who tries pot at a Saturday night party because someone has some and passes it around and everyone else tries it, may be very foolish, but he isn't a criminal – at least not in the sense that I think of criminals."[42] Since he did not define this "foolish" act as a criminal one, change was required.

Was it possible that the government would favour legalization? Although the minister of national health and welfare mentioned this possibility if "a significant minority of the Canadian people smoke marijuana," it did not take long for Munro to discover that it was not the preferred option.[43] Legalization was unlikely because of strong opposition within the federal government. Also, Canada had signed the 1961 Single Convention on Narcotics. Because the Single Convention designated marijuana an illegal drug and Canada had agreed to design its drug policy accordingly, the options that the federal government could exercise in revising its drug policy were restricted.

Outside the state apparatus, Canadians rejected legalization, as revealed by public-opinion polls on drugs, even though only two were conducted between 1966 and 1975. In the April 1970 Gallup poll, Canadians were asked whether they favoured the legalization of marijuana. Of the respondents, 77% opposed it, a percentage similar (although a little lower, at 73%) to that found among those between the ages of 21 and 29. Five months later, Canadians surveyed by Gallup were divided over the issue of decreasing penalties, such as replacing jail terms with fines. Those Canadians in favour totalled 41%, and 45% were opposed. A significant cultural gap was noticed, with 50% of francophones, 38% of anglophones, and 35% of those categorized as "other" (the term was probably used to refer to people who spoke neither French nor English) approving this solution. There was also an age gap, with 51% of people aged 21 to 29, 39% of those aged 30 to 39, 35% of those aged 40 to 49, and 40% of those over 50 giving their approval.

John Munro and his officials supported the option of softening the penalties for marijuana offences. To enlarge the debate and build a consensus around this possibility, Munro convinced the Trudeau Cabinet to go ahead with the appointment of the Commission of Inquiry into the Non-Medical

Use of Drugs in 1969. It took five years for the commission to deliver its conclusions, which were not unanimous. When the federal government appointed the commission, it expected to receive a report paving the way to possible changes to its drug legislation. It got more than expected because the Le Dain Commission was unable to reach a strong consensus on the marijuana issue. The divisions that affected the medical profession over the issue were reflected in the Interim Report and the Report on Cannabis, released by the commission in 1970 and 1972 respectively. On health effects and how the state should handle the marijuana issue, commissioners disagreed. For Marie-Andrée Bertrand, legalizing the possession of marijuana was the best solution since criminalization caused more harm to users than the substance itself. For the majority of commissioners, as stated in the Cannabis Report, cannabis posed certain health dangers, such as its negative impact on the maturing process of youth and its role as a stepping stone to the use of other drugs. Under these circumstances, it was prudent to advocate moderate change to the law. Since it was crucial for the state to weigh the costs and benefits of its approach, law enforcement and repression did not seem appropriate, especially in the case of the crime of possession. A partial decriminalization was a more appropriate course of action, such as in the case of possession.[44] However, commissioners agreed on the need for information and education campaigns, based on facts instead of fear.[45]

When the federal government introduced Bill S-19 in November 1974, it made official its views on the marijuana debate. The option of legalization was categorically rejected. The federal government chose to transfer marijuana from the Narcotic Control Act to the Food and Drugs Act. The new classification of marijuana meant reduced penalties for the crime of possession. Fines, instead of jail terms, would be the punishment for first and second offences. However, the offender who could not pay the fine would be sent to jail.

The choice made by the federal government reflected divisions among interest groups and the influences of these groups. The RCMP and other supporters of the law enforcement approach won the debate; Bill S-19 never became law. However, changes took place in how law enforcement was implemented. The federal government allocated more resources to the RCMP, and the manpower dedicated to drug enforcement increased from 105 officers in 1968 to 256 in 1972. The Crown also had more flexibility in sentencing marijuana offenders in the case of possession since penalties were reduced.[46]

National Health and Welfare officials could not impose their solutions because their allies, notably the CMA and the medical community at large, were divided. Schwarz and others denounced the CMA's call for an amendment to Bill S-19 favourable to the decriminalization of marijuana.[47] This denunciation undermined the CMA's stand. However, this was not a total loss for the CMA since it could be credited for changes to the administration of public drug policy by the justice system. Controversy, division, and an unclear consensus meant that the political will disappeared, as did the window of opportunity that had opened in 1974, as other priorities took precedence.

Conclusion

In 1975, like today, marijuana was an illegal substance. Moral judgments about hippies and drugs came to prevail and prevented significant change. This meant that health arguments could not provoke an important shift in the objectives of public drug policy. In fact, divisions among health professionals undermined the efforts to change the objectives.

Although I have focused on only two interest groups, many other groups, such as university students, parents, social workers, lawyers, and pharmacists, intervened in the debate. This shows that morality politics had a great facility to mobilize social groups in the 1960s. That the discussion of the drug issue did not lead to fundamental changes demonstrates the point made by Meier that morality politics produce inefficient morality policies.

However, the drug issue was a complex one, with many other factors playing a part in the process of the revision of public policy. Good examples are the impact of mass media, relations between the provinces and the federal government, and the influential role of federal bureaucrats. The debate that took place in Canada affected other societies. It illustrated that other influences, such as the implications of the 1961 Single Convention on Narcotics, constrained Canada's ability to design its policy. This "international constitution" that governed the classification of drugs reflected the choice made by countries to prefer repression and control in handling drug use. This choice showed that internal debates had international consequences since it led some countries to carry onto the world stage various interest groups' views on drug use.

Acknowledgment
This chapter is part of a larger project on the marijuana debate in the 1960s in Canada, supported by a standard research grant from the Social Sciences and Humanities Research Council of Canada. I would like to thank Magda Fahrni and Robert Rutherdale, the editors of this volume, and the two anonymous reviewers for their useful comments and suggestions.

Notes
1 Brief to the Commission of Inquiry on the Non-Medical Use of Drugs by the University of British Columbia Law Students Association, 30 October 1969, Library and Archives Canada (LAC), RG 33/101, vol. 15, file 1710.
2 The Non-Medical Use of Drugs: A Report to the Commission of Inquiry prepared by the Vancouver City Policy Department, October 1969, LAC, RG 33/101, vol. 15, file 1702.
3 See Becki Ross, "Men Behind the Marquee: Greasing the Wheels of Vansterdam's Professional Striptease Scene, 1950-75," in this volume. Ross demonstrates that moral reformers

denounced strip-club businesses. The intervention of moral reformers and other groups in the debate illustrates that moral issues have the potential to mobilize large segments of society. K.J. Meier, *The Politics of Sin: Drugs, Alcohol, and Public Policy* (Armonk, NY: M.E. Sharpe, 1994), 3.

4 A. Hunt, *Governing Morals: A Social History of Moral Regulation* (Cambridge, Cambridge University Press, 1999), 4.

5 Meier, *Politics of Sin,* 3-19.

6 M. Valverde, *The Age of Light, Soap, and Water: Moral Reform in English Canada, 1885-1925* (Toronto: McClelland and Stewart, 1991), 165.

7 Ibid., 44.

8 See C. Heron, *Booze: A Distilled History* (Toronto: Between the Lines, 2003).

9 L. Beauchamp, *Les drogues: Les coûts cachés de la prohibition* (Montreal: Lanctot Éditeur, 2003); N. Boyd, "The Origins of Canadian Narcotics Legislation: The Process of Criminalization in Historical Context," *Dalhousie Law Journal* 8, 1 (1984): 102-36; D.J. Malleck, "'Its Baneful Influences Are Too Well Known': Debates over Drug Use in Canada, 1867-1908," *Canadian Bulletin of Medical History* 14 (1997): 263-88.

10 For a history of the Canadian Medical Association that gives a broad description of the context of the 1960s, see J.S. Bennett, *History of the Canadian Medical Association, 1954-94* (Ottawa: Canadian Medical Association/Association médicale canadienne, 1996).

11 A. Prentice et al., *Canadian Women: A History* (Toronto: Harcourt Brace, 1996); R. Tatalovich, *The Politics of Abortion in the United States and Canada: A Comparative Study* (Armonk, NY: M.E. Sharpe, 1997).

12 B. Clow, "'An Illness of Nine Months' Duration': Pregnancy and Thalidomide Use in Canada and the United States," in G. Feldberg, M. Ladd-Taylor, A. Li, and K. McPherson, eds., *Women, Health and Nation: Canada and the United States since 1945* (Montreal and Kingston: McGill-Queen's University Press, 2003), 47.

13 E. Dyck, "Psychedelic Psychiatry: LSD and Post-World War II Medical Experimentation in Canada" (PhD thesis, McMaster University, 2005), 228.

14 Submission by Dr. Lionel Solursh, Toronto Western Hospital, 7 November 1969, LAC, RG 33/101, vol. 16, file 1735.

15 J.R. Unwin, *Review and Position Paper Re Non-Medical Use of Drugs with Particular Reference to Youth* (N.p.: CMA Council on Community Heath Care Special Committee on Drug Misuse, 1969), 4.

16 Ibid., 5.

17 Interim Brief, submitted by the CMA to the Le Dain Commission, 6 November 1969, LAC, RG 33/101, vol. 16, file 1851.

18 Unwin, *Review and Position Paper,* 43.

19 Ibid., 56.

20 Ibid.

21 Canadian Medical Association, Proceedings of General Council, 1971, 67.

22 Ibid., 1972, 71-72.

23 ibid., 1974, 137.

24 Commission of Inquiry Into the Non-Medical Use of Drugs, *Interim Report* (Ottawa: Information Canada, 1970), Appendix B, 9.

25 Ibid., Appendix B, 46, 47.

26 A Critique of the Interim Report of the Le Dain Commission by Conrad J. Schwarz, 30 June 1970, LAC, RG 33/101, vol. 13, file 1536.

27 *The Journal,* Addiction Research Foundation of Ontario newspaper, 1 June 1974, 2.

28 RCMP, Report of the Royal Canadian Mounted Police Fiscal Year Ended 31 March 1968, 20, 22.

29 D. Marshall, "The Cop and the Hippie: Arms and the Man," *Maclean's,* July 1968, 64.

30 E.W. White, "Youth in Action Days," *RCMP Quarterly* 34, 4 (April 1969): 49; P.J. Winship, "The Problems of Youth Are the Problems of the Police," *RCMP Quarterly* 35, 1 (July 1969): 10-20.

31 In her chapter on striptease in this volume, Ross, "Men Behind the Marquee," provides another example of "methodical suspicion." Nightclubs in Vancouver's low-income and reputedly seedy East End were targeted by police.

32 Letter to Gerald Le Dain, Chairman of the Commission of Inquiry Into the Non-Medical Use of Drugs, from J.R.R. Carriere, Deputy Commissioner (Criminal Operations), RCMP, 9 December 1969, LAC, RG33/101, vol. 9, file 1.

33 Memorandum to the Deputy Commissioner OPS from the DCI, 20 August 1969, LAC, RG 18, vol. 4831, file GC 310-10 (1969), part 1.

34 Memorandum to the Deputy Commissioner OPS from the DCI, 20 August 1969; Memorandum to the OIC CIB Attn: Insp. Macauley, 6 August 1969, LAC, RG 18, vol. 4831, dossier GC 310-10 (1969), part 1.

35 F.G. Kilner, "Undercover Operation," *RCMP Quarterly* 34, 3 (January 1969): 6.

36 J.C. Pinet, "A Trip to Hippyville," *RCMP Quarterly* 35, 3 (January 1970): 41. In his study of the FBI and the New Left in the US, Davis mentions that FBI undercover agents insisted in their reports about New Left activists on "neglect of personal cleanliness, use of obscenities ... publicized sexual promiscuity." These reports reflected the views of J. Edgar Hoover, who insisted in a May 1968 memo that "every avenue of possible embarrassment must be vigorously and enthusiastically explored." This emphasis on physical characteristics in order to undermine the New Left movement reflects similar tactics by the RCMP toward hippies. See J.K. Davis, *Assault on the Left: The FBI and the Sixties Antiwar Movement* (Westport, CT: Praeger, 1997), 46-47.

37 Report from D.B. Meggison, Calgary Drug Section and A.J. Sismey, Calgary Drug Section, 24 October 1969, LAC, RG 18, vol. 4831, dossier GC 310-10 (1969), part 1.

38 Memorandum to the Deputy Comm's (OPS) from the DCI, subject: Le Dain Commission, 20 October 1969, LAC, RG 18, vol. 4831, file GC 310-10 (1969), part 1; Letter from J.R.R. Carriere, A/Comm's., Director, Criminal Investigation, to James J. Moore, Executive Secretary, Le Dain Commission, 3 November 1969, LAC, RG 18, vol. 4831, file GC 310-10 (1970), part 2; Comments by NH&W Working Party on Interim Report of the Le Dain Commission, n.d., LAC, RG 29, vol. 1540, file 1003-1-1-2, part 1.

39 The National Council of Women of Canada, March 1975, LAC, MG 32 C-55, vol. 5, file: Drugs Correspondence from Ontario.

40 Letter from J. McGinnis, Corporation of the City of Woodstock, to Gerald Le Dain, 5 June 1970, LAC, R 923, vol. 12, file 4.

41 City of Toronto Executive Committee Report No. 25, City Council Minutes, Toronto, 1972, vol. 2, 10 May 1972 to 27 September 1972, 1888-93.

42 Speech by John Munro, Minister of National Health and Welfare, to Canadian Pharmaceutical Association Annual Convention, Regina, 19 August 1968, Centre for Addiction and Mental Health Archives, Addiction Research Foundation Collection, box 63-25, file: John Munro.

43 *Toronto Star,* 29 January 1970, 1.

44 Commission of Inquiry into the Non-Medical Use of Drugs, *Cannabis Report* (Ottawa: Information Canada, 1972).

45 Commission of Inquiry into the Non-Medical Use of Drugs, *Interim Report,* 189, 467, 537.

46 Summary of Measures to Control the Heroin Abuse Problem, by J.A. Hunter, January 1972, LAC, RG 29, vol. 1549, file 1006-5-1, part 4.

47 *The Journal,* Addiction Research Foundation of Ontario newspaper, 1 March 1975, 1, 4.

Contributors

Dimitry Anastakis teaches history at Trent University, in Peterborough, Ontario. His primary research examines post-Second World War Canadian politics, trade, and economic policy, particularly Canada's role in the North American auto industry. He is the author of *Auto Pact: Creating a Borderless North American Auto Industry, 1960-1971* (2005).

Éric Bédard is an associate professor of history and social sciences in the distant learning faculty (TÉLUQ) at the Université du Québec à Montréal. He is the author of *Chronique d'une insurrection appréhendée: La crise d'Octobre et le milieu universitaire* (1998) and the co-editor of *Parole d'historiens: Anthologie des réflexions sur l'histoire au Québec* (2006).

Joel Belliveau is a senior researcher at the Canadian Institute for Research on Public Policy and Public Administration in Moncton, New Brunswick. His PhD thesis (Université de Montréal, 2007) deals with 1960s student movements and their impact on Acadian political culture.

Michael Dawson is chair of the History Department at St. Thomas University. He is the author of *The Mountie from Dime Novel to Disney* (1998) and *Selling British Columbia: Tourism and Consumer Culture, 1890-1970* (2004).

Karen Dubinsky teaches in the History Department at Queen's University. Her chapter in this volume is drawn from her current project, entitled *Babies without Borders: Adoption and the Symbolic Child in Canada, Cuba and Guatemala*.

Magda Fahrni is an associate professor in the Department of History at the Université du Québec à Montréal. She is the author of *Household Politics: Montreal Families and Postwar Reconstruction* (2005).

Steven High is Canada Research Chair in Public History at Concordia University. He is the author of *Industrial Sunset: The Making of North America's Rust Belt* (2003) and co-edited with Barbara Lorenzkowski a special issue of *Histoire sociale/ Social History* on "Culture, Canada and the Nation" in 2006.

Marcel Martel is an associate professor and holds the Avie Bennett Historica Chair in Canadian History at York University. His research interests are political, intellectual, and cultural history. Most recently, he has published *Not This Time: Canadians, Public Policy and the Marijuana Question, 1961-1975* (2006) and *Envoyer et recevoir: Lettres et correspondances dans les diasporas francophones* (2006).

Steve Penfold is an assistant professor in the Department of History at the University of Toronto. His research examines the history of mass consumption and car culture in North America.

Becki L. Ross is jointly appointed in women's and gender studies and sociology at the University of British Columbia. She has published in a range of journals, including *Journal of Women's History, Canadian Review of Sociology and Anthropology,* and *Journal of the History of Sexuality*. She is completing a book manuscript entitled *The Shake, the Rattle, and the Pole: Vancouver's Striptease Past*. Her new research concerns the expulsion of sex workers from Vancouver's West End, 1975-85.

Robert Rutherdale is a member of the Department of History and Philosophy at Algoma University College, Laurentian University. He is a specialist in postwar Canadian society and in consumerism and family life since 1945. He is the author of *Hometown Horizons: Local Responses to Canada's Great War* (2004) and is now completing a book on fatherhood in Canada during the postwar baby boom and consumer era.

Joan Sangster teaches history and women's studies at Trent University, Peterborough. She has published on women's, working-class, and legal history; her most recent book is *Girl Trouble: Female Delinquency in English Canada* (2002). She is currently researching a book on women and wage labour in the post-Second World War period.

Christabelle Sethna is a historian and associate professor with the Institute of Women's Studies and the Faculty of Health Sciences at the University of Ottawa. Her research and publishing focus is on the history of sex education, contraception, and abortion. She is currently working on a project on the history of the birth control pill and its impact on single, university-aged women in Canada between 1960 and 1980.

Robert Wright teaches in the History Department at Trent University. He is the author of several books on Canadian politics and culture. His most recent book is *Three Nights in Havana: Pierre Trudeau, Fidel Castro and the Cold War World* (2007).

Index